# Women & Music

# Women & Music

A HISTORY

EDITED BY

KARIN PENDLE

INDIANA UNIVERSITY PRESS BLOOMINGTON & INDIANAPOLIS

Manufactured in the United States of America

Library of Congress Cataloging-in-Publication Data

Women and music : a history / edited by Karin Pendle.
        p.    cm.
    Includes bibliographical references (p.     ) and index.
    Discography: p.
    ISBN 0-253-34321-6 (cloth)
    1. Women musicians.   2. Women composers.   3. Music—History and
criticism.   I. Pendle, Karin, XXXX.
ML82.W6   1991
780'.82—dc20                                                      91-8413

1 2 3 4 5   96 95 94 93 92

# CONTENTS

# Modern Music in the Americas

# The Special Roles of Women

# Illustrations

# Preface

*Women and Music: A History* is a survey of women's activities in music performance, composition, teaching, and patronage from the times of the ancient Greeks to the present, with an emphasis on art music in Europe and the Americas. This focus is not meant to suggest that women's musical activities, or even their most significant ones, are in any way limited to these areas of the world, but rather to enable students and teachers in standard music history courses to coordinate the material in this book with the topics normally covered in undergraduate surveys. As such surveys have broadened in accordance with today's educational goals, so *Women and Music* moves beyond Western art music to include chapters on women in popular music and jazz, women as financial supporters of the arts, and women's roles in non-Western music. Finally, a chapter on feminist aesthetics introduces a subject that has begun to arouse the interest of many creative scholars.

The feminist movement of the 1960s and 70s was the driving force behind the emergence of a wide range of studies and theories centering on the lives, positions, and contributions of women in society through the ages. As in other fields, so in music, scholars began to show an interest in the work of the half of the world's population that had been ignored in earlier studies of music history and development. Women's Studies came to the fore more slowly in music than in many other fields, perhaps because musicology was (and in some countries still is) dominated by men schooled in traditional methodologies. Even a decade ago, *Women and Music* could not have been written, for serious, thorough, reliable sources on women musicians were too few in number and their subjects too widely spread across music's history to support a continuous chronological narrative. Fortunately, these conditions no longer apply; hence, this textbook.

The present book, based largely on recent scholarship, can serve not only as the basis for formal course work but can represent a summing-up of many areas into which our studies of women in music have taken us. Much has been done: the latest scholarship has been remarkable for both its

x PREFACE

quantity and its quality. Much remains to be done: the narrative still lacks some continuity, faces, voices, and names. Our authors, all recognized specialists in some area or aspect of women's musical activities, have created a framework for current study and future exploration. In so doing, they have added some new colors and shone some new lights on the history of music, past and present.

*Historical Anthology of Music by Women* (1987), edited by James R. Briscoe, and the set of cassettes (1991) he assembled to accompany it may be used to great advantage in conjunction with the present book. Both the *Anthology* and the tapes provide valuable examples of compositions by women from all historical periods in Western music since decipherable notation came into use. When works discussed in *Women and Music* appear in the *Anthology,* page numbers for the scores are given in the text, indicated by the abbreviation HAMW. The three cassettes present most of the music included in the *Anthology;* a complete list of the selections is given at the end of this book.

People too numerous to mention have encouraged this project and have assisted each of us in our search for materials. Though we cannot acknowledge everyone personally, we thank you no less sincerely for your help. My special thanks go to the Friends of Women's Studies, University of Cincinnati, for the grant that covered the cost of the book's pictorial and musical illustrations.

KARIN PENDLE

# Ancient and Medieval Music

# I.
# Women and Music in Greece and Rome

*Ann N. Michelini*

Music had a central and widely diffused importance in ancient Greek culture, and it was just this importance that created strong resistance to the notion of music as an art in its own right. A fifth-century B.C.E. lyric fragment attributed to Pratinas states that "song is queen," while the pipe "should dance after, since it is the servant." Music was an integral part of much Greek poetry, and Greek poetry was the basic raw material of Greek education. Even after Greek prose writing began to become important in the fifth century B.C.E., the works of Homer and Hesiod were the textbooks for schools; and in the earliest period (700–450) poetic works were the source of almost all knowledge about history, religion, morality, philosophy, and geography. The word "music" *(mousikê)* was used virtually as a synonym for education, and a painting of a school scene was as likely to feature a lyre as it was a book. The history of Greek women in music is therefore inseparable from the history of Greek poetry.

Investigating the role of Greek women in music is difficult because it is difficult to generalize about Greek culture. "Greece," never a united nation in the classical period, consisted of many tiny or medium-sized states. These little states differed greatly in their social, political, legal, and ritual life; they were united only by a common language, which expressed itself in a common literature. Poetry was thus doubly important because it was the major source of pan-Hellenic culture. Although the roles of Greek women differed widely from city-state to city-state, in most early Greek cultures women and men tended to work, play, and socialize in single-sex groups. On the one hand this meant rather strict lines of segregation, amounting in some Greek societies to virtual seclusion for women. On the other hand, this same segregation left room in some areas and periods for a rich cultural life within female society, including the production by women and for women of poetry and its musical accompaniment.

We know of one such group from the fragmentary remains of the poetry of Sappho, who lived in Mytilene on the island of Lesbos at about the turn of the sixth century B.C.E. and who was one of the greatest lyric poets of all time. Sappho's work centers on homoerotic experience among a circle of women; as a result it has often been misunderstood, both in antiquity and in modern times. Marriage may have marked a change in a girl's role in these homoerotic societies: Sappho wrote wedding songs that emphasize the pathos of the bride's separation from family and friends; and several times we hear of grief for absent friends or lovers, who may have left Mytilene because of marriage. It is also apparent that an older married woman such as Sappho herself, who wrote poems to her daughter, Kleis, could continue to function as a poet and as self-proclaimed lover.

Sappho, in one of her most famous works, sings that she envies anyone who can sit opposite her beloved and listen to the beloved's enticing words—she herself becomes helpless when faced with such beauty. (The last stanza is missing several lines.)

> To me he seems equal to gods,
> the man who sits facing you
> and listens as you speak
>     softly close by,
>
> and laugh enticingly. That is what
> startles the heart in my breast,
> for, as I look at you an instant, then
>     I can no longer speak.
>
> My tongue is broken, and a thin
> fire quickly suffuses my skin.
> My eyes see nothing; my ears
>     are buzzing.
>
> Sweat covers me, and trembling
> possesses me entire.
> I am paler than grass,
> and I seem to myself
>     just short of death.
>
> But all must be endured,
> for [?] even a poor man. . . .

This sophisticated poem points up the paradox of eloquence and emotion, love and writing about love. Just as in Shakespeare's sonnets, the poet hopes to win love through the power of her words, while complaining that as a sincere lover she finds it difficult to speak except through her verse.

We know of no other female poetic social groups like the one in Mytilene; but we do hear of other female poets, such as Corinna of Thebes, Praxilla of Sicyon, and Telesilla of Argos. These women all worked in the fifth century B.C.E., and Corinna has left substantial parts of several lyric poems. Her work seems aimed at male society and includes narrative of heroic myth; but the legends are local and the work is striking for its simplicity, compared with the very complex and sophisticated poetry of Pindar, a contemporary Theban male lyric poet. The contrast suggests that after Sappho's day the poetry of women continued to flourish in some areas without taking part in the development of male poetry, which was performed at the great Panhellenic festivals, from which female poets were excluded.

While Greek male poets had the dominant role in relation to music, women were active as performers on musical instruments and sometimes as singers and dancers in the *choros*. In Sparta in the mid-seventh century B.C.E., the poet Alkman was famous for his "maiden songs" *(parthenia)*, designed for performance by a chorus of unmarried girls. Fragments show that members of the chorus described each other's beauty and expressed erotic adoration for their chorus leader. Boys attended school but, in the fifth century, Greek girls did not; nevertheless, some of them seem to have learned to play the lyre and to recite poetry (such as the songs of Sappho) to the music. Paintings on fifth-century pottery show well-dressed matrons sitting around with lyres, sometimes apparently as part of bridal ritual. Women were also strongly associated with aulos playing, but here the aspect of class stratification becomes more prominent. A large class of professional female aulos players, most of whom seem to have been slaves, were hired out to perform at all-male drinking parties; often the piper is depicted nude, suggesting that she functioned as a prostitute as well. Segregation of the sexes meant that women who came into the male world, like those hired to play music, received little pay and were accorded low status. In the classical period, the most famous lyre players and pipers were male, just as all the actors in Athenian drama were male; they wore masks and wigs when playing women's parts.

In the second half of the fourth century B.C.E. the forces of Alexander of Macedon destroyed the great Persian empire. Greek-speaking Macedonians gained control of the civilized world, and the resulting spread of Greek culture has caused this era to be called "Hellenistic." New styles of poetry turned away from male concerns, such as war stories of heroic myth, to everyday life and romantic sentiment. At the same time, from the fourth century on, the increasing prevalence of schooling for girls as well as boys led to an apparent increase in female participation in musical and poetic life.

An important figure seems to have been Erinna, a young female poet who, probably in the mid-fourth century, wrote a touching poem to a childhood friend, taken from her first by marriage and then by early death. Erinna resumed some of Sappho's themes in a new style, apparently influencing such famous third-century poets as Theocritus and Callimachus. Among female poets in this period were Anyte, who wrote epitaphs for pet animals, and Nossis, whose poems reflect a distinctly Sapphic emphasis on female society. We also hear by the second century B.C.E. of female poets who traveled to such Panhellenic festival sites as Delphi and won prizes for public recitations there.

In the Roman period (roughly 250 B.C.E. to 300 C.E.), the relation between women and music continued to center on poetry, but it was complicated by the ambivalent reaction of Roman culture to Hellenic influence. While trumpets, pipes, and even the lyre were already known to the Romans, the great influx of Greek culture, including Greek music, dates from the second century B.C.E., when Rome began to dominate the civilized world. The Romans thought of dancing, singing, and lyre playing as undignified activities, effeminate for men and perhaps corrupting even for women. When the historian Sallust refers to someone who "played the lyre and danced more beautifully than is necessary for a respectable woman," he implies that respectable women were supposed to know and perform Greek music but that there was concern about these foreign arts. The ambivalent attitudes toward music guaranteed its importance in one aspect of cultural life: Roman erotic poetry, by definition in opposition to traditional Roman cultural values, glorifies the *docta puella*, or learned lady, who is both connoisseur and love object. The poet Ovid advised women to use their vocal and instrumental skills to captivate lovers, performing lyrics from the tragic theatre, from Hellenistic Greek poets, or from Sappho. Because Roman women were less segregated, we hear more about them from Roman men; but we find few female poets who speak of their own experience. Only one, Sulpicia, has left some poems addressed to a male lover.

## SUGGESTIONS FOR FURTHER READING

Groden, Susy Q. *The Poems of Sappho*. New York: Bobbs-Merrill, 1966.

Maas, Martha, and Snyder, Jane McIntosh. *Stringed Instruments of Ancient Greece*. New Haven: Yale University Press, 1989.

Pomeroy, Sarah. *Goddesses, Whores, Wives, and Slaves: Women in Classical Antiquity*. New York: Schocken Books, 1976.

————. "*Technikai kai mousikai.*" *American Journal of Ancient History* 2 (1977):51–68.

Skinner, Marilyn. "Sapphic Nossis." *Arethusa* 22 (1989):5–18.

Snyder, Jane McIntosh. *The Woman and the Lyre: Women Writers in Classical Greece and Rome.* Carbondale: Southern Illinois University Press, 1989.

Starr, Chester. "An Evening with the Flute-Girls." *La Parola del Passato* 181 (1978):401–10.

# II.
# Women in Music
# to ca. 1450

*J. Michele Edwards*

## SECULAR MUSIC

### Resources

Developing a portrait of the musical activities of women in western Europe from the first to the fifteenth century is rather like creating a tapestry from a variety of fibers and textures. No single type of resource provides comprehensive information on the range of their participation. We can, however, bring together an array of resources: iconographic and literary references, wills and financial accounts, guild records and religious documents, didactic treatises and chronicles by travelers, tax records and song texts, and music treatises and manuscripts. Since there are problems in understanding and interpreting each type of resource, they can best be used to clarify each other. For example, limiting a study to music manuscripts produces an unrealistic view of musical activity, because written preservation for some types of music was irrelevant. Much secular music of this era was easily learned by rote or was of transitory interest, so that notation was unnecessary. Early liturgical music, on the other hand, called for continuity and was preserved in larger quantities. Since women's roles were particularly curtailed in the area of institutional religion, reliance on music manuscripts alone distorts our understanding of women's contributions to the music culture. In addition to unjustly emphasizing liturgical music, a bias toward written documentation also gives unwarranted weight to music of the aristocracy, who, along with the clergy, were more likely than working people to be literate or to have access to a copyist. Finally, medieval music manuscripts, even when available, omit many details of sound and performance. Coupling the study of manuscripts with other resources reveals more clearly the range and nature of activities in which women of various classes made music during these fifteen centuries.

## Musical Roles

Women played many roles in music: amateur and professional singers, dancers, and instrumentalists; composers; benefactors; educators; and copyists. In a late fourth-century sermon, St. John Chrysostom, patriarch of Constantinople, described the importance of popular song in the lives of working people, specifically mentioning lullabies sung by wet nurses and songs performed by women weavers—"sometimes individually and to themselves, sometimes all together in concert."[1] Music making by women was woven into the fabric of life and linked with two important events: birth and death. *Book of the Pious,* by thirteenth-century Rhenish Jews, almost certainly referred to singing by women in condemning the singing of Gentile lullabies to Jewish infants. Women's choirs sang at both pagan and Christian funeral rites.

Women are especially visible in descriptions of social dancing. Their participation in dance-songs is known from the beginnings of Christianity in both liturgical and nonliturgical situations. The two most common forms of medieval dance-song preserved in writing are the *carole* and the *rondeau,* which were enjoyed by workers and nobility alike. Song texts—e.g., those in *Carmina Burana* and in an eleventh-century manuscript called the Cambridge Songs— frequently refer to circle dancing, one of the oldest styles. A woman is most often cited as dance leader. For example, in a secular Latin dance-song on the last page of the Cambridge Songs manuscript, a woman leads the dance as solo singer in the center of the ring. The verses are a love song, and the refrain is quite simple, yet with interesting dramatic potential: "With ah! and oh!" Most dance-songs were performed with voices only, but the pipe and tabor and the vielle were also commonly associated with dancing.

Another example of music as part of the social exchange between women and men comes from a biography of St. Jón, the first bishop of northern Iceland (d. 1121). "There was a favourite game of the people— which is unseemly—that there should be an exchange of verses: a man addressing a woman, and a woman a man—disgraceful strophes, mocking and unfit to be heard."[2] These love songs retained their popularity despite Bishop Jón's admonition against them. This game of love songs, as they were called by the biographer, probably presented an opportunity for women and men to sing simple improvised dialogues.

Prominent women were frequent benefactors of music, and several connected with French courts during the late Middle Ages were especially important. Married first to Louis VII of France and later to Henry II of England, Eleanor of Aquitaine (1122–1204) had substantial political power. She and two of her daughters, Marie and Aelis (Countess of Blois), influenced the cultural climates of their courts, thus shaping the values and behavior of the nobility.

Writings by a fifteenth-century Dominican friar provide confirmation of women as skilled copyists and scribes. He cites at least a dozen convents with active scriptoria; and he singles out two nuns at Colmar, in northeastern France, who were especially proficient at copying choir books. In his eulogy for Sister Lukardis of Utrecht, the friar praises her work as a copyist:

> She busied herself with . . . writing, which she had truly mastered as we may see in the large, beautiful, useful choir books which she wrote and annotated for the convent and which has caused astonishment among many fathers and priests who have seen the missal she prepared, written in a neat correct script.[3]

His astonishment need in no way imply that women scribes were rare; it is, instead, more a comment on his own misunderstanding of the activities and contributions of women.

## Medieval Lyric

The medieval lyric—songs of personal poetic expression—continued traditions which had flourished throughout western Europe for centuries. The lyric was part of a performing/aural tradition rather than a written/visual one, with poetry and music being inseparable. During the late Middle Ages the lyric was international in scope, yet it formed a diverse repertoire, making simple definitions impossible. Current scholarship about lyric traditions has produced the most information on the trobairitz and troubadours of southern France. Though women appear to have participated in smaller numbers than men as composers of the medieval lyric, they were more active than has often been reported: "For each language and culture, we are much at the mercy of the selectors—the predominantly male world of chroniclers and copyists."[4]

A thirteenth-century anthology of goliardic poetry, *Carmina Burana*, preserves over 200 poems. Included among them are Latin lyrics from many European lands, especially England and France, and a number of verses in a German dialect. Subjects range from moral questions to satire, and include love, drinking, and gambling. There are also dance-songs, parodies of religion, vagabond songs, and six religious plays. Although these poems, a collection spanning more than 200 years, were meant to be sung, only a few include music—in staffless, unheighted neumes (nondiastematic notation)—while others have space left above the text for a melody.

The following pregnancy song, "Huc usque, me miseram!" like most of the poems in *Carmina Burana,* is anonymous but was most likely written by a woman; it resembles poems about pregnancy written in other European languages. It has no musical notation and is preceded by a brief introduction:

> Here begins a flowery song
> As it rises like a bird so it gives solace.
> Eve, how many are the joys of love?

The poem itself functions much as a response (literally a *reflexus,* or refrain) to this question.

> I loved secretly, but now the pain! My belly is huge, and birth is near.
> Mother yelled, Father slapped me. Both fumed. I'm alone in this room, and can't play outside.
> Neighbors look at me as at a monster. They stare, poke each other, and clam up till I walk by.
> They always point at me with fingers. I'm a wonder. They wink obscenely. They damn me for one sin.
> Why am I talking? I'm gossip in every mouth. Pain grows and now my friend is gone.
> He ran off for good, back to France. Without him I hurt, almost die. I cry for myself.[5]

Literary scholar Peter Dronke has reconstructed a possible recitation-performance of another item from *Carmina Burana,* the dance-song "Tempus est iocundum, O virgines modo congaudete" (The time is joyful; O girls, rejoice now!).[6] The narrative presents a social event. In the first strophe, the chorus leader calls the young women and men together and introduces the refrain, which the chorus sings at the end of the remaining seven strophes. Women soloists are featured in the second, fifth, and sixth strophes; men in the others. Each stanza ends with the word *floreo* (to flower [with love]), which rhymes with the refrain's *pereo* (to die [from love]). This constant signals the entrance of the chorus.[7]

Trobairitz, or women composer-poets, lived in Occitania (now southern France) in the region with the largest concentration of troubadours, wrote lyrics in Provençal *(langue d'oc),* and flourished during the late twelfth and thirteenth centuries. Of the twenty-one trobairitz known by name, most were members of the nobility and had various ties with troubadours. We have twenty-nine extant lyrics, a long religious poem by Gormonda de Montpellier, and contemporary biographical sketches of seven trobairitz. A Paris manuscript contains portraitlike illustrations of the Comtessa de Dia and of Castelloza. The music of trobairitz and troubadours was less frequently written down than was their poetry. Among the trobairitz materials, only "A chantar m'er de so q'ieu no volria" (I have to sing of what I would not wish) by the Comtessa de Dia includes music notation (see HAMW,* pp. 11–13). This poem is preserved in more than one manuscript; however, the music appears only in *Le manuscrit du roi,* a collection of songs copied around 1270 for Charles of Anjou, brother of Louis IX. Literary scholars have particularly high praise for this lyric, in which a woman struggles to understand her lover's rejection. Even in her lament she affirms her self-worth, and she makes a rare claim of her own beauty in the first and last stanzas.

Of the surviving lyrics by trobairitz, twelve are *tensos*—debate songs or dialogues involving questioning and an exchange of views—and seventeen are *cansos*—songs or, more specifically, love songs. Three of the *tensos* are by women—two by pairs and one by a trio of women—in which advice is either sought or given. The poem by the three women challenges two important social values of male-dominated medieval society: Lady Alais wishes to remain unwed, and Lady Iselda wishes to have a husband but no children. The remaining *tensos* are dialogues between a woman and a man, and are written by more than one author. Generally the speakers alternate stanzas; however, one of the anonymous poems and the *tenso* between Lombarda and Barnat Arnaut d'Armagnac are divided into two longer sections, one by each of the writers. The form of the *tenso,* designed for debate, highlights "the battle of the sexes." In the *tensos* by the trobairitz, women and men are frequently set in opposition, using rather conventional terms. In language and imagery the trobairitz remained close to the troubadours, as if constricted by the rules and traditional male language of the *tenso.*

Using the more open form of the *canso,* women found more distinctive voices, and their distance from *fin'amors* (fine or courtly love) is more apparent. Neither the women nor the men in the poems are idealized, but are true to life. The trobairitz lyric most often speaks directly to the beloved rather than to a general audience. The poems by women articulate their desire for recognition as individuals and for a voice in their relationships with men. Perhaps the most substantial transformation of *fin'amors* is the *canso* by Bieiris de Romans, who probably lived during the first half of the thirteenth century. The song is addressed to a woman named Maria—who

---

*This abbreviation is used throughout this book to refer to *Historical Anthology of Music by Women,* edited by James R. Briscoe (Bloomington and Indianapolis: Indiana University Press, 1987).

is clearly not the Virgin Mary. "Na Maria, pretz e fina valors" (Lady Maria, in you merit and distinction) is the only known medieval lyric that gives expression to lesbian love. (Despite the lack of supporting evidence, some scholars have expended considerable energy in an effort to prove that this lyric was written by a man.) Retaining the language of the courtly tradition, the lyric elevates the beloved through Bieiris's words of praise and speaks of physical desire. The tone of this love lyric, however, is more positive than much of the repertoire of either the trobairitz or the troubadours: there is no deceit, no infidelity, no bitterness or anger toward the beloved. For example, the second stanza reads:

> Thus I pray you, if it please you that true love
> and celebration and sweet humility
> should bring me such relief with you,
> if it please you, lovely woman, then give me
> that which most hope and joy promises
> for in you lie my desire and my heart
> and from you stems all my happiness,
> and because of you I'm often sighing.[8]

By the early thirteenth century, love songs in many languages emerged in imitation of the trobairitz and troubadours. The trouvères of northern France wrote in *langue d'oïl*, or the medieval French language, which developed into modern French. *Le manuscrit du roi* preserves at least one, and perhaps three, items by women trouvères. Two include music: "Mout m'abelist quant je voi revenir" (It pleases me much when I see), by Maroie de Dregnau of Lille; and "Chanterai por mon corage" (I shall sing for my courage), attributed in another manuscript to Dame de Fayel but here ascribed to Guiot de Dijon. Although the text is presented from a woman's point of view, this approach was sometimes used by men, leaving the attribution uncertain. "Jherusalem, grant damage me fais" (Jerusalem, you do me a great wrong)—without music—is attributed to two different men, but Peter Dronke tentatively ascribes this woman's lament to a female trouvère.[9] Among ten known *jeu-partis*, or debate songs, which have women authors or coauthors, three survive with music: an anonymous work by a woman and her lover; one by Perrot de Beaumarchais and an unnamed woman; and "Je vous pri dame Maroie" (I beg you, lady Maroie), by Dame Margot and Dame Maroie. Additional women trouvères include the Duchesse de Lorraine, Agnes de Navarre-Champagne, Comtesse de Foix, and Blanche of Castile (1188–1252), granddaughter of Eleanor of Aquitaine and twice Regent of France.

Like the trobairitz, most of the female trouvères were noblewomen, and some were among the most influential and powerful people in western Europe during the twelfth and thirteenth centuries. Marie de France (fl. 1160–1215) was most likely a member of the court of Eleanor of Aquitaine and Henry II of England. Preservation of her writings in languages other than the original French attest to the popularity of her lyrics. Marie accompanied herself on the harp to perform poetry from *Les lais,* one of her most important works. Written music apparently existed for these narrative *lais,* but the manuscript is lost.[10] Marie began her literary work making translations into French from Latin and perhaps from English to entertain and edify Henry II and the people of his court. She moved on to compose *lais,* for which she is best known, because she found them more difficult, hence more of a challenge to her artistry.

Marie's *lais* are relatively short and are the earliest known western European narrative poetry in the vernacular by a woman. Marie's distinctive forms, narrative twists, and female perspective differentiate her from both female and male contemporaries who composed *romances* or *lais.* Rather than relate a long series of adventures, she focuses on a single, unified episode. Her *lais* include the typical themes of her era: heroines and heroes, love and sex. "But when she sang of this world of lovers, she showed its unpredictability, its effects on individuals, not just the moral lessons it might teach. She chose to emphasize character and situation over narrative."[11] Marie recounted stories from women's points of view, and her women are involved as active agents. In *Lanval,* her hero is a woman, not a knight. In most versions of *Laüstic,* at least one of the lovers dies in the end, but Marie substitutes the death of a nightingale, a symbol of the couple's love.

Available documentation suggests considerable literary and musical activity at the major Spanish courts during the late Middle Ages. Women participated in various ways in this cosmopolitan culture, which integrated Muslims, Jews, and Christians. For example, in Castile at the court of Sancho IV (reigned 1284–95), palace account books show salaries for twenty-seven minstrels: two Arabic women, twelve Arabic men, one Jewish man, and twelve Christian men. The association of dark skin with *jougleresses* suggests a special prominence of Moors among women minstrels, even beyond the borders of Spain. Frederick II, Holy Roman Emperor and King of Sicily, employed Moorish musicians in his Norman-Saracen court at Palermo. In several medieval romances a noblewoman disguises herself as a *jougleresse* by darkening her face and becomes a traveling musician, singing as well as playing an instrument. Such episodes occur in *Aucassin et Nicolette* and *Bueve de Hantone,* written in Provençal, and in *Bove d'Ancona,* in Italian.

Two women play chess while a slave or servant entertains with lute music. Source: *Libro de los juegos* (Book of games) from the Iberian court of Alfonso the Wise (1221-84); Escorial, MS j. T. 6. Reproduced from Julian Ribera, *La Musica de las Cantigas* (Madrid: Tipographia de la Revista de Archivos, 1922), vol. 3.

From at least the eleventh century onward, women singers at the courts of Andalusia entertained with bilingual lyrics. They concluded *muwash-shahs* (love poems in classical Arabic or Hebrew) with vernacular stanzas using colloquial Arabic or Spanish. These final stanzas, or *kharjas*, talk directly and frankly of complex feelings and present women as active lovers, and are the earliest known examples of so-called women's songs (*cantigas de amigo* or *chansons de femme*), in which male authors put words into women's mouths. This type of medieval lyric raises interesting questions about authorship, preliterate expressions, and gender systems, and suggests the willingness of men to speak for or define women.

Accounts of Arabic and Jewish women who wrote lyrics in medieval Spain indicate the importance of being in a creative environment. Most of these women can be linked with other accomplished poets: a father or lover, a woman teacher, or even a slave master. Although not all were noblewomen, they were usually connected with a court. Kasmúnah, daughter of a Jewish poet, studied with her father and was considered an outstanding writer. Her two-part dialogues with her father parallel the form of some Provençal *tensos*.

While a resident of Cordova, Zeynab Al-murabiyyah (d. 1009), who never consented to marriage, composed several verses praising Al-mudhfer, a son of Al-mansúr Ibn Abí A'mir, who eventually usurped the throne of Cordova. Waládah, daughter of the King of Cordova and the beloved of poet Ibn Zaidún, was among the most famous poets of her day. Hind (mid-twelfth century), a slave woman in Xátiva who excelled in poetry and music as a lutenist and singer, was praised by a famous Arabic poet in an invitation to his house: "The nightingale, after hearing thy performance, envies thee, and wishes to hear again the deep intonations of thy lute."[12] A freed slave, Al-'arúdhiyyah (d. eleventh century), learned grammar and rhetoric from her master in Valencia, then surpassed him as a poet. Unfortunately, neither medieval Arabic music nor secular music attributed to medieval women on the Iberian peninsula are known to have survived.

Until at least the mid-fourteenth century no music for the Italian secular lyric has survived. Texts for two sonnets and part of a *tenzone* in Italian from the mid-thirteenth century are attributed to a woman known only as "the accomplished damsel" (Compiuta Donzella).

Study of the medieval lyric is revealing about gender systems. Repeatedly, song texts relay what it meant to be a woman or a man, but women and men differed in their perspectives. Women's choice and treatment of form also differed from that of their male contemporaries. To gain a more comprehensive understanding of medieval western Europe, the views of women must be added to the male concept of *fin'amors*.

## Performers

Information is sketchy about musical performance by men as well as by women in the medieval period and earlier. Though evidence of women's roles as performers is scarce, women seem to have engaged in many of the same secular activities as their male counterparts. Distinct musical activities appear to be due at least as much to class as to gender. For example, medieval French literary sources identify aristocratic women as singers of dance-songs, troubadour and trouvère chansons, motets, and *lais*. In Cordova, during the reign of Al-mansúr Ibn Abí A'mir (939–1002), well-educated women played instruments, such as the organ, to entertain their husbands. Didactic treatises aimed toward middle- and upper-class women encouraged singing and playing some instruments as a pastime. French treatises do not generally condemn public performance by women, but one early fourteenth-century Italian treatise by Francesco da Barberino, *Del reggimento e costumi di donna,* seeks to limit women's musical activity to the private sphere. On the other hand, women from lower social classes are known largely as professional performers, either traveling minstrels or servants at court.

Provençal, Old French, Spanish, Galician-Portuguese, and Middle English each have words that refer specifically to women minstrels: *jougleresse, ménestrelles, juglaresa* or *juglara, jograresa,* and *gliewméden.* In addition to singing and playing instruments, minstrels possessed an array of entertainment skills—tumbling, juggling, recitation, dancing, acrobatics, and mime. Some minstrels were slaves; others were hired by courts. The eleventh-century court of Poitiers, in Occitania, included hundreds of Moorish *jograresas,* received as a reward for the count's assisting Aragon in the campaign against the Moors in 1064. Payment records verify the presence of women singers and instrumentalists at various courts, especially in France. For example, in 1239, Louis IX paid Mélanz to be a *cantatrix,* or woman singer, to the Countess of Blois. Mahaut d'Artois hired a woman singer for Christmas 1319; she also employed a woman organist named Jehanne. Mahaut's granddaughter, a princess of France, employed three female singers and a woman bellringer. Women and men were treated equally in the articles of incorporation for the guild of minstrels in Paris (1321). The articles, which regulated such activities as apprenticeships and hiring until 1773, consistently refer to *ménestreus et ménestrelles* or *jougleurs et jougleresses.* At least eight of the thirty-six original signers to the articles were women.

## Instruments

Iconography, French literary sources, and financial accounts of the English court all indicate that a single instrument, rather than an ensemble, most frequently accompanied voice(s) in monophonic music of the twelfth and thirteenth centuries. Medieval women are represented as performers of percussion instruments, organ, and especially string instruments. Wind instruments, which were specifically discouraged as not feminine (and not even appropriate for aristocratic men) during the Renaissance, must already have been a rarity for women. Percussion instruments, which by the fifteenth century were also viewed as inappropriate choices for women, were linked with two activities in which women were prominent: processionals and dancing. A late fourteenth-century illumination from a Vienna manuscript shows five women in a procession. They are singing and playing small drums and handbells, two of the most common medieval percussion instruments.

Women are linked with the organ from very early in music history.

Thaïs, a Greek from the third century B.C.E., is the earliest known organist. Her husband is said to have invented the hydraulis, an early organ. Depictions of organs on sarcophagi identify several women from the Roman Empire (second and third centuries C.E.) as organists: Aphrodite, Julia Tyrrania, and Gentilla. In Hungary, the inscription on the tomb of Aelia Sabina (probably third or fourth century C.E.) reads: "She herself remaining, as she was seen among the people, playing the hydraulis so well."[13] The early Christian church rejected the use of instruments in worship as pagan, and the organ was not widely used in church services until the fourteenth century. However, wealthy monasteries owned and used organs much earlier, and perhaps this was also true for convents. Beginning in the Middle Ages, both the positive and the portative were deemed appropriate instruments for domestic entertainment by women.

According to French romances and recommendations in didactic treatises, medieval women most frequently played strings: vielle, harp, psaltery, gittern, rote, lyre, rebec, and citole. Illuminations in thirteenth-century French sources show women playing a similar group of string instruments: vielle, harp, rebec, and gittern. Iconography from the Iberian peninsula offers some of the richest sources on medieval instruments and instrumentalists, and women are quite visible in many. In a Galician-Portuguese manuscript called *Cancioneiro da Ajuda,* twelve of the sixteen miniatures include women performers, most frequently as singers. Often the women accompany themselves with castanets or tambourine. In perhaps the most significant collection, *Las Cantigas de Santa Maria,* compiled at the court of Alfonso the Wise (1221–84), every tenth song—singing general praise to Mary—is accompanied by a painting of performing musicians.

# RELIGIOUS MUSIC

## Women in Judaism

Women's prayer-songs had a prominent place in the Hebrew Bible (Old Testament): the songs of Deborah (Judges 5), Miriam (Exodus 15:20–21), Jephtha's daughter (Judges 11:34), and Hannah (1 Samuel 2:1–10). Each of these is a spontaneous acclamation or celebration: for example, Miriam's song celebrates the Israelites' crossing the Red Sea and their escape from Pharaoh when he and his horsemen were swept into the sea. According to biblical accounts, as worship became more formal, women's roles diminished. By the early Rabbinic period, in the third century C.E., singing by women in worship was forbidden because a woman's voice was considered "sexual incitement" (Babylonian Talmud, treatise *Berakot,* chap. 3, para. 24a).

Miriam and each of the women at the Red Sea played a *tof,* often called a timbrel, the only membranophone (a percussion instrument whose sound is produced by striking or rubbing a stretched skin) mentioned in the Hebrew Bible. Among Egyptians the *tof* was played only by women or eunuchs, and it may have been exclusively a woman's instrument among the Jews. Perhaps its association with women helps to explain why this instrument was excluded from the music of the Second Temple (late sixth century B.C.E. to 70 C.E.). Outside of worship, Jewish women participated in music both as singers and as instrumentalists. Even in the most restrictive situations women sang among themselves, before weddings and at funerals, and Jewish instrumentalists, including women, were highly visible from the second century B.C.E. onward.

## Women in Early Christianity

Women's participation in and contributions to early Christianity were extensive. In its earliest days, this new religion primarily attracted people who lacked economic and social privilege—women of all classes and lower-class men. Particularly in the communities of widows and virgins associated with early Christianity, women redefined themselves and rejected traditional gender roles and class divisions. For women, conversion to Christianity meant chastity, defying the traditional definitions of woman as wife and mother. Cross-class participation by women in Christianity brought together slave and slaveholder, challenging the patriarchal Roman family. By the end of the second century, men within Christianity recognized the challenge to gender roles by women and began working to rebuild the system so as to exclude women and give religious authority to men. The growing institutionalization of Christianity, which might have given women a greater voice in an important cultural sphere, instead restricted women's religious activities. The establishment of Christianity as a state religion brought more extensive participation and control by men. Ironically, women were increasingly excluded from the very institution they had been so instrumental in establishing.

Women's activities in music paralleled their overall opportunities in the Church. During the early centuries of Christianity both women and men sang during worship. Ignatius of Antioch (first–second century) spoke in terms of the congregation singing with one voice, women and men together. By the late fourth century, however, many church councils and individual churchmen sought to silence women's singing during the worship service.

Patristic literature frequently cited "women should keep silence in the churches" (1 Corinthians 14:34) as justification for the exclusion of women from singing and preaching activities.[14] Many, but not all, early Christian writers continued to encourage extraliturgical singing of psalms by women as a deterrent to singing secular music. From the fourth century, the opportunity for women in public churches was further inhibited with the shift from congregational singing to music provided by select choirs, solely of men and boys.

The gradual suppression of singing by Christian women can be linked with various factors: a reaction to the singing among women in other religious groups; the characterization of women musicians as prostitutes and courtesans; the identification of women with the arousal of sexual desire and worldly temptation; and, chiefly, the political victory of the Roman Church over heretics and Gnostics. The Gnostics, who treated women and men in an egalitarian fashion, were the dominant Christian community in Egypt and northern Syria from the third century until the time of Augustine (354–430) and posed the greatest threat to the Roman Church. The subjugation of women by the Roman Church occurred simultaneously with its suppression of the Gnostic community. The exclusion of women from the music of public worship was also deeply rooted in patriarchy: the domination of women was viewed as a means of retaining and enhancing the power of the Latin church fathers.

Despite actions that were likely to thwart compositional creativity, some women did emerge as composers. Names of individual composers— from the first millennium of Christianity—are seldom known. At least seven women can be identified as composers of Byzantine Christian chant between the ninth and fifteenth centuries: Martha, a ninth-century abbess at Argos; Thekla, a nun who probably lived during the late ninth century and was known for her *kanones*; Kassia, a well-educated ninth-century poet and composer (see HAMW, pp. 1–5); Theodosia, another ninth-century composer, who wrote a song in honor of St. Johanna; Kouvouklisena, a singer and *domesticos* (or leader) of a women's choir; a singer and composer from the late fourteenth or early fifteenth century whose name is not known but who is identified as the daughter of Ioannes Kladas, a leading composer of Byzantine chant; and Palaeologina, a nun from the late fourteenth or the fifteenth century who probably founded the convent of St. Theodora in Thessalonika.

Women composers contributed to hymns, the major genre of Byzantine chant. When *troparia*, originally short intercalations between psalm verses, grew, they became independent hymns: especially *stichera* and *kanones*. Like a *troparion*, a *sticheron* is sung between psalm verses, but only during the last few verses. Some have unique melodies, while others share melodies with other *stichera*. A Byzantine *kanon* is a verse form of nine sections, each alluding to one of the nine biblical canticles. Each section contains several stanzas with a repeated melody. Palaeologina, a cultured and intelligent woman, composed *kanones* in honor of St. Dimitri, St. Theodora, and others. Music by only two of the women is preserved: one song is ascribed to the daughter of Ioannes Kladas; and forty-nine liturgical compositions are attributed to Kassia, though only twenty-three are considered authentic. Twenty are *stichera*, but her most famous work, "The Fallen Woman" (see HAMW, pp. 4–5), is a *troparion*.

Religious music-drama was one of the most interesting accretions to medieval Christian religious rituals. Women characters have especially significant roles in the Easter drama *(Quem quaeritis)*, the earliest and most popular story. Although clerics generally took the roles of both female and male characters, nuns also participated, creating more realistic, mixed casts. For example, the Marys were portrayed by three nuns in fourteenth-century performances at the collegiate church at Essen and at Barking Abbey in Essex (England) during the time when Lady Katherine of Sutton was abbess (1363–76). Participation by nuns is indicated in the rubrics of the Wilton Processional and in the fourteenth-century St. Quentin drama from the nunnery of Origny-Sainte-Benoîte. The St. Quentin drama and the *Visitatio Sepulchri* (Visit to the tomb) in the Wilton Processional, a manuscript created for and by Benedictine nuns ca. 1300, led to a rethinking of the traditional conclusion that development in music-drama was accomplished through the inclusion of additional scenes and characters. The story in the Wilton Processional focuses on the single scene of the three Marys and the angel at the tomb, but it is longer and more complex than many other dramas with this plot. It is not surprising that nuns retained the emphasis on women rather than add scenes in which men predominate.

## Women's Faith Communities

In both Judaism and Christianity, women found opportunities for musical participation in religious life through women's communities when their participation was limited in municipal houses of worship. Only one community of Jewish women from late antiquity is known, while Christian women's communities were more numerous and documented from at least as early as the second century.

In *On the Contemplative Life* (first century C.E.), Philo of Alexandria described a monastic community of Jews: *Therapeutrides* (women) and *Therapeutae* (men). The women and men of this double house on Lake

Mareotis, outside Alexandria, prayed, studied scriptures, and composed and sang hymns and psalms. Both sexes participated separately but equally, except on the Sabbath and for the festival of Shavuot, when they worshipped together. The festival music is quite interesting. Prayers, commentary on scripture given by the president, and the first round of singing preceded a meal of bread and pure water. After the president offered a hymn to God,

> all the others take their turn as they are arranged and in the proper order while all the rest listen in complete silence except when they have to chant the closing lines or refrains, for then they all lift up their voices, all the men and all the women.[15]

Since the Therapeutic society emphasized equality, it is reasonable to assume that both women and men sang as soloists during this ritual. Philo continues, describing the sacred choral vigil after supper as the peak:

> They rise up all together and standing in the middle of the refectory form themselves first into two choirs, one of men and one of women, the leader and precentor of each being the most honoured among them, and also the most musical.

These separate choirs sang both in unison and antiphonally. Then, in what was clearly a rare occurrence, the women and men joined together in one chorus, singing until dawn in an ecstatic state.

Christian women's communities took on new significance from the fourth century, when the nunnery offered women virtually their only opportunity to sing and compose music in praise of God. The convent nourished leadership and creativity among women: "The impulse toward leadership which kept the men in the world sent the women out of it."[16] Between 500 and 1500, the convent was the only acceptable alternative to marriage for European women, and it "fostered some of the best sides of intellectual, moral, and emotional life."[17] Singing liturgical music was the central communal activity in most convents. The education of novices focused on reading and singing, to encourage participation in collective worship. In singing eight Offices plus Mass together each day, making and sharing music was at the very core of women's communal lives. One woman served as *cantrix*, assuming a leadership role not open to women outside the convent. More than a conductor, she also chose repertoire, held rehearsals, supervised the copying of music and illumination work, managed the library, and supervised liturgy. She would have been among those most likely to compose texts and music for religious services.

In addition to the many anonymous nuns who provided religious leadership and who created embroidery, tapestries, sculpture, illuminations, and songs, several nuns stand out during the period of intense creative activity in the twelfth century: Hildegard, who was exceptional in both the depth and the breadth of her intellectual and creative scope; Héloise, perhaps the most famous nun of the era; Marie of Oignies, the mother of the Beguine movement; Constance of Le R 	onçeray, a lyric poet; and Abbess Herrad of Hohenbourg, who conceived and planned the impressive illuminated religious encyclopedia *Garden of Delights*.

## Hildegard of Bingen

Hildegard of Bingen was a twelfth-century visionary theologian in addition to being a composer of seventy-seven religious songs and a lengthy music-drama that has no medieval parallel. At the age of eight, Hildegard became an oblate in the Benedictine double house at Mount St. Disibode, and at fifteen she entered the novitiate. Her first official position as a leader was in 1136, when she succeeded her mentor as superior at Disibodenberg. Against the wishes of the monks at St. Disibode, Hildegard founded her own community at St. Rupertsberg. Construction for the new convent began in 1148; and when she and her sisters moved in two years later, they took with them rich endowments and greater independence for themselves. Hildegard was so successful that by 1167 she had founded a daughter house at Eibingen. Often called a mystic, she chronicled her visions and wrote on medical and scientific matters as well as on the lives of saints. Hildegard almost certainly supervised the large number of detailed illuminations in a famous manuscript recounting her visions. She was well known throughout Europe, responding to theological questions, making prophecies, corresponding with popes and monarchs, offering spiritual guidance, and speaking out for reform.

Hildegard disavowed an educational background and claimed that all her writings and music came to her in visions. Her works, however, reveal a familiarity with two medieval music theorists, Boethius (ca. 480–524) and Guido of Arezzo (eleventh century). Her comments can be more fully understood in the context of monastic life and the medieval world. Hildegard grew up surrounded by a visionary tradition of Rhine mystics and deeply aware of biblical dreamers, so it is not surprising that she too had visions. Since she lived in an era that prohibited women from teaching or holding authority over men, her need to deny human instruction is no mere topos of humility, but a claim to high authority. . . . Only through visions could a religious or intellectual woman gain a hearing. . . . while men might perhaps heed a divinely inspired woman, they would have little patience with a mere presumptuous female.[18]

For Hildegard, music was an avenue of access to mystical experience. She composed music as a way to make palpable God and divine beauty. Her poetry and music, dating from as early as the 1140s, were written largely for Offices and Mass at her convent. A few pieces celebrated saints important in nearby Trier and were perhaps written on commission. Her chant cycle, *Symphonia armonie celestium revelationum* (Symphony of the harmony of celestial revelations), is preserved in two different versions: one manuscript containing fifty-seven chants (1175) and another containing seventy-five pieces (1180s). These chants are distinctive and idiosyncratic, though they are also linked with the medieval chant repertory. Her texts, modeled on the prayers and songs of the liturgical Office, "contain some of the most unusual, subtle, and exciting poetry of the twelfth century."[19] Their resulting free-verse or prose quality is echoed in her freely spun melodic lines with their irregular, unpredictable gestures. Like her contemporaries, Hildegard built her works from a small number of melodic formulae; however, her development process resulted in more-continuous, through-composed musical lines. Musical stability arises from organic melodic unity rather than from conventional factors such as strophic form or regular poetic meter. Hildegard's songs often encompass a wide range, covering two octaves or more. Her frequent use of ascending and descending leaps of a fifth is also exceptional for chant. Though Hildegard's hymns and sequences are not bound by traditional forms, her works in other genres, such as the Kyrie (see HAMW, p. 10), have identifiable precedents in Gregorian chant repertoire.

When church officials interviewed the nuns at Bingen to gather evidence for Hildegard's proposed canonization (which was never completed), three nuns claimed to have seen the abbess chanting "O virga ac diadema" (see HAMW, pp. 8–9) while illuminated by the Holy Spirit. Analysis of this chant shows both Hildegard's independence and her connections with contemporaries and tradition. Textually, "O virga" has ties with the typical formal pattern of sequences from the tenth and eleventh centuries, in which the first and the last verses stand alone while the other verses are paired (a bb cc dd . . . n). Hildegard balances the salutation in the first strophe with a prayer to Mary as *Salvatrix* (a feminine savior) in the last. In content, the central ten strophes form sections of three, four, and three strophes respectively, not the expected pairs. Melodically, "O virga" also modifies the form common in the sequences of Hildegard's contemporaries: her form is governed by a variant of the binary principle, comprising only strophic pairs (aa bb . . . ff). Her strophes are not rhymed, nor are they alike structurally. In "O virga" each pair of verses employs a single melodic idea, transformed to fit the differing texts. The resulting sound is unified through recurring melodic fragments, but literal repetition is avoided.

Hildegard's awareness of herself as a woman among women seems evident in the texts of her songs. Many of her seventy-seven extant chants honor women: sixteen are addressed to the Virgin Mary; thirteen to St. Ursula and her women followers; and four to various groups of women. Sixteen are addressed to local or individual male saints, leaving only twenty-eight to such traditional Christian figures as God and the Holy Spirit. Her poetic imagery is frequently woman-centered, and women take an active role in the spiritual story of salvation Hildegard presents. In this way she inspired women to become aware of their power in the material world and to exercise that power. Working within a women's community, Hildegard developed remarkable leadership and extraordinary creativity. Only as a member of a religious community of women could she have brought together her scientific, artistic, and theological creations.

## Polyphony

Whether women sang polyphony is a matter of scholarly debate. Three manuscripts of polyphonic music from fourteenth- and fifteenth-century England have slim ties with nunneries but at least suggest the possibility that nuns in England sang in parts. Continental sources, on the other hand, give strong evidence that nuns sang polyphony. This information is derived from sixteen manuscripts from convents, spanning over 300 years and originating in locations throughout Europe. As with other repertoires by women, the genres represented coincide with those of men composers from the same era: conductus, motets, Mass movements, sequences, and hymns.

The Las Huelgas Codex is the most extensive source of polyphony known to have been owned by a nunnery. The manuscript, dating from the fourteenth century, was copied from a manuscript that Maria Gonzalez de Aguero had transcribed earlier in the century. The complex music reflects the skill of the nuns and girls in the choir of Las Huelgas, near Burgos, Spain. This convent had a trained choir of young girls similar to the boys' choirs in cathedral schools. From 1241 to 1288, the time of Abbess Beren-guela, daughter of Beatrix of Spain and Ferdinand III, one hundred nuns sang in the choir and forty girls were in training. Records indicate that the nuns sang in three parts.

## SUMMARY

Throughout the centuries of the Roman Empire and the European Middle Ages, music was viewed as a powerful enterprise as well as a source of entertainment and pleasure. The spiritual power and moral suasion ascribed to music gave it special significance and encouraged its regulation. Thus the same institution that proclaimed, "God established the psalms, in order that singing might be both a pleasure and a help,"[20] suppressed the voices of women. Middle- and uppper-class women were restricted from public performance, yet their education and leisure gave them the opportunity to cultivate music as a personal accomplishment. Women musicians among slave and servant groups had considerable visibility as professional performers, but they were subjected to a loss of liberty and were often treated as sexual objects. Music is a major way to articulate status and is closely connected with both class and gender systems. The presence of skilled musicians at court along with the creation of elaborate melodies and complex forms were marks of power and prestige. Gender and class differences contribute to and help to explain differences in musical activities between women and men or among women during the first to the fifteenth centuries.

### NOTES

1. As translated in Oliver Strunk, *Source Readings in Music History* (New York: W. W. Norton, 1950), p. 68.

2. *Biskupa Sögur* (Copenhagen, 1858) I:165–66, as quoted in translation by Peter Dronke, *Women Writers of the Middle Ages. A Critical Study of Texts from Perpetua (†203) to Marguerite Porete (†1310)* (Cambridge: Cambridge University Press, 1984), p. 105.

3. As quoted in translation by Margaret Wade Labarge, *Women in Medieval Life. A Small Sound of the Trumpet* (London: Hamish Hamilton, 1986), p. 224.

4. Peter Dronke, *Women Writers*, p. 98.

5. As translated by Willis Barnstone, in Aliki Barnstone and Willis Barnstone, eds., *A Book of Women Poets from Antiquity to Now* (New York: Schocken Books, 1980), p. 61.

6. This poem is among those set by Carl Orff in *Carmina Burana* (1936).

7. Peter Dronke, *The Medieval Lyric* (London: Hutchinson University Library, 1968), pp. 192–93, expanding on Joseph Bédier's reconstruction of another early thirteenth-century dance-song.

8. As translated in Meg Bogin, *The Women Troubadours* (New York: W. W. Norton, 1980), p. 133; first published as *Les femmes troubadours* (Paris, 1978).

9. Peter Dronke, *The Medieval Lyric*, pp. 106–107, including note 1.

10. Jean Maillard, *Evolution et esthétique du lai lyrique, des origines à la fin du XIVème siècle* (Paris: Centre de Documentation Universitaire, 1963), p. 66.

11. Bonnie S. Anderson and Judith P. Zinsser, *A History of Their Own: Women in Europe from Prehistory to the Present,* 2 vols. (New York: Harper & Row, 1988), 1:309–10.

12. Ahmed Ibn Mohammed Al-Makkari [al-Maqqari], *The History of the Mohammedan Dynasties in Spain,* translated and edited by Pascual de Gayandoes, 2 vols. (1840; reprint New York: Johnson Reprint Corp., 1964), 1:166–67.

13. Friedrich Jakob, *Die Orgel und die Frau* (Männedorf, Switzerland: Orgelbau Th. Kuhn, 1972), p. 14, as quoted by Jane Schatkin Hettrick, "She Drew an Angel Down: The Role of Women in the History of the Organ 300 B.C. to 1900 A.D.," *The American Organist* 13/3 (March 1979):40.

14. Consensus scholarship now indicates this admonition is most likely a later insertion to Paul's letter (deutero-Pauline).

15. As quoted in translation by Ross S. Kraemer, "Monastic Jewish Women in Greco-Roman Egypt: Philo Judaeus on the Therapeutrides," *Signs* 14/2 (Winter 1989):346.

16. Emily James Putnam, *The Lady: Studies of Certain Significant Phases of Her History* (1910; reprint Chicago: University of Chicago Press, 1970), p. 78.

17. Lina Eckenstein, *Woman under Monasticism* (1896; reprint New York: Russell & Russell Inc., 1963), p. vii.

18. Barbara Newman, "Hildegard of Bingen: Visions and Validation," *Church History* 54 (1985):169, 170.

19. Peter Dronke, *Poetic Individuality in the Middle Ages: New Departures in Poetry 1000–1150* (Oxford: Oxford University Press, 1970), p. 151.

20. St. John Chrysostom, as translated by Oliver Strunk, *Source Readings,* p. 68.

Special thanks are due to those who provided research assistance for this chapter: Jane Lohr (University of Iowa graduate student) and Melissa Hanson (Macalester College, class of 1990). I am also grateful to colleagues and friends who read the manuscript and offered suggestions, especially Barbara Newman, Calvin Roetzel, and Dorothy Williams.

## SUGGESTIONS FOR FURTHER READING

For surveys on trobairitz, see Meg Bogin, *The Women Troubadours* (New York: W. W. Norton, 1980); William D. Paden, ed., *The Voice of the Trobairitz: Perspectives on the Women Troubadours* (Philadelphia: University of Pennsylvania Press, 1989). For interpretive work that challenges Bogin, see Marianne Shapiro, "The Provençal *Trobairitz* and the Limits of Courtly Love," *Signs* 3/3 (Spring 1978):560–71.

On Castelloza, see Peter Dronke, "The Provençal Trobairitz: Castelloza," in *Medieval Women Writers,* edited by Katharina M. Wilson (Athens: University of Georgia Press, 1984), pp. 131–52.

On Hildegard, see Barbara Newman, *Sister of Wisdom: St. Hildegard's Theology of the Feminine* (Berkeley: University of California Press, 1987); and Saint Hildegard of Bingen. *Symphonia: A Critical Edition of the Symphonia armonie celestium revelationum,* edited by Barbara Newman (Ithaca: Cornell University Press, 1988), which includes text translations and commentary.

For Hildegard's music, see Pudentiana Barth, Maria-Immaculata Ritscher, and Joseph Schmidt-Görg, eds., *Hildegard von Bingen: Lieder* (Salzburg: Otto Müller Verlag, 1969). A modern edition of *Ordo virtutum* has been prepared by Audrey Ekdahl Davidson (Kalamazoo: Medieval Institute Publications, 1985); a modern edition of nine chants is available in Christopher Page, ed., *Sequences and Hymns,* No. MCMI (North Harton, England: Antico Edition, [1982]).

Anne D. Bagnall, "Musical Practices in Medieval English Nunneries," Ph.D. diss., Columbia University, 1975 (University Microfilms, 75–25, 648), includes material on music-drama and polyphony.

John F. Plummer, ed., *Vox Feminae: Studies in Medieval Woman's Song,* Studies in Medieval Culture, vol. 15 (Kalamazoo: Medieval Institute Publications, 1981), offers eight essays on songs using a woman's "voice."

# The
## Fifteenth
## through the
## Eighteenth
## Centuries

# III.
# Women in Music,
# ca. 1450–1600

## Karin Pendle

## INTRODUCTION

"Did women have a Renaissance?" Answers to this question, posed by historian Joan Kelly-Gadol in a path-breaking article, have led to significant reassessments of the concepts of periodization that most students absorb from their earliest encounters with history. Until Kelly-Gadol asked this question, most people's ideas about the period 1450–1600—which is still most often referred to as the Renaissance—were formed by the writings of relatively wealthy, educated men aimed primarily at readers of similar sex and class. The best known among these scholars was the German historian Jacob Burckhardt (1818–97), whose influential *The Civilization of the Renaissance in Italy* was first published in German in 1860. In a chapter entitled "The Position of Women," Burckhardt put forth his claim that the sexes in Renaissance Italy were regarded as equal, at least among the educated classes. This view reappeared so often in the works of subsequent scholars that its truth was never seriously questioned until Joan Kelly-Gadol proposed a new, woman-centered point of view.

Renaissance. Rebirth. What was in fact reborn in the so-called Renaissance? The learning and literature of classical authors, the ancient Greeks and Romans, though not unknown to some scholars of the early Christian era, now came to dominate the education and thinking of men of fourteenth-, fifteenth-, and sixteenth-century Europe. Boys learned Latin, even Greek, so that they could study the ancient authors in their original tongues. The liberal arts emphasis of classical education became this period's ideal as well: grammar, rhetoric, logic, mathematics, astronomy, and music theory were its central components; physical education and modern languages and literature might be added. Such knowledge was not to be acquired for its own sake, however. It was regarded as practical: it dealt with man, hence was humanistic, and prepared the young scholar for his duties as a citizen. The Renaissance Man was not to be a specialist but a generalist, one who had absorbed the best ideas of classical civilization in order to enhance his own humanity.

Civic and artistic values as well as personal goals were affected by this reborn humanistic spirit. The period 1450–1600 witnessed the emergence of strong European states and of empires acquired when explorers pushed beyond the boundaries of their known world. Throughout Europe, capitalism began to undermine the earlier, manor-based economy. Some of the greatest religious art and music ever known was created under a humanistic aesthetic that encouraged a greater range of individual expression than had been common heretofore; and painting, sculpture, song, and dance adorned brilliant courts and enhanced public spectacles.

Yet this was a time not of unity of spirit but of diversity and contradiction. During the century that saw the discovery of America, most Europeans were born, lived, and died in the same geographical area, for travel within Europe was slow and often treacherous. The humanistic view of life spread broadly throughout the Continent, yet it was shared only by the monied or the titled, those who valued education and had access to it. Classical learning affected enlightened views of man and society, yet widespread persecution of witches, most of them women, stained much of the sixteenth century and continued into the seventeenth. The same factors that freed and empowered Renaissance Man caused the lines of separation to be drawn ever more closely around Renaissance Woman, and too many experienced not a rebirth but an increasingly confined existence.

## Women in Society, 1450–1600

How then did women participate in the society of their time? There is no single answer to this question, just as there is no single answer to the question of men's participation. A woman's experience was influenced by her social or economic class as well as by her sex. Yet there were certain constants that cut across class lines, for gender was of supreme importance in defining a woman's life: in other words, certain things happened to women simply because they were women. The central position of the family in both public and personal spheres of life influenced the degree to which women's position was subordinate to men's. The fact of this subordination, however, was unquestionable; and woman's position could now be justified not only by supposedly objective observations of her inferiority but by the beliefs and practices of the ancients. A highly born girl or the daughter of a wealthy merchant might receive the same humanistic education as her brothers. Yet whereas the education of a boy was designed to make him a good citizen, a girl studied the classics to make herself a more attractive prospect for marriage and to enable her to take charge of her children's education. Sir Thomas More, sixteenth-century England's leading advocate of humanistic education for women, took pleasure in his daughters' scholarly accomplishments, but he still expected them simply to get married, have children, and run their households intelligently. And the noted Mantuan educator Vittorino da Feltre (1378–1446), though impressed by the precocious intelligence of his young pupil Cecilia Gonzaga, realized that society would allow her to continue her studies beyond her teen years only if she fulfilled her desire to become a nun.

For the requirement that society placed on all women in the years 1450–1600 was that they consider marriage, motherhood, and household management their life's vocation. The possibility of an unattached woman of marriageable age was not entertained. Entering a convent was an option open only to wealthy Roman Catholics, for a novice was expected to bring with her a suitable dowry, perhaps even her own furniture or clothing. Most titled or wealthy girls married at sixteen to eighteen years of age, usually to men ten to fifteen years older than themselves. Thus, although one reads of academically, artistically, or musically talented women during this period, they are almost always prodigies who retreat into obscurity by the age of twenty.

Upper-class girls, then, could be as well educated as their male contemporaries, but they used this education in a passive way for most of their lives. Also passive were the virtues prescribed for young women: modesty, humility, silence, patience, piety, obedience, and—above all—chastity. Every girl, no matter how high her birth, was educated in domestic tasks and household management. Though upper-class boys as well as girls usually learned to sing, dance, and play one or more instruments, too much emphasis on these skills in a boy's education was thought to lead to effeminacy. The arts that occupied women—weaving, needlework, music, perhaps drawing or painting—required talent and practice to produce good results; yet many authorities still considered them trivial, intended only to keep idle hands busy.

From the beginning, then, and throughout her early years, a girl was made aware that her life was meant to be spent in the private sphere, while her brother would enter the public sphere as a full participant in the activities of society. At every turn the girl was educated to be obedient and submissive, first to her father, later to her husband. In practice, however, women still assumed some of the public roles open to them in earlier centuries. Noblewomen might be called upon to rule in their husbands' absences, as was Eleonora of Aragon, Duchess of Ferrara; or to serve as regents, like France's Queen Catherine de' Medici. Some women were still permitted to inherit kingdoms and to rule in their own right—Elizabeth I of England and Isabella of Castile, for example. Wives of rich merchants often contributed their knowledge and skills to the family business; and women married to members of the landed gentry were expected to oversee many of their estates' operations, to supervise and educate the servants, to serve tenants as physicians and apothecaries, and to keep the household accounts. Clearly, such women were neither unskilled nor passive. Yet neither were they independent or employed in furthering their own interests. Rather, they came increasingly to serve the purposes of male-dominated institutions.

Academically or artistically gifted women of the fifteenth and sixteenth centuries might be tolerated, accepted, or even praised for their accomplishments, but only as exceptions to the rule of female inferiority. Women rulers themselves often went to great lengths to demonstrate that they had moved beyond their sex. The few women artists who had sustained careers, such as Sofonisba Anguissola (1532/35–1625) and Lavinia Fontana (1552–1614), still suffered restrictions on seeking commissions or other forms of patronage in cities or courts at any distance from their families. Academically talented women, particularly if they tried to continue their studies and writing beyond their teens, were decried for trying to become men.

Verona's Isotta Nogarola (1418–66), a humanistically educated woman who chose to live the life of a nun, though in her family home rather than in a convent, was attacked by men for going against nature and rejected by women for her supposed pretensions. Even those who praised her did so not because of the quality of her writing but simply because she, a woman, could write at all. One misogynistic critic even accused her of incestuous relations with her brother, on the grounds that "an eloquent woman is never chaste."[1] A younger sister, Ginevra, who also showed promise as a scholar, chose to marry rather than to follow Isotta's lonely path. In truth, even the Virgin Mary, whose position among Roman Catholics was greatly enhanced beginning in the late fifteenth century, was revered as an exception to the rule, a woman above all women whose status had no noticeable effect on that of the rest of her kind.

Despite a lot of talk about humanistic education and women's scholarly accomplishments, the large majority of women were illiterate. Even among the wealthier families, there was opposition to teaching girls to read and write. Though the new Protestant sects encouraged all members to learn to read, the better to study the Bible at home, much of what passed for knowledge of Scripture, prayers, or hymns must have been a matter of simple memorization. It would be some time before the numbers of literate European women would rise.

## WOMEN AS MAKERS OF MUSIC

Music making has never been limited solely by class, race, or sex. Throughout history, peasants have improvised their own dance tunes, women have hummed lullabies, and men have danced to the sounds of pipe and tabor. Yet at various times in the past, restrictions on musical activities by women have confined them to certain types or spheres of music. Though wealthy or titled women during the period 1450–1600 were expected to be able to read music, to sing, to dance, and to play at least one instrument, they were also expected to limit their music making to home or court. Musical ability was a social asset for both sexes, but regardless of how well one performed, to sing or play before a paying audience would not have been thought proper for a member of the upper classes. Nor did many titled or wealthy people compose music—Henry VIII of England, Anne Boleyn, and Carlo Gesualdo come to mind as exceptions—although they probably could have improvised melodies to their own lute accompaniment. To have studied composition, a technical skill acquired for vocational purposes, or to publish one's own music would have been another unseemly activity for the wealthy.

Yet music instruction must often have been on a high level. Mary of Burgundy was a pupil of Busnois, while Isabella d'Este studied with Johannes Martini, and later with one of his French pupils. Beatrice of Aragon, future Queen of Hungary, is said to have been a pupil of Johannes Tinctoris.[2] Anne Boleyn attracted notice at the court of Henry VIII in part for her musical skills. Her daughter, Elizabeth, was an able performer. Elizabeth's half-sister, Mary Tudor, was a capable singer to the lute; and Isabella d'Este danced and sang to the lute before an audience at the festivities surrounding the marriage of her brother Alfonso to Lucrezia Borgia. Lucrezia herself was particularly fond of dancing. An earlier Lucrezia, Lucrezia de' Medici, is known to have written texts for *laude,* which she or someone in her court sang to improvised or popular tunes.

Musicologist Nino Pirrotta has observed: "Of all the mythical powers of music, only one seems to have been most familiar to the humanists, that of diverting the mind and bringing relaxation."[3] Ancient Greek authors had noted music's ability to move listeners and repeatedly stressed the intimate relationship between text and tune. The desire to cultivate these ancient properties of music led humanistically educated Italian noblewomen and noblemen to choose singing to the lute as their favorite mode of music making. This sort of entertainment involved not just reading music from the printed page but improvising an entire composition—at times both the poem and its musical setting. Hence, what Claude Palisca calls "some of the most characteristic music of the period" is not music we can study, for it was not written down.[4] Though women like Isabella d'Este, Marchesa of Mantua, and Elisabetta Gonzaga, Duchess of Urbino, were well known for their ability to improvise songs,[5] the practice was so widespread that there must have been scores of other court ladies and gentlemen who could perform at least adequately. In all likelihood their songs would have been strophic, perhaps based on a reiterated succession of harmonies or even on a popular song from the written tradition (like the *basse danse* in vogue during the same years). Melodies were probably simple but are likely to have been ornamented; and accompaniments would have been essentially chordal, though the performer's aptitude would determine the degree of elaboration.

Although women undoubtedly played an important role in this unwritten tradition, it is not surprising that no fifteenth-century woman has yet been discovered who actually wrote vocal music, despite the fact that many had been well trained in the art. Only in the last half of the sixteenth century do women emerge as composers within the previously all-male fields of sacred and secular vocal polyphony. Still, women were influential in the development of Italian polyphonic music by men around 1500. Through their patronage, both Isabella d'Este and Lucrezia Borgia encouraged the cultivation of the *frottola,* a type of music rooted in improvised practice and destined to become the major antecedent of the madrigal.[6]

Domestic music making involving what we would call art music was not limited to the nobility, but was also an important part of the family lives of merchants, landholders, and other wealthy and educated people. Iconographic evidence shows middle-class women singing, playing keyboard or plucked string instruments (lutes or harps, for example), pumping the bellows of portative organs, or making music on flutes, dulcimers, or bowed strings. In Protestant households, singing psalms and hymns in harmony or with instrumental accompaniment was a popular pastime and formed a part of domestic devotional services. In these activities women participated equally with men, though some censorious souls might criticize a woman who displayed too much skill or vaunted that skill to gain public approval.

Anonymous (sixteenth century), "Le Concert cham-
pêtre: Le chant." Bourges, Musée DuBarry. Photo
courtesy of Giraudon/Art Resource.

## Music Making as a Profession

Outside the domestic sphere, women performers could be found in
many circles. The famous courtesans of this era counted music making an
indispensable skill. Courtesans were not simply prostitutes, but women who
also wined, dined, and entertained their male guests with music and witty
conversation. The famous courtesan Imperia (1481–1512) was known for
her ability to sing to the lute; and Tullia d'Aragona, a courtesan of the
mid-sixteenth century, headed an intellectual salon, wrote and published
poetry, and was commended for her lovely singing voice and her abilities as
a lutenist. Another published poet, the courtesan Veronica Franco (d.
1591), was an accomplished singer and instrumentalist.

Actresses in the professional *commedia dell'arte* troupes, which began
to emerge in mid-sixteenth-century Italy, were also expected to sing and
dance. Music was an integral part of a *commedia* performance, and music

and dances were performed before the drama began and between its acts. The typical *commedia dell'arte* troupe of the sixteenth century included three women and seven men, many of whom became famous even outside Italy for their lively portrayals of the *commedia*'s stock characters. Isabella Andreini (b. 1562) was one of the finest performers. In addition to acting, she wrote poetry and plays and was quite knowledgeable about music. She also led a notably virtuous life, something that could not be said about most of her female colleagues. Another comedian, Vincenza Armani, was both a singer and an instrumentalist.

Italian actresses were performing in London and Paris by the 1560s, though they were not universally accepted. Reports of a *commedia* company in London in 1577 noted that the actresses scandalized many members of the audience (who would not see English women on their own public stages until after the Restoration, in 1660). The scandal, however, was not due simply to the presence of women on a public stage but to the sorts of parts they played. Whether young lovers or saucy maids, these women were not the passive, chaste, obedient ladies described in Renaissance manuals on female behavior. Little wonder that even in Italy, respectable women usually stayed away (or were kept away) from the lusty *commedia* shows.

Women performers were not absent from the stages of the courts, for dramatic and musical entertainments in connection with private celebrations included women in their casts. France's court ballets were performed by both male and female dancers, and dramas produced at Italian courts included women musicians and dancers if not actresses. Wolfgang Osthoff tells of five men and women who sang a *strambotto* and a *barzelletta* during the production of a comedy, *Trinumo,* in 1499. He mentions one Barbara Salutati, who helped organize and performed in the musical interpolations to a 1526 production of Machiavelli's *La Mandragola.*[7] Whereas the 1499 performers were probably amateurs (they could even have been men in female costumes), Salutati and the women who participated in the 1526 drama appear to have been professionals. Osthoff also mentions that on another occasion Salutati was paid for her services. Elsewhere, amateurs of both sexes were known to have joined the professional performers at many court functions. Both Ippolita Sforza, Queen of Naples, and Catherine de' Medici, Queen of France, took their places as dancers; and Marguerite of Navarre wrote her own morality plays and farces, all of which contained music.

In the *intermedii* that graced the performance of a drama to celebrate the marriage of Ferdinand de' Medici to Christine of Lorraine in 1589, most of the musicians were male, and men took many of the supposedly female roles as well. There were two outstanding female performers among the soloists, however: Lucia Caccini and Vittoria Archilei (1550–1620s or later), both professional artists and both married to men who were composers and performers. "Dalle più alte sfere" (From the most exalted spheres), perhaps written by Antonio Archilei for his wife, gave Vittoria an outstanding vehicle for her vocal virtuosity; and Lucia Caccini improvised her own accompaniment on the lute for the aria composed for her by her husband, Giulio.[8] Later in the entertainment, Margherita Loro Alleluia joined the two Archileis for the trio portions of a madrigal; and she sang along with Vittoria and Lucia in segments of a *ballo,* during which they accompanied themselves on a Spanish chitarrina, a Neapolitan chitarrina, and a small harpsichord respectively.

There were a few women among the hired musicians at some Italian courts in the sixteenth century. Dalida de' Putti, a singer who entered the service of Lucrezia Borgia in 1507, was to become the mistress of Cardinal Ippolito d'Este, whose musical establishment she joined in 1512. Even earlier, a Madama Anna, also referred to as Madama Anna Inglese, appeared on the rolls of royal musicians in Naples in 1471, and reappeared there at various times through the end of the century.[9] Though hers is the only woman's name to be specified, there must have been more women singers or musicians at Naples during this period, for special lodgings were built to house them. Possibly the women were relatives of male musicians at court, since wives and daughters of male performers are known to have been hired elsewhere without officially having their names added to the payrolls. Virginia Vignoli, for example, worked with her father, also a performer, in Venice, where she was considered his "adjunct." By the 1560s she was pursuing the career of professional singer, though she later gave up her music to marry.[10]

## Ferrara's *concerto delle donne*

At Ferrara, women singers had been performing for some years before Duke Alfonso II established the famous *concerto delle donne* (women's ensemble) in 1580. Anthony Newcomb lists Lucrezia and Isabella Bendido, Leonora di Scandiano, and Vittoria Bentivoglio, along with bass Giulio Cesare Brancaccio (b. 1515–20), as court singers active as early as 1577.[11] Since Brancaccio had been brought to court specifically because of his singing talents, the women may also have been professionals. Yet paid or not, the women, all either noble or wealthy, would have been members of the court regardless of their musical ability. Members of the *concerto delle donne,* on the other hand, had in common with Brancaccio that they were invited to Ferrara specifically to perform vocal music at the court's chamber

Andrea Solario (1465–after 1515), "The Lute Player." Rome, Galleria Nazionale. Photo courtesy of Art Resource.

music concerts. Though members of the *concerto* were given court appointments as ladies-in-waiting to Duchess Margherita, there is no doubt that they were in fact hired singers.

The first members of the *concerto delle donne* to arrive in Ferrara were Livia d'Arco (d. 1611); Anna Guarini (d. 1598), daughter of the poet Giovanni Battista Guarini; and the much-honored Laura Peverara (d. 1601). Their first recorded performance took place on November 20, 1580, though only Guarini and Peverara sang at that time. Livia d'Arco was thought to be in need of further training and did not appear with the group until mid-1582. Finally, Giulio Cesare Brancaccio joined the new ensemble in December 1580, and the group began regular performances during Carnival 1581. In 1583 the fabled Tarquinia Molza (1542–1617) joined the ensemble, but she was forced to leave in 1589 when her affair with composer Giaches de Wert became known. For nearly two decades the fame of Ferrara's singing ladies spread, and admirers attempted to establish similar groups in Mantua and Rome. By mid-1589 Alfonso's sister Lucrezia, probably envious of the attention paid to performers who had come to be associated with her sister-in-law's private concerts, founded a rival ensemble in Ferrara.

The women in Duchess Margherita's *concerto* differed from earlier female singers, whether amateurs or professionals, in the particularly virtuosic vocal style they espoused. Performing in the Duchess's *musica secreta* (private music)—for so the nightly chamber-music concerts were called—they specialized in music decorated with numerous *passaggi*, trills, and cadenzas, which were probably improvised in rehearsal and then committed to memory. *Madrigali . . . per cantare a uno, e duo, e tre soprani* (Madrigals to be sung by one, two, and three sopranos), of 1601, by the court composer Luzzasco Luzzaschi, contains examples of the sort of music with which the women astounded their listeners. The trio "O dolcezze amarissime d'amore" (O most bitter sweetness of love), though less virtuosic than some of the solo numbers, gave each singer a chance to display her artistry. In addition, there must have been some music for female voice or voices and bass, for Brancaccio, already well versed in this luxuriant style, performed with the women until he was dismissed for insubordination in 1583.

The women of the *concerto* were skilled not only in singing their memorized repertoire, which was extensive, but also in sight-reading polyphonic music from partbooks. Each woman also played at least one instrument and was able to accompany herself or the ensemble. The group had few idle hours, for rehearsals and performances occupied from two to six hours a day. In addition, they took part in court *balletti* as both singers and dancers.

Perhaps this work was tiring, but the rewards could be considerable, and prestige must be counted among them. Laura Peverara was both the subject and the dedicatee of three anthologies of madrigals: a manuscript collection (ca. 1580) and two published volumes, *Il Lauro secco* (The dry laurel, 1582) and *Il Lauro verde* (The green laurel, 1583). The printed works were compiled by one of Laura's admirers, the poet Torquato Tasso, and all three collections contained music by the best and best-known male madrigalists of late sixteenth-century Italy.

Financially, the women also reaped great benefits. Though society would not yet allow them to exist as independent professionals (all except Molza, a widow, married not long after the arrival of the *concerto* in Ferrara), they were rewarded with excellent salaries and what we might classify as fringe benefits. Laura Peverara received a dowry, an apartment in the ducal palace, and stipends for her mother and husband; while Tarquinia Molza was given an apartment and a salary more than twice Luzzaschi's.

EXAMPLE 3-1.    Luzzasco Luzzaschi, "O dolcezze amarissime d'amore," mm. 12–17. From Alfred Einstein, *The Italian Madrigal* (Princeton: Princeton University Press, 1949), 3:311. Used by permission of the publisher.

She later became the first woman to receive Roman citizenship. The fate of Anna Guarini was not so fortunate. Despite her enviable position at court, she was murdered by her jealous husband.[12]

Luzzasco Luzzaschi was not the only composer to write music specifically geared to the virtuosic performing style of the three women. The *concerto delle donne* and rival groups drew forth numerous volumes of pieces for accompanied female soloists well into the seventeenth century. Equally important was the influence of the Ferrarese *concerto* on the polyphonic madrigal for mixed voices. Among the composers who applied this manner of ornamented singing to the madrigal was Giaches de Wert, whose "Vaghi boschetti" (Delightful groves) from his seventh book of madrigals for five voices (1581) features vocal ornamentation in all voices. The idea of women as public performers, spurred no doubt by the employment of actresses in the *commedia dell'arte,* and the sort of virtuosity

EXAMPLE 3-2.    Giaches de Wert, "Vaghi boschetti," mm. 27–32. © 1965 by the American Institute of Musicology/Hänssler Verlag. All rights reserved. International copyright secured. From *Corpus mensurabilis musicae* 24, Giaches Wert, *Opera omnia*, vol. 7, *Madrigals of 1581,* edited by Carol MacClintock. Used by permission of the publisher.

associated with women's singing surely influenced composers like Jacopo Peri, Caccini, and Claudio Monteverdi to give women key roles in their operas.

The death of Duke Alfonso II in 1597 left Ferrara without a ruler, as the duke had no sons. Alfonso's musical establishment, one of the largest and best in Italy, was dissolved along with his court. Its legacy was such that one historian has suggested "that the formation of a virtually professional group of [female] madrigal singers at the Ferrarese court . . . was the most important single development in the history of Italian secular vocal music during the last third of the [sixteenth] century."[13]

## The Nuns of San Vito

Ferrara was the home of another group of female performers, the nuns of San Vito Convent under the leadership of organist and composer Sister Raffaella Aleotti. While Ferrara's court ladies were fascinating audiences with their vocal virtuosity, the nuns of San Vito were presenting concerts by an instrumental and vocal ensemble of an excellence that led one admirer, Ercole Bottrigari, to speak of them as "not human, bodily creatures" but "truly angelic spirits."

> When you watch them come in . . . to the place where a long table has been prepared, at the end of which is found a large clavicembalo, you would see them enter one by one, quietly bringing their instruments, either string or wind. They all enter quietly and approach the table without making the least noise and place themselves in their proper place, and some sit, who must do so in order to use their instruments, and others remain standing. Finally the Maestra of the concert sits down at one end of the table . . . with a long, slender and well-polished wand . . . , and when all the other sisters clearly are ready, gives them without noise several signs to begin, and then continues by beating the measure of the time which they must obey in singing and playing. And at this point . . . you would certainly hear such harmony that it would seem to you either that you were carried off to Heliconia or that Heliconia together with all the chorus of the Muses singing and playing had been transplanted to that place.[14]

At first the friend Bottrigari is addressing is unwilling to believe that such music could be made by a group of women, and he is amazed that concerts of this kind have been going on for some time. Even the instruments the nuns play surprise him: not the usual "women's instruments," keyboards or bowed and plucked strings, but cornetti and trombones as well. Giovanni Maria Artusi, who also attended the San Vito concerts, notes that the ensemble included cornetti, trombones, violins, viole bastarde, double harps, lutes, cornamuses, flutes, harpsichords, and singers; and he declares that the performance was exceptional not just for women: "Most of the people in Italy could not . . . have done more than what was done by these nuns. . . ."[15] The twenty-three nuns in the ensemble, says Bottrigari, worked under the supervision of Sister Raffaella, who also saw to their instruction. Unfortunately, he says nothing about their repertoire, which could have included any sacred or secular polyphonic vocal or instrumental pieces of the day.

Other fifteenth- and sixteenth-century convents known for their excellent music included all those of Milan (but especially Santa Maria Maddalena and the Assunta detto del Muro), San Gemiano in Modena, and San Lorenzo and San Giovanni in Monte in Bologna.[16] Ferrara itself boasted two convents besides San Vito whose music was deemed superior: San Silvestro and San Antonio. Outside the public eye, nuns performed liturgical and extraliturgical music for their own ceremonies. Works included devotional *laude,* particularly those published in the sixteenth century by Serafino Razzi of Venice, and sacred dramas with music.[17]

The spirit of the Council of Trent (1545–63), which was conservative at times to the point of repression, began to make itself felt during the last decades of the century. Increasing restrictions were placed on convents with regard to music and the nuns' relationship with the outside world. Public concerts such as those at San Vito were prohibited, and no outsiders—not even women—were permitted inside the convent to instruct the nuns in music. Nor were the nuns to continue their common practice of performing at court or in the homes of the wealthy. As for instruments, only organ and harpsichord were allowed. Though it is likely that, as in earlier times, these proscriptions were not followed to the letter, they doubtless had a dampening effect on music making in convents. Raffaella Aleotti continued as organist at San Vito far into old age, but her ensemble had long since disbanded.

## WOMEN COMPOSERS, 1450–1600

Women creators of music in the written tradition did not emerge until rather late in the period 1450–1600.[18] Some of the reasons for this are easy to find. The emphasis on improvised singing to lute accompaniment at court meant that writing down a piece of music had no particular priority in circles in which women with sufficient musical education might have done so. Also, as with classical education, so with musical education: its availability to girls depended in large part on their families' attitudes. Even under the best circumstances a girl's training might not have extended to theory and composition. In addition, one major source of a thorough musical education was completely closed to girls: the *cappella,* the group of musicians employed by a church or court to create and perform music for church services, processions, or other ceremonial or civic occasions. A boy appointed to a court *cappella* at a young age would receive a liberal arts education and might even travel to a distant university at his patron's expense. He would be trained not just to sing and play, but to compose and to take on other court duties as well. As for the Church, it remained a major provider of musical training through the eighteenth century. Though members of a *cappella* might also be asked to perform chamber music for court functions, chamber groups like the *concerto delle donne* were never asked to augment the *cappella,* for that institution and its educational opportunities were reserved for boys and men.

Without access to the *cappella* there were few outlets for a budding composer's products and limited access to the best musicians. Thus young women were kept from an important part of any apprenticeship: learning by doing. Unable to hear their music rehearsed and performed, they had little reason to write it in the first place. Music publishing, a growing industry after 1500, might have provided access to audiences; but if there were no demand for a composer's music, the publisher was unlikely to want to print it; and if the music remained unpublished, there would be no demand. It should be noted, however, that a great deal of music was still circulated in manuscript, and that numerous works in both manuscript and printed sources of the fifteenth and sixteenth centuries were anonymous. Thus women may have written more music than we know. That women began to write down, sign, and publish their music during the final decades of the sixteenth century is surely another manifestation of the same spirit that moved women to become professionals in other artistic and creative fields—literature, painting, acting, and musical performance.

Among the earliest known women composers of this period is Caterina Willaert. She may have been related to the Venetian composer Adrian Willaert, but she was not his daughter, as he had no children. In 1568 Orlando di Lasso, director of music at the court of Ludwig of Bavaria, had a madrigal by Caterina and one by her countrywoman Maddalena Casulana performed at court. Unfortunately, neither work is named in the report of this event, and Caterina's has not been preserved. Both Paola Massarenghi and Cesarina Ricci de' Tingoli published madrigals: Massarenghi a single piece in a 1585 Ferrara anthology, Tingoli a complete volume in Venice in 1597. Though Sister Raffaella Aleotti is the only San Vito nun whose music remains, others at the convent apparently wrote music too.

It is difficult to determine whether two pieces attributed to sixteenth-century noblewomen were actually written by them. Anne Boleyn (1507–

36), to be sure, was capable of writing a piece of the quality of "O Deathe, Rock Me Asleepe" (HAMW, pp. 16–17). Though she was a member of England's minor nobility, at the age of twelve she had been sent to the French court, where her royal education included music. The sadness expressed in both the text and the music of "O Deathe" seems to prophesy the fate that awaited Anne. The minor mode, the inexorable, ostinato-like quality of the figure G–Bb–A–G in the accompaniment, and the repetitions of "now I dye" or just "I dye," usually to a descending minor third, give the piece a flavor not unlike that of the famous lament in Purcell's opera *Dido and Aeneas* (1689).

Italy's Leonora Orsina (fl. 1560–80), like Anne Boleyn, was surely competent to write music. Yet the song "Per pianto la mia carne" (With sobs my body), which appears in a Modena manuscript, may only have been dedicated to her by an unnamed composer.[19] The piece has some historical importance, as it is one of the first to provide both plain and ornamented versions of the melodic line. These *passaggi* are neither expressive nor pictorial, but merely decorate the song's major cadences. The piece, for solo voice and lute, is short and rather simple except for the ornamentation, and it anticipates the virtuosic style of singing that was to become so popular after 1580. Another Italian noblewoman, Isabella de' Medici, may have written a song included in the same Modena manuscript. She will appear again in a musical context, as the dedicatee of the first published book of madrigals by a woman.

## The Music of Maddalena Casulana

Maddalena Casulana (ca. 1540–ca. 1590) is the first woman to publish her music as well as the first to consider herself a professional composer. Born at Casola d'Elsa near Siena (hence the name Casulana), she received her musical training there and in Florence, the city that also heard her first compositions.[20] In 1566 four of her madrigals appeared in the collection *Il Desiderio*, published by Girolamo Scotto of Venice. These four-voice pieces, sharing a volume with works by such masters as Cipriano de Rore and Orlando di Lasso, were the first pieces by a woman ever printed. A third book in the *Il Desiderio* series (1567) contained another of Casulana's madrigals. It was followed one year later by a volume devoted solely to her music, her *First Book of Madrigals for Four Voices*, also published by Scotto and destined to be reprinted twice, both times in 1583. At about the same time Casulana appears to have moved to Venice, where she gave private lessons in composition. In Vicenza she is reported to have played the lute for a private entertainment. Her next home may have been Milan, for her second collection of madrigals is dedicated to a Milanese government official. Another source, also from Milan, notes that Casulana was making her living as a composer.

For more than ten years after the publication of her *Second Book of Madrigals for Four Voices* (Venice: Girolamo Scotto, 1570), little was heard of Casulana, and no new works appeared in print. She apparently married, as documents of the 1580s refer to her as either Signora Maddalena Casulana di Mezarii or Maddalena Mezari detta Casulana, the latter on the title page of her *First Book of Madrigals for Five Voices* (Ferrara: Angelo Gardano, 1583). Her last known madrigal, a piece for three voices, appeared in a collection now known only in its second edition: *Il Gaudio* (Venice: Erede di Girolamo Scotto, 1586). After that, nothing more of her life is recorded. Though a publisher's catalogue of 1591 lists two volumes of sacred madrigals by a Casulana, the composer cited could be another person by the same name or from the same area of Italy.

Maddalena Casulana was a respected and honored composer, as is amply demonstrated by the reprinting of her music, the many works by others that were dedicated to her, and the poems written in her praise. Yet she was still all too aware of society's attitudes toward women and their accomplishments. In dedicating her *First Book of Madrigals for Four Voices* to Isabella de' Medici, Casulana wrote:

> I truly know, most illustrious and excellent lady, that these first fruits of mine, because of their weakness, cannot produce the effect I would like, which would be not only to give some testimony to Your Excellency of my devotion but also to show the world (for all that has been granted to me in this profession of music) the vain error of men, who so believe themselves to be the possessors of the high arts of the intellect that they cannot believe themselves to have the least thing in common with women.[21]

While most dedications of music to noble patrons include any number of standard expressions of the unworthiness of both the composer and the music being offered to so exalted a person, Casulana's dedication is much more specific: she is publishing her (apparently not so weak) music to show men that a woman is capable of creating such works. Also clear from her words is the fact that she considers herself a professional composer, undoubtedly the first woman in the history of music to do so.

Maddalena Casulana's music is finely crafted and worthy to stand beside that of any other composer of her day. Her genre of choice, the madrigal, engaged the best creative talents of the sixteenth century. Choosing the finest Italian poems of past or present, madrigalists attempted to reflect the imagery of those texts in their music. Casulana was particularly well attuned to the sentiments of the poems she chose, writing music with an expressive content that ranged from simple madrigalisms (for example, running eighth notes on words like "singing," "circling," "flying") to the passionate, declamatory outpourings that begin such pieces as "Morir non può il mio cuore" (My heart cannot die) or "Morte—Che vôi?—Te chiamo" (Death—What is your wish?—I call to you; HAMW, pp. 20–21). In the latter, the separate cries to Death in soprano, tenor, and bass voices (the tenor in quite a high range) and Death's reply, "What is your wish?" set to a very disjunct alto line, aptly establish the mood for the rest of the piece. The work is compact, intense, and free of trivial word painting. The intellectual/musical device of using on the syllable "fa" notes that are *fa* in different hexachords intensifies the poetic dialogue between Death and the supplicant.

## Vittoria/Raffaella Aleotti

Some confusion still exists over the identities of two published composers of the sixteenth century, Raffaella (ca. 1570–after 1646) and Vittoria Aleotti (ca. 1573–after 1620). Some scholars maintain that the two women were in fact one person, and that Vittoria simply took the name Raffaella upon entering Ferrara's San Vito Convent.[22] A major source of this confusion is the dedication written by Giovanni Battista Aleotti for his daughter Vittoria's *Ghirlanda de madrigali a quattro voci* (Garland of madrigals for four voices), published by G. Vicenti in Venice in 1593. Telling of the musical talents of his five daughters, Signor Aleotti relates that since the oldest girl had already decided to become a nun, he thought it a good idea to provide her with music lessons. "It so happened that while she was learning, my second daughter was always present, along with her sister Vittoria (a child of four going on five). . . ."[23] From this translation it would seem that Aleotti has spoken thus far of a total of three daughters; but other translations have rendered the passage, "my second daughter and her sister who is called Vittoria was always present," assuming that "her sister Vittoria" simply modifies "my second daughter."[24] Most scholars have assumed the oldest daughter to be Beatrice, who did enter the convent for a time, perhaps only as a student, and who later married.

Young Vittoria so astonished her parents and the music teacher with what she absorbed from her sister's lessons that she was given lessons of her own. At the age of six or seven Vittoria was sent to San Vito to continue her musical education, and by the age of fourteen she had decided to become a nun herself. Meanwhile, she had made such progress in her study of music theory that her father asked the poet Giovanni Battista Guarini for some verses, which Vittoria soon set to music as four-voice madrigals; hence the *Ghirlanda,* the work of a composer not yet out of her teens.

Soon thereafter the name Vittoria Aleotti drops from sight, and we hear only of Raffaella. Raffaella too brought out a volume of vocal music in 1593, *Sacrae cantiones quinque, septem, octo, & decem vocibus decantande* (Motets for five, seven, eight, and ten voices singing together; Venice: Ricciardo Amandino), the first sacred music by a woman to appear in print. After that date, all references to Raffaella are consistent with what we know of Vittoria: she is cited as a composer of both madrigals and motets, an exceptional organist and teacher in the convent, and a performer of both vocal and instrumental music in the homes of wealthy citizens of Ferrara. It is not possible to say with certainty whether Vittoria and Raffaella are two separate individuals or not, for the documents uncovered to date are inconclusive. However, existing evidence lends most support to the conclusion that they were in fact one person. For purposes of discussion, however, we shall use the name Vittoria when referring to the madrigals and Raffaella when referring to the motets.

Vittoria Aleotti's first published composition appeared in 1591: a single madrigal in an anthology of works by Ferrarese composers, brought out by Giacomo Vincenti of Venice. Her complete volume of 1593 contains twenty-one madrigals, all for four voices. Though written during the years when Ferrara's *concerto delle donne* was helping to change the complexion of the madrigal, Vittoria's pieces do not reflect these or other progressive trends. Instead, they reveal a solid grasp of basic sixteenth-century compositional technique and a youthful exuberance that is contagious. "Baciai per haver vita" (I kissed to have life), one of the pieces with text by Guarini, is typical. Each textual idea is given a musical setting that clearly differs from that which precedes or follows it yet complements the surrounding material. The lively imitative texture of the opening gives way to chordal declamation; then a sustained texture introduces the idea of death—but "so welcome a death" that gloom disappears as the voices ascend, the bass drops out, and the soprano even sings a two-bar ornament. The harmonies and rhythms are quite straightforward. Though Vittoria is not an innovator, her music reveals a lively talent that could have taken on new challenges had the opportunity arisen.

Most of Raffaella Aleotti's sixteen motets use biblical or liturgical texts associated with Matins services during the Christmas season or on one of the Feasts of the Virgin Mary. Though the specific times and places of their performance are unknown, the motets were probably used by the San Vito nuns in their chapel. "Facta est cum angelo" (And suddenly there was with the angel), for SAATB choir, uses familiar lines from Luke 2:13–14 describing the angels' visit to the shepherds outside Bethlehem. Like most motets of this period, "Facta est" contains contrasting chordal and imitative segments. The changes in texture are pictorial, for all the voices sing together in chordal fashion when they represent the "multitude of the heavenly host" singing "glory to God in the highest," whereas the narrative portions of the text are most often set imitatively. Other motets in Raffaella's collection are more strictly contrapuntal and less sectional than "Facta est," while still others are polychoral. On the whole, they seem more mature than Vittoria's madrigals. Yet like the madrigals, the motets exhibit a good grasp of technique and style and convey a more than superficial understanding of their subjects.

Vittoria/Raffaella Aleotti cannot be considered a professional composer, since her intention in entering the convent was to lead the life of a nun. Yet she was among the small but growing number of women whose works were published, not just as isolated pieces here and there, but in full volumes. In addition, Sister Raffaella was known as a performer, teacher, and conductor, and her activities continued into old age despite the dampening effect of the Counter-Reformation.

## WOMEN MUSICIANS AND THE CONCEPT OF THE "RENAISSANCE"

If women's status as composers and musicians improved during the final decades of the sixteenth century, the course of this improvement was irregular and its effects were confined to certain areas of music. By 1600, women could aspire to positions as court musicians or opera singers, but the professions of instrumentalist or church musician would remain almost exclusively male for some time. The field of composition had opened up to women, but only in a restricted way, limited as it was to music for vocal soloists or ensembles. Finally, the necessity to pursue a vocation as wife or nun led most young women to give up their music studies and disappear from recorded history at an early age. At the same time, however, women played an active and influential role in the unwritten tradition of fifteenth- and sixteenth-century music, creating texts, musical settings, and manners of performance that were not only part of the artistic mainstream but even in its vanguard. Singing to the lute was a pastime women shared with men, and the vocal virtuosity of such women as the *concerto delle donne* influenced both the written tradition and performance practice. In these areas, then, women could be said to have had at least something of a Renaissance.

NOTES

1. Margaret Leah King, "Thwarted Ambitions: Six Learned Women of the Italian Renaissance," *Soundings* 59 (1976):284.

2. Allan Atlas's comment that Beatrice was probably uninterested in Tinctoris's ideas concerning music theory seems unwarranted given the evidence presented. In the end, even Atlas concludes that one cannot really judge "either the level at which Tinctoris may have tutored the princess or the skill at music that [she] . . . may have attained." *Music at the Aragonese Court of Naples* (Cambridge: Cambridge University Press, 1985), p. 112.

3. Nino Pirrotta, "Music and Cultural Tendencies in Fifteenth-Century Italy," *Journal of the American Musicological Society* 19 (1966):144.

4. Claude Palisca, *Humanism in Italian Renaissance Musical Thought* (New Haven: Yale University Press, 1985), p. 5.

5. Nanie Bridgman, *La Vie musicale au Quattrocento et jusqu'à la naissance du madrigal (1400–1530)* (Paris: Gallimard, 1964), p. 134.

6. William Prizer, "Isabella d'Este and Lucrezia Borgia as Patrons of Music: The Frottola at Mantua and Ferrara," *Journal of the American Musicological Society* 38 (1985):1–33.

7. Wolfgang Osthoff, *Theatergesang und darstellende Musik in der italienischen Renaissance* (Tutzing: Hans Schneider, 1969), 1:10, 219–20.

8. Archilei's and Caccini's arias are published in D. P. Walker and J. Jacquot, eds., *Les Fêtes du mariage de Ferdinand de Médicis et de Christine de Lorraine* (Paris: Editions du Centre National de la Recherche Scientifique, 1963), pp. 1–8, 156.

9. Atlas, pp. 105–106.

10. Anthony Newcomb, "Courtesans, Muses, or Musicians? Professional Women Musicians in Sixteenth-Century Italy," in Jane Bowers and Judith Tick, eds., *Women Making Music* (Urbana: University of Illinois Press, 1986), p. 108.

11. Anthony Newcomb, *The Madrigal at Ferrara* (Princeton: Princeton University Press, 1980), 1:8–13.

12. Newcomb, "Courtesans," pp. 95–96.

13. Newcomb, *Madrigal,* 1:3.

14. Ercole Bottrigari, *Il Desiderio; or, Concerning the Playing Together of Various Musical Instruments,* translated by Carol MacClintock (Rome: American Institute of Musicology, 1962), pp. 57–59.

15. C. Ann Carruthers-Clement, "The Madrigals and Motets of Vittoria/Raphaela Aleotti," Ph.D. diss., Kent State University, 1982, p. 10.

16. Carl Gustav Anthon, "Music and Musicians in Northern Italy during the Sixteenth Century," Ph.D. diss., Harvard University, 1943, p. 77.

17. Kathi Meyer-Baer, *Der chorische Gesang der Frauen, mit besonderer Bezugnahme seiner Betätigung auf geistlichen Gebiet* (Leipzig: Breitkopf & Härtel, 1917), pp. 17–27.

18. Jane Bowers, "The Emergence of Women Composers in Italy, 1566–1700," in Bowers and Tick, *Women Making Music,* pp. 162–63.

19. Carol MacClintock, ed., *The Solo Song, 1580–1730* (New York: W. W. Norton, 1973), No. 4.

20. Biographical information from Beatrice Pescerelli, *I Madrigali di Maddalena Casulana* (Florence: Leo S. Olschki, 1979).

21. Ibid., p. 7 (my translation).

22. Most of the information on this controversy is taken from C. Ann Carruthers-Clement. The birth and death dates for Vittoria and Raffaella are those

in *The New Grove Dictionary of Music and Musicians*, which considers them to be two separate individuals.

23. Carruthers-Clement, p. 160.

24. "Sempre presente v'era la seconda mia figliuola, & sua sorella Vittoria detta (bambina di quattro in cinque Anni). . . ." The first translation is mine; the second is from Bowers, "Emergence," p. 130.

### SUGGESTIONS FOR FURTHER READING

In addition to the items mentioned in the text or cited in the notes, the following sources provide authoritative information on women during the period 1450–1600.

Campori, Giuseppe. "La figlia del Guarini [Anna Guarini]." *Nuova antologia* 12 (1869):321–32.

Castiglione, Baldesar. *The Book of the Courtier*. A number of editions are available.

Cook, Susan, and LeMay, Thomasin. *Virtuose in Italy, 1600–1640*. New York: Garland, 1984.

Elias, Cathy Ann. "Musical Performance in Sixteenth-Century Italian Literature: Straparola's *Le piacevoli notti.*" *Early Music* 18 (1989):161–73.

Kelly-Gadol, Joan, "Did Women Have a Renaissance?" In *Becoming Visible: Women in European History,* edited by R. Bridenthal and C. Koonz. Boston: Houghton Mifflin, 1987.

Kelso, Ruth. *Doctrine for the Lady of the Renaissance*. Urbana: University of Illinois Press, 1956.

Labalme, Patricia A., ed. *Beyond Their Sex: Learned Women of the European Past*. New York: New York University Press, 1980.

Lea, Kathleen. *Italian Popular Comedy*. 2 vols. Oxford: Clarendon Press, 1934.

Masson, Georgina. *Courtesans of the Italian Renaissance*. New York: St. Martin's Press, 1975.

Prizer, William F. *Courtly Pastimes: The Frottole of Marchetto Cara*. Ann Arbor: UMI Research Press, 1980.

### Music

Aleotti, Raffaella. "Angelus ad pastores ait," "Ascendens Christus in altum," "Facta est cum angelo," edited by C. Ann Carruthers-Clement. New York: Broude Brothers, 1983.

Aleotti, Vittoria. "Baciai per haver vita," "Hor che la vaga aurora," edited by C. Ann Carruthers-Clement. New York: Broude Brothers, 1983.

# IV.
# Musical Women of the Seventeenth and Eighteenth Centuries

*Barbara Garvey Jackson*

## Introduction

Women participated in most of the major developments of both Baroque and Classic styles in the seventeenth and eighteenth centuries, from composition in the new forms and styles to music publishing and instrument building. The period also saw the rise of an important new career for women, that of opera singer, because a well-trained soprano was the favored voice for most solo vocal music. Opera was the major new form of the early seventeenth century, one that always required women singers. Some women composed operas—Francesca Caccini sang in the first operas and was an opera composer as well. Despite two centuries of competition with male castrato singers and such minor setbacks as the ban on women's appearances on the stages of the Papal States, women opera singers flourished throughout Europe. The great stars had international careers from London to St. Petersburg, and little traveling companies (often family enterprises) provided opera to smaller courts and cities.

The contemporary dramatic and virtuoso singing styles also found their way into the music of Catholic, Lutheran, and Anglican church services, and the practice of combining instruments with voices in church music spread from Venice throughout Europe. Particularly in Italy and Austria, Catholic women responded to operatic, and later symphonic, influences when they wrote for the Church, just as did their male contemporaries. The only Protestant women active as church music composers were German Lutheran aristocrats, and they wrote mostly devotional music for home use, not service music. A noblewoman might have time and opportunity for musical training and was in a position of sufficient authority not to be restrained from religious composition if that was her bent. Anglican service music by women is practically unknown before the nineteenth century, while in the denominations emphasizing congregational singing, women sang as worshippers but were not allowed in choirs. There was never a Protestant equivalent for the musical opportunities afforded Catholic women by the convent.

In seventeenth-century Italy, musical performances in the convents of Milan and other northern cities were often splendid. Nuns published Masses and other liturgical music as well as paraliturgical motets; even Barbara Strozzi and Francesca Caccini, known largely for secular music, composed Catholic religious songs. During the eighteenth century, however, musical life in the convents declined for many reasons—from ecclesiastical disapproval of their musical activities to the dissolution of convents and the destruction of libraries that took place during the French Revolution and the Napoleonic wars.

There were some composers of religious music active outside the convents; in the latter half of the eighteenth century, Marianne von Martinez wrote several symphonic Masses and other liturgical music in Vienna. However, the accession of Emperor Joseph II in 1780 led to restrictions that discouraged elaborate musical settings of the liturgy, the use of instruments in church, and the involvement of women in the performance of church music. In France and England there were some women organists by the late eighteenth century, such as Elisabeth Lechanterie at the church of Saint-Jacques de la Boucherie in Paris. There were a few women soloists in churches in Hamburg as early as 1716, and at Eszterháza and Salzburg in the late eighteenth century. However, only men and boys were allowed to be members of most Catholic or Protestant church choirs.

During these centuries there was an increase in public secular music making and more musical careers not directly tied to the Church (although not all were open to women). Catholic church musicians were no longer required to be celibate clergy, and the Protestants never had been; so these married church musicians began to contribute to the networks of musical families so characteristic of the era. Male and female members of these musical dynasties pursued a wide variety of musical activities and formed support systems fostering the education and employment of their talented children. Families like the Caccinis, the Bachs, and the Bendas usually married within the profession. The daughters of musicians were often professionally trained, usually as singers. They often married other musicians, and their children tended to inherit musical talent, while the family setting provided professional apprenticeship. Although in the Bach family the professional activities of most of the women ceased at the time they married (except for J. C. Bach's wife, the soprano Cecilia Grassi, who had a long professional career), the women in families of court singers (like the Caccinis) often continued their musical careers after marriage. Professional activities within extended families included the creation and performance of various types of music, instrument building, and music engraving and publishing. There were active and successful women in every one of these activities (although church performance was rare).

No court musical establishment was complete without well-trained female singers, even if it did not maintain an opera. Female instrumentalists were sometimes court musicians, especially in the musical establishments of women aristocrats, such as Queen Marie Antoinette. However, violinist Regina Strinasacchi, who worked in the ducal orchestra at Gotha, was a rare exception to the general pattern that women were not hired as orchestral musicians at court or in the opera house.

Until the mid-eighteenth century, the harpsichord and the organ were the main keyboard instruments, both for solo music and as continuo in virtually all ensemble music. There were renowned women harpsichord players and some important composers for that instrument, but there were few female organists except in convents. In the late eighteenth century, the rise of the piano, with its solo role in concertos and sonatas, was accompanied by the rise of women pianist-composers, and some of the best performers were women.

The academies in Italy from the mid-sixteenth century onward were societies of intellectuals, under aristocratic sponsorship, which considered literary, philosophical, and musical matters and often fostered musical performance, especially of works that represented their aesthetic ideas and experiments. Their membership was all male, but women sang in their musical presentations. Members of the Caccini family in Florence and Barbara Strozzi in Venice were among the women musicians for whom academy performance was important.

By the eighteenth century, the salon, an aristocratic or middle-class gathering of intellectuals and music lovers, had become a means of fostering new music as well as art and literature in such cities as Paris, Vienna, and Berlin. Unlike the male academies, the salon was often under the patronage of an art-loving or intellectual woman who gathered brilliant representatives of the culture about her in a sort of private sponsorship, as in the soirées of Marianne von Martinez in Vienna. Most of the concert life of eighteenth-century Vienna took place in salons, private homes, and musical instrument shops (like the showroom of the piano builder Nannette Stein Streicher).

The seventeenth century also saw the rise of public concerts. By 1678 Thomas Britton was holding some in the loft over his London small-coal shop, and these included many women performers. In Venice the girls of the conservatories performed orchestral music and oratorios within their institutions for enthusiastic public audiences. By the early eighteenth century the Concert Spirituel series in Paris used male and female musicians, both Parisians and touring artists. Similar concert series were soon organized in London, Edinburgh, Frankfurt, Hamburg, and even such American cities as Boston and Charleston.

The mixed chorus—a choir of both men and women—was established in the eighteenth century. At the beginning of the seventeenth century virtually all choral music was for all-male choirs, with boy choristers and adult male falsettists and castrati singing the treble parts. There were female choirs, but only in convents or in the Venetian conservatories, while the Church viewed the whole idea of men and women singing together in church choral music with suspicion. Even in the convents, much of the polyphonic music that has survived seems to have been for groups of soloists. Since established choral groups existed only for religious music, mixed choral groups could be found only in *ad hoc* secular court festivities. But in opera, which grew out of such *ad hoc* festive occasions, the chorus was always mixed—although it disappeared from the Italian stage not long after the opening of public opera houses (Venice, 1637), no doubt for reasons of economy. Women remained on the stage as soloists, often as fabulously well-paid stars. In France, where opera was a court activity supported by the royal purse, the mixed chorus was retained. At the Concerts Spirituels choral works were performed with the same chorus that sang in the opera.

In Germany Johann Mattheson (Hamburg) and Johann Adam Hiller (Leipzig) argued strongly that women's voices should be well trained and used in all choral music, including that of the Church, but it was only outside the Church that the mixed chorus could develop. Hiller opened a singing school in 1771 in which he trained male and female singers for his public concerts in Leipzig; and in Berlin, in 1790, C. F. C. Fasch organized a *Singakademie* of professional musicians and capable amateurs that demonstrated the viability of a permanently organized mixed chorus and became a model for choral societies throughout Europe and even in America.

The establishment of these choruses was facilitated by the strong musical interests of amateurs in the growing middle class, which was also affluent enough to pay for music instruction, buy instruments (especially pianos and harps), attend public concerts, and purchase printed music. Eighteenth-century amateurs were often very fine performers and sometimes quite good composers; their ranks included both aristocratic and middle-class women and men. There was a wide range of abilities, of course, from girls for whom music was merely a social adornment to make them more marriageable, to such excellent pianists as Barbara von Ployer, Marianne von Grenzinger, and the Archduke Rudolph, for whom Haydn, Mozart, and Beethoven wrote demanding masterpieces. It was the connoisseurs and amateurs who created the vigorous market for widespread domestic and public music making of the late eighteenth century.

## THE EARLY SEVENTEENTH CENTURY IN ITALY

Music theorists in the early seventeenth century distinguished between *prima prattica* (the first practice), the old contrapuntal art of the church musician, and *seconda prattica* (the second practice), the new dramatic style for solo singer accompanied by figured bass. The *prima prattica* had been largely a male art, composed and sung for church, and access to formal instruction in this art was not easily available to women. Nevertheless, some women learned counterpoint through private study, among them Isabella Leonarda, the most prolific woman composer of the seventeenth century, who apparently studied with the *maestro di cappella* of the local cathedral. Her work shows her sound training in the art, for eleven of her compositions are entirely in strict *a cappella* counterpoint, as are sections of two of her Masses. She also uses imitative counterpoint freely in instrumentally accompanied choral works, such as the second Kyrie of Messa Prima from Op. 18 (HAMW, pp. 51–53).

The *seconda prattica* was the modern music of the day and the style of the new forms of monody and opera. Although it originated as a secular style, it quickly invaded church music and may be seen in religious music by Francesca Caccini and Barbara Strozzi. Most women musicians, both performers and composers, cultivated the *seconda prattica* in secular musical works and learned the new art as singers. Their theoretical training emphasized the newly invented figured bass technique rather than the older contrapuntal style.

### The Caccinis

The remarkable Caccini family led in the development of the dramatic style of solo song accompanied by figured bass at the beginning of the seventeenth century. The musically active family members included the father, his two wives, a son, two daughters, and at least one granddaughter. Giulio Caccini, the father, had developed a style of musical declamation that aimed to "almost speak in tones." The "certain noble negligence of song" of this new music required a new manner of singing, which he taught to his first and second wives—Lucia and Margherita—and to his children—Francesca, Settimia, and Pompeo. He also taught his daughters composition and the continuo instruments—harpsichord and lute. Through the mastery of these instruments they acquired the technical tools necessary for composition in the new style, as well as for the improvisation of vocal ornamentation. When the spectacular virtuosa Vittoria Archilei sang at the Medici court in Florence in 1588, Caccini associated himself with her by proudly claiming that she performed his music, bragging in the preface to his opera *Euridice* of "the new manner of passages and redoubled points, invented by me, which Vittoria Archilei, a singer of that excellence to which her resounding fame bears witness, has long employed in singing my works" (although a contemporary witness, Giustiniani, claimed it was Archilei herself who had "almost originated the true method of singing for females").[1]

Giulio's oldest daughter, Francesca Caccini (1587–1640?), made her professional debut at the age of thirteen in *Euridice,* an opera by her father's rival Jacopo Peri. When the ensemble of family musicians, "il concerto Caccini," traveled to Paris in 1604, Francesca's singing so impressed the French king that he sought to keep the young woman in Paris, but the Florentine court would not release her, and she formally entered the service of the Medicis in 1607. The same year she married singer Giovanni Battista Signorini. She collaborated with Michelangelo Buonarroti (nephew of the artist), setting his poetry to music for several court entertainments (all of which have been lost). She, her sister, and Vittoria Archilei performed in a trio (now lost) said to have contained splendid contrapuntal passages. In 1616 Francesca and her husband went to Rome to perform in the entourage of Cardinal Carlo de' Medici, and the following year they traveled to other Italian cities. They were thus among the earliest artists to tour, an activity that later became common for professional musicians and in which women were active from the beginning.

Francesca Caccini composed and published both sacred and secular music. At a time when women were generally barred from singing in church, she and her sister, Settimia, were soloists in the Church of San Nicola in Pisa during the Holy Week performances directed by their father. Francesca was described as "singing perfectly in the interpretation of music of every style, sacred as well as secular, and contrapuntal as well as monodic."[2]

Francesca's first publication was *Il primo libro delle musiche a una e due voci* (1618). It contains thirty-two solo songs and four duets for soprano and bass (perhaps for performance with her husband). The dedication to Cardinal de' Medici may explain the inclusion of many religious pieces—twelve settings of Italian devotional poetry (some of which Francesca may have written) and seven Latin liturgical texts (see the Italian spiritual madrigal "Maria, dolce Maria" and the Latin Psalm "Laudate Dominum" in HAMW, pp. 25–34). In 1622 she collaborated with Giovanni Battista da Gagliano on *Il martirio di Sant' Agata,* a *sacra rappresentazione,* or sacred piece in dramatic style foreshadowing oratorio; unhappily, the work has been lost.

The music in *Il primo libro* combines musical declamation Caccini had learned from her father with the virtuoso embellishment practiced by Archilei and the Ferrarese singers. She uses many forms of the period: simple canzonettas, which are completely strophic in form; strophic variations, in which the bass line, though somewhat varied, is repeated while the succeeding stanzas of the poem are set to a freely worked melody; and sectional pieces foreshadowing the cantatas of Barbara Strozzi, in which the changing emotions of the text are reflected in contrasting sections. Some pieces were completely through-composed. Caccini characteristically wrote out all ornamentation (at a time when it was often left to the singer to improvise), and she often used embellishment for expressive rather than purely decorative effect, as in "Maria, dolce Maria" (HAMW, pp. 31–34). From 1618 to about 1623 she trained singers for court performances. The transmission of a new style to a circle of followers and students is an important stage in the development of any art form, and her teaching role is thus another indication of her significance. In 1621 she bore a daughter, Margherita, who became a singer (no doubt trained by her mother) and a nun at San Girolamo in Florence.

The most famous of Francesca Caccini's stage works was *La liberazione di Ruggiero dall' isola d'Alcina,* the first extant opera by a woman (see "Aria of the Shepherd" from this opera in HAMW, pp. 35–37). It was commissioned by the joint regents, Christine and Maria Maddalena de' Medici, mother and widow, respectively, of Cosimo de' Medici. The occasion was the state visit of Prince Ladislas Sigismund of Poland to the Pitti Palace on February 2, 1625. The opera was repeated in Warsaw three years later, the first Italian opera performed outside of Italy. It was also the first opera based on Ariosto's *Orlando Furioso,* a popular source of Renaissance madrigal texts, which remained a literary inspiration for composers and librettists for more than a century.

The cast of six sopranos, two altos, seven tenors, and one bass exemplifies the seventeenth-century delight in high voices, although the large number of natural male voices and the absence of a castrato are unusual. The many short arias commonly bracket the sections in which the singer is accompanied by continuo with instrumental ritornelli, as in the "Aria of the Shepherd" (HAMW, pp. 35–38). The choice of three recorders for the ritornello is another example of the taste for treble ensembles. There are several short five- and six-part choruses (probably sung by an ensemble of soloists), a brief chorus for six sopranos, and a double-chorus madrigal in eight parts. Francesca Caccini disappeared from the pay list of the court after 1627, although she continued to perform occasionally. She probably died in 1640.

The career of Settimia Caccini (1591–ca. 1638) was centered in Mantua. Her husband was the singer Alessandro Ghivizzani, and both of them were in the service of the Gonzaga family at Mantua, where they worked with Monteverdi (for whom Settimia created the role of Venus in *Arianna* in 1608). Settimia was employed to perform in the cities in which her husband worked, so when he became *maestro di cappella* at Lucca and later went to the court of Parma, she sang professionally in those cities. After she was widowed in 1632, she returned to the payroll of the Medici court in Florence. Later court account books list a Settimia Ghivizzani, who was probably her daughter. Both Settimia and Alessandro composed, and two manuscripts survive with their songs. The aria "Già sperai, non spero hor' più" is attributed to her in a seventeenth-century published collection. Although short, it displays the multisectional structure that was later to characterize the cantata.

## A Cantata Composer outside the Theatre—Barbara Strozzi

Barbara Strozzi (1619–after 1664) was a Venetian composer and singer, renowned as the "virtuosissima cantatrice" (most virtuosic singer). She was the adopted daughter of the poet Giulio Strozzi. Although she lived in Venice, where public opera was born, and studied composition with an opera composer (Francesco Cavalli), she herself neither performed nor composed opera. For unknown reasons, she sang only in her father's house for the academy he founded. She made her public career in a quite new way—entirely by publishing her compositions. Eight volumes of her music were published in Venice between 1644 and 1664. They contain over a hundred works, all vocal music, mostly for solo voice and continuo, with a few ensemble pieces among her early publications. The continuo accompaniments could have been performed on lute or chitarrone, and were probably originally played by the composer herself. Although Strozzi did not perform publicly, her published work circulated outside Italy, and she rated an entry in Walther's German *Lexikon* decades after her death. More than a century after her death, the English historians Charles Burney and John Hawkins both considered her a noteworthy composer.

Barbara Strozzi was a precocious talent, singing for her father's musical and literary friends by the age of fifteen (when Nicolò Fontei wrote songs for her to texts by her father). Her father's Accademia degli Unisoni (Academy of the like-minded) met at the Strozzi house for their witty and rhetorical discussions, at which Barbara sang, often performing her own compositions, and served as their mistress of ceremonies.

This sheltered career may have been an attempt to protect Strozzi from the slander to which Venetian women musicians were vulnerable. If so, it was not successful, for association with her father's free-thinking and libertine circle subjected her to malicious rumors and satire at the tender age of sixteen (although references to her in her adult life do not allude to the early spiteful rumors). Perhaps it was this bitter experience that kept her from a public performing career.

Strozzi's early publications were underwritten by her father, and later volumes were dedicated to high-ranking patrons in Venice and across the Alps. Some of her works also appeared in seventeenth-century collections. Most of her music is secular, except Op. 5, *I sacri musicali affetti,* which contains settings of fourteen Latin poems with sacred themes tied to specific seasons of the church calendar.

Strozzi was one of the most prolific composers of secular chamber music in the century, ranking above Giacomo Carissimi, Luigi Rossi, and Marc' Antonio Cesti in number of published works. She used many of the forms and vocal styles in use in the period, ranging from long works labeled "cantata" or "lamento" to simpler, even strophic, forms. Her expressive melodic style and her strong, active bass lines are both illustrated in Example 4-1, an excerpt from "Tradimento!" from Op. 7, *Diporti di Euterpe overo cantate e ariette a voce sola.* The one-word refrain, "Tradimento" (betrayal), opens the piece, appears again before the second stanza, and concludes the work. The martial, trumpetlike melodic figure to which it is set is varied each time it is used. New musical material is used for each of the three stanzas of the poem, expressing its specific emotional content. In the last stanza the martial motive from the refrain is used for the words "To arms, my heart." The section shown here, the second refrain and the beginning of the second stanza, illustrates the text painting on the word "legarmi" (to tie me) and the writhing embellishment of "lusinga" (entices).

EXAMPLE 4-1.        Barbara Strozzi, "Tradimento!" mm. 24–31, from *Diporte di Euterpe* (Venice: Francesco Magni, 1659). Copy in the Civico Museo Bibliografico Musicale di Bologna. Text: "Betrayal! Hope, to tie me, with great things entices the more I believe."

## Women and Music in Italian Convents

More than half the music published by women in northern Italy in the seventeenth century was by nuns, especially in Milan, Bologna, Pavia, and Novara. Splendid musical performances took place in the convents despite the Council of Trent's strong disapproval in its decree of 1553:

> [In convents] the Divine Office should continue to be sung by them [the nuns] and not by professionals hired for that purpose, and . . . they should answer in . . . the Mass [only] whatever the choir is accustomed to answer, but they will leave to the Deacon and Subdeacon [male clergy] the office of chanting the Lessons, Epistles, and Gospels. *They will abstain from singing either in Choir or elsewhere the so-called "figured chant"* [polyphonic music]. . . .[3]

The rule was not enforced uniformly, but it was always a real threat to musically active convents and the basis for sporadic or continuous harassment by conservative churchmen. However, when local authorities permitted it, music in the convents flourished.

As musical styles changed in the outside world, the new developments were immediately taken up by the nuns. The solo motet (for one to four solo voices with basso continuo) seems uniquely well suited for convent use, since it was so often written for treble soloists, although when there was more than one solo voice in the published works, bass and sometimes tenor voices were likely to be included. The composing nuns wrote Psalms, Magnificats, and Masses, as well as motets with extraliturgical texts, often contemporary devotional poetry they had also written; virtually all their music was for use in the church service. The composers Caterina Assandra, Claudia Sessa, and Chiara Margarita Cozzolani were from convents in or near Milan. Cozzolani's Op. 3 (1650) calls for splendid forces of up to eight voices, and some of her works used violins with voice and organ, combining voices and instruments in the modern, concerted style. These composers were known as far away as Strasbourg and even Protestant Leipzig, where their works were published in seventeenth-century collections.

For most of the nun composers only single volumes of published music have survived, but Isabella Leonarda (1620–1704) published over 200 works in twenty volumes. The earliest were two dialogues for alto, tenor, and basso continuo, which appeared in 1640 in a collection by Gasparo Casati, *maestro di cappella* of the Novara Cathedral and probably Leonarda's teacher. It was common practice for a teacher to introduce works of a maturing student by including them in his own publication. Although Leonarda's first two independently published volumes have been lost, all her printed music from 1670 on is extant. A gap of several years in her published output may indicate that Leonarda ceased composing for a time, but her style gives no evidence of a creative hiatus. Rather, like her younger contemporary Arcangelo Corelli, she probably selected pieces for publication from works she had already composed, a supposition borne out by the neatly balanced arrangement of the works within her volumes. In 1693 she published twelve church sonatas (eleven trio sonatas and one solo sonata), the earliest instrumental works by a woman to have survived complete.

Leonarda's family was of the minor nobility and had strong church ties. Two of her brothers were churchmen at the Novara cathedral, and two sisters were nuns in her convent. Leonarda entered the convent at the age of sixteen, and her first music was published four years later. She eventually rose to administrative office in the convent, and the title pages of her publications chronicle her successive titles of *madre, madre superiora* (mother superior), *madre vicaria* (perhaps a provincial administrator), and finally *consigliera* (counsellor). Her strong personal devotion to the Virgin Mary is indicated in the unusual double dedications of her works—to the Virgin and to a human dedicatee (from city officials in Novara to the Emperor Leopold I). She may well have written many of her motet texts, as the very personal text of "Quam dulcis es" from Op. 13 suggests. In it she addresses Mary directly:

How sweet you are, how dear—my loving heart!—o holy Mother.
. . . . . . . . . . . . . . . . . . . . . . . . . . . . . . . . . . . . . . . . .
If I sing, if I make sounds, they are songs through you.
With the music I give you, you take me back again.
Melodious accents are fashioned by me so that my harmonies magnify you.
Therefore my music is always wholly yours, Virgin Mary. Amen.[4]

As in this piece, many of Leonarda's vocal works use two violins and continuo to accompany the voice. This combination, the "church trio," survived to the end of the eighteenth century as a common and practical instrumental grouping in much church music.

All of Leonarda's vocal volumes included pieces requiring tenor and/or bass voices. Even the books that are entirely for solo voice (Opp. 12, 14, 15, 17, 20) include works for bass. Leonarda may have revised works originally written for the nuns to make the published volumes useful outside convents, but it seems much more likely that for special occasions extra singers were hired by the convent (a practice also found in other church institutions). Perhaps the male clergy serving the congregation sang these parts. Since church authorities constantly complained about nuns' contacts with outside musicians, one can assume that the use of outsiders did in fact occur. The

Ursuline order to which Leonarda's convent belonged was a teaching order (founded to educate girls); it was probably associated with a school in which the girls may have been musically trained. Santa Orsola, like so many convents, was dissolved during the Napoleonic era; most of the records were destroyed, and its library was scattered. No manuscript music survives, and many fascinating questions about the institution and its music remain unanswered.

Most of Leonarda's music is written in the highly expressive dramatic, sectional style favored in the mid-seventeenth century (see HAMW, pp. 41–56). In the Credo of the *Messa Prima* from Op. 18, tempo changes even within sections are used for text expression. The word "Crucifixus" (He was crucified) is marked *adagio* and is floridly set, but the next phrase, "etiam pro nobis" (also for us), is marked *spiritoso* (animated), a term Leonarda uses frequently. The syllabic text setting also increases the animation, to express joy that the sacrifice was "for us." The violins echo both emotions. Dynamics are marked; see the word *piano* at measures 94 and 108. Tutti and solo markings make clear that this is truly a choral work, which seems to be a rarity among the surviving works of seventeenth-century nuns.

Copies of Leonarda's works are in libraries in northern Europe as well as in Italy. Sébastian de Brossard (1655–1730) owned several of her works (which he gave to the Bibliothèque Nationale), and he thought highly of them. At the time Beethoven was growing up in Bonn there was a set of part books for one of her Masses in the court library inventory, though by then the music was too old-fashioned to be in use. Long after her death Leonarda's works were known to Fétis and Gerber, and her name appears in both of their biographical dictionaries.

### The Venetian Conservatories

Among the most remarkable institutions in seventeenth- and eighteenth-century Europe were the four *ospedali*, or conservatories, of Venice: the Ospedale della Pietà; i Mendicanti; gli Incurabili; and i Derelitti, or l'Ospedaletto. They cared for many persons in need, including orphaned or abandoned boys and girls, as did charitable institutions in other cities. In the Venetian institutions, girls who showed musical talent were given remarkable educations, apparently because music performed by the children had proved useful in encouraging the giving of alms. Similar institutions in Naples and elsewhere provided musical training for boys only.

In the seventeenth and eighteenth centuries, money to run the institutions was raised by private donations and public funds (such as gondola rental fees and the sale of indulgences), while the alms collections financed dowries for the girls who married—this was a remarkably enlightened concern at a time when a respectable marriage without a dowry was impossible. Girolamo Miani (St. Emiliani), the Venetian nobleman who founded l'Ospedaletto, believed in teaching the poor and considered the arts important in their education. Thus, at l'Ospedaletto the girls had enough musical training by the mid-sixteenth century to perform the daily Offices at the institution, and by 1600 about forty girls were admitted into a special program to learn music.[5]

In the early seventeenth century, music had become very important in all four institutions, each of which had its own choir and orchestra of girls. Famous musicians (for example, Antonio Vivaldi at la Pietà) were employed as teachers; and each institution presented concerts of both instrumental and vocal music, which visitors from all over Europe came to hear. The rigorous curriculum took ten years to complete. At the end of this time the most accomplished could remain in the institution as licensed *maestrae*. This gave the musically talented woman an alternative to marriage: a teaching career in an institution that was not a convent. The teaching was shared by the outside masters and the *maestrae*. Sometimes the *maestrae* were celebrated artists, well known to the public through their performances at the *ospedali* concerts, though they never toured in the outside world. Vivaldi wrote at least twenty-two violin concertos to display the virtuosity of Maestra Anna Maria della Pietà, which were heard only in the concerts of that institution. Incidentally, her name illustrates the use of the title of an institution or instrument as a surname for a foundling.

The central instrumental form cultivated in the conservatory concerts was the concerto. Hundreds were written for soloists with string orchestra and continuo, using almost every instrument of the period (except organ and harpsichord) in solo roles. The performances clearly demonstrated that women could perform on any instrument, a fact mentioned with delight and surprise by many visitors. Choral music was also performed in the conservatories, including much liturgical music, a valuable and virtually unexplored repertoire for treble voices. Some of the music of Galuppi, Hasse, Porpora, and Vivaldi for the conservatories exists in two versions: one for treble voices, and another that includes tenor and bass voices. There was music in the conservatory libraries that called for male voices, but it was sung entirely by women, sometimes with the lower parts transposed, sometimes with instruments performing the bass parts. There is no record that men were ever hired to sing at the Venetian *ospedali*, and the markings on many performance parts confirm that the performers were all women. This appears to be another indication of the horror with which the Church viewed mixing male and female voices.

Oratorio provided edifying religious recreation in the operatic style during Lent, when the theatres were closed. Although oratorio in other parts of Italy was often performed for audiences of all-male confraternities (religious clubs for laymen), in Venice they were written for the women conservatory students to perform for mixed public audiences. The great popularity of the conservatory oratorios may be judged by the fact that the libretti for more than 200 have survived.

There were restrictions for students educated in the institutions. If a conservatory musician left to marry, she had to agree not to perform in public, at least not in Venice, and even if she became a nun she had to go to a convent outside the Republic of Venice. The violinist Anna Maria della Pietà could continue a performing career only by staying as a *maestra* at the institution; while Maddalena Lombardini, who was educated at i Mendicanti, achieved a distinguished international reputation performing in Paris, London, Dresden, and as far away as Russia.

Maddalena Lombardini, later Sirmen (1745–85), was a virtuoso violinist and the only known woman composer trained in the Venetian conservatories. Her parents were impoverished aristocrats, who had her admitted to the Ospedale dei Mendicanti at the age of seven. During her fourteen-year stay at the conservatory, she was granted special permission to leave occasionally to study with Giuseppe Tartini (1692–1770). The earliest critical notice she received as an adult performer was from Quirino Gasparini, who wrote: "She won the hearts of all the people of Turin with her playing. . . . I wrote to old Tartini last Saturday telling him the good news. It will make him all the happier, since this student of his plays his violin compositions with such perfection that it is obvious she is his descendant."

At twenty-one, Lombardini was a licensed *maestra* at the conservatory, so she had to ask permission from the Board of Governors when she decided to marry and to pursue a career in the outside world. She married violinist Ludovico Sirmen in 1767, and they toured together. In London she performed her own violin concerti, was a member of the Italian opera orchestra, and even took leading roles as a singer in works by Pergolesi and Gluck. Other successes were as a violinist in Paris at the Concerts Spirituels in 1768–69 and again in 1785, when she performed a concerto by Viotti in which the most modern violin techniques were exemplified. She was enormously successful as a composer. Leopold Mozart considered her concertos "beautifully composed," and her works were published in France, England, the Netherlands, Germany, and Austria. Many of her works were still in print sixty years after her death, some having gone through as many as five editions. Her works included violin concertos and chamber music, and display the violin with brilliant virtuosity in the new style of the early Classical period. According to family archives, the daughter of Maddalena Lombardini Sirmen married a distant relative of the seventeenth-century composer Isabella Leonarda.

## Opera Singers

Except in France, opera in the seventeenth and eighteenth centuries was dominated by Italian singers. The careers of hundreds of women singers are documented, although there was competition for high-voice roles from the castrati. Baroque opera typically used high voices for most of the roles, regardless of gender, so the hero was commonly a mezzo-soprano or an alto, and could be either a castrato or a woman. The contralto Francesca

Rosalba Carriera (1675–1757), portrait of Faustina Bordoni. Used by permission of the Civici musei veneziani d'arte e di storia, Venice.

Bertolli, one of Handel's singers, was described in London in 1729 as "a very genteel Actress, both in Men's and Women's Parts." On the other hand, early seventeenth-century Venetian opera often used the male tenor voice for comic old women's roles. The gender of characters in opera, as in Elizabethan spoken drama, in which boys played the women's roles, was sufficiently ambiguous to facilitate the disguise plots that the audiences of the time relished.

Women opera singers were usually privately trained, as was the case with Faustina Bordoni (later Hasse, 1700–81). She was from a noble Venetian family, which was unusual for any woman professional other than a nun. Her family background ensured that she did not suffer the moral problems associated with sponsorship by a nobleman (a common pattern for French actresses and singers) or need to worry about her reputation. Her family's position also assured Bordoni an excellent education. Her musical talent was recognized early, and she studied with the singer Antonio Bernachi, the aristocrat-composer Benedetto Marcello, and Michelangelo Gasparini, brother of one of the important teachers at the Pietà. Since she had not actually been educated in the conservatory, she could begin her career in Venice, where she made her debut at age sixteen. She was soon an international star, singing for very high fees in other Italian cities, as well as in Munich and Vienna. She went to London in the 1720s, where she sang for Handel for nearly a decade. Although her family name was distinguished, she was often referred to merely as Faustina, a first-name-only form of address common in the theatrical world.

In 1730 Faustina married the composer Johann Adolph Hasse, in whose operas she had been a great success. Both were hired at the court of Dresden, where she was paid twice as much as he. Their two daughters became singers, though they were not the superstars their parents were. The Hasses were able to retire with financial security to Vienna and later to Venice.

## FROM THE *GRAND SIÈCLE* TO THE REVOLUTION IN FRANCE

The latter half of the seventeenth century in France began the "great century" of Louis XIV, during which Jean-Baptiste Lully was the monarch of French music. Among Lully's innovations was the use of professional female dancers on the stage in 1681, replacing the aristocratic amateurs of earlier French productions. The stunning performances of de La Fontaine, Pasant, Carré, and Leclercq brought women permanently onto the French stage as professional *danseuses*.

The French did not care for the castrato voice, so soprano roles in French opera were sung by women. As Le Cerf said, "a third of the leading roles in the operas of Lully are those of ordinary tenors; our women are always women; our basses sing the roles of Kings, Magicians, solemn and older Heroes; and our tenors and *hautes-contre* are the young gallant heroes and the amorous gods."[6] Female alto roles were not used in French opera until Campra's role for Mlle. Maupin in 1702, although the very high male tenor voice (*haute-contre*) was common. Women were part of the French opera chorus from its beginning in the 1670s. The normal chorus used female sopranos, *hautes-contre*, tenors, and basses for the *grand choeur* (with baritones added if there were five parts), and two sopranos and *haute-contre* for a *petit choeur* of select singers, the same arrangement found in French religious motets of the period.

The singing of French nuns at convents like the Feuillants in Paris and the Abbey of Longchamps was much praised, but no French nun composers are known. Nuns also sang outside the convent walls, as soloists in liturgical music at the chapel of Versailles. Even more surprising, laywomen sang sacred solos both in convents and at Versailles, where Anne-Renée Rebel and her two daughters sang regularly for the King's Mass, as did Louise Couperin, a cousin of François Couperin *le grand*. François's eldest daughter, Marie-Madeleine Couperin, was a musical nun, probably an organist, at the royal abbey of Maubisson.

The Concerts Spirituels were founded in 1725 to perform instrumental music and sacred choral works at the Salle des Suisses of the Tuileries Palace during Lent and on other religious holidays when the opera was closed (hence the name). The grand motets with Latin texts performed at these concerts were some of the earliest sacred works to enter the concert hall, and the choir included women. Women also performed as solo singers and instrumentalists. Among the performers were harpists Anne-Marie Steckler Krumpholz (who also had a brilliant career in England after the Revolution) and Countess Stéphanie-Félicité de Genlis, violinists Mme. Gautherot and Maddalena Lombardini Sirmen, many harpsichordists (and, later in the century, fortepianists), and singers. Many works by women composers were also heard in the Concerts Spirituels.

Women were active in the business of engraving and publishing music in France, and young girls could be apprenticed in the craft of engraving. One such was Louise Roussel, who married the violinist Jean-Marie Leclair and engraved and published much of his music, as well as works of many other composers. She came under suspicion (though she was apparently innocent) when Leclair was murdered with a sharp object that might have been an engraver's tool. Frequently women were partners in business with their husbands and quite prepared to take over the shop when they became widows. In the important Boivin firm, publisher François Boivin married Elizabeth Ballard, who worked with him in the shop. Her father was the music printer Jean-Baptiste-Christophe Ballard, who represented the fifth generation of another important publishing house. Women in the family had been active in the Ballard business since its founding, so Elizabeth undoubtedly learned the profession as she was growing up. When her husband died in 1733, she ran the Boivin company for twenty years, during which time the value of the stock skyrocketed. In the Erard family, most noted for piano and harp building, Marie-Françoise Erard and Catherine-Barbe Erard Marcous were active as publishers from 1798 to 1833.

Aristocratic Frenchwomen learned to play the "feminine instruments"—lute, harp, harpsichord, or, later in the century, piano—or to sing. Some reached a high level of artistry, while others remained inept. The number of serious amateurs created a market for music teachers (a few of whom were women), especially since it was the custom for dedicated, wealthy dilettantes to have daily lessons. Lady amateurs, as well as some professional singers, published numerous songs of varying quality in fashionable collections or in journals like the *Mercure de France*.

The two most impressive French women composers before the Revolution, in terms of the quality as well as the quantity of their surviving works, were Elisabeth-Claude Jacquet de la Guerre and Antonia Bembo, both of whom were writing in the late seventeenth and early eighteenth centuries.

### Elisabeth-Claude Jacquet de la Guerre

> For four years a wonder has appeared here. She sings at sight the most difficult music. She accompanies herself, and accompanies others who wish to sing, at the harpsichord, which she plays in a manner that cannot be imitated. She composes pieces, and plays them in all the keys asked of her . . . and she is still only ten years old.[7]

The prodigy described in this review in the *Mercure galant* in July 1677 was Elisabeth Jacquet (ca. 1666–1729), daughter of the French organist Claude Jacquet and his wife, Anne de la Touche. Both parents were from families of performers, teachers, and, in the case of the Jacquets, harpsichord builders. Elisabeth took her first lessons with her father, a harpsichord and organ teacher. By the time she made her Versailles debut in 1673 she was well prepared to accept the offer from Mme. de Montespan, the king's mistress, to reside at Versailles. There Elisabeth performed and completed her general education, perhaps with Mme. de Maintenon (the governess of Montespan's children by the king and later his secret wife). In

1684, probably aged eighteen, Elisabeth married Marin de la Guerre, also an organist and harpsichord teacher, and moved back to Paris. She maintained her contacts with the court without having to live there, enjoying the best of both worlds.

Marriage did not end professional activities for La Guerre. She wrote a ballet (now lost), which was performed at Versailles, and a successful opera. In 1687 she published a book of harpsichord pieces that included several suites of French dances, unmeasured preludes, chaconnes, and toccatas. In some movements she exhibits the marriage of French and Italian styles which is also found in music of her contemporary François Couperin *le grand*. A second set of harpsichord pieces, which appeared in 1707, includes "La Flamande," an elegant allemande. It is fully marked with the French symbols for little embellishments *(agrémens)* and is followed by a *double*, or variation, on each of the two sections (HAMW, pp. 59–62). The Chaconne, in the same volume, is a variation dance form in which the first *couplet* returns between each new statement, combining variation and rondeau principles in the characteristic French manner (HAMW, pp. 63–65).

La Guerre also wrote violin solo and trio sonatas around 1695, which is within five years of the first such music in France. She published three volumes of cantatas in the first wave of French cantata production (the first printed collections appeared in 1706, La Guerre's first volume in 1708). Her first two books are unique in France in that the texts are based on Bible stories, with three of the twelve on biblical women—*Esther, Susanne et les vieillards* (Susannah and the elders), and *Judith*. The mythological texts of the third volume are more typical of French cantatas. The first piece in this volume is *Semelé*, based on the Greek myth of Semele, the mistress of Zeus whose desire to see her lover destroys her (see HAMW, pp. 66–76). The last air, as in most French cantatas, is the moral of the story (often a rather cynical one, although not in this example). The cantata calls for one singer, although the text alternates between the narrator and the protagonist, which is typical of the French form. Although many of La Guerre's cantatas are for singer and continuo only, this one is "avec Simphonie," that is, with an instrumental part (violin or violins in unison, with optional flute in the second air). The violin plays the prelude and the interludes between the airs, and forms a duet with the singer in all but the last air. The instrumental pieces in La Guerre's cantatas are often vividly descriptive, as in the agitated prelude to the accompanied recitative "Mais quel bruit étonnant" (But what an astonishing noise), in which the violin and voice alternately portray the thunder and lightning of Zeus's appearance.

Jacquet de la Guerre was widowed in 1704, and her only son, a young musical prodigy, apparently died at about the same time. In her years of widowhood she was professionally active, and many of her publications date from the period after her bereavement. She performed publicly at the popular fair theatres, for which she wrote some songs, and gave concerts in her home. Her last known work (now lost) was a choral Te Deum celebrating the recovery of Louis XV from smallpox. Such a work would only have been commissioned from a composer of undoubted importance. At her death in 1729 a medal was struck in her honor, and Evrard Titon du Tillet wrote:

> She had a very great genius for composition, and excelled in vocal music the same as in instrumental; . . . One can say that never had a person of her sex had such talents as she for the composition of music, and for the admirable manner in which she performed it at the harpsichord and on the organ. . . .[8]

La Guerre apparently never left France, but her music was known in Germany. She performed for Max Emanuel, Elector of Bavaria, when he visited Paris in 1713, and dedicated the mythological cantatas to him (see *Semelé*). Walther's German *Lexikon* (1732) has a longer article for La Guerre than for François Couperin *le grand*. Although her rediscovery took longer than Couperin's, today she is probably the woman composer of the period best known to modern audiences, through performances of her harpsichord works and cantatas and several fine recordings.

## Antonia Bembo

In striking contrast to the highly visible Elisabeth Jacquet de la Guerre, Antonia Bembo is a mysterious figure. She lived during the reign of Louis XIV, but her dates are unknown. She was from Venice, although her family connections there cannot be traced, and when and why she found herself in France is unclear. Nothing is known of her musical training. She wrote large-scale works (an opera and two Te Deums), though no record exists of performances. She lived in a convent, although she was not a nun, and her "career" as a composer was secluded to an incredible degree. She was under the protection of the king, as the young Elisabeth Jacquet had been, but no record of payment of royal support has been found.

All that is known of Bembo is the impressive group of surviving works and the biographical information in their prefaces. Five volumes of manuscript scores, dating from the late 1690s to after 1707, all but one dedicated to Louis XIV, are now in the Bibliothèque Nationale. We know only that Bembo was a Venetian noblewoman who had been "abandoned by him who drew me from Venice."[9] Whether he was a lover, a husband, an artistic associate, or a relative is unknown. Bembo says that she had arrived at the court many years before, that the king had heard her sing and, learning of her present distress, gave her a pension. He found shelter for her at the Comunità di Nostra Signora di Buone Nouelle (Community of Our Lady of Good Tidings), "a holy retreat. . . . until such a time as the occasion presented itself for me to place myself in some more distinguished lodgings." Although Bembo bears the name of a distinguished Venetian family, no reference to her has been found in family archives.

Bembo's music is unavailable in modern publications, except for a few tantalizing excerpts in a 1939 article by Yvonne Rokseth.[10] The first manuscript volume contains forty-one vocal compositions, of which five are to Latin texts, a pair of couplets are French, and the rest are Italian. They are mostly songs for soprano (often quite high) and continuo, perhaps written for her own voice, a few duets, a trio (a cantata for the marriage of the Duchess of Burgundy), and a few pieces with added violins. The continuo parts frequently explore low ranges, even descending to low A, which would indicate a seven-string French gamba as the accompanying string instrument. Some of the texts are religious, some are in praise of the monarch, and some seem to have more personal emotions, as in the da capo aria "Habbi pietà di me, non mi lasciar morir" (Have mercy on me, do not let me die), from which an excerpt of the A section is given in Example 4-2. There is an unusual double key signature (F♯ minor and F minor), apparently so that the performer could choose the key in which she wanted to perform it. In our example only the F♯ minor signature has been shown.

EXAMPLE 4-2.     Antonia Bembo, opening aria from "Habbi Pietà," *Produzione armoniche*, MS, pp. 157–58. Paris: Bibliothèque Nationale. Used by permission.

In her last works Bembo used increasingly developed and sophisticated techniques in large-scale pieces. She wrote two Te Deums, one for a *petit choeur* of two sopranos and a bass accompanied by two violins and figured bass (the church trio instrumentation), and the second a vast *grand motet* for five-part chorus. Her opera, *L'Ercole amante* (1707), is based on the same text Cavalli had used more than forty years earlier to celebrate the marriage of Louis XIV in 1662. Although composers of that time did not write an opera without a performance in view, we do not know why Bembo composed an opera, why she set that particular text, or even whether the piece was ever performed.

Bembo's last known work is a setting of French translations of seven Penitential Psalms. The progression from the Italianate style of her first volume to the increasing use of French style traits in the Te Deums and the psalms suggests that Bembo had opportunities to hear music of her contemporaries, either within the convent in which she had taken refuge or

EXAMPLE 4-3.    Antonia Bembo, Venus' first aria from *L' Ercole amante*, MS score, p. 166. Paris: Bibliothèque Nationale. Used by permission.

through outside performances. French translations of the psalms were very fashionable in the French court at this time. The ones Bembo used had been made by the painter and musician Elisabeth-Sophie Chéron (1648–1711). Although Chéron had renounced her Huguenot religion to continue in court life, these serious psalms probably had special meaning for her, and Bembo responded to the intense texts with expressive musical settings.

## COMPOSERS OF THE GERMAN ARISTOCRACY

The musical education of girls in the Lutheran parts of Germany in the eighteenth century prepared them to sing psalms and other spiritual songs in the church congregation and at home in order to provide a Christian atmosphere for their children. For a daughter of an aristocratic family, musical skills were at the bottom of the list of accomplishments for which tutors and governesses were responsible. The aim was that music should be cultivated just enough so that the girl "could do little airs and Lieder . . . without many runs and variations."[11] Nevertheless, in households in which the family valued music as more than part of good Christian domesticity or a social skill enhancing marriageability, children of both sexes could and did receive much better musical educations than this wary minimum.

## Anna Amalia, Princess of Prussia

When Anna Amalia, Princess of Prussia, was growing up in the court of her music-hating father, the soldier-king Frederick William I, she received little musical instruction in her childhood, and formal study was possible only after her father died. Yet, thanks to the clandestine aid of Queen Sophia Dorothea, many of the king's fourteen children developed into musicians. The three most musical were Princess Wilhelmina Sophie (later Margravine of Brandenburg, 1709–58), the son and heir Frederick (1712–86), and the youngest princess, Anna Amalia (1723–87). The king treated all the children with great cruelty, and in his rages even dragged little Anna Amalia across the room by her hair. Music was the secret consolation of the children. Frederick and Wilhelmina both learned the flute and played duets away from their father's watchful eyes; and Frederick gave his little sister Anna Amalia her earliest music lessons, which she always remembered with affection. She learned harpsichord, flute, and violin and turned to the harpsichord for release from the constant family strife around her.

When the old king died in 1740, Frederick came to the throne, bringing a great throng of musicians into the court with him. What had been forbidden was now richly available. Anna Amalia could at last hear Italian opera, study with cathedral organist Gottlieb Hayne, and devote herself to other pleasant pursuits. Alas, she also met a young army officer with whom she fell deeply and unwisely in love. Her brother was furious and imprisoned her lover for ten years. Anna Amalia was made abbess of a religious community in Quedlinburg, although she could live in her own house in Berlin. Her only joy for the rest of her life was music. In 1758, at the age of thirty-five, she finally began systematic and serious study of music theory and composition and had an organ built in her home. She hired Johann Philipp Kirnberger, a student of J. S. Bach, as her Kapellmeister and teacher. She learned the techniques of four-voice settings of chorales and of old-fashioned counterpoint, at a time when the music around her was galant, elegant, and sentimental. She wrote an opening chorale and chorus for the oratorio *Der Tod Jesu*, which Kirnberger used as a models in the theory book he dedicated to her; her brother's court composer, Graun, later set the whole libretto. Her chamber music includes a lovely flute sonata (the first movement is in HAMW, pp. 86–87). This work is more galant in style than her other works and may have been written before her studies with Kirnberger. The choice of solo instrument for this sonata was a natural one for a composer in a flute-playing family.

Anna Amalia was an ardent collector of the old music she loved, and she preserved over 600 volumes of musical treasures by J. S. Bach, Palestrina, Handel, Telemann, and other composers of the past, as well as works by a few moderns like C. P. E. Bach—a significant contribution to European culture. After World War II her library was split between East and West Berlin, where, except for some items lost in storage during the war, it remains a priceless heritage. Only a small bundle of her own works remains, perhaps because, being very "timorous and self-critical," she may have destroyed some of her own compositions.

## Anna Amalia, Duchess of Saxe-Weimar

In contrast to the Princess of Prussia, with her conservative tastes, the Duchess of Saxe-Weimar, also named Anna Amalia (1739–1807), was dedicated to fostering new developments in both literature and music. Her parents were Philippine Charlotte (a sister of Anna Amalia of Prussia) and Duke Karl I of Brunswick; both valued musical training as part of the excellent education they gave their children. When she married the Duke of Saxe-Weimar, Anna Amalia had need of her good education, for by the age of nineteen she was a widow with two sons to raise. For the next seventeen years she was responsible for running the state as Regent. When her elder son came of age, she turned her energies to artistic and intellectual endeavors, so successfully that Weimar came to be known as the "Court of the Muses." While her aunt Anna Amalia of Prussia had preserved the legacy of the glorious Baroque past in her magnificent library, the court of Anna Amalia of Saxe-Weimar pointed to the future thriving German cultural life, for which her court circle had planted the seeds of literary romanticism, nourished by rich musical activity.

Throughout her life the duchess pursued intellectual interests, composed music, played the harpsichord and the new fortepiano, and encouraged the most brilliant young poets, playwrights, and musicians of Germany to come to Weimar. Twenty-four-year-old Johann Wolfgang von Goethe came to the court as an advisor and minister of state for the duke and remained under the regency of the duchess. Many plays by Wieland and Goethe were first staged in the Weimar court theatre. Anna Amalia's most successful composition was music for the 1776 production of Goethe's Singspiel *Erwin und Elmire,* for which Johann André had written a setting a year earlier. One of the songs in the work, "Das Veilchen," is now best known in Mozart's setting of a decade later.

Artists from many of the great musical families came to Weimar. The *Kapellmeister* when Anna Amalia arrived was Johann Ernest Bach, nephew and student of J. S. Bach. She hired Ernest Wilhelm Wolf (who had worked with Hiller in Leipzig) to be her sons' music tutor; he later was her own teacher as well as *Kapellmeister*. His wife, Maria Carolina Benda, was a harpsichordist and singer, a sister of composer Juliane Benda (later Reichardt).

## EIGHTEENTH-CENTURY ORATORIO COMPOSERS OF NORTHERN ITALY AND VIENNA

During the reigns of Leopold I (d. 1705), Joseph I (1705–11), and Charles VI (1711–40), and again during the reign of Maria Theresa (1740–80), oratorios by several women were performed in Vienna. The composers were the Austrian nun Marianne von Raschenau; the Italians Caterina Benedetta Gratianini, Camilla de Rossi, and Maria Margherita Grimani; and, in the late eighteenth century, the Viennese composer Marianne von Martinez. Of the compositions by Raschenau, *Chormeisterin* (choir director) at the convent of St. Jakob auf der Hülben in Vienna, only the printed libretti from the performances survive for two oratorios and two secular stage works. Two oratorios by Gratianini have survived in manuscript; one was "sung before the Highnesses of Brunswick and Modena . . . and wondrously received," according to a note on the score.

Camilla de Rossi and Maria Margherita Grimani composed the largest amount of surviving music. Absolutely nothing is known about the life of either composer. The manuscripts by Rossi identify her as Roman; and Grimani bears the name of a famous Venetian family, although like Antonia Bembo, she cannot be officially connected to it. All we know is that their music was used in the court at Vienna, and that some of the best singers of the court participated in the performances.

The oratorios of both composers are large works in the formal scheme used by Alessandro Scarlatti after 1700. They are divided into two large sections, each introduced by a single-movement or a multimovement sinfonia. Within each half are a succession of *da capo* arias alternating with *secco* recitatives. There are occasional duets and usually a final ensemble of soloists. Many of the arias are continuo arias with orchestral ritornelli, while others are accompanied by a larger group of instruments. There is no chorus. The dramatic style is the same as that used for opera in the same time period.

The orchestra consists of strings, harpsichord, and a few other instruments, sometimes adventurously used. Rossi's *Il Sacrifizio di Abramo* (Abraham's sacrifice), composed in 1708, calls for two *chalumeaux* (predecessors of the clarinet) just one year after the instrument had been introduced into the opera in Vienna. Rossi also uses instrumental color for

EXAMPLE 4-4.    Camilla de Rossi, "Quanto, quanto mi consola un oggetto lontananza," mm. 32–40, from *Santa Beatrice d'Este*, MS score, Vienna, Austrian National Library, Musiksammlung. Text: "If by itself hope were so beautiful, what then would be the reward?"

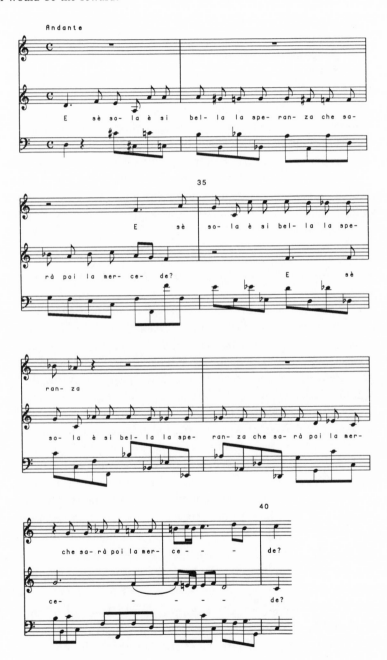

characterization: the lute is associated with Isaaco's innocence in *Il Sacrifizio di Abramo,* while trumpets are used for the villain, a military man, in *Santa Beatrice d'Este* (1707). Rossi uses striking key relations and chromaticism for expressive effects, as in the chromatic excerpt from *Santa Beatrice d'Este* shown in Example 4-4.

Two oratorios and an opera, *Pallade e Marte,* by Maria Margherita Grimani are extant. The manuscript of the opera is inscribed "Bologna, April 5, 1713," apparently the time and place of the completion of the work. It was performed in Vienna later in 1713 to celebrate the emperor's name day (a prestigious occasion for a composer), but all that is known of the composer's connection with any particular place is that both her oratorios were also performed in Vienna. The opera is her shortest extant work, and calls for only two singers, soprano and alto. The Sinfonia (see HAMW, pp. 79–83) is a miniature Italian overture: a short, brilliant flourish of sound in the opening G major allegro; a largo in the relative minor in sarabande rhythm; and, returning to major, a binary-form presto movement in a lively 3/8 meter.

## SONG COMPOSERS IN BERLIN AND WEIMAR

The confluence of literary and musical talents in mid-eighteenth century Berlin and Weimar was conducive to the development of the Lied. Berlin was the center for a literary aesthetic that called for simple, often strophic songs with unobstrusive accompaniment. The style of the songs was often deliberately folklike *(volkstümlich).* The accompanying instrument was usually the piano, although the clavichord, a popular instrument of sentiment and feeling in this period, was also well suited to accompany the melody. *Volkstümliche* songs in Berlin, Leipzig, and Weimar were written for intimate private performances, usually by amateur singers. A more sophisticated style, more Italianate and with greater demands on the singer and more elaboration of the piano part, developed in Vienna. Lieder were published in collections of all kinds, and music magazines (a new development in the eighteenth century) often included the latest new songs. Many women composed and published songs, among them Corona Schröter (1751–1802) in Weimar and Juliane Benda Reichardt (1752–83) in Berlin.

### Corona Schröter

Corona Schröter grew up in a musical family. Her father, an oboist, taught his children—Corona (a singer), Johann Samuel (a pianist), Johann Heinrich (a violinist), and Marie Henriette (a singer). He took the whole family on concert tours to Leipzig, the Netherlands, and England, as a few years later Leopold Mozart would take his *Wunderkinder* Nannerl and Wolfgang. When Corona was thirteen the family moved to Leipzig. Johann Adam Hiller, a leading figure in the musical life of the city, was distressed about the generally poor training of German singers as well as the exclusion of women from choral singing, especially in the Church. He argued: "If God primarily gave man the splendid talent of producing a melodic tone with his throat in order to praise Him, then it is highly unfair to exclude the other sex which has received this gift to a great extent from its creator, from worshiping him too. . . ." To encourage improvement of choral singing, he advocated that: "Concert societies and weekly rehearsals could be established . . . with the main focus directed upon the improvement of singing. One should not again, however, make the mistake to exclude women."[12] He founded a singing school in 1771 to which both sexes were admitted. The curriculum included vocal technique, solfege, diction in choral music from operas and oratorios, aria performance, keyboard playing, and Italian. His most famous student was Corona Schröter.

When Goethe went to Weimar from Leipzig, he took Schröter to Anna Amalia's court as an actress and a singer. Her closest friends at the Weimar court were the poets Goethe and Schiller. She acted and sang in Goethe's plays and composed the incidental music for *Die Fischerin* (1782). She also taught singing and drama there in the last two decades of the century.

Schröter published two collections of Lieder, in 1786 and in 1794. Goethe's "Der Erlkönig," which she was the first to set, is in the 1786 collection. It was a stage song in *Die Fischerin*, originally sung by the character Dortchen (played by Schröter) as she sits by the hearth. Goethe wanted the piece to be a folklike ballad, as if "the singer [had] learned to sing it somewhere by memory."[13] As a stage ballad Schröter's setting is very successful, aiming at an aesthetic goal totally different from that of Franz Schubert's more famous setting. Not all of Schröter's Lieder are in the *volkstümliche* style of "Der Erlkönig," however, and the piano has much more independence in the songs of her second volume. In "Das Mädchen am Ufer," from her first book, the voice and piano parts are notated together on two staves, a normal convention for the early Lied (see Example 4-5). The piano usually doubles the singer's line, and in this example, there are additional small notes for the pianist. The soprano clef used in the right hand is the normal convention of the period.

## Juliane Benda Reichardt

The Benda family was one of the largest and most complicated musical dynasties of the period. Juliane was one of four musical children of the

EXAMPLE 4-5.    Corona Schröter, "Das Mädchen am Ufer," *Fünf und zwanzig Lieder* (Weimar: the author, 1786), p. 14. Facsimile from the copy in the Goethe-Museum, Anton und Katharina Kippenberg Stiftung, Düsseldorf. Text: "The ocean was wildly howling; the storm groaned with woe. There sat the maiden weeping; on the hard rock sat she. Far over the ocean's roar she cast her sighs and gaze. Since naught could still her sighs, the echo came back to her."

violinist Franz Benda, concertmaster to Frederick the Great. Her grandmother was from the Brixi family of Czech musicians, her aunt Anna was a singer, and she had at least a dozen musician cousins, several of whom were composers. The Benda family was related by marriage to other musical dynasties of Bohemia and Germany, and Juliane's daughter Louise Reichardt was to be a prolific Lied composer in the next century.

When Juliane was only six, her mother died, and she received her music instruction from her father. A young composer named J. F. Reichardt came to Berlin as court *Kapellmeister* in 1775. His first love had been Corona Schröter, who had refused him and in fact never married, but in Berlin he heard Juliane Benda sing and play the piano and fell in love with her. Within a year they were married, when both were twenty-three years old. Juliane was already composing songs and piano music. She published Lieder in a collection with her husband as well as in musical magazines. In 1782 she published two piano sonatas and seventeen songs that showed great promise for the future. The normal life of a young married woman of the eighteenth century included frequent pregnancies, with their attendant risks, so the births of three children in the seven years of her marriage were not unusual, nor was her early death after the birth of the third child, in 1783. Juliane Benda Reichardt was buried on her thirty-first birthday.

## LATE EIGHTEENTH-CENTURY VIENNA

In the latter half of the eighteenth century Viennese women composers cultivated many musical forms: concertos and sonatas for piano, chamber music, oratorios, Masses, operas and other large works, and a few symphonies. Women performed as singers, fortepianists (the piano was gradually replacing the harpsichord), harpists, and (a few) violinists. As the piano gained ground, many of its best players were women, several of whom also were composers. Vienna was also the workplace of the great piano builder Nannette Stein Streicher, who, with her younger brother, André Stein, had moved their shop to Vienna from Augsburg in the 1790s.

Although the financial problems of the Empress Maria Theresa (1740–80) led to decreased support for court music, so that it no longer dominated the Austrian musical scene, a rich musical life was dispersed throughout the city, and the most glorious period in Vienna's musical history was under way. Noble and middle-class homes alike rang with music, and much of the concert life of the city took place in private houses, from the grand events at Baron Gottfried van Swieten's palace to more intimate evenings at the Martinez house. Concert societies sprang up, beginning with Florian Gassmann's Tonkünstler-Sozietät in 1772, providing public concerts modeled on the Concerts Spirituels in France. In the churches music for the Mass often used large orchestras, and elaborate settings of religious music took place all over Austria, not just in the Cathedral of St. Stephen in Vienna.

By the end of the eighteenth century there are scattered references to women as soloists in Austrian church music. At the Esterhazy court, solos in Joseph Haydn's Masses were sung by women, among them Thérèse Gassmann (later Rosenbaum), who was also the soprano soloist for the first Austrian performance of Haydn's *The Seven Last Words*. At Salzburg, Michael Haydn's wife, Maria Magdalena Lipp Haydn (daughter of the court organist), was hired by the archbishop as a soloist for both sacred and secular music.

## Marianne von Martinez

The largest extant body of music by a Viennese woman of this period is that of Marianne von Martinez (1744–1812). She composed Masses and other liturgical music (mostly in symphonic style), oratorios, cantatas, concertos for piano and orchestra, sonatas, a symphony, arias, and other vocal works—almost every genre of the period except opera. Of her more than 200 known works, only about seventy survive.

Martinez was born into a Spanish family of minor nobility; she was the daughter of the master-of-ceremonies to the papal nuncio. She lived in a house on the Michaelplatz that was an interesting microcosm of Viennese society. On the first floor lived the Dowager Princess Esterhazy (mother of Joseph Haydn's patron). As one went up the floors, the social level of the occupants declined. The Martinez family lived on the third floor in a spacious apartment that also housed the court poet and opera librettist Pietro Metastasio. The attic apartments were rented to poorer tenants, tradespeople, or music teachers. In 1750 a young fellow who had just been dismissed from the choir school at St. Stephen's took an attic room there: his name was Joseph Haydn.

The bachelor Metastasio took a great interest in the family, especially in the education of the children. He was struck by Marianne's talent, and by the time the little girl was ten years old he had arranged for her to study singing with the great Italian opera singer and composer Niccolò Porpora, and for harpsichord lessons with Joseph Haydn, the young man in the attic room, who also accompanied her singing lessons. Marianne showed talent for composition, which she studied with Hasse (Faustina Bordoni's husband, who had now retired to Vienna) and Giuseppe Bonno. Charles Burney heard her sing in 1772 and praised both her singing and her compositions.

By the 1760s Martinez was writing large church works. Four symphonic Masses, six motets, and three litanies for choir and orchestra are extant. It has been suggested that the "Christe" of her Mass No. 1 in D major may have been known to the young Mozart and that his 1768 Mass, K. 139, is modeled on it.[14] One of her Masses, probably her third, was performed at St. Michael's Church, the court chapel, in 1761. It is a large work (more than one hundred and fifty pages of score) with soprano, alto, and tenor solos; four-part chorus; and an orchestra of two natural trumpets, two oboes, two flutes, violins, and organ continuo. Her fourth Mass was composed in 1765. When Emperor Joseph II came to the throne, his reforms led to a simpler style of church music, without orchestras, and brought back the old rule against women "speaking" (that is, singing) in church. So Martinez wrote no more Masses, although she did make several psalm settings, using Italian translations by the Neapolitan poet who commissioned the compositions.

The fame of Martinez spread to Italy, especially after she was admitted to the Accademia Filarmonica of Bologna in 1773, for which she wrote a psalm and a *Miserere* as her admission test pieces. By this time, she is spoken of as a pianist rather than as a harpsichordist. Mozart probably wrote his Piano Concerto in D major (K. 175) for her to perform in Dr. Mesmer's garden in 1773. Her keyboard music was mostly for piano, although the early A-major and E-major sonatas were published in a harpsichord anthology in 1765. The same two sonatas were included in a piano anthology some seventy years after her death, when they were reedited with the dynamics of piano music.[15] The first movement of the A-major sonata (HAMW, pp. 90–93) shows rococo embellishment of the thematic material, with a development section that exploits spicy little mordents and trills in bright, idiomatic passages split between the hands, alternating with roulades of triplets (see measures 16–26).

Martinez was active as a performer, particularly as a pianist, and was a prolific composer, but she never held a professional appointment, which would apparently have been unacceptable in her social class. She and her sister provided a household and care for their family friend and benefactor Metastasio until his death. He wrote the libretti for two of Martinez's oratorios, *Santa Elena al Calvario* (St. Helen at Calvary, 1781) and *Isacco figura del Redentore* (Isaac, Symbol of the Redeemer, 1782). The latter work is written for an orchestra consisting of a full Classic wind section—pairs of trumpets, horns, oboes, flutes, and bassoons; timpani; and a full string section. A performance by the Tonkünstler-Sozietät used a large orchestra and a choir of about 200 singers.

In 1782 Metastasio died, and the Martinez siblings inherited his large estate. Their home was a center for weekly musical soirées, with the most distinguished musicians in town as guests and performers. Haydn and Mozart were often there, and Mozart wrote four-hand piano sonatas to perform with Marianne. Foreign visitors, such as the tenor Michael Kelly, made sure to go to these events when they visited Vienna. In 1796 Martinez opened a singing school in her home and produced singers of professional quality. Many fine female singers—amateur and professional, choristers as well as soloists—were trained in such private schools.

Martinez's last known public appearance was also that of her old teacher Haydn—to hear Salieri conduct Haydn's *Die Schöpfung* (The Creation) on March 27, 1808. Martinez and her sister, neither of whom ever married, died within two days of each other in 1812. Although Martinez held no professional posts, she was a thoroughly trained and serious musician and a significant composer. Her musical evenings were important events in the cultural life of Vienna during its golden age, and her own performances were splendid. She took teaching seriously and in this way promoted the continued vitality of the cultural life she had helped to shape.

In the nineteenth century, when most of her music was forgotten, Martinez's creative contributions were downgraded in the fashionable debate about whether or not women possessed creativity. In 1844 the publication of Caroline Pichler's memoirs provided ammunition for the negative side of the argument, with their spiteful criticism of feminine creativity generally and of Martinez in particular. Pichler had been a salonière of the 1780s whose gatherings competed with those of Martinez and Paradis, and the biased memories and aesthetic judgments of her old age should have been read with skepticism. Modern critics have viewed Martinez's accomplishments more favorably and should help to restore a more balanced view.

## Maria Theresia von Paradis

Maria Theresia von Paradis (1759–1824) was born into the family of the royal court secretary of Empress Maria Theresa, for whom the little girl was named. When she suddenly became blind at the age of three, various cures were attempted (including efforts by Dr. Mesmer), but she never regained her sight. The empress provided an annual stipend for her (it was stopped during the reign of Joseph II but was restored by Leopold II), and she was given the best musical education possible, perhaps in the belief that her blindness was an impediment to marriage. Paradis studied piano with Leopold Kozeluch, singing with Vincenzo Righini and Antonio Salieri, and composition with Salieri, Carl Friberth, and Abbé Vogler. Her theoretical studies included dramatic composition, harmony, counterpoint, and figured bass. By the age of sixteen, Paradis was astonishing the Viennese public with her talent as a piano virtuoso and singer. Mozart composed a piano concerto for her—probably the one in B♭ major, K. 456; and Salieri composed his only organ concerto for her.

In 1783 Paradis, her mother, and her friend and librettist Johann Riedinger started a three-year concert tour of Europe. Her 1784 visit to Paris was significant for more than musical reasons, for while there she met Valentin Haüy, an educator who was soon to open a pioneering school for the blind. In his *Essay on the Education of the Blind,*[16] he referred frequently to the methods that had been used to teach Paradis reading, mathematics, geography, and music.

In the 1790s Paradis worked with Riedinger to develop a peg board on which she could set down her musical compositions, which could then be transcribed by a copyist. Her first extant works are the songs written during her concert tour, *Zwölf Lieder auf ihrer Reise in Musik gesetzt (1784–86)*. "Morgenlied eines armen Mannes" (Morning song of a poor man) is a particularly moving song from this collection (see HAMW, pp. 97–98). Her compositions were not limited to the works that she herself performed. Paradis composed at least five operas and three large cantatas (one in memory of the unfortunate Louis XVI of France), and her dramatic works were performed at major theatres in Vienna. Her last opera, a comic magic-opera, *Rinaldo und Alcina,* was produced in Prague in 1797. It is based on Ariosto's *Orlando Furioso,* the same literary source used by Francesca Caccini for *La liberazione di Ruggiero* nearly 200 years earlier.

Unfortunately, much of Paradis's music has been lost. All that survives of her dramatic works is an excerpt from the Singspiel *Der Schulkandidat* (The school candidate), a very successful work that had six performances at the Marinelli Theatre in Vienna in 1792–93. Had Paradis published more of her music, more might have survived, but she responded self-deprecatingly when asked why she had not done so, saying, "Would male fellow artists withdraw from me if I, as a woman—and especially as a blind woman—dared to compete with them?"[17] Among the lost works are two piano concertos, several sonatas, songs, and a piano trio. Her name was still so illustrious in our own century that Samuel Dushkin borrowed it for a work that he attributed to her, the *Sicilienne* (see HAMW, pp. 99–100).

Paradis's circle of friends included many musicians, such as the Mozart family, and literary figures, including the novelist and poet Sophie de Laroche (one of whose texts Paradis set in *Zwölf Lieder*). Like Martinez before her, Paradis opened a music school in 1808 in which she taught many outstanding women pianists and accepted both blind and sighted students. The school was noted for its Sunday house-concerts. Paradis was buried in St. Mark's Cemetery, where the site of her grave—like Mozart's, in the same cemetery—is unknown.

## SUMMARY

In the year 1800, one could look back over the two preceding centuries and see increased roles for women in music in many areas. They were especially active as opera singers, composers, harpsichordists and pianists, violinists, teachers, and publishers and engravers. Their ranks included an important instrument builder and even a few impresarios and theatre managers. The various activities of women in music are well documented in Italy, France, Germany, Austria, and England (there mainly as performers), although they may have been active in other regions where records have been lost or are still inadequately studied.

Women worked in convents (whose importance was greatest during the seventeenth century but had fallen sharply by 1800), courts (which declined after the French Revolution), and the new and growing public concert series. The eighteenth century saw early examples of touring artists, like Maddalena Lombardini Sirmen. Extended musical families provided opportunities for training and networks of related professionals. Husbands, wives, and children (as in the Caccini family) might all work in a court; wives and husbands might be partners in musical businesses, especially publishing; and within an extended family one might find a wide variety of musical professions, as was the case among relatives of Elisabeth Jacquet de la Guerre. Formally organized educational opportunities for women outside the convent were found first in the Venetian conservatories. Singing schools for both sexes were established in Leipzig and Berlin; and private music schools—for example, those of Martinez and Paradis—developed in Vienna and elsewhere.

Although some of the most productive women did not have paid professional careers in the modern sense, their activities helped shape the whole musical society in which they lived. Neither Barbara Strozzi in the seventeenth century nor Marianne von Martinez in the eighteenth performed in public or held official positions of any sort, yet both contributed significantly to the musical societies in which they worked. The academies of seventeenth-century Italy and the French and German salons of the eighteenth century provided private forums for artistic work, and the leadership in the salons was often by women. The expanding activities of noble and middle-class amateurs enriched musical life in many ways, including the fostering of mixed choral organizations at the end of the eighteenth century.

As composers, women wrote Masses and other Catholic service music (from the seventeenth-century nun Leonarda to the Viennese laywoman Martinez in the eighteenth century), devotional music for use outside the service, opera (Francesca Caccini, in the earliest days of the form), oratorio (especially Italians for Vienna in the early eighteenth century), harpsichord music (Elisabeth Jacquet de la Guerre), and piano music. They were especially active as composers of vocal music, writing in almost every form in vogue during their lives—the monodies of the Caccini sisters; the French cantatas of La Guerre; the German Lieder of Corona Schröter and Juliane Benda Reichardt; and, of course, opera. The number of women composers of purely instrumental music is smaller, although there are chamber works by Leonarda and La Guerre, violin concertos and chamber music by Lombardini Sirmen, military marches by Anna Amalia of Prussia, and symphonic music by Martinez. Many doors had opened for women in music during the seventeenth and eighteenth centuries, and the nineteenth century was to see a further blossoming of their activities.

## NOTES

1. Giulio Caccini, dedication to *L'Euridice* (1600), translated in Oliver Strunk, *Source Readings in Music History* (New York: W. W. Norton, 1950); and Vincenzo Giustiniani, *Discorso sopra la musica* (1628), edited and translated by Carol MacClintock, Musicological Studies and Documents 9 (Rome: American Institute of Musicology, 1962), pp. 70–71.

2. Maria Giovanna Mesera, "Una musicista fiorentina del seicento: Francesca Caccini," *La Rassegna musicale* 14/5 (May 1941):197; and *The New Grove Dictionary of Music and Musicians*, s.v. "Caccini [Giulio Romano]," by H. Wiley Hitchcock.

3. Italics added. Quoted in Jane Bowers, "Music in the Italian Convents," *Helicon Nine: The Journal of Women's Arts and Letters* 9 (1983):69–70, reprinted from liner notes for *Music for the Mass by Nun Composers*, Leonarda LPI 115 (1982).

4. Isabella Leonarda, "Quam dulcis es," from Op. 13 (1687), for high voice, two violins, and organ, edited and translated by Barbara Garvey Jackson (Fayetteville, AR: ClarNan Editions, 1984).

5. Jane Berdes, "The Women Musicians of Venice," in *Eighteenth-Century Women and the Arts*, edited by Frederick M. Kenner and Susan Lorsch, Contributions in Women's Studies No. 98 (New York: Greenwood Press, 1988), p. 156.

6. Jean Laurent Le Cerf de la Viéville, *Comparaison de la musique italienne et de la musique françoise* (Brussels, 1704–1706).

7. *Mercure galant*, July 1677, pp. 107–108, translated in Edith Borroff, *An Introduction to Elisabeth-Claude Jacquet de la Guerre* (Brooklyn: Institute of Medieval Music, 1966), p. 6.

8. Evrard Titon du Tillet, *Parnasse française* (Paris, 1732), translated in Borroff, pp. 17–18.

9. From the Preface to *Produzioni armoniche*, translated in Yvonne Rokseth, "Antonia Bembo, Composer to Louis XIV," *Musical Quarterly* 23 (1937):149.

10. Ibid.

11. F. Guthmann, "Grad der musikalischen Bildung bei Frauenzimmern," *Allgemeine musikalische Zeitung* 9 (1807):380ff.; cited in Eva Weissweiler, *Komponistinnen aus 500 Jahren* (Frankfurt am Main: Fischer, 1981), p. 114.

12. Johann Adam Hiller, *Anweisung zum musikalisch-zierlichen Gesange*, translated in Suzanne Julia Beicken, "Johann Adam Hiller's 'Anweisung zum musikalisch-zierlichen Gesange,' 1780: A Translation and Commentary," Ph.D. diss., Stanford University, 1980, pp. 9–10.

13. Marcia J. Citron, "Corona Schröter: Singer, Composer, Actress," *Music and Letters* 61 (1980):23.

14. Bruce MacIntyre, *The Viennese Concerted Mass of the Early Classic Period* (Ann Arbor: UMI Research Press, 1986), p. 81.

15. First published in *Raccolta musicale contenente XII sonate per il cembalo solo d'altretanti celebri compositori italiani* (Nürnberg: Haffner, 1756–65). The word "cembalo" and the early date show that they were harpsichord music, although by the end of the composer's life they would have been performed as piano music. Emil Pauer included them in *Alte Meister: Sammlung wertvoller Klavierstücke des 17. und 18. Jahrhunderts* (Leipzig: Breitkopf & Härtel, 1868–85), reedited as piano music. This version of the first movement of Martinez's Sonata in A major is reprinted in HAMW, pp. 90–93.

16. Valentin Haüy, *Essai sur l'education des aveugles* (Paris, 1786). The first volume of this work had embossed letters for the blind to read. Louis Braille, who invented the Braille system, was one of Haüy's students.

17. "Nachrichten," *Allgemeine musikalische Zeitung* 12 (1810):471–74; translated in Jane Bowers and Judith Tick, eds., *Women Making Music* (Urbana: University of Illinois Press, 1986), p. 230.

## SUGGESTIONS FOR FURTHER READING
### Books and Articles

Bates, Carol Henry. "The Instrumental Music of Elisabeth-Claude Jacquet de la Guerre." Ph.D. diss., Indiana University, 1978.

Berdes, Jane L. "Music and Musicians in the Four Ospedali Grandi of Venice, 1525–1855." Ph.D. diss., Oxford University, 1989.

Carter, Stewart Arlen. "The Music of Isabella Leonarda (1620–1704)." Ph.D. diss., Stanford University, 1981.

Fremar, Karen Lynn. "The Life and Selected Works of Marianna Martines (1744–1812)." Ph.D. diss., University of Kansas, 1983.

Jackson, Barbara Garvey. "Oratorios by Command of the Emperor: The Music of Camilla de Rossi." *Current Musicology* 42 (1968):7–19.

Laini, Marinella. "Le produzioni armoniche di Antonia Bembo." Ph.D. diss., University of Pavia, 1988.

Larson, David. "Women and Song in Eighteenth-Century Venice: Choral Music at the Four Conservatories for Girls." *Choral Journal* 18 (October 1977):15–24.

Lorenz, Franz. *Die Musikerfamilie Benda: Franz Benda und seine Nachkommen.* Berlin: W. de Gruyter, 1967.

Matsushita, Hidemi. "The Musical Career and the Compositions of Maria Theresia von Paradis." Ph.D. diss., Brigham Young University, 1989.

Raney, Carolyn. "Francesca Caccini, Musician to the Medici, and Her Primo Libro (1618)." Ph.D. diss., New York University, 1971.

Rosand, Ellen. "Barbara Strozzi, virtuosissima cantatrice: The Composer's Voice." *Journal of the American Musicological Society* 31 (1978):241–81.

Silbert, Doris. "Francesca Caccini, called La Cecchina." *Musical Quarterly* 32 (1946):50–62.

Ullrich, Hermann. "Maria Theresia Paradis in London." *Music and Letters* 43 (1962):19–23.

Whittemore, Joan Margaret. "Revision of Music Performed at the Venetian Ospedali in the Eighteenth Century." DMA thesis, University of Illinois at Champaign-Urbana, 1986.

## Modern Editions and Facsimiles of Music

Anna Amalia, Princess of Prussia. Sonata in F major for flute and continuo, edited by Gustav Lenzewski. Munich: Chr. Friedrich Vieweg, 1975.

Caccini, Francesca. "Aure volanti," edited by Carolyn Raney. In *Nine Centuries of Music by Women*. New York: Broude Brothers, 1977.

————. *Il primo libro delle musiche a una e due voci di Francesca Caccini ne' Signorini* (facsimile). In *Italian Secular Song: 1606–1636*, vol. I: *Florence*. Introduction by Gary Tomlinson. New York: Garland, 1986.

————. *La Liberazione di Ruggiero*, edited by Doris Silbert. Northampton, MA: Smith College Archives, 1945.

Harbach, Barbara, ed. *Women Composers for the Harpsichord*. Bryn Mawr: Elkan-Vogel, 1986. Works by Gambarini, Martinez, Auenbrugg.

Jackson, Barbara Garvey, ed. *Arias from Oratorios by Women Composers*. Fayetteville, AR: ClarNan Editions, 1987. Works by Rossi, Grimani, Grazianini.

————. *Lieder by Women Composers of the Classic Era*. Fayetteville, AR: ClarNan editions, 1987. Works by Liebmann, Westenholtz, Paradis, Schröter.

La Guerre, Elisabeth-Claude Jacquet de. *Pièces de Clavecin* [1707], edited by Paul Brunold, 1938, and Thurston Dart, 1965. Monaco: Oiseau Lyre, 1965.

————. *Pièces de Clavecin* [1687], edited by Carol Henry Bates. Paris: Le Pupitre, 1986.

————. "Raccommodement comique de Pierrot et de Nicole," edited by Carolyn Raney. In *Nine Centuries of Music by Women*. New York: Broude Brothers, 1978.

————. Sonata No. 1 in G minor for two violins and continuo, edited by Robert P. Block. London: Nova, 1985.

Leonarda, Isabella. "Ave Regina Caelorum," edited by Stewart Carter. In *Nine Centuries of Music by Women*. New York: Broude Brothers, 1980.

————. Messa Prima from Op. 18 (1696), edited by Barbara Garvey Jackson. 2d ed. Fayetteville, AR: ClarNan Editions, 1988.

————. "Quam dulcis es," from Op. 13 (1687), edited by Barbara Garvey Jackson. Fayetteville, AR: ClarNan Editions, 1984.

————. *Selected Compositions of Isabella Leonarda*, edited by Stewart Carter. Recent Researches in the Music of the Baroque Era 59. Madison: A-R Editions, 1988.

————. Sonata Duodecima for violin and continuo from Op. 16 (1693), edited by Barbara Garvey Jackson. Baroque Chamber Music Series No. 16. Ottawa: Dovehouse Editions, 1983.

Lombardini Sirmen, Maddalena. *Three Violin Concertos*, edited by Jane Berdes. Madison: A-R Editions, 1991.

Martinez, Maria Anna. Sonatas in A and E, edited by Traud Kloft. Düsseldorf: Frauenmusikvertrieb, 1990.

Paradis, Maria Theresia von. *Lenore*, edited by Hidemi Matsushita. Fayetteville, AR: ClarNan Editions, 1989.

————. *Zwölf Lieder auf ihrer Reise in Musik gesetzt (1784–86)*, edited by Hidemi Matsushita. Fayetteville, AR: ClarNan Editions, 1987.

Rieger, Eva, and Walter, Kate, eds. *Frauen komponieren: 22 Klavierstücke des 18.–20. Jahrhunderts*. Mainz: Schott, 1985. Works of La Guerre and Martinez.

Rossi, Camilla de. *Dori e Fileno,* edited by Barbara Garvey Jackson. Fayetteville, AR: ClarNan Editions, 1984.

———. *Il Sacrifizio di Abramo* [1708], edited by Barbara Garvey Jackson. Fayetteville, AR: ClarNan Editions, 1984.

———. *S. Beatrice d'Este* [1707], edited by Barbara Garvey Jackson. Fayetteville, AR: ClarNan Editions, 1986.

Strozzi, Barbara. *Cantatas by Barbara Strozzi* [facsimile]. Introduction by Ellen Rosand. New York and London: Garland, 1986.

———. "Con le belle non ci vuol fretta" and "Consiglio amoroso," edited by Carolyn Raney. In *Nine Centuries of Music by Women.* New York: Broude Brothers, 1978.

———. *Diporte di Euterpe, overo Cantate e ariette a voce sola, opera settima. Venezia 1659* [facsimile]. Introduction by Piero Mioli. Florence: Studio per edizioni scelte, 1980.

———. *I sacri musicali affetti* [facsimile]. Introduction by Ellen Rosand. New York: Da Capo Press, 1988.

———. "Lagrime mie." In *The Solo Song, 1680–1730,* edited by Carol MacClintock. New York: Norton, 1973.

# The Romantic Period

# V.

# European Composers and Musicians, ca. 1800–1890

*Nancy B. Reich*

## INTRODUCTION

The political, social, and economic events that followed in the tumultuous aftermath of the French Revolution offered women many opportunities in musical life but also presented them with additional problems. Patronage of the arts, formerly a prerogative of the aristocracy, was moving to the middle class. The consequent growth of public concerts; the establishment of music festivals, concert halls, and concert societies; and the increasing number of opera houses open to paying audiences enabled musicians, both men and women, to reach a larger public. The founding of music schools throughout Europe brought a new professionalism to the art. The development of the railroad and the steamship made it possible for the touring artist to travel with greater ease. Imperialist expansion permitted musicians to tour not only on the European Continent but throughout the world, and tour they did, journeying by steamer or traveling by carriage, camel, and elephant to bring European music to Africa, Australia, North America, and India.

Because of the increasingly prosperous middle class, more women took part in amateur musical activities during the first half of the nineteenth century. Their numbers gave an impetus to all the businesses that served music: the number of piano builders swelled, music publishing houses proliferated, and music journalism became a thriving enterprise. Indeed, books, almanacs, dictionaries of music, and music magazines designed especially for the needs and interests of "the fair sex" became popular in every country of Europe and in England.

Prosperous and aspiring bourgeois families discovered that music lessons for their daughters could be an asset in their climb to social acceptance. The leisure created by new technology and industry afforded middle-class girls and women the opportunity to cultivate music (primarily voice and piano) to improve their marriage possibilities as well as to provide entertainment. Although this led to a large group of amateurs out of which some real talents emerged, upper- and middle-class women were discouraged from taking music too seriously. Even the most competent were forbidden by husbands or fathers to appear in public, to publish music under their own names, or to accept fees for their teaching lest these activities reflect badly on the social status of the family. The advice and support of a man was still a necessity in the musical career of a woman no matter how talented she was. Men still held the important posts in music teaching and publishing, formed the committees making decisions for concert organizations and festivals, and held the power in the musical world despite the entrance of some women into positions of prominence as performers and teachers.

The movement we call Romanticism dominated all the arts in the nineteenth century, although its roots extend well back into the eighteenth century. The writings of social and educational philosopher Jean-Jacques Rousseau (1712–78) influenced developments in all the arts in the nineteenth century and shaped attitudes toward women and their place in society. Such pronouncements as, "There are no good morals for women outside of a withdrawn and domestic life"; "The peaceful care of the family and the home are their lot"; "The dignity of their sex consists in modesty"; "Shame and chasteness are inseparable from decency"; and "The whole education of women ought to be relative to men"[1] affected the roles and education of women in every sphere, but were particularly damaging to the development of women composers and performers.

The Romantic ethos idolized the artist-genius—always male—who was seeking self-expression. Woman was idealized; her function was to serve as a Muse for the creator, to inspire and nurture the man. The women who befriended and inspired Beethoven—Eleonore von Breuning, Antonie Brentano, Countess Marie Erdödy, Dorothea von Ertmann, Marie Bigot, among others—were well-educated, skilled, and talented musicians, but theirs was always a supporting role. In 1795, Wilhelm von Humboldt—a German linguist, statesman, and educator—described the difference between the sexes in these terms:

Creative force is more attuned to aggressive movement while receiving force is more attuned to regressive movement. That which animates the former we call male; that which inspires the latter—female. All that is male shows more spontaneous activity; all that is female more passive receptivity. . . .[2]

Fortified by the words of these eminent thinkers, most men (and women) accepted this point of view. Women who attempted creative work suffered societal displeasure; consequently, even among professional women musicians who were supported and encouraged by family and friends, there were internal and external conflicts about composing. This may explain why such a gifted composer as Clara Schumann was ambivalent about her creative work and could declare that women should not compose. The prevailing views on proper feminine behavior (passive and submissive) were so firmly entrenched that she was uncomfortable about her role as a composer, although she had no qualms about appearing as a performer, which she considered a re-creative activity. Indeed, newspaper accounts of the work of successful professional women musicians almost always assured the readers that the musician was not only accomplished but also "womanly."

## EDUCATION

The establishment of largely state-supported music schools to train the professional musician created new environments for the woman performer. Very few schools, however, accepted women as composition students. Women composers of the first half of the nineteenth century studied privately, just as their forebears had. By the 1870s, however, conservatory classes in orchestration and composition began to admit women. Only at this point do we see women trained as professional composers emerging from the educational institutions.

The forerunners of the nineteenth-century conservatories were the Venetian *ospedali* and music schools established in Germany and France primarily to educate professional singers. By the time the first group of pupils entered the Paris Conservatoire, founded in 1795 to educate musicians who would help preserve and maintain the ideals of the French Revolution, it was understood that women would be among the students. The Royal Academy of Music in London accepted an equal number of boys and girls at its opening in 1823. Conservatories in Milan (founded in 1807), Vienna (1817), Brussels (1832), Leipzig (1843), Cologne (1850), Dresden (1856), Bern (1857), Berlin (1869), Naples (1872), and Frankfurt (1878) admitted female students subject to special conditions. In all these schools, boys and girls received instruction in separate divisions and often in separate quarters. In Brussels, for example, in 1877, girls and boys attended the Conservatory on alternate days. Joint classes for both sexes, such as French declamation and mixed chorus, were held on Mondays, Wednesdays, and Fridays, the girls' days. Although restrictions were rarely spelled out in the statutes of organization, it was assumed that the girls were studying to become performers or teachers rather than composers or conductors, and that they would limit their studies to voice, piano, or harp. By the 1870s, more women were studying the violin; and soon they were winning prizes and awards in Paris, Brussels, and Berlin and serving on the faculties of major institutions.

Policies regarding the study of such subjects as theory, harmony, and composition varied widely. In most conservatories, the women were required to study these subjects, but since the sexes were separated it is doubtful whether the curriculum was equal. In Leipzig, for example, entrance requirements were the same for boys and girls but male students were required to take a three-year course in theory, while women took a two-year course "especially organized for their requirements."[3] In some schools, there were no classes in composition for women, and those who wished to study did so privately; in other schools, such as the Brussels Conservatory, women could study composition with the director himself at designated hours on Wednesday afternoons. By 1883, we find counterpoint and score reading listed as major studies for several women on the student roster of the Hoch Conservatory in Frankfurt; thus, it seems clear that attitudes had changed.

Regulations regarding participation in student orchestras also varied from city to city. In certain schools women instrumentalists were not permitted in the orchestra or ensemble classes; in others they were required to participate. Over the years, and after some bitter battles, the restrictions were lifted.

The numbers of female music students swelled in the course of the century. When the Leipzig Conservatory opened in 1843, the first class consisted of thirty-three male and eleven female students. By 1868, twenty-five years after its founding, this conservatory had graduated 1,420 students: 975 males and 445 females. In 1878, the first year of the Hoch Conservatory in Frankfurt, there were ninety-seven female and forty-two male students. It is difficult to say how many of the women went on to professional careers and remained in those careers after marriage.

With the opening of the new conservatories, teaching opportunities for the professional woman musician were expanded. Some—Marie Pleyel and Pauline Viardot, for instance—joined faculties on retiring from the concert stage. Others—like Louise Farrenc, professor at the Paris Conservatoire for over thirty years—taught throughout their careers. There were, however, restrictions on these professors: in general, women taught only women, though male professors could teach both women and men. Even though the Brussels Conservatory boasted of procuring such a star as Marie Pleyel for its faculty, she was restricted to teaching the "classe des jeunes filles." Except for superstars like Clara Schumann, women professors were generally not accorded the respect, rank, and salaries of their male counterparts.

## Writers and Scholars

There were few women musical scholars in the nineteenth century; more than most branches of music, the field of scholarship was dominated by men. Nevertheless, several women musician/writers made valuable contributions to music history. The works of La Mara (pseudonym for Marie Lipsius, 1837–1927), Florence May (1845–1923), and Amy Fay (1844–1928), for example, have become standard documents for study of the nineteenth century. La Mara knew Liszt and Wagner, wrote more than twenty volumes and many essays, and edited letters of musicians. *Music Study in Germany* by Amy Fay had more than twenty printings and was translated into French and German. Florence May's biographies of Clara Schumann and Johannes Brahms are major sources for these nineteenth-century musicians. Michel Brenet (pseudonym for Marie Bobillier, 1858–1918), a highly respected music historian, was one of the few women musicologists of her time. Under her male *nom de plume* she wrote many important articles and over twenty monographs.

## COMPOSERS

In the early decades of the nineteenth century, a number of women composers achieved professional status—that is, their music was published and performed, and they received money for their work. Most of them were from families of professional musicians: parents of these creative women were composers or performers. In fact, many of the mothers of nineteenth-century musicians, both male and female, were themselves skilled and talented artists, a circumstance long neglected in discussions of composers. It is also interesting to note that the majority of women musicians were also wives and mothers, some bearing as many as eight children. These exceptional women managed home and professional responsibilities and were often the sole support of their families.

Many professional women composers were concert artists who, like the male virtuosi of their day, wrote to display their performing skills. They introduced their own works as well as compositions by others. Some well-known women composers of the nineteenth century who performed their own works in public concerts were Maria (Wolowska) Szymanowska, Clara (Wieck) Schumann, Léopoldine Blahetka, Josephine Lang, Pauline (Garcia) Viardot, Louise Farrenc, Luise Adolpha Le Beau, and Agathe Backer-Grøndahl. A smaller number composed for other groups: some wrote for their students (Louise Reichardt), others for home performance (Fanny Hensel), and still others for orchestras and opera companies (Louise Farrenc, Loïsa Puget, Louise Bertin). Emilie Zumsteeg (1796–1857), Johanna Kinkel (1810–1858), Annette Droste-Hülshoff (1797–1848), Emilie Mayer (1821–1883), and Louise Héritte-Viardot (1841–1918) were also active as composers.

## COMPOSERS OF VOCAL MUSIC

### Song Composers

The art song (in German, Lied) was considered a particularly appropriate genre for women composers, partly because it was associated with home music making, thereby remaining within women's domain, and partly because, as a relatively simple form it did not compete with the more complex, "masculine" genres such as sonatas or symphonies, which required the more intensive study frequently denied to women musicians. Throughout the nineteenth century, the great majority of published works by women were art songs and—equally suitable for the female—short pieces for piano, which will be discussed below.

Louise Reichardt (1779–1826) grew up in a musical and literary home and received her education in that household. Her mother, Juliane (1752–88), a keyboard player and composer who died when Louise was only four, was one of several talented daughters of Franz Benda, concertmaster to Frederick the Great. Louise's father, Johann Friedrich Reichardt, *Kapellmeister* at the same court and a composer, conductor, and writer, encouraged his eldest daughter in her musical interests but offered her no formal training in composition. Political outspokenness caused Reichardt to lose his court position in 1794, and the Napoleonic invasion of Germany (1806–15) brought great financial difficulties to the family, including the temporary loss of their home near Halle. Louise Reichardt, who never married, left home in 1809, moved to Hamburg, and established a private voice studio. She was able to support herself and even assist her family by her teaching, composing, and other musical activities. For the sake of her pupils, she became involved with the Hamburg Gesangverein, a choral group that she helped organize. Reichardt conducted the chorus at rehearsals but not at concerts. Modest, very pious, and holding firmly to traditional patterns of feminine behavior despite her financial independence, she barely acknowledged her accomplishments as a composer or musician.

The earliest printed songs by Louise Reichardt were in a joint collection with her father in 1800, but she published on her own thereafter. More than seventy of her songs, most in the *volkstümlich* (folklike) style popularized by the Romantic poets, are known to have been published, though not all have been found. Her texts were by the leading German poets she knew personally—Wolfgang von Goethe, Ludwig Tieck, Novalis, Clemens Brentano, and Achim von Arnim. Reichardt's songs are among the best of the early *volkstümliche* songs by any composer; most of them are strophic, with the words never obscured by the melody or the simple piano accompaniment. The harmonies are diatonic and the phrases regular. Her songs demonstrate an unforgettable melodic gift and were beloved by generations of Germans who sang them in the belief that they were folk songs. A number were reprinted in collections of German folk songs, which proliferated in the nineteenth century. Louise Reichardt also published a collection of more dramatic Italian songs, with texts by Metastasio, and some religious choral works for women's voices. Forty-two of her songs have appeared in a recent American collection.

The next generation of song composers—Josephine Lang, Fanny Hensel, and Clara Schumann—wrote in a more sophisticated style. Like their male contemporaries, they used texts from such Romantic poets as Goethe, Eichendorff, Rückert, and Giebel. Romantic (often thwarted) love and the beauties of nature formed the subjects of the texts but, unlike their male counterparts, women generally avoided poetry extolling heroism or war. Piano parts no longer served merely as a support for the voice but were of greater technical difficulty and formed an integral part of the composition; chromaticism was regularly employed in both voice and piano parts, and all the elements—piano, voice, and poem—blended into the artistic unity that characterized the mature song style.

The grandparents and aunts of Josephine Lang (1815–80) were professional musicians, and both her parents were employed as musicians at the Munich court. In 1836, Lang herself joined the court as a singer. Almost entirely self-taught in composition, she attracted the attention of Felix Mendelssohn and Robert Schumann, whose encouragement aided her determination to continue to compose. During the fourteen years of her marriage (1842–56) to poet Reinhard Köstlin, she bore six children and virtually ceased all creative work. When her husband died she resumed teaching and composing, producing piano works as well as songs. As a girl and later, during her widowhood, the support of Ferdinand Hiller, a composer and friend of Mendelssohn and the Schumanns, helped Lang make the necessary contacts with publishers.

Josephine Lang wrote her first songs at the age of thirteen, and some of her best work stems from her adolescent years. (See "Frühzeitiger Frühling," composed in 1830, in HAMW, pp. 111–12.) More than 150 of her songs were published during her lifetime. In 1882, the prestigious firm of Breitkopf & Härtel brought out a two-volume collection of her songs.

The older sister of Felix Mendelssohn and the daughter of a prominent and wealthy Berlin family, Fanny Hensel (1805–47) was heir to a distinguished musical tradition carried on by accomplished women amateurs. Grandmother, mother, aunts, and great-aunts were all skilled musicians, and Fanny too had the best training Berlin afforded. Her general and musical education was practically identical to that of her brother, but her father, who encouraged Felix's professional aspirations, forbade her to perform for fees or to have her music published. Her first songs appeared in a collection of her brother's and under his name. Both her father and her brother held that professional work had no place in the life of a woman of their class and status and believed that Fanny Hensel's responsibilities were to home and child rather than to art. Nevertheless, Hensel continued composing, and her works were performed at the Sunday musicales she organized and directed in her home. Her mother and her husband, Wilhelm Hensel, an artist whom she married in 1829, encouraged her creative work. At the age of forty, she summoned up the courage to defy both her father and her brother and accepted an offer from a Berlin publisher for her compositions. Only a few works were printed; Fanny Hensel died at age forty-one, one week before a review of a number of her piano compositions appeared in a leading Leipzig music journal.

Hensel's music was influenced by her study of Bach and her close relationship with her brother, but she developed her own distinctive style, particularly in her songs and piano miniatures. Her songs (about 300) have a confidence and melodic ease lacking in Felix Mendelssohn's works in that genre, gifts that her brother acknowledged when he wrote: "She has composed several things, especially German lieder which belong to the very best we have."[4] Though numbered Op. 1, No. 1, "Schwanenlied" (HAMW, pp. 115–18) is not an early work; it is, however, a beautiful example of her lyrical style.

Fanny Hensel was exceptionally prolific: her *oeuvre* includes songs;

works for piano, including several sonatas; music for organ; chamber music; choral works with and without orchestra; and an overture for orchestra. The greater part of her output is unpublished. The manuscripts remained in the hands of her family, who kept almost all (the Piano Trio, Op. 11, was an exception) from public view for several generations. Publications and recordings of her music have been appearing in recent years.

Clara (Wieck) Schumann (1819–96) was born in Leipzig to Marianne Tromlitz Wieck (pianist, singer, and daughter and granddaughter of a well-known musical family) and Friedrich Wieck (eminent music pedagogue and music merchant). Clara entered the musical world as a child prodigy. Her ambitious father saw to it that she had a superb musical education: he taught her piano, and she studied theory, harmony, counterpoint and fugue, composition, orchestration, and voice with the best available teachers in Leipzig, Dresden, and Berlin. Following a long and bitter lawsuit with her father, who refused his consent, in 1840 she married composer Robert Schumann (1810–56). She continued to compose, teach, and perform during their marriage, despite the births of eight children. After her husband's death, Clara ceased composing but resumed her career on the concert stage and remained a sought-after teacher and editor.

All of Clara Schumann's extant songs except "Walzer" were written after her marriage to Robert. The first song group was written as a Christmas gift for her husband in 1840; soon afterward he suggested that Clara join him in writing a collection of songs based on texts by Friedrich Rückert. This publication, called Op. 37/12—that is, his Op. 37 and her Op. 12— was followed several years later by Clara Schumann's own collection of six songs dedicated to Queen Caroline Amalie of Denmark. Her last published Lieder, *Six Songs from Jucunde,* were written in 1853. Of her twenty-five songs, seven were unpublished but autograph scores survive. Her *oeuvre* encompasses songs, choral works, a concerto for piano and orchestra, chamber music with piano, and short piano works. (Examples of her work in three different genres appear in HAMW, pp. 122–42.)

Though her melodies lack the spontaneity of those of Louise Reichardt or Fanny Hensel, the songs of Clara Schumann are powerful and expressive. When appropriate, she employs a brilliant piano style, as befits a concert artist of her rank (as in "Er ist gekommen" and "Am Strande"). Some of the most moving of her songs are in a declamatory style with a sparse accompaniment; their strength derives from her bold harmonies and sensitivity to the texts, as in "Ich stand in dunklen Traümen," "Sie liebten sich beide," and the unpublished "Es fiel ein Reif in der Frühlingsnacht." Her last songs, the least known, capture, in skillfully interwoven voice and piano parts, the joyful evocation of love and nature so beloved by the Romantics.

Although Pauline (Garcia) Viardot (1821–1910) was best known as an international opera star, she was also a composer, a pianist of concert rank, a great actress, a graphic artist, and a voice teacher. Born into a family of musicians, she was surrounded with singers and opera from her earliest years. Her father, Manuel Garcia, was a renowned singer, vocal pedagogue, and impresario; in 1825 he brought the first Italian opera company to the United States. Her mother, born Joaquina Stiches, was an actress and a singer; and her sister, Maria Malibran, was a fabled opera star. Pauline studied voice with her father and mother, piano with Franz Liszt, and composition privately with Anton Reicha, the famed composition teacher at

Pauline Viardot. Reproduced by permission of Music Division, The New York Public Library for the Performing Arts, Astor, Lenox and Tilden Foundations.

the Paris Conservatoire. Her career was first guided by her father and later by her husband, Louis Viardot (1800–83), a writer and theatre producer who gave up his own career to work with hers. The Viardots had several children, one of whom, Louise Héritte-Viardot, was a singer and a composer.

Unlike other women composers of her time, who tended to be rather serious and introverted, Pauline Viardot had a colorful, compelling personality. She had friends in artistic, literary, and musical circles throughout the European Continent. After hearing two operettas that Viardot had composed, accompanied, and produced, Clara Schumann, a lifelong friend, wrote, "She is the most gifted woman I have ever met."

Viardot composed vocal works in several styles and languages: German Lieder, French chansons, operettas on libretti by Russian novelist and friend Ivan Turgenev, short works for piano, and several interesting arrangements for voice and piano. Her songs, like her life, are distinguished by her flair for color and drama. (A brilliant example of her song writing is "Die Beschwörung," HAMW, pp. 154–57.)

## Composers of Opera and Operetta

Only a few women essayed opera and operetta, but of those who did, a surprising number had their works produced. Among the nineteenth-century women who wrote operas were Loïsa Puget (1810–89), Louise Bertin, Marie de Grandval, Pauline Viardot, and Ingeborg von Bronsart.

Daughter and sister of the editors of the prestigious *Journal des débats,* Louise Bertin (1805–77) lived her entire life in Paris. Encouraged by her family and her teacher, François Fétis, the writer and critic, Bertin wrote four operas. Three were produced at the Opéra-Comique and the Opéra between 1827 and 1836: *Fausto,* based on Goethe's *Faust; Le Loup-garou,* with libretto by Scribe and Mazères; and *Esmeralda,* based on Victor Hugo's *Notre-Dame de Paris,* for which the author himself adapted the text. However, the young composer found the lack of critical acclaim discouraging, and after the performance of her last opera, *Esmeralda,* she turned to other genres. She wrote twelve cantatas, a piano trio, ballades for piano, and a number of chamber symphonies.

Although Marie (de Reiset) de Grandval (1830–1907)[5] was a serious and prolific composer with professional skills and accomplishments, her aristocratic background and social class doomed her to amateur status. She studied with Friedrich von Flotow and later, when she recognized her need for further tutelage, with Camille Saint-Saëns. A number of her operas were produced in Paris but, for the early works, she used *noms de plume,* both male and female. By 1869, however, Grandval had enough confidence to use her own name; her compositions—operas, oratorios, a Mass, and other large choral pieces—were published, performed, and favorably reviewed. She also wrote chamber music, symphonies, and other works for orchestra. The last grand opera she composed, *Mazeppa* (ca. 1892), was highly praised by contemporary critics. Her works have been characterized as "essentially French, energetic, vibrant, and melodic."[6]

Ingeborg (Starck) von Bronsart (1840–1913) was born in St. Petersburg to Swedish parents. She was best known as a pianist, although she had been composing since she was a child. While studying with Liszt, Ingeborg Starck met Hans Bronsart von Schellendorf, a musician, and they married in 1862. She continued her career but was forced to give up public appearances when her husband became director of the Hanover court theatre. Ingeborg von Bronsart composed vocal music, works for piano, chamber music, and orchestral works, but she achieved her greatest success as a composer of operas. Her *Jery und Bätely,* based on a Goethe libretto, was published in 1873 and performed throughout Germany.

## Choral Works by Women

Secular choral singing by groups of men or women was a nineteenth-century phenomenon resulting from the efforts of the middle class to participate in musical life and from the Romantic revival of interest in music of earlier periods. As women joined in this activity, women composers took up this genre. Secular choral groups for men were founded in the late eighteenth century; many were choral societies organized by alumni of the great church choirs in which only men and boys participated. Women's choral groups began to appear in the first decades of the nineteenth century and soon merged with the male choruses; by the middle of the century almost every city that professed a musical life had a choral society. These large mixed choruses were a mainstay of two- or three-day festivals, which were particularly popular in England and Germany. It may be of interest to note that Felix Mendelssohn organized, conducted, and wrote his large choral works for performances at these festivals, whereas his sister Fanny conducted her choral works at her Sunday home musicales. Among them are several cantatas and an oratorio, as well as shorter works for mixed chorus.

Other women who wrote choral music for public consumption include Louise Reichardt, whose compositions are scored for women's voices. Johanna Kinkel (1810–58), who founded and conducted a mixed chorus with an extensive repertoire of old and new works, wrote choruses, secular cantatas, and sacred works. Clara Schumann accompanied the Dresden

Gesangverein and composed three *a cappella* choruses for that group. Luise Adolpha Le Beau, who wrote in many genres, composed secular choral works as well as choruses on biblical subjects. Other composers of choral music included Pauline Viardot, Agathe Backer-Grøndahl, and Ingeborg von Bronsart.

## COMPOSERS OF INSTRUMENTAL MUSIC

### *Women and the Piano*

The Romantics held instrumental music to be superior to music with words, and the piano was the instrument that seemed best to exemplify Romantic ideals. By 1830, it had a greater range, bigger sound, and more strength than the keyboard instruments of the previous century and could express intimate emotion as well as display dazzling virtuosity. It was as suitable a musical vehicle for the great virtuosi as it was for the amateur. The lingering echoes of the sustaining pedal could project "the infinite longing which is the essence of romanticism."[7] The piano, seen and heard in concert hall, palace, and parlor, was considered a particularly appropriate instrument for women to play because of its association with domestic music making.

The women who composed for piano employed, for the most part, the short lyric forms so beloved of the age: songs without words, etudes, romances, ballades, intermezzos, nocturnes, scherzos, and dance forms such as the polonaise and the mazurka. Although these works were frequently associated with what was derogatorily called "salon music," they were, in the hands of the best composers, elegant and expressive pieces. Particularly popular among concert pianists who performed their own works was the theme-and-variations form, in which the artist could demonstrate versatility and brilliance. Among the composers who wrote for the piano—all of them successful concert artists as well—were Maria Szymanowska, Louise Farrenc, Léopoldine Blahetka, Fanny Hensel, Clara Schumann, Luise Adolpha Le Beau, and Ingeborg von Bronsart.

Maria (Wolowska) Syzmanowska (1789–1831) was the first Polish pianist to gain a European reputation. Although neither of her parents was a musician, as a child she was given the best musical education Warsaw had to offer. Beginning in 1810 she toured throughout continental Europe and England. She married in 1810, but her husband was not interested in her career and she left him in 1820, taking her three children with her. Szymanowska supported herself and her family by concertizing, composing, and teaching. In 1828 she settled in St. Petersburg, where she had an official position as court pianist to the tsarina. She died in that city during a cholera epidemic.

Szymanowska's published piano works include nocturnes, waltzes, and etudes; they were known and played throughout Europe. (Her B♭-major *Nocturne* is published in HAMW, pp. 103–108.) Szymanowska was one of the first composers to write concert music employing such Polish dance forms as the mazurka and the polonaise. Polish scholars credit her with enormous influence on the young Frédéric Chopin. She also composed songs and chamber works.

Louise (Dumont) Farrenc (1804–75) was born in Paris, and that city remained the lifelong center of her activities. She studied piano with her godmother, and harmony and theory privately with Anton Reicha. Though the Paris of Farrenc's youth was a city where opera reigned supreme, her interests and those of her husband, Aristide Farrenc (1794–1865), a flutist and music publisher, were in music of the Classical and earlier eras. With Aristide, Louise co-edited a historical anthology of piano music, *Trésor des pianistes,* which brought keyboard music of previous centuries to the attention of the French public.

Shy, serious, and essentially conservative, Louise Farrenc devoted herself to composing and teaching piano at the Paris Conservatoire, where she was a professor for over thirty years. Her few public appearances as a pianist were urged on her by her husband, who hoped that her compositions would become better known as a result. Her creative work reflects her activities: she wrote etudes in a wide variety of styles to use at the Conservatoire for teaching purposes. She also composed rondos, variations for piano, sonatas, chamber music, symphonies, and other works in Classical forms. Her contemporaries praised her craftsmanship and erudition, and she was awarded many honors during her lifetime.

Léopoldine Blahetka (1811–87),[8] an Austrian pianist and composer, grew up in an intellectual environment. Her father taught mathematics and history, and her maternal grandfather was the Viennese composer Andreas Träg. Beethoven heard Léopoldine perform when she was five years old and convinced her parents that she should study with Joseph Czerny (not related to Carl Czerny). She later studied piano with Friedrich Kalkbrenner and Ignaz Moscheles and composition with Simon Sechter, the highly respected pedagogue who taught Franz Schubert and other eminent Viennese musicians. Between 1825 and 1827, Blahetka performed throughout Germany and was acclaimed by the critics as a pianist and a composer.

Blahetka wrote for voice, for violin and piano, for piano and orchestra, and for solo piano. Her opera, *Die Räuber und die Sänger,* was produced in

Léopoldine Blahetka. Reproduced by permission of Music Division, The New York Public Library for the Performing Arts, Astor, Lenox and Tilden Foundations.

Vienna in 1830. For the piano, she composed polonaises, many sets of variations, and piano transcriptions of popular operatic arias. Her "Souvenirs d'Angleterre" uses "God Save the Queen" as the basis of brilliant and pianistic variations. Her piano trio is a joyful work with a rollicking polka finale. Her writing, reminiscent of both Beethoven and Mendelssohn, exploits the singing tone of the piano and the brilliant upper range of the keyboard. Blahetka retired from active concertizing and composing at the end of the 1830s, settled in Belgium, and turned to teaching.

Fanny Mendelssohn Hensel's piano works were composed for her own home Sunday musicales. Strongly influenced by Bach and Beethoven and the tutelage she received together with her brother, she composed studies, contrapuntal works, sonatas, and character pieces for the piano, including her *Lieder ohne Worte* (Songs without Words). Scholars believe that it was Fanny, not her brother Felix, who gave the name to the genre, but the influence of one upon the other is so great that it is impossible to determine the origin of the term. A group of her last *Lieder ohne Worte* was chosen for publication by Felix after her death. Hensel's experimentation in these works has been described as "an original attempt at elevating the genre to one of greater musical significance."[9] Two large works for piano, a piano sonata in C minor and one in G major, survive but have not been published.

The keyboard works of Clara Schumann delineate the changing styles of piano music in the first half of the nineteenth century. Among her girlhood works are several in variation form—typical of the period—in which popular melodies were employed to demonstrate the prowess of the pianist. At the same time, however, the young pianist was writing short lyric pieces characteristic of the New Romantic School, a group that included Chopin, Mendelssohn, Robert Schumann, and Clara herself. After her marriage, she chose to write in more traditional forms, reflecting her joint studies with her husband of Bach, Mozart, Haydn, and Beethoven. In these years she wrote several romances and character pieces, a sonata for piano (unpublished until 1991), preludes and fugues (Op. 16), and the *Variations on a Theme by Robert Schumann,* Op. 20, a serious and formal work (HAMW, pp. 130–42) unlike the flashy variations of her youth.

## Women and Chamber Music

Like the art song and piano music, chamber music was considered an acceptable genre for women. In the first decade of the nineteenth century it was still associated with private music making rather than with concerts for paying audiences. In fact, public chamber music concerts were not given until the 1820s. Nevertheless, only a few women composed chamber music. Léopoldine Blahetka, who performed with chamber groups in Vienna between 1823 and 1830, composed for chamber ensembles that included piano. Louise Farrenc's best works may have been the pieces she wrote for various combinations of instruments: sonatas, trios, quintets, a sextet, and a very successful nonet for winds and strings. All of them have been performed but not all have been published. (The first movement of Farrenc's Trio, Op. 45 for flute [or violin], cello, and piano can be found in HAMW, pp. 145–51.)

Clara Schumann, who programed Beethoven's piano and violin sonatas and piano trios in her recitals as early as the 1830s, organized a trio in Dresden for which she was the pianist. The concerts she arranged were among the first public chamber music performances given in that city. Her own Piano Trio, Op. 17, undoubtedly inspired by the works she had played, was well received by reviewers. Many commented on the gender of the composer, and several expressed surprise that a woman could write an instrumental work so skillfully and with such effect. "Let us look at this trio," wrote one critic; "the basic foundation has been designed with confidence, the individual parts have been fashioned with taste, and throughout the whole, there is a tender, poetic quality that pervades the entire piece and consecrates it as a work of art."[10] (See HAMW, pp. 124–29, for the first movement of the Trio.)

For her home musicales Fanny Hensel composed duos, a piano quartet, a string quartet, and—her last major work—a piano trio, her Op. 11, published posthumously. This piece demonstrates, in the words of one Hensel scholar, her "formidable compositional skill and inventiveness."[11] Other composers who wrote for chamber combinations were Bronsart, who wrote a number of duos, and Le Beau, whose chamber works, including sonatas, trios, and a string quintet, were considered some of her best compositions.

## Women and Orchestral Music

Rare was the woman who ventured into the realm of orchestral music in the nineteenth century. There were several reasons for this. First, symphonies and works for large groups were considered masculine forms to be performed in public concert halls. Second, orchestral works required skills that many women musicians had not had the opportunity to learn. Third, women rarely had access to the groups that would rehearse and perform their works. All composers—male and female—needed (indeed, still need) connections to the men who held power in the musical world. This posed a special difficulty for women: they were less likely to know the right people and would, moreover, undoubtedly antagonize the influential conductors and managers if they stepped out of their traditional submissive female roles.

Because most women composers were pianists, their works for orchestra most often involved the piano as well. Consequently, we find that concertos and fantasies for piano and orchestra, which the composer herself could introduce, were among the most frequently performed orchestral works by women. Clara Schumann's Piano Concerto, Op. 7, was just such a piece; written as a vehicle for her girlhood concerts, it was first played, to great acclaim, in 1837.

Later in the century, as women had more opportunity to study composition and orchestration, a number of composers had the courage to essay orchestral music, Farrenc and Le Beau among them. Farrenc's three symphonies (written between 1841 and 1847) were performed but not published. According to Friedland, who has studied the autograph scores, these works are modeled on those of the great Classical masters—Haydn, Mozart, and Beethoven—and share with the symphonic productions of her contemporary Felix Mendelssohn "the classical ideal of formal and textural lucidity."[12]

Luise Adolpha Le Beau (1850–1927) did not shun large musical forms and persevered in her composing despite opposition from the musical establishment in her native Germany. Supported by her parents, who were not professional musicians but who were musical and totally devoted to her, Le Beau studied piano and composition privately with such eminent teachers as Clara Schumann, Franz Lachner, and Josef Rheinberger. As was the case with other nineteenth-century women composers, her first career steps were as a pianist, and she earned a living as pianist, teacher, and music critic, though she saw her true vocation as that of composer.

Le Beau wrote an opera and songs as well as works for piano, chorus, orchestra, and chamber groups. Her Cello Sonata, Op. 17, won first prize in a Hamburg competition in 1882, and she received much critical acclaim for her chamber works. Her compositions tended to be conservative, reflecting her studies with Rheinberger. Among her best works are a piano sonata (1879); a sonata for violin and piano (1882); the Cello Sonata, Op. 17; and a Symphony in F minor for Large Orchestra, Op. 41. Le Beau received praise for the energy and power of her works, which critics found very masculine. She lived until 1927 but withdrew from musical life in 1903.

## PERFORMERS

### Singers

Of all the professional women performers in the nineteenth century, the largest number were singers. Most prominent were those who sang opera, but many great vocalists also performed in public concerts and in church. The opera singers were the great stars of the period: lionized, adored, they had international reputations and appeared in opera houses throughout Europe and North and South America. Most singers were related to professional musicians or actors and continued the family tradition as a matter of course. Few singers from middle-class families went into opera because they feared the opprobrium visited upon women, whereas aspiring opera singers from professional musical or theatrical families (who were already déclassé) were not discouraged by such attitudes. The stage was a means to money, fame, and even marriage into the aristocracy, though it was generally understood that a career was to be relinquished upon marrying.

The vocation of singer could begin at an astonishingly young age: stars of the Paris Opéra might appear as early as age fifteen and be used up by twenty-five. Some then turned to provincial opera houses; others taught or made good marriages at retirement in their twenties. Among the prominent and influential singers who appeared in opera and concert in the first half of the nineteenth century were Angelica Catalani (1780–1849), who dubbed herself the "prima cantatrice del mondo" and managed the prestigious Théâtre des Italiens in Paris for a brief period; Anna Milder-Hauptmann (1785–1838), who created the role of Leonore in Beethoven's *Fidelio;* and the vocal phenomenon Giuditta Pasta (1798–1865), who sang the title role at the premiere of Bellini's *Norma.*

Henriette Sontag (1805–54), the first German to have an international reputation in a field dominated by Italian singers, was eighteen when she sang in the first performance of Beethoven's Ninth Symphony. Sontag's husband, Count Rossi, was an Italian nobleman who, an English critic wrote, "did not publicly announce the marriage until after his wife (in 1830) had made a very lucrative concert tour."[13] Sontag returned to the stage in 1848, when Rossi was in financial difficulty. She died a few years later in Mexico while on a North American tour.

Wilhelmine Schröder-Devrient (1805–60), also German, had a particularly colorful career. The daughter of a well-known actress in Vienna, she made her debut at the age of seventeen in that city as Pamina in *The Magic Flute.* Schröder-Devrient created roles in three Wagner operas, including that of Venus in *Tannhäuser;* and she was associated with Wagner and other revolutionaries in the uprising against the Saxon king in 1849. She made fiery political speeches, which are still remembered, and was exiled from Dresden.

Other renowned singers who sang opera but were better known for their activities on the concert stage were the English soprano Clara Novello (1818–1908), a favorite singer of Felix Mendelssohn and Robert Schumann; and Jenny Lind-Goldschmidt (1820–1887), the "Swedish Nightingale." Because of her gifts and popularity and the fact that her personal reputation remained unsullied, Lind was able to dispel to some degree the aura of disrepute associated with the stage. For this, several generations of singers are indebted to her.

Among the eminent singers who were members of family dynasties and passed the musical tradition down to younger sisters, daughters, nieces, and cousins were Maria Malibran and her younger sister Pauline Viardot, members of the Garcia family. Malibran, like Viardot, also composed; her brilliant career—the subject of novels, plays, songs, and movies—was cut short by a riding accident. Though Viardot was a more versatile musician

Jenny Lind's triumphant arrival in New York City. Reproduced by permission of Music Division, The New York Public Library for the Performing Arts, Astor, Lenox and Tilden Foundations.

than her sister, she never inspired the wild adoration that surrounded Malibran.

In the latter part of the century the Patti sisters, Carlotta (1835–89) and Adelina (1843–1919), both coloratura sopranos, were celebrated in Europe and North America. Carlotta pursued a career as a concert artist rather than an opera singer, while Adelina was considered the successor to Pasta and Giulia Grisi as an international star and "Queen of Song." Although she was distinguished for the sweetness and purity of her voice more than for her dramatic gifts, she triumphed equally in the opera and the concert hall.

## Pianists

A number of women pianists of the nineteenth century were celebrated as world-class artists. First and foremost was Clara Schumann, who had a blazingly successful career as a concert pianist for over sixty years, longer than that of any other musician, male or female, in the nineteenth century. The works she programed changed the character of the piano recital from a lengthy potpourri of virtuoso works based on popular melodies to a serious, composer-centered event concentrating on a few works by such composers as Bach, Beethoven, Mendelssohn, Chopin, Robert Schumann, and Brahms. Clara Schumann was one of the first pianists to play from memory and to play without any assisting artists. She had a direct influence on later generations of pianists through her teaching: among her women students who had professional careers in Europe and North America were Fanny Davies (1861–1934), Ilona Eibenschütz (1872–1967), Mathilde Verne (1865–1936), and Natalia Janotha (1856–1932).

Schumann was not without female rivals. As a child she was compared to Léopoldine Blahetka, Anna de Belleville (later Belleville-Oury, 1808–80), and above all, Marie Pleyel (1811–75, born Marie Moke). Among the outstanding women of a later generation were Wilhelmine Clauss-Szarvardy (1834–1907) and the English pianist Arabella Goddard (1836–1922). In 1873 Goddard, famed as a Beethoven interpreter, began a three-year world concert tour that took her to America, Australia, and India; within weeks of her return she gave two London recitals.

Some of the most celebrated women pianists of the latter half of the century were as well known for their tempestuous personalities as for their musicianship and formidable techniques. Among them were Sophie Menter (1846–1918), a student of Carl Tausig and Liszt and later professor at the St. Petersburg Conservatory; and Teresa Carreño (1853–1917), a Venezuelan pianist and composer who was considered a world-class artist. In the last decades of the century, there were so many outstanding female keyboard artists that it is difficult to single out individuals from among the talented crowd. Two who were particularly influential were Anna Essipoff (also known as Annette Essipova, 1851–1914), a Russian virtuoso who toured throughout the world and was the favorite partner of violinist Leopold Auer. She taught at the St. Petersburg Conservatory from 1893 to the end of her life. Agnes Zimmermann (1847–1925), born in Germany, built her career in England, edited sonatas of Mozart and Beethoven, and was considered a great classical pianist.

## Harpists

Along with the piano, the harp was considered eminently suitable for women. It was played almost exclusively by women, in part because the movements required to play it were graceful and because audiences enjoyed the sight as well as the sound. A recital in Vienna in 1809 by Caroline Longhi was reviewed by Johann Friedrich Reichardt in a style typical of the period:

> She played very well, and what is more, looked very well, because she understood how to show off a beautiful figure to its greatest advantage, especially at the harp, where she managed to place herself and deport herself in so many varied and yet still graceful positions that we received a good view of her entire beautiful figure from all sides. Her harp playing itself was quite delicate and pleasing.[14]

The first women to play in orchestras were harpists. Josefa Müllner (1769–1843) was a soloist in the Vienna court orchestra and harp teacher of the archduchesses (sisters and daughters of the emperor). Dorothea (Scheidler) Spohr (1787–1834) toured with her husband, Ludwig Spohr, the violinist, composer, and conductor; both Spohrs were employed in the orchestra of the Theater an der Wien between 1813 and 1815.

## Violinists

String instruments were considered unfeminine in the early nineteenth century in large part because it was thought that the performers did not look attractive while playing. Nevertheless, Italy's very talented and well-trained Milanollo sisters, Teresa (1827–1902) and Marie (1832–48), were celebrated throughout Europe. After Marie's death, Theresa toured alone until 1857, when she married and retired from the stage.

By 1870, the violin was more acceptable, and many women came to Berlin to study with Joseph Joachim, despite the ban on their participation in the orchestra of the Hochschule. Marie (Soldat) Roeger (1863–1955), a favorite Joachim student, won the prestigious Mendelssohn prize at the Hochschule, as did Gabriele Wietrowetz (1866–1937), another Joachim pupil. Both these violinists and many others who studied at the Paris and Brussels conservatories went on to have careers as soloists and to play in all-women string quartets in the last decades of the century. Perhaps the best known European woman violinist of her time was Wilma (Neruda) Norman, later Lady Hallé (1839–1911). She made her debut at the age of seven and subsequently appeared in all principal cities of Europe. After her first husband died she married Sir Charles Hallé, continued with her career, and played an important part in the musical life of London.

Teresa and Marie Milanollo. Reproduced by permission of Music Division, The New York Public Library for the Performing Arts, Astor, Lenox and Tilden Foundations.

## Other Instrumentalists and Orchestra Players

Although women were not encouraged to study orchestral instruments in the conservatories until late in the century, there were a number of instrumentalists, usually daughters of professional musicians, who studied privately and had professional careers in the early decades of the nineteenth century. Occasionally we find a woman on the roster of a provincial orchestra, but more often women instrumentalists played as soloists. From the programs of the Leipzig Gewandhaus, a renowned concert hall, we learn that between 1781 and 1881 there were a number of women soloists: eighteen violinists, two cellists (1845 and 1875), one flutist (1832), and two concertina players (1851 and 1870). Another instrumental soloist was Caroline (Schleicher) Krähmer (1794–ca. 1850), one of the few women wind players of the nineteenth century. When her father died, she took over his duties as town musician and later played in the orchestra of the Duke of Baden. Schleicher, who embarked on a concert tour as a clarinet soloist at the age of twenty-eight, met and married Ernst Krähmer, an oboe player, in Vienna. The couple (who had two children) gave annual concerts in Vienna between 1827 and 1837.[15]

By the 1870s women instrumentalists denied entry into orchestras began to form their own string quartets and all-female orchestras. Although these women had had the best conservatory training—many graduating with the highest honors—the women's orchestras were rarely given the same serious attention and respect enjoyed by their male counterparts.

## Conductors

The art of conducting as we know it developed in the nineteenth century, and the first modern conductors were composers, such as Mendelssohn, Weber, Berlioz, and Wagner. As far as is known, women of the time were not invited to conduct professional instrumental groups but a number of women established and conducted choral groups. Because many women musicians held positions as teachers, they may have conducted student groups. In some rare circumstances a composer might have conducted her own work; Louise Héritte-Viardot, for example, describes her experience with a Stockholm orchestra.[16] Women were not admitted to conducting classes, nor were they welcomed as apprentices. It was to be many years before a woman would be accepted on the podium.

## SUMMARY

Despite social, educational, and economic restrictions, women participated in every aspect of musical life in the nineteenth century. Songs, keyboard music, chamber music, symphonies, and operas composed by women were performed and published. Performers were seen and heard on concert stages throughout Europe, and women artists traveled to and performed on five continents. Women students flocked to the great conservatories established in the nineteenth century and availed themselves of the professional training now open to them. Women were employed as teachers in the public conservatories and founded their own schools as well. Denied membership in symphony and opera orchestras, they established their own ensembles. Women writers and scholars produced basic studies on music and musical life. As in previous centuries, however, most of the professional women musicians were from families of musicians with a generations-long tradition.

The new prosperity of the middle classes afforded a great many women the time to study music. A large group of amateurs developed, some rising to the highest levels of musical proficiency but not given the opportunity to work professionally because of the prevailing attitudes toward feminine behavior. Most often, the well-to-do musical amateur, no matter how talented, was forced to limit herself to domestic music making. The accomplishments of professional and amateur women musicians of the nineteenth century have largely been ignored by historians. They are only now beginning to be recognized.

## NOTES

. 1. Jean-Jacques Rousseau, *Politics and the Arts: Letter to M. d'Alembert on the Theatre (Lettre sur les spectacles)*, translated by Allan Bloom (Glencoe, IL: Free Press, 1960), pp. 82–83, as quoted in Mendel Kohansky, "Introduction," *The Disreputable Profession: The Actor in Society* (Westport, CT: Greenwood Press, 1984); and Jean Jacques Rousseau, *Emile*, bk. 5, in *Oeuvres complètes*, edited by Michel Launay, 3 vols. (Paris, 1967–71), vol. III: *Oeuvres philosophiques et politiques: de l'Emile aux derniers écrits politiques, 1762–1772*, pp. 243–47, as quoted in Susan Groag Bell and Karen M. Offen, *Women, the Family, and Freedom: The Debate in Documents*, 2 vols. (Stanford: Stanford University Press, 1983), 1:49.

2. Wilhelm von Humboldt, "Ueber der Geschlechtsunterschied und dessen Einfluss auf die organische Natur," in *Die Horen*, vol. I, pt. 2 (Tübingen, 1795), p. 111, as quoted in Bell and Offen, 1:68.

3. *Das Conservatorium der Musik in Leipzig* (Leipzig, 1843), p. 6.

4. Quoted in Victoria Sirota, "The Life and Works of Fanny Mendelssohn Hensel," DMA thesis, Boston University, 1981, p. 85.

5. I am indebted to Lydia Ledeen of Drew University for information about Marie de Grandval. Prof. Ledeen's paper on the composer was read at a regional meeting of the College Music Society at Trenton State College on March 26, 1988.

6. Quoted by Ledeen from Hippolyte Buffenoir, *La Comtesse de Grandval* (Paris, 1894), pp. 10–11.

7. E. T. A. Hoffmann, as quoted in *Source Readings in Music History*, edited by Oliver Strunk (New York: Norton, 1950), p. 777.

8. I am indebted to Lydia Ledeen for information on Blahetka.

9. Sirota, p. 177.

10. *Allgemeine musikalische Zeitung* 50 (April 5, 1848):233 (my translation).

11. Sirota, p. 246.

12. Bea Friedland, *Louise Farrenc, 1804–1875: Composer, Performer, Scholar* (Ann Arbor: UMI Research Press, 1980), p. 163.

13. H. Sutherland Edwards, *The Prima Donna* (London, 1888; reprint New York: Da Capo, 1978), p. 237.

14. Johann Friedrich Reichardt, *Vertraute Briefe geschrieben auf einer Reise nach Wien und den Oesterreichischen Staaten zu Ende des Jahres 1808 und zu Anfang 1809*, edited by Gustav Gugitz, 2 vols. (Munich: Georg Müller, 1915), 1:193–95 (my translation).

15. Pamela Weston, *Clarinet Virtuosi of the Past* (London: Pamela Weston,

1971), pp. 175–77; and *More Clarinet Virtuosi of the Past* (London: Pamela Weston, 1977), pp. 226–28.

16. Louise Héritte-Viardot, *Memories and Adventures* (London: Mills and Boon, 1913; reprint New York: Da Capo, 1978), pp. 224–25.

## SUGGESTIONS FOR FURTHER READING

Bushnell, Howard. *Maria Malibran: A Biography of the Singer*. University Park: Pennsylvania State University Press, 1979.

Citron, Marcia. *The Letters of Fanny Hensel to Felix Mendelssohn*. Stuyvesant, NY: Pendragon, 1987.

FitzLyon, April. *Maria Malibran: Diva of the Romantic Age*. London: Souvenir Press, 1987; distributed in the United States by Indiana University Press.

———. *The Price of Genius: A Life of Pauline Viardot*. New York: Appleton-Century-Crofts, 1964.

Hensel, Sebastian. *The Mendelssohn Family (1729–1847) from Letters and Journals*. 2d rev. ed. Translated by C. Klingemann and an American Collaborator. 2 vols. New York: Harper and Brothers, 1882; reprint Westport, CT: Greenwood Press, 1968.

Krille, Annemarie. *Beiträge zur Geschichte der Musikerziehung und Musikübung der deutschen Frau (von 1750 bis 1820)*. Berlin: Triltsch & Huther, 1938.

Loesser, Arthur. *Men, Women, and Pianos: A Social History*. New York: Simon and Schuster, 1954.

Mackenzie-Grieve, Averil. *Clara Novello, 1818–1908*. London: Geoffrey Bles, 1955; reprint New York: Da Capo, 1980.

Pendle, Karin. "A Night at the Opera: The Parisian Prima Donna, 1830–1850." *Opera Quarterly* 4 (Spring 1986):77–89.

Reich, Nancy B. *Clara Schumann: The Artist and the Woman*. Ithaca: Cornell University Press, 1985.

———. "Louise Reichardt." In *Ars Musica, Musica Scientia: Festschrift Heinrich Hüschen*, edited by Detlef Altenburg. Cologne: Gitarre und Laute Verlagsgesellschaft, 1980.

Ware, W. Porter, and Lockhard, Thaddeus C. *P. T. Barnum Presents Jenny Lind: The American Tour of the Swedish Nightingale*. Baton Rouge: Louisiana State University Press, 1980.

# VI.
# European Composers and Musicians, 1880–1918

*Marcia J. Citron*

## Introduction

The status of European women generally improved between 1880 and 1918. Women benefited from many of the far-reaching political, social, and economic forces that were reshaping the attitudes and conventions of Western society. Politically, nationalism yielded to internationalism, a trend capped by the global reach of World War I (1914–18). Socially, increased urbanization accompanied a new wave of industrialization. Women entered the labor pool in ever-greater numbers, and the figures swelled during the war, as women filled jobs vacated by men at the front. This proved a very important stage in women's move from supportive to primary work roles. After the war, however, the numbers dropped drastically as Western Europe reverted to more traditional notions of women and work.

In the late nineteenth century, increased industrialization led to the need for social reform. Although most reforms focused on the typical laborer, who was male, women figured as incidental beneficiaries. A strong wave of feminism swept through Europe in this period, notably in England, as middle-class women in particular perceived a growing discrepancy between themselves and men. Ironically, this perception arose as a result of women's greater access to education and because increased wealth exaggerated the split between the male world of the public sphere and the female world of the domestic. The various feminist movements culminated in the granting of the vote to women, which generally occurred by 1920. Economic reliance on women during World War I probably played a major role in bringing the long struggle to a successful conclusion. Nonetheless, suffrage functioned more as a symbol than as a barometer of widespread change. With few exceptions, women still lacked such basic legal rights as holding office, owning property, and suing for divorce.

Increased access to birth control devices proved critical in women's expanded array of options. The production of cheap rubber for use in condoms as well as the development of the diaphragm in the 1880s marked an important stage in women's reproductive freedom. Birthrates, especially in the middle and upper classes, dropped markedly by the early years of the twentieth century. With infant and maternal mortality in decline, women felt less of a need to produce large numbers of children in order to ensure familial succession. Industrialization alleviated the necessity for children to work at home for the family's livelihood. These factors gave women greater control in the timing and number of children—a necessary condition for sustained creative work.

Although reproductive freedom was probably the single most important factor in the emergence of the modern woman, other signs were in evidence. The drastic social upheavals during World War I led to radical changes in women's appearance, reflecting their expanding options. Short skirts and short hair, for example, allowed for greater freedom of movement and thus placed fewer restrictions on women's activities. At the same time the stigma of makeup—the sign of a "loose woman"—began to vanish, and women could enjoy additional possibilities for physical individuality.

What was the typical profile of the European woman composer in this period? In many ways she resembled her prototype earlier in the century. She was likely to come from the middle or upper class and from an artistic home environment, where encouragement by knowledgeable family members helped instill the motivation and self-confidence needed for artistic fulfillment. This was especially important for women. Whereas society still took male success for granted, talented women continued to be viewed as exceptions and thus lacked the support systems long established for men. Men also had the benefit of a long history of role models; women still had few female role models or colleagues and tended to feel isolated and unsure of group identity. Still, aspiring female creators had the advantage over their predecessors of better access to education, especially in the burgeoning music conservatories. Although women were still a rarity in theory or composition classes, a few, such as Ethel Smyth and Lili Boulanger, took advantage of these opportunities.

Women composers were active in various musical cultures. One of the most interesting was *fin-de-siècle* France, with its mixture of the new and the old: the resurgence of a specifically French style fanned by nationalism after the Franco-Prussian War (1871), an interest in the operas of Richard Wagner as well as in instrumental music, and the continuation of academic values as promulgated by the Paris Conservatoire.

## AUGUSTA HOLMÈS

Augusta Holmès (1847–1903) flourished in this rich atmosphere. Of Irish extraction, Holmès was born in Paris but spent her formative years in Versailles. Although neither of her parents was especially musical, Augusta nonetheless reaped the benefits of a home that attracted leading writers, artists, and musicians. Unfortunately, Augusta's mother discouraged her interest in music; but after Mme. Holmès's death, when Augusta was a young teen, her father encouraged her to develop her talent. Despite the proximity of Versailles to Paris, the center of French musical life, Augusta studied with local musicians. The poet Alfred de Vigny, her godfather (possibly her natural father), played a major role as mentor and adviser, a kind of substitute for her mother.

As Holmès approached her twenties, she became an ardent Wagnerian and fought hard to have works by Wagner included on the Concerts Populaires, an important Paris series. She had the opportunity to meet Wagner at his home on Lake Lucerne; and she corresponded with Franz Liszt, who admired her musical talents. In the mid-1870s Holmès joined the circle of César Franck—it is unclear whether she actually studied with him—and began to compose in earnest. Her lifelong attraction to the grand French vocal tradition and its lofty ideals is exemplified in her early works, including the symphonic poem *Hymn to Apollo* (1872). Many of her large orchestral works are subtitled "dramatic symphony" and include chorus and vocal soloists; others, such as *Triumphal Ode,* composed for the Paris Exposition of 1889, also include vocal forces. Among her large works that appeared on programs of major concert series, such as the Concerts Populaires, was *Les Argonautes* (1881).

Like many a French composer, Holmès tried her hand at opera. Strong literary talent as well as admiration for Wagner probably influenced her decision to write her own libretti. She completed four operas but only one was produced: *La montagne noire,* a work of four acts, performed at the Paris Opéra on February 8, 1895. Along with Louise Bertin's *Fausto* (1831) and *La Esmeralda* (1836), it was one of the few operas by women introduced in Paris in the nineteenth century. Unfortunately, *La montagne noire* was poorly received, and Holmès suffered a great disappointment. Some have attributed its lack of success, which contributed to Holmès's physical decline, to the fact that it was actually composed some twelve years earlier, and by the time the performance materialized its Wagnerian subject matter and musical treatment had become passé.

Holmès's interest in vocal genres extended well beyond dramatic music, however. She composed approximately 130 songs (most of them after 1880), many to her own texts. The large number published attest to her popularity, and Ethel Smyth was one contemporary who greatly admired them. The songs that are readily available[1] exhibit typical traits of the period as well as individual characteristics. Many texts deal with idealized love, heroism ("Ogier le Danois," 1900), or exotic locales ("Garci Perez," 1892). These were standard conventions in contemporary French song, although Holmès's attraction to heroism also reflects her strong Irish patriotism. Her musical style displays great variety. The Christmas song "Noël" (1885), for example, features an appropriate folk style. The exotic flavor of Morocco in "Charme-du-jour" (1902) comes through in the drone bass and the improvisatory turns in the vocal line. The ghost of Wagner hovers in "La Haine," from *Les sept ivresses* (1882), where the markedly dramatic style builds on a left-hand pattern similar to an important Leitmotiv in *The Ring*. In contrast, a neoclassical vocabulary found in much French music around 1900 permeates the playful "À Trianon" (1896). Holmès composed only a few small-scale instrumental pieces, including *Fantaisie* for clarinet and piano, written as a competition piece for the Paris Conservatoire in 1900.

Throughout her life Augusta Holmès mixed easily in leading artistic circles. She had a vibrant personality and was described as a real beauty.[2] Although she never married, she had a lengthy affair with the poet Catulle Mendès (1841–1909) and reputedly had three children with him. The typical posthumous assessment dwells on her beauty, to the exclusion of her music. Consequently, posterity has idealized Holmès's persona and feminine charms and thereby ignored or at best marginalized her creative achievements. A truer assessment can emerge only when we peel away the layers of idealization to expose the human characteristics and creative energy of this interesting woman.

## CÉCILE CHAMINADE

The professional paths of Holmès and Cécile Chaminade (1857–1944) crossed in the 1880s, when the orchestral works of both women appeared on the programs of major concert series. For the most part, however, their careers remained distinct. Chaminade was born in Paris to an upper middle-class family that valued the arts. Both parents were amateur musicians, and her mother taught her to play the piano. Chaminade's earliest pieces may date from 1865, composed for her first communion. Félix Le Couppey, an important Paris musician, recommended that she study at the Conservatoire. Although M. Chaminade would not permit his daughter to attend the school because of his views on proper female decorum, he allowed her to study piano and theory privately with professors on the faculty.

By the late 1870s Chaminade began to perform publicly as a pianist in chamber music. Her compositional debut occurred in April 1878 and was well received by the press. Throughout her active career as composer-pianist, which lasted until the outbreak of World War I, these two genres formed her mainstay. In the 1880s she produced several large-scale works as well, including *Suite d'orchestre* (1881) and *La Sévillane* (1882), a one-act opéra-comique performed privately in concert version. *Callirhoë*, a ballet, premiered in Marseilles (1888) and probably was Chaminade's greatest success. The decade also included the dramatic symphony *Les Amazones*

Cécile Chaminade. Photo courtesy of the Vicomtesse J. de Cornulier-Lucinière. Used by permission.

(1884–88) and the *Concertstück* for piano and orchestra, both introduced in April 1888 in Antwerp. *Concertstück* proved highly successful and enjoyed numerous performances before World War I. Except for the still-popular Concertino for flute and orchestra, written as a competition piece for the Conservatoire (1902), Chaminade composed no other orchestral works.

Around 1890 Chaminade embarked on a career as a concert pianist, performing almost exclusively her own compositions. She toured the Continent and began annual visits to England in 1892. She focused on piano works and songs, and the widespread exposure created a market for their publication. In fact, Chaminade was one of the most published women composers. She became extremely popular in the United States, where her pieces were also printed. Around 1900 the first of many Chaminade Clubs came into existence, and her growing popularity led her to make the long journey to America. Between October 24 and December 15, 1908, Chaminade gave concerts in twelve cities, traveling as far west as Minneapolis. Audiences flocked to see her, although press reception was mixed. During this period Chaminade won several awards, including the Jubilee Medal from Queen Victoria (1897) and the Chefekat from the Sultan of Turkey (1901). In the summer of 1913 she was admitted into the prestigious Legion of Honor, the first female composer so honored. Advancing years and the outbreak of war curtailed Chaminade's concertizing. The rest of her life was played out in increasing debilitation and isolation, exacerbated by her belief that she was forgotten. Chaminade died in Monte Carlo on April 13, 1944, at the age of eight-six.

Personally, Chaminade preferred solitude or the company of her family and enjoyed a close relationship with her mother. Her platonic marriage (1901–1907) to Louis-Mathieu Carbonel, a Marseilles music publisher twenty years her senior, shocked her family yet apparently suited Chaminade, who later declared that "it is difficult to reconcile the domestic life with the artistic. . . . When a woman of talent marries a man who appreciates that side of her, such a marriage may be ideally happy for both."[3] Thus we have Chaminade's views on a classic dilemma facing women.

Chaminade was extremely prolific. Of her approximately 400 compositions, about 200 are piano pieces and about 135 are songs. Like many women she was drawn to these intimate genres, whose expressive potential holds special appeal for female culture. Almost all of Chaminade's piano works are character pieces with descriptive titles that capture the flavor of *la belle époque*. The harmonic language is diatonic and functional, with frequent color chords to add spice. The forms are simple and traditional, while the melody, their most prominent element, is generally elegant and tuneful.

Like many a French work of the period, Chaminade's piano pieces often exploit exoticism, such as the Spanish flavor of "Sérénade" (1884) or "La Lisonjera" (The flatterer, ca. 1890). Standing apart is the Sonata (composed ca. 1888 and published in 1895), her only work in this genre. Since Chaminade did not perform the complete piece in public, she may have considered it an experimental work.

The Sonata consists of three contrasting movements (entire piece in Da Capo reprint, *Three Piano Pieces* [1979]; second movement in HAMW, pp. 213–17), with the leisurely pacing typical of Romanticism. The third movement, a virtuosic showpiece, was first published in 1886 as the fourth of the *Six Études de Concert,* Op. 35. The first movement takes its cue from Chopin, and in its sweep and grandeur resembles an extended ballade more than a classically structured first movement. The piano writing is bold and idiomatic for the instrument. Built on two ideas that are subjected to various manipulations, including thematic transformation, the movement stands out within Chaminade's piano *oeuvre* on several accounts. First, it emphasizes thematic development rather than melody, the composer's mainstay (melody is supreme in the second movement). Second, it sports structural experimentation. Third, it deploys fugal procedure, probably attributable to the influence of Saint-Saëns, whom Chaminade greatly admired, and Moritz Moszkowski, the Polish-German composer soon to become her brother-in-law.

Chaminade's songs are tuneful and appealing, and fall into the same categories as those of Holmès. Chaminade also composed several choral works with piano, which were performed by choral societies and were popular in the home, and a few chamber pieces, including two successful piano trios. *Concertstück,* Op. 40, for piano and orchestra, which opens with a reference to Wagner's opera *The Flying Dutchman,* belongs to the tradition of the one-movement rhapsody for this combination begun by Carl Maria von Weber.

Chaminade's art largely reflects the culture of the middle- to upper-class woman of *la belle époque.* Despite great success and popularity in her heyday, however, Chaminade has not fared well in music history. If mentioned at all, she is dismissed as a composer of charming salon pieces. Such assessments rest on the assumption of a two-tiered hierarchy of music making, the professional and the amateur, in which the former takes precedence. Since the word *amateur* implies the domestic world inhabited by women, critics and historians have thus placed less value on women's activities. In order to evaluate Chaminade we will have to gain a firmer understanding of the sociology of the domestic sphere: its activities, conventions, and value systems.

## AGATHE BACKER-GRØNDAHL

Another composer-pianist whose music mirrors feminine culture near the end of the century is Agathe Backer-Grøndahl (1847–1907). At the height of her career she told the astonished George Bernard Shaw, then a London music critic, that her artistry grew out of her life as wife and mother. Indeed, Backer-Grøndahl managed to combine a rich domestic life and a fulfilling musical career—a feat that would make her the envy of many a modern woman.

Born near Oslo, Norway, into an artistic home, Backer-Grøndahl showed early talent for the piano. She studied with Theodor Kullak in the mid-1860s, then with Hans von Bülow and Franz Liszt. Her performing career took flight in the early 1870s, and she received high praise for her renditions of Beethoven and Chopin. In 1875 she married. From this point Backer-Grøndahl solved the family-career dilemma by devoting a block of years to one activity and then concentrating on another. Thus she stayed at home until 1883 to raise her three sons, then returned to public performing. From 1890 to 1898 Backer-Grøndahl immersed herself in composition and produced most of her works. In 1898 she returned to concertizing, this time (like Chaminade) emphasizing her own works, and enjoyed great success throughout Scandinavia. She undoubtedly received encouragement from her husband, who became a choral conductor.

Parallels with Chaminade can be seen in the music of Backer-Grøndahl. Both composers stressed piano works and songs, and both were prolific in these genres. The piano music in particular exhibits stylistic similarities, as in Backer-Grøndahl's early collection *Trois morceaux* (Three pieces) Op. 15, published in 1882.[4] It features the directness of expression typical of much music by women. The evocation of dance rhythms in various guises represents another feminine connection: women's centrality in ballet, an art form then at its height, and in dance in general. Although considered a leading artistic representative of her country, Backer-Grøndahl did not write in a noticeably nationalistic style. Her music is cosmopolitan and, like many a Chaminade work, betrays its debt to Chopin and Mendelssohn.

## LILI BOULANGER

The music of Lili Boulanger (1893–1918), on the other hand, reflects a post-Romantic world. Born two generations after Chaminade and Backer-Grøndahl, Boulanger inhabited the Paris of Fauré and Debussy, Diaghilev and Stravinsky. In her short lifetime this remarkable composer accomplished a great deal, buoyed by a combination of prodigious talent, sheer will, and a supportive family environment. Lili was born in Paris into a family with musical roots. Her paternal grandmother was an opera singer; and her mother, a Russian, came to Paris to study voice with Ernest Boulanger, a professor at the Conservatoire and a winner of the Prix de Rome in composition (1835). Boulanger married his pupil in 1877, despite an age difference of more than forty years. Lili was the youngest of their three children, of whom the first died in infancy. Lili's close relationship with her older sister, Nadia (1887–1979), had a profound impact on her musical outlook. Nadia provided a strong female role model, instilling a sense of unlimited possibilities. Among relationships between musical siblings this pair of sisters is unique. As a child Lili experienced the death of her father, with whom she was also quite close, and survived a life-threatening case of bronchial pneumonia. The psychological and practical effects of chronic illness would play major roles in molding Boulanger's self-identity and her relationship to the creative process.

Both Lili and Nadia received a wealth of encouragement and support for the development of their musical abilities. In the late 1890s Lili often accompanied Nadia to her classes at the Conservatoire. Her own, private training began with solfege lessons and moved on to include instruction in several instruments. She had the good fortune to be exposed to a broad range of historical styles, and her first pieces date from this period. As Lili grew older, frequent bouts of illness prevented sustained music training, and she lived largely in isolation imposed by Mme. Boulanger to protect her daughter from contamination. Catholicism became especially meaningful to Lili and found its way into some of her works of this period.

The year 1910 marked a turning point. The seventeen-year-old, increasingly aware of the likelihood of an early death, decided to devote all her energies to becoming a composer. To Boulanger this included winning the Prix de Rome, the prestigious annual prize in composition awarded by the Conservatoire on the basis of a grueling competition. No matter that the competition had only recently begun admitting women, or that she lacked the stamina to survive such an expenditure of effort. Over the next two years Boulanger pursued a systematic course of preparation. She took theory lessons and practiced setting the types of texts given in the competition. More formalized training occurred in early 1912, when she entered the Conservatoire. Boulanger attempted the Prix de Rome that spring, but illness forced her to drop out. The next year, however, she was successful, and she became the first woman to win the prize (Nadia had earned second place in 1908). One wonders whether it is mere coincidence that two "firsts" for French women composers occurred around the same time: Boulanger's winning the Prix de Rome and Chaminade's admission to the Legion of Honor.

Boulanger garnered the honor with her cantata *Faust et Hélène,* which was premiered in November 1913. Although she encountered sexual prejudice in the first months of the fellowship residency in Rome, Boulanger gradually became acclimated and worked on several compositions, including the song cycle *Clairières dans le ciel.* War broke out in August 1914, and Boulanger returned to Paris. The next year she and Nadia participated in the war effort by keeping colleagues and friends at the front abreast of musical news. She spent the spring of 1916 in Rome in an attempt to complete her interrupted fellowship. Deteriorating health forced her return to Paris in late June, and over the next two years she was able to work only sporadically. On March 8, 1918, the Paris premiere of *Clairières* took place. One week later Lili Boulanger died. Despite her tragically short life, she was a prolific composer. Of her twenty-nine extant completed works, twenty-one have been published. She also left an incomplete opera, *La Princesse Maleine,* based on a Maeterlinck play. Of the extant works approximately three-quarters are vocal, many with orchestra. This preference places her squarely in the French tradition.

Boulanger's major work during her 1914 residency in Rome was the magnificent song cycle *Clairières dans le ciel* (Rifts in the sky). The thirteen poems come from the larger collection *Tristesses* (1902–1906) by the Symbolist Francis Jammes. The poetry elicited a powerful response from Boulanger, who identified with the heroine. Narrated by a male (a tenor voice), the texts speak in delicate floral metaphors of the hope, tenderness, joy, fulfillment, loneliness, and desolation of fleeting love. Boulanger's settings are subdued, almost somber, and the range of contrasts is narrow. Text expression emerges as the most important element. With suppleness and a responsiveness to the nuances of the French language, the semideclamatory vocal lines approach the rhythms of speech. In this Boulanger is typically French and resembles Debussy. She also shows her nationality in the cycle's emphasis on color and sonority: exploring new combinations, registers, and textures in the piano; and utilizing the Impressionists' harmonic palette of nonfunctional seventh and ninth chords, parallel chords, and modal progressions. Most of the songs are through-composed or at best in a loose AB form.

The twelfth and thirteenth songs (HAMW, pp. 234–44) exemplify Boulanger's mastery. "Je garde une médaille d'elle" (I keep a medallion of hers), only sixteen bars long, depends for its unity on a one-bar harmonic progression, set in strict contrary motion, juxtaposing the sonorities of the stark open fifth, the major seventh chord, and the minor ninth chord. The vocal line resembles recitative and moves brilliantly to the dramatic setting of "prier, croire, espérer" (to pray, believe, hope). The last song, "Demain fera un an" (Tomorrow will be a year), is the longest of the set. The poetry is often painful, as it speaks of nothingness and death. Tonally the song begins in D minor, where No. 12 ends. Boulanger matches the retrospective text with retrospective music, namely, three substantial references to earlier songs: a *Tristan* section from No. 6; an accompaniment pattern from No. 11; and, near the end, a quotation of the poetry and music from the beginning of the cycle. Although the song features greater contrasts than do the preceding numbers, Boulanger deploys a repeating bass rhythm of quarter note, half note, quarter note that provides continuity. Her sense of impending death colors the song and leaves the listener stunned by the final line: "Nothing more. I have nothing more, nothing more to sustain me. Nothing more. Nothing more."

Boulanger grew up in a transitional culture, and many of her works express the changes that were taking place. *Clairières,* for example, hints at the isolation and alienation that were to become hallmarks of modernism and displays many of the traits we single out in Debussy as harbingers of twentieth-century style. As a woman, Boulanger ignored confining gender stereotypes in her quest for personal achievement. Her total absorption in her art provides an inspiring model for female creators. One cannot help but wonder what this remarkable woman would have composed had she lived longer.

## ALMA MAHLER-WERFEL

Although Paris witnessed many moments of modernism, Vienna lay much closer to the heart of the movement. From 1900 to the end of World War I, the twilight of the old artistic order and the birth of the new intermingled in fascinating ways. Gustav Mahler's music, for example, embodied the excesses of post-Romanticism and hinted at the alienation of modernism. It was but a short step to the compositions of Schoenberg and Berg, the art works of Klimt and Kokoschka. Freud's theories of the unconscious, conceived around 1900, reflect the modernist tendencies of this culture.

Alma Mahler-Werfel (1879–1964) was a product of this fascinating period. Her father, Emil Schindler, was a noted portraitist. Alma adored him and claimed that he always took her seriously. She spent much of her time in his studio and remembered fondly his fine tenor voice singing

Schumann Lieder. Perhaps this early musical association played a part in her creative attraction to that genre. In any case, the Schindler home regularly hosted the leading cultural figures in Vienna, providing the young girl with an invaluable understanding of the artistic world and the artistic personality. Alma found music irresistible and, according to her memoirs, began composing at the age of nine. Her early compositions were for various media, both instrumental and vocal. As a teen she passed through a Wagnerian phase, in which she described herself as "screaming Wagner parts until my beautiful mezzo-soprano had gone to pieces."[5] Alma fed her literary passion by assembling a personal library that ranged from the classics to the avant-garde.

Around 1900 Alma began composition lessons with Alexander Zemlinsky, a young composer-conductor who also taught Schoenberg. Zemlinsky introduced her to Gustav Mahler, and Alma was smitten by this temperamental celebrity who was head of the Vienna Opera and nineteen years her

Alma Mahler Werfel. The Alma Mahler Werfel Collections, Department of Special Collection, Van Pelt Library, University of Pennsylvania.

senior. Mahler asserted his dominance, whether it concerned what she was reading or whether she would be permitted to compose. As Alma later wrote: "He considered the marriage of Robert and Clara Schumann 'ridiculous,' for instance. He sent me a long letter with the demand that I instantly give up my music and live for his alone."[6]

After their marriage in March 1902, Alma gave up composition and became copyist and helpmeet to her husband. Mahler apparently could not brook competition, especially from a woman, which he took as a threat to his fragile ego. As to why Alma agreed to such a marriage, we must remember that she was young and less confident of her own needs, and that she gravitated toward a father substitute: in this case a much older man, a famous man, an artistic man. Shortly after a marital crisis in 1910, which prompted Mahler to consult with Freud, Gustav begged her to resume composing and insisted on helping to get her works published. It is difficult to believe that Mahler, who had not even heard Alma's music when he demanded that she stop composing, experienced a sincere change of heart. Rather it was a plea of desperation—fear of losing his wife to another man. In any case, Alma's *Five Lieder* (1910) resulted.

Mahler died in 1911, and Alma began a relationship with the artist Oskar Kokoschka, once again subordinating herself to a man's work. In 1915, after she broke with Kokoschka, she married Walter Gropius, a young architect who was to found the Bauhaus school of art in 1919. While he was serving in the war, Alma met the poet Franz Werfel, whom she eventually married in 1929. This was her only happy, long-lasting relationship. In the intervening years she published two other collections: *Four Lieder* (1915) and *Five Songs* (1924).

Mahler-Werfel's later years continued to be filled with adventure. Because Werfel was Jewish the couple left Vienna in 1938, settling first in France and eventually in southern California in a community of European refugees that included Schoenberg and Bruno Walter. After Franz's death in 1945 Alma moved to New York, where she died in 1964.

Mahler-Werfel's keen intellectual faculties made her a focal point of leading cultural circles, especially through 1920. She relished the avant-garde. In her memoirs she prided herself on her ability to single out and marry men whom posterity would later consider great. As she wrote about Gustav Mahler after the successful performance of his Symphony No. 8 at the Hollywood Bowl: "I saw once more how instinctively right I had been to cast my lot with Mahler when people thought of him as just a conductor and opera director and would not believe in his creative genius."[7] In her relationships with artistic greats Alma believed she had a mission to nurture their talent. She did not see herself as some passive Muse, a contemporary gender stereotype, but as an active participant in building artistic fulfillment and success.

What of her own artistic fulfillment? Alma is surprisingly reticent about her own music, except for the period with Mahler. We find a few allusions in her memoirs, but they convey little. She also says little about other musical activities, such as playing the piano. In part this is because her memoirs were intended for a broad readership and best-seller success. Yet the reticence signifies more: deep-seated ambivalence about her own creativity. Her background was ripe for such conflict. On the one hand she had support from her father, her teacher, and her environment; on the other she had few female role models and internalized the debilitating attitudes of her first husband. She implies that Werfel was more supportive, but by that time in her life (1930s) it was probably too late. Despite youthful confidence and enthusiasm, and above all great talent, Mahler-Werfel produced a relatively small number of compositions over her eighty-four years. Most were probably early works. Only fourteen pieces in three sets were published, all Lieder. These and two other songs in manuscript constitute her existing creative output (other musical manuscripts were destroyed in the bombing of Vienna in World War II).

The collection of 1915, *Four Lieder,* exemplifies Mahler-Werfel's glorious contribution to the art song.[8] Typically, each song is based on a poem of a contemporary writer and displays her perceptive grasp of literary values, especially declamation, imagery, and symbolism. Musically we find a broad stylistic range. One of her main devices is the skillful control of dissonance. Her vocal lines often proceed in large leaps, a manner that accords well with dissonance and a harmonic idiom that verges on atonality. Such a daring vocabulary places Mahler-Werfel in the company of contemporary experimentalists like Schoenberg and Berg. The third song, "Ansturm" (Assault), on a text by Richard Dehmel, is particularly bold. Composed in 1911, it is perhaps the earliest work by a woman set to a text that centers on sexual desire and release. In this flouting of social convention, Mahler-Werfel deploys a fascinating mix of musical styles, including recitative, Brahmsian lushness, sharp dissonance, and an unresolved dominant seventh chord at the end.

"Der Erkennende" (The one who is aware; HAMW, pp. 248–50) was composed in 1915 and published in *Five Songs* (1924). Set to a poem by Franz Werfel, it reveals Mahler-Werfel's brilliant ability to translate poetic imagery into musical terms. The desolation of the text is captured through spare musical language: even rhythms, repeated pitches, ostinato-like patterns, and economic thematic material. This stylistic simplicity, which also includes an ABA form and scalar melodies, contributes to a sense of irony that reflects the *Angst* of the era. Above all, Alma Mahler-Werfel's songs show passion—passion corresponding to the person. The addition of her songs to the repertoire will provide singers a wonderful vehicle of expression.

## ETHEL SMYTH

While Vienna and Paris were encouraging experimentation, England was continuing to pursue an insular tradition that perpetuated ideals of the early nineteenth century. In addition, England lacked a native tradition and an institutionalized structure for music making—it could boast only a few opera houses, very brief opera seasons, and a paucity of operas by English composers. This musical culture formed the backdrop to the indomitable Ethel Smyth (1858–1944).

Of the same generation as Chaminade, Smyth came from a middle-class

John Singer Sargent, portrait of Ethel Smyth. National Portrait Gallery, London. Used by permission.

Victorian family with little artistic bent. From the first she was a noncon-formist. Not only did she overcome paternal objections to her attending the Leipzig Conservatory (1877), but after her return she broke convention by deciding to devote herself to the composition of opera, a bold decision for her time, nationality, and gender. Smyth broke gender conventions in other ways. Her dress was as much masculine as feminine, and she liked to smoke cigars. She participated actively in the suffragist movement in England (1910–12) and even spent some time in jail. Her "March of the Women" became a rallying call for the movement. Sexually she was a lesbian, a fact she did not attempt to conceal. Through autobiographical writings, includ-ing several books and numerous articles, Smyth revealed in a forthright manner her shrewd understanding of gender conventions as they affected women's attempts to attain success in a man's world.

Smyth's student works included chamber music, piano sonatas, and Lieder, genres that reflect the traditionalist Germanic leanings of the Leipzig Conservatory and of her subsequent teacher, Heinrich von Herzogenberg. After two successful orchestral pieces in England (1890), Smyth composed one of her best works, the Mass in D. Although its premiere in 1893 received some very good reviews, the Mass was not performed again until some thirty years later. Smyth identified genre, Germanic style, and sexual prejudice as causes:

> Year in year out, composers of the Inner Circle, generally University men attached to our musical institutions, produced one choral work after an-other—not infrequently deadly dull affairs—which, helped along by the im-petus of official approval, automatically went the round of our Festivals and Choral Societies. . . . Was it likely, then, that the Faculty would see any merit in a work written on such very different lines—written too by a woman who had actually gone off to Germany to learn her trade?[9]

Perhaps Smyth found solace in the fact that Sir Donald Francis Tovey included the Mass in his analytic volume on choral music, comparing it to Beethoven's Missa Solemnis and noting that both are spiritual, not liturgi-cal, works. He admired the vocal writing and declared that "the score should become a *locus classicus* for the whole duty and privileges of choral orchestration."[10]

Around the time that her Mass was introduced, Smyth was working on the first of her six operas, *Fantasio* (1892–94). Dissatisfied with this "fantastic comedy," which was set in German and had been performed in Weimar in 1898, Smyth destroyed all the copies in 1916. Her next opera was *Der Wald* (The forest), a one-act tragedy composed between 1899 and 1901. In its Germanic traits—language, symbolism, and compositional technique—the opera betrays her musical roots. In 1902 *Der Wald* was performed in Berlin and London. The next year, with Smyth as conductor, it was staged at the Metropolitan Opera in New York, the first opera by a woman to be performed there.[11]

*The Wreckers* (1903–1904) is Smyth's best opera. After a personal experience at the caves off the coast of Cornwall, Smyth was inspired to sketch a story and give it to her friend and collaborator Henry Brewster to fashion into a libretto. Smyth, ever practical, assented to Brewster's wish to write in French because she sensed the possibility of a performance under conductor André Messager. This fell through, as did projected performances in Monte Carlo and Brussels. Arthur Nikisch, the opera director in Leipzig, liked the work and engaged it for the 1906–1907 season. It was premiered successfully in November 1906, with the German title *Standrecht* (Martial law). Smyth nonetheless withdrew the work by removing the music from the players' stands when the conductor refused to reinstate cuts she opposed, an incident that reveals Smyth's character and her unyielding commitment to principles. The opera, translated into English, was introduced to England in May 1908 in a concert version of Acts I and II, and it received a fully staged performance in June 1909.

*The Wreckers* embodies Smyth's dual loyalties to English and German traditions. Its subject matter melds the English people and the forces of nature. In this Smyth laid the groundwork for later English composers, notably Benjamin Britten in *Peter Grimes* (1945). The tonal clarity reflects English conservatism as well as Smyth's training in Leipzig. Her powerful orchestration and emphasis on thematic development exemplify the Germanic tradition, and the legacy of Wagner is evident in the absence of traditional divisions into separate numbers. Smyth creates unity through the use of recurring motifs, although the practice differs from Wagner's full-fledged Leitmotiv technique. She does, however, emulate Wagner in the symbolic importance assigned the power of nature. Smyth may have modeled the heroine, courageous and willing to defy conventional morality, on Wagner's Isolde as well as on herself.

The overture, constructed as a medley, introduces many of the important themes of the opera. It opens with the Wagner-like motif that the chorus intones during the storm scene of Act I (HAMW, pp. 222–31). The orchestra is exploited for color and evokes many pictorial effects. The harmonic language is largely functional, although modal progressions provide occasional contrast. Counterpoint is one of the chief compositional devices. In 1910, John Fuller Maitland concluded his enthusiastic assessment of *The Wreckers* with the following statement: "It is difficult to point to a work of any nationality since Wagner that has a more direct appeal to the emotions, or that is more skilfully planned and carried out."[12] Unfortunately this opera has lain dormant for many years. A fine counterpart to *Peter Grimes,* it could strike a resonant note, especially with English audiences.

In 1910 Smyth suspended her creative activities for a few years to participate in the suffragist movement. World War I forced the cancellation of some planned performances of her music, especially in Germany. Between 1919 and 1940 she concentrated on writing about her life and expressing her views, completing ten books. Her style is direct, perceptive, witty, and practical. She also continued as an activist, as in her persistent attempts to keep women orchestra players in the jobs they had held during the war. All in all Ethel Smyth counts as one of the most striking figures in women's history. A pathbreaking composer and feminist, she had the courage to live up to her convictions regardless of consequences. She is the first woman to articulate in so direct a manner the subtle and overt types of discrimination facing women musicians. Even increasing deafness could not dampen the energy and pluck of this iconoclast.

## SUMMARY

As we have seen, European women musicians around the turn of the century participated vividly in musical life. Their impressive achievements round out our picture of musical creativity at that time. Taken as a whole they might suggest a new model for historical periodization. In any case, these achievements serve notice that factors particular to women's experience—career-marriage relationship, mothering, role models, and access to training and to audiences—must be added to the variables of historical evaluation. Only a very small percentage of their compositions is known today. The most obvious reason is that very little of their music is available, but that is a symptom rather than a cause and reflects various attitudes about art music, canon formation, and women themselves. Fortunately, these complex issues are being explored; they hold out the promise of a better appreciation of women's accomplishments in their own right.

### NOTES

1. See Augusta Holmès, *Selected Songs* (New York: Da Capo, 1984).
2. See Ethel Smyth's narration of Holmès's attraction to Smyth's friend Henry Brewster in her essay "Augusta Holmès," in *A Final Burning of Boats* (London: Longmans, Green & Co., 1928), pp. 126–36.

3. Interview in *The Washington Post,* November 1, 1908, Magazine section, p. 4.

4. Reprinted in Agathe Backer-Grøndahl, *Piano Music* (New York: Da Capo, 1982).

5. Alma Mahler Werfel, *And the Bridge Is Love* (New York: Harcourt, Brace and Company, 1958), p. 9.

6. Ibid., p. 19.

7. Ibid., pp. 301–302.

8. A modern edition of all Alma Mahler-Werfel's published songs was brought out by Universal Edition of Vienna in 1984.

9. Ethel Smyth, *As Time Went On* (London: Longmans, 1936), p. 172.

10. Donald Francis Tovey, *Essays in Musical Analysis,* Vol. 5: *Vocal Music* (London: Oxford University Press, 1937), p. 236.

11. See excerpts from the review that first appeared in *Musical Courier* (March 18, 1903), in *Women in Music,* edited by Carol Neuls-Bates (New York: Harper and Row, 1982), pp. 225–26.

12. *Grove's Dictionary of Music and Musicians,* 2d ed., s.v. "Smyth, Ethel," by J. A. Fuller Maitland.

## SUGGESTIONS FOR FURTHER READING

Citron, Marcia J. *Cécile Chaminade: A Bio-Bibliography.* Westport, CT: Greenwood Press, 1988.

Filler, Susan. "A Composer's Wife as Composer: The Songs of Alma Mahler." *Journal of Musicological Research* 4 (1983):427–41.

Hyde, Deryck. "Ethel Smythe [*sic*]: A Reappraisal," in *Newfound Voices.* London: Belvedere Press, 1984. Pp. 138–206.

Kravitt, Edward. "The Lieder of Alma Maria Schindler-Mahler." *Music Review* 49 (1988):190–204.

*The Memoirs of Ethel Smyth.* Abridged and introduced by Ronald Crichton. London: Viking, 1987.

Meyers, Rollo. "Augusta Holmès: A Meteoric Career." *Musical Quarterly* 53 (1967):365–76.

Rosenstiel, Léonie. *The Life and Works of Lili Boulanger.* Rutherford, NJ: Fairleigh Dickinson Press, 1978.

St. John, Christopher [Marie]. *Ethel Smyth: A Biography.* London: Longmans, Green and Co., 1959.

# VII.
# Women in American Music, 1800–1918

*Adrienne Fried Block*
*assisted by Nancy Stewart*

## INTRODUCTION

Music in the New World, except for that of native American tribes, was a transplanted tradition with roots in Europe and Africa. In the United States, as in Europe, the dawn of the nineteenth century found women in music in two separate worlds: the amateur, who made music at home; and the professional, usually a woman from a musical or theatrical family. An unbridgeable divide separated the middle- or upper-class amateur from the professional: respectable women did not perform in public. Under the prevailing American doctrine of domestic feminism, man's sphere was the world, woman's the home. Victorian middle- and upper-class women were trained for marriage, for playing a supportive yet dependent role in a patriarchal society, not for careers.

However, American middle-class women soon began to demand an education, the better to train their children, and training in music in order to bring the beneficent influence of the "divine art" into the home. Musical training for girls and women gradually improved, becoming institutional-ized and more accessible. Gradually, too, a few American-born women emerged as professional performers and composers of vernacular and parlor music and later of art music. Their emergence was aided by the women's movement that developed in the decades following the Civil War, creating an ideology that offered an alternative to domestic feminism and empower-ing women to move into the public sphere. This chapter will trace those changes over a dozen decades.

## THEATRE AND CONCERT SINGERS:
## FROM VISITORS TO NATIVES[1]

During the Federal period (ca. 1780–1820), professional women from England and the Continent appeared on American stages as members of touring troupes. Typically they had grown up in the English theatre, served their apprenticeships under the watchful eyes of parents and siblings who were themselves professional artists, and married stage people. A singing actress was always under the management of her closest male relative, who signed contracts and collected her wages. Whatever her status, she called herself "Mrs." as a badge of respectability. Despite this, every aspect of her life, from her morals to her finances to her weight, was open to scrutiny by the diverse public that attended her performances. Gender, class, national origin, and mores were all shaping factors in her public as well as her private life.

English theatre companies first introduced ballad operas, among them *The Beggar's Opera* (1728), into America in 1735. Comic opera soon followed. In 1791, French opera came to New Orleans and was introduced in the North as well. Roles for women included heroines, fine ladies, chambermaids, old women, and hoydens (ill-bred, demanding, ready-for-fun, out-of-control women). In addition, women appeared dressed as men in trouser roles.

The leading singing actress on the American stage before 1800 was Mary Ann Pownall (Wrighton) (1751–96).[2] Famous as an opera and concert singer in England, after coming to America in 1792 she performed in cities along the Atlantic Coast as a member of the Old American Theater Company. Pownall's concert repertoire included her own compositions, which exhibit flowing melodies and strophic forms typical of English popular song as well as operatic ornamentation and dramatic climaxes. Eight of her songs appeared in print, three in a joint publication with James Hewitt, an English-born concert manager, violinist, publisher, and composer.

Italian opera soon began edging out English opera on American stages. The Garcia troupe, a Spanish family of professional singers who arrived in 1825, presented Mozart's *Don Giovanni* and operas by Rossini, among others. The company gave about eighty performances in a matter of months. In the troupe were the father, Manuel Garcia, and his son, Manuel, later renowned as a voice teacher; the prima donna and star of the company was his seventeen-year-old daughter Maria (1808–36). Because New York audiences did not accept Italian opera immediately, the Garcias met with mixed reception. However, Maria Garcia had an outstanding personal success as both a concert and an opera singer. After marrying she returned to Paris and a fabled career in opera under her husband's name, Malibran.

The Garcia troupe was followed by other foreign companies performing Italian opera in English, a change that turned the genre into popular entertainment. Occasionally husband-and-wife teams ran the companies. Among them were the Seguin Opera Company, which toured the States from 1841 to 1852, and the hundred-member Parepa-Rosa English Opera Company, which appeared between 1869 and 1871.[3] Because of the popularity of Italian opera, publishers began issuing arias and ensembles separately for amateur parlor pianists and vocalists, among whom were large numbers of women. The result was that Italianate stylistic elements were absorbed into the American musical stream.

It is significant that the first American-born singer came from America's first family of professional musicians. Eliza Ostinelli Biscaccianti (1824–96), who made her debut in New York as Amina in *La Sonnambula,* was the daughter of the pianist and organist Sophia Hewitt Ostinelli and the granddaughter of James Hewitt. Thanks to the money raised by a group of Bostonians, Eliza Ostinelli was able to go to Italy to study voice. After her marriage and return in 1847, she became a favorite of American audiences, singing in opera and concert from New York to San Francisco.

In the 1840s opera singers from abroad began touring the United States as solo artists. Most famous was the charismatic Jenny Lind (1820–67), who in September 1850 began an eighteen-month tour. She sang all over the United States and brought enormous numbers of Americans into concert halls for the first time. Her programs included orchestral works, opera arias and ensembles, and parlor songs like "Home, Sweet Home"—a democratic mix that contributed to her broad appeal. Although she was known as "the Swedish nightingale," a nickname that suggests the mindless singing of a bird, she was a hard-working and first-rate musician. P. T. Barnum, her concert manager for the tour, shrewdly played up Lind's piety and impeccable personal reputation, advertising her as "the musical saint." As a result, Jenny Lind succeeded almost single-handedly in convincing Americans that a woman could go on the lyric stage and still retain her virtue. Lind's visit also was the stimulus for the building of opera houses in many cities across the United States, thus opening up further opportunities for women. Because of her success, European singers like Henriette Sontag and Marietta Alboni also made American tours.

Lind, who was famous for her generosity, made European study possible for an American singer. The English-born contralto Adelaide Phillips (1833–82) came to Boston as a singing, acting, and dancing child prodigy. Lind heard Phillips sing and gave her $1,000 to study in London with

Manuel Garcia. After a debut in Europe, Phillips become a leading opera, oratorio, and concert singer, and she ran her own opera company for a season. Hers became the typical pattern of singers—early training in the United States, followed by study and a debut in Europe, and finally a return to the United States—their professional calibre validated by their European success.

This pattern, however, rarely applied to African-American singers. Before Lind's American tour ended, Elizabeth Taylor Greenfield (ca. 1817–76) made her debut in Buffalo in 1851 singing operatic arias as well as several of the songs Lind made popular. Greenfield's label as "the black Swan" not only attempted to transfer some of Lind's appeal but also exploited the novelty of a black singing a classical repertoire. Born in slavery, Greenfield was freed while still a child when her owner, a Quaker, moved north to Philadelphia. Although she had a rich voice and an enormous range, poverty and prejudice left her no choice but to teach herself. Following her debut, Greenfield embarked on concert tours, first in the United States, then in England. There she finally found a temporary teacher in Sir George Smart, but she was never able to raise enough money for further study in Europe. She returned to Philadelphia in 1854 to teach voice and give occasional concerts. Even though prejudice prevented her from fulfilling her potential, she broke ground for later African-American singers of art music.

Clara Louise Kellogg (1842–1916) did succeed, both in America and in Europe, following an all-American education, the first opera singer to do so. She also epitomized the new American vocal artist. Born into a white middle-class American family without a tradition of professional performance, she overcame the Puritanical censure of women who went on the stage, finally achieving the highest international stature as well as social acceptance. Kellogg was born in Sumterville, North Carolina, of an educated and musical family who supported her musical aspirations. She displayed musical talent as a child and soon began lessons in piano, at which she excelled. Later she joined a church choir, and in a less traditional vein, learned to sing minstrel songs to her own banjo accompaniment. After hearing Lind's first concert in New York in 1850, the eight-year-old Kellogg determined to be a professional singer.[4] Her family moved to New York in 1857, where she studied with leading voice teachers.

Sensitive to social attitudes about stage people, Kellogg called her friends together before her debut to announce that she was going on the stage, and that if they never spoke to her again she would understand and forgive them. Kellogg added that she hoped some day to overcome their rejection and make them proud of her. Her debut in New York in 1861 as

Gilda in *Rigoletto* was enormously successful. She sang Marguerite in the American premiere of Gounod's *Faust* in 1863 and in London's Covent Garden in 1867. In all she sang forty roles and was in demand for concert and oratorio work as well.

Despite her family's love of music, their attitudes about her career were ambivalent, as Kellogg noted years later:

> My mother hated the atmosphere of the theatre even though she had wished me to become a singer, and always gloried in my successes. To her rigid and delicate instinct there was something dreadful in the free and easy artistic attitude, and she always stood between me and any possible intimacy with my fellow singers.[5]

Her mother accompanied her on tour until Kellogg's marriage to her concert manager and simultaneous retirement at age forty.

Emma Abbott (1850–91), a protégée of Kellogg's, studied in both the United States and Europe. She never relaxed her Victorian moral standards; indeed, her European career ended when she refused on moral grounds to sing the role of Violetta in *La Traviata*. On her return she found a way to continue in opera without violating her moral code: she formed her own opera company and gave abridged—and sanitized—versions of operas in English translation to audiences in America's West, with enormous success and handsome financial returns.

Sissieretta Jones (1869–1933), like Greenfield before her, had to deal with the societal limitations placed on African-Americans. However, she had fine training, especially from the famous New York voice teacher Luisa Cappiani. Following her New York debut in 1888, she toured with the Jubilee Singers, the Patrick Gilmore Band, and other groups, and gave solo recitals, including appearances at the White House for President Benjamin Harrison and in London for the Prince of Wales. Nevertheless, opera was never an option for her because of prejudice. From 1896 to 1916, Jones toured with a troupe of African-American performers called the Black Patti Troubadours. Although her colleagues offered vaudeville-type acts, Jones sang only opera excerpts and popular songs, as had Lind before her.

Among the other black concert singers of the period were Nellie Brown Mitchell (1845–1924), Marie Selika (1849–1937), Anna Madah Hyers (1853–1934), her sister Emma Louise Hyers (1855–1904), and Flora Batson (1864–1904). The Hyers sisters ran their own company, presenting a drama interspersed with songs about the Underground Railroad entitled *Out of Bondage*, the final act of which gave them the opportunity to sing opera arias. Despite this beginning, after 1880 support for black artists in the United States diminished, and most African-American singers found their best opportunities in Europe.

By 1918, many American women had aspired to operatic careers for fame and fortune. Among those who succeeded—as expected, all white—in addition to Kellogg and Abbott were Annie Louise Cary (1841–1931), Emma Thursby (1845–1931), Minnie Hauk (1851–1925), Lillian Nordica (1857–1914), Marcella Sembrich (1858–1938), Emma Nevada (1859–1940), Emma Eames (1865–1952), Louise Homer (1871–1947), Olive Fremstad (1871–1951), Lillian Blauvelt (1874–1947), Mary Garden (1874–1967), Geraldine Farrar (1882–1967), and Alma Gluck (1884–1938). By 1900, divas were lionized as celebrities and cultural heroines, and the doors of high society were open to them. Even without careers in opera, singers found opportunities as church and oratorio soloists, as voice teachers, and as concert artists. The period 1880 to 1920 was a golden one for singers on the recital stage. These women's lives testify to the changes that had taken place in American society in the late nineteenth and early twentieth centuries. The seeds that Lind had planted bore significant fruit.

There were in addition opportunities for women in popular theatre—vaudeville, musical comedy, and operetta—beginning in the latter part of the nineteenth century. Outstanding performers were Lillian Russell (1861–1922), who sang in all three genres, including Gilbert and Sullivan operettas; Eva Tanguay (1878–1947), a performer of "exuberant sexuality," and Sophie Tucker (1884–1966), both featured in Tony Pastor's vaudevilles; Fay Templeton (1865–1939), who starred in musical comedy, most notably in George M. Cohan's *Forty-Five Minutes from Broadway* (1906); and Fritzi Scheff (1879–1954), who left the Metropolitan Opera to appear in operettas and was famous for her role in *Mlle. Modiste* (1906), written for her by Victor Herbert.

## MUSIC TRAINING AND EDUCATION

Before ca. 1830, music making by amateurs was considered a social grace in imitation of English high society. Only wealthy families could offer their daughters music instruction—superficial as it usually was—or buy the harpsichords, harps, guitars, or pianos women played. Women who sang and played in society as part of the rite of courtship or at home to relieve boredom and isolation usually abandoned music after marriage. However, as cities grew in the nineteenth century, the merchant class grew along with them, and musical accomplishment became middle class. Lessons in music as well as in dancing, embroidery, drawing, and rules of deportment became all but mandatory for well-bred young ladies. Although music continued to have a role in courtship, women now played at home to promote domestic harmony and to uplift and charm their children. Indeed, music was associated with the ideal of woman as "angel in the house." The abundant literature about women in music included advice about maintaining the image of the "angel"—modest, patient, sober, unselfish, and submissive—who sang only parlor songs with chaste words. If she played piano for others, she was counseled to avoid long and complex works. As Judith Tick wrote, "Tradition simultaneously encouraged [women] to take up music, yet discouraged them from aspiring to any meaningful standards and repressed artistic ambition."[6]

Music was first taught at seminaries as an ornamental course along with embroidery. In the early nineteenth century a typical music curriculum consisted of instruction in piano, harp, guitar, and voice. However, training gradually improved at female seminaries and academies where middle- and upper-class teen-agers studied. Violin and organ also were offered, especially in better schools, like the Moravian Seminary in Bethlehem, Pennsylvania, the Cherry Valley Seminary in New York, and Music Vale in Connecticut. As a result of the women's widespread participation in amateur music making, girls' schools offered better training in music than did boys'. Troy Seminary in New York progressed from an ornamental curriculum for amateurs to a rigorous music program for professionals during the course of sixty years. By 1900, its music department had become a conservatory, and its catalog stipulated that its curriculum was suitable not only for aspiring professionals but also—and apparently secondarily—for amateurs. These changes also reflected the increased professionalization of women in music.

As music teaching became a preferred field for women during the second half of the nineteenth century, the need for better teacher preparation became apparent. Music Vale at some point became Salem Normal School and enjoyed a national reputation. It offered training in notation, harmony, thoroughbass, counterpoint, and composition. At its peak it drew students from a wide geographical area, and its graduates fanned out all over the country, effectively raising the level of music teaching. The Crane Normal Institute of Music of Potsdam, New York, founded in 1886, was the first music school in the country to become affiliated with a teacher-training college. Its aim was to offer thorough preparation to future public school music teachers, primarily women. Founded and directed by Julia Ettie Crane (1855–1923), the school is now known as the Crane School of Music of the State University of New York at Potsdam.[7] Schools like Crane helped professionalize the field for women: by 1910 women constituted sixty percent of all music teachers, the highest percentage in the history of the United States. However, men occupied the prestigious teaching positions, were better paid, and were considered better qualified to teach advanced students.

The establishment of American conservatories after the Civil War was an important development for women, who predominated as students. Oberlin College-Conservatory opened in 1865, followed in 1867 by the Cincinnati, Boston, and New England conservatories, in 1868 by Peabody, in 1885 by the National Conservatory of Music in New York, and in 1886 by the American Conservatory in Chicago. The music schools offered high-calibre training, often with European-educated teachers. Because many parents would not send their daughters abroad without a chaperone— usually the mother—yet were loath to disrupt family life, American conservatories provided an alternative. The year after the New England Conservatory opened, its student body consisted of 1,097 females and 317 males, but its violin scholarships were reserved for two boys between eight and fourteen. On the other hand, the Boston Conservatory opened its string classes to women, an action that forever changed prospects for women as instrumentalists. Founded by Julius Eichberg, Boston's curriculum was modeled on that of the Brussels Conservatory, which was renowned for training violinists.

Among those who set up American conservatories were two women, Clara Baur (1835–1912) and Jeannette Thurber (1850–1946). Before leaving Germany at the age of fourteen, Baur studied piano and voice at the Stuttgart Hochschule für Musik, and in 1867 she founded the Cincinnati Conservatory in its image. Offering training to both amateurs and aspiring professionals, the conservatory drew students from all parts of the country. After Clara Baur's death, her niece Bertha Baur (1858–1940) directed the school. Jeannette Thurber, who founded the National Conservatory of Music in New York, had studied violin at the government-supported Paris Conservatoire. Noting that no such support existed for comparable American conservatories, Thurber determined to establish a school on the Parisian model. In 1885 she opened the New York school, but she had to assume the role of patron herself: the government support she actively sought was never granted. Like Baur, she included a number of women on her faculty. Because she believed, with Antonin Dvořák, who led the school from 1892 to 1895, in the importance of the music of African-Americans for the future of American music, the school offered scholarships to talented blacks.

However, many believed that nothing took the place of European training. Amy Fay (1844–1928) left Cambridge, Massachusetts, in 1869 to study piano in Europe. Her letters to her sister from Germany, written during her six-year stay and published in her *Music Study in Germany,*[8] are especially valued for their vivid descriptions of Franz Liszt's piano classes. At the same time, Fay painted a picture of student life and the marvelous opportunities such a sojourn offered for absorbing music and European culture. Her book inspired hundreds, perhaps thousands, of women to go and do likewise.

Almost two generations later, in 1905, another American woman told of her experiences as a music student in *An American Girl in Munich.*[9] Mabel Wheeler Daniels (1878–1971), who like Fay began her studies in Boston, completed them at the Munich Conservatory. Unlike Fay, she had gone to study composition, but she met long-standing prejudices against the admission of women to composition classes. Fortunately, she had the preparation and courage to overcome those obstacles and so paved the way for the women who followed her.

# RELIGIOUS MUSIC

Most women who studied music—in the United States or abroad—remained amateurs who played and sang at home. But for both black and white women, religious rituals offered opportunities for music making outside the home: singing in the congregation or the choir, or playing the organ. In the late eighteenth century, women and men attended singing schools in New England, where they learned the rudiments of musical notation using shape notes. The practice of shape-note, or "fasola," singing soon spread to the South and West. In these hymns, the tenors sang the melody, the women the two upper parts. Of the many tune books that contained the fasola repertory, the first to include hymns by women was the famous *Southern Harmony,* compiled by William Walker (1835). Among the several hymns by women is the shape-note piece for three voices shown in Example 7-1.

As religious activists and guardians of society's morals, women naturally became important as hymnists—that is, authors of hymn texts—and occasionally as composers of the music. Most of these women were amateurs, but because the texts were religious, they could allow their names to appear in print with impunity—something that amateur composers of secular music tended to avoid.

*Woman in Sacred Song,* the first retrospective collection of hymn tunes and texts by women, reflects the extent of activity by women in this field.[10]

EXAMPLE 7-1.    Miss M. T. Durham, "The Promised Land." Excerpt from *American Women Composers before 1870*, copyright © 1983 by Judith Tick, is reprinted by permission of UMI Research Press, Ann Arbor, MI, p. 117. Text: "On Jordan's stormy banks I stand, And cast a wishful eye, To Canaan's fair and happy land, Where my possession lie. I am bound for the promised land, O, who will come and go with me?"

It contains about 2,500 religious poems and about 103 hymn tunes by fifty composers. Phoebe Palmer Knapp (1839–1908), an outstanding writer of gospel hymns, is represented by several, most notably her "Blessed Assurance," with text by the leading poet of gospel hymnody, Fanny Jane Crosby.

While women contributed heavily to evangelical hymnody, their participation in more traditional churches was limited. In the more ritualistic Protestant churches, only males sang in the choirs. Many women served as church organists, but often for little or no pay; the large churches tended to hire men, and concert organists were almost invariably male. One notable exception was Lillian Frohock, who pursued a concert career in the 1860s and 70s in Boston and New York City and in Germany.

Choral singing was initially a male activity for amateurs. Eager to perform major choral works by leading European composers, but frustrated by the musical limitations of church choirs, in the eighteenth and nineteenth centuries men organized private singing societies. The Handel and Haydn Society of Boston became the model for many later groups. It was run by its all-male membership, and women sang by invitation. At its first concert, in 1815, the chorus numbered ninety men and ten women.[11] Usually men sang the alto, tenor, and bass parts, and women, reinforced by a few male falsettists, sang the soprano. Beginning around mid-century, German and

Scandinavian men newly arrived in the United States also formed singing societies, inviting women to join them in performances of Haydn's *Creation* or Handel's *Messiah*.

In the women's music clubs, however, of which the first was organized in Portland, Maine, in the 1870s women were able to organize and run their own choruses. Some female choruses, like the St. Cecilia Society of New York, founded in 1906, became polished performing organizations. Composers—many of them women—responded to the increased demand for music for women's voices, building up a substantial repertoire that was issued by publishers in special series. During the 1909–10 season, the' ninety-five-member chorus of the Rubinstein Club of Cleveland gave a program that featured the violinist Maud Powell as soloist, and a performance of *The Mermaid,* a cantata by Fannie Snow Knowlton. Women also functioned as conductors: in 1900, the Dominant Ninth Chorus of Alton, Illinois, assisted by a male chorus, gave a concert at which Mrs. C. B. Rohland conducted Samuel Coleridge-Taylor's *Hiawatha's Wedding Feast*.

While these choral singers were all amateurs, around mid-century a few talented women were able to assume public roles while remaining in the bosom of the family—as members of professional singing families. These groups brought professional polish to the performance of vernacular music. As usual, their model was European: the Rainer Family from the Tyrolean Alps. As a result of their tour in the early 1840s, several American singing families became active, among them the Baker Family of New Hampshire and the Luca Family Singers, a black family from New Haven, Connecticut. The most famous, however, was the Hutchinson Family Singers: three brothers and their sister, Abby Hutchinson. She composed, arranged, sang, and sometimes accompanied the group on the guitar. In the Hutchinson repertoire were glees, sentimental songs and ballads, and the yodeling Tyrolean songs popularized by the Rainer Family. But they also presented topical songs in support of equal rights for women, temperance, and the abolition of slavery.

The Fisk Jubilee Singers, organized in 1871 to raise funds for Fisk University in Nashville, Tennessee, eventually became a professional touring group. They began with four men and seven women, a conductor, and an accompanist, Ella Shepherd, who trained but did not conduct the choir. The Jubilee Singers offered concert arrangements of spirituals at the World Peace Jubilee in 1872, for President Grant, and for Queen Victoria, who became one of their patrons. The group thus brought spirituals into the mainstream of American concert music and became the model for other black choirs.[12]

## PIANISTS AND VIOLINISTS

In the latter part of the nineteenth century a few American women emerged as concert artists. The special conditions that fostered their development included an active feminist movement that supported women's aspirations for professional careers, improved opportunities for high-quality training, and a wave of visiting virtuosas from overseas who served as models.

The mother of the singer Eliza Biscaccianti, Sophia Hewitt (1799–1845), was an early exception: she was one of the first American women to become a professional keyboard player. Sophia, James Hewitt's eldest child, first appeared in New York and Boston as a seven-year-old prodigy. Later she taught piano, harp, organ, and singing, and served as organist at two churches in Boston. In September 1820 she was appointed organist of the Handel and Haydn Society, a position she filled for ten years. Her husband, violinist Louis Ostinelli, had to collect her pay, for according to the law, married women had no economic independence.

Beginning in mid-century, instrumental virtuosas began to appear, at first foreign-born, later American-born and -bred. Teresa Carreño (1853–1917) emigrated to the United States with her family in 1862.[13] Within a month of their arrival in New York the child was presented to the public as a prodigy. Audiences were entranced. So too was the pianist Louis Moreau Gottschalk, whom she worshipped as a performer and a composer, and who gave her lessons when he was in town. Following a concert with orchestra in Boston, the conductor called Carreño the "freakiest prodigy . . . since Mozart." A creative as well as a performing talent, she regularly included her own works on her programs. After two years of American tours, her family took her to Paris, where she captivated Rossini with one of her piano pieces and where Liszt, in a symbolic laying on of hands, declared her a genius. Carreño's frequent tours of the United States allowed the American public to watch her development from a performer of somewhat slapdash brilliance to a mature but always intensely energetic pianist of acknowledged greatness.

In the 1870s, a number of eminent European pianists toured the United States, playing solo with the famous Theodore Thomas orchestra. Among them were the German pianists Anna Mehlig and Marie Krebs, and the English pianist Madeleine Schiller. During that decade, Julie Rivé-King (1854–1937) became the first American-born woman to succeed on the concert stage.[14] Harold Schonberg states that she "was to the piano what Theodore Thomas was to the orchestra, and she helped to establish a new standard in repertoire and performance."[15] Rivé-King was born in Cincinnati to parents who had come from France in 1850. Because of their professional involvement in the arts, they were important models for their daughter. She displayed her prodigious gifts at the piano early, and her mother soon began to give her lessons. In 1871 Rivé studied in New York; later she studied in Europe, where she delighted Liszt with her playing. Shortly after she made her debut in Leipzig, her father died quite suddenly; Rivé cancelled her projected European tour and sailed for home, never to return.

In 1874, she began a series of concert tours of the United States and Canada, including several with Theodore Thomas and one with conductor Anton Seidl. Many of her concerts were arranged by her husband, Frank King, whom she married in 1877 and who managed her career until he died in 1900. Thereafter, unused to being her own manager, she gave up touring and took a position at Chicago's Bush Conservatory, where she taught for the rest of her life. Her playing was notable for its clear, precise, facile touch and its technical perfection.

Fannie Bloomfield Zeisler (1863–1927), who came to America from Austria as a child, fused strong European influences with an equally strong sense of identity as an American.[16] Zeisler grew up in the Midwest and studied in Chicago. At fourteen she played for the touring Russian pianist Annette Essipoff, who urged her to study in Vienna with Essipoff's husband, the famous Theodore Leschetitzky. After study in Europe, Bloomfield Zeisler returned to make her American debut in 1884. During her long and brilliant concert career, she struggled to overcome stereotypes, such as those that assumed that women lacked men's physical power at the keyboard, all the while branding women who exhibited such power and energy as boisterous Amazons. Zeisler projected an image to Americans of a woman who could "play like a man" yet remain a woman concerned with husband, home, and family. Indeed, women felt compelled at the time to assure their audiences that they were "real women" as well as artists.

Until the late nineteenth century, women were told they should not play orchestral instruments other than the harp because they did not look good playing them (the flute, for example) or did not have the required strength (lower woodwinds and brass). Violins were considered instruments of the devil that no self-respecting woman would play. But thanks primarily to the influence of Camilla Urso, the violin became not only an accepted but even a preferred instrument for female musicians.

Urso (1842–1902) arrived in New York from Paris in September 1852, just a few months after Jenny Lind ended her American tour. Then a ten-year-old prodigy, she was the first professional female violinist to perform in the United States, and she soon became an inspiration and role model for others. Born in Nantes into a family of professional musicians, Urso decided at age five to study violin. Her father objected because he believed that no respectable girl played the instrument. She insisted, and finally he agreed to find her a teacher. After fighting her way into the Paris Conservatoire, where she was a scholarship student, she graduated in two years with high honors. Her New York debut was the start of a series of American concert tours, interrupted by an eight-year hiatus (1855–63), when she returned to Europe for further study. While there she married the man who became her concert manager. During her many years of touring, she also gave concerts in Europe, Australia, and South Africa.

In 1867 Urso, who performed frequently in Boston, received an extraordinary honor: the members of the Harvard Musical Association presented her with a written testimonial declaring her the equal of the best male violinists. Yet as a woman she could not play in that orchestra; she later attacked this discriminatory practice.[17] Urso had qualities that resembled Lind's, including dignity and an artistic integrity that generated respect from audiences, as well as a warmth that reached the musically sophisticated and the untutored. Her extensive repertoire included concerti by Beethoven, Mozart, and Mendelssohn and many of the now-standard solo works by Paganini and Vieuxtemps. She never lowered her standards. As a result she was an effective educator of the American public.

Urso's artistry and personality may have influenced Julius Eichberg in 1867 to open string classes to female students at the Boston Conservatory. By 1894 *Freund's Weekly* could report that between 400 and 500 young women were studying violin in Boston, and that many had already gone beyond the student level. The writer also noted that this was of great benefit to professional [male] "fiddlers," who as a result could find all the students they wanted. Several of Eichberg's students who went to Europe to work with Joseph Joachim later became solo or ensemble players. Geraldine Morgan, who played quartets with Joachim, and Lillian Shattuck, who returned to teach at the Boston Conservatory, each formed her own string quartet. Another Eichberg student, Olive Mead (1874–1946), later became a protégée of Franz Kneisel, whose string quartet was the most famous in the United States. Mead had a distinguished career both as soloist and as leader of the highly regarded Olive Mead Quartet.

The outstanding American woman violinist of the late nineteenth century was Maud Powell (1867–1920).[18] As a girl she had heard Urso play and became a violinist because of Urso's example. Born in Uniontown, Pennsylvania, Powell grew up in Aurora, Illinois, and went to Europe to study at the Leipzig and Paris conservatories and with Joachim, with whom she made her debut in 1885. But like many concert artists, she and her family paid a high price for her European training and career. At fourteen she terminated her general education to concentrate on the violin. Her mother accompanied her to Europe on a tour of duty as chaperone that ended seventeen years later and all but destroyed Maud's parents' marriage. Like many other professional women of the time, Maud Powell believed that she must choose between marriage and family and a career. Like many others, when she finally married, at thirty-seven, it was to her concert manager. During her intensely hard-working yet gratifying life, she played with leading orchestras in Europe and the United States, toured the world, and organized and led her all-female string quartet and later her own trio.

String players at the Boston Conservatory also learned orchestral skills in the Eichberg Lady Orchestra (organized in 1884), a string ensemble that played both classical and popular music. By training all these women, their male teachers also were creating competition for professional jobs. That competition, however, was not actual but potential, since women were effectively barred from all-male orchestras. Black and white women found other solutions, among them all-women orchestras and bands, segregated by color and, almost without exception, marginal and underpaid even when fully professional.

True to pattern, the first such group was an imported one, the Vienna Ladies Orchestra, or Damen-Orchester, formed in 1867 and on tour in the United States beginning in 1871. Although they were concert artists, they found it necessary to play in beer halls and restaurants. In 1880, Marion Osgood of Chelsea, Massachusetts, organized her own Ladies' Orchestra to play at dances and parties. Four years later, Caroline B. Nichols, one of Eichberg's violin students, formed the outstanding and long-lived Boston Fadette Lady Orchestra. By ca. 1920, about 600 women had played in the Fadettes, and some of them went on to form their own orchestras.

Of course, women's orchestras needed more than strings. Some employed men to play the missing instruments. Others made do with whatever female instrumentalists they could find. The New York Ladies' Orchestra, active in 1888, included strings, guitars, mandolins, harp, kettle drum, banjo, piano, and organ. Such a combination was appropriate for a light classical and popular repertoire, which all the orchestras found they had to offer—whether or not they also played more serious music—in order to get work. Indeed, some, like the Fadettes, included not only a mixed repertoire but vaudeville acts as well. The number of women's orchestras continued to grow: in 1908 there were thirty orchestras active in the United States.

In 1917–18, when many men were in uniform, women trained in female orchestras were hired and paid union wages to play in hotel orchestras, but they had to give up their jobs to men at the end of the war. Maud Powell noted at the time the persistence of discrimination against women in orchestras:

> When I first began my career as a concert artist I did pioneer work for the cause of the woman violinist, going on with the work begun by Camilla Urso. . . . A strong prejudice then existed against women fiddlers, which even yet has not altogether been overcome.[19]

With few exceptions, women only began to have opportunities as orchestral musicians during World War II.

## WOMEN AS COMPOSERS

Women were publishing songs as early as the 1790s. For the next several decades most of their songs and dances, some with variations, marked them as accomplished amateurs with minimal training in music. Often the pieces were attributed to "A Lady" or "Mary," thus preserving their composers' anonymity and amateur status while making clear that the composer was a woman. Whereas concert music was beyond most women's skills, and genres such as minstrel songs were too vulgar, the parlor song, the quintessential musical expression of the Victorian era, occupied a central position in women's amateur music making.

Most parlor songs are about love—romantic, filial, maternal, sisterly, platonic, or unrequited. Most call for a woman's voice, employ a limited range, are in strophic form with regular phrases, and are simple enough to be sung by an amateur. An occasional parlor song from early in the century had a fairly demanding piano accompaniment, while vocal lines in more elaborate songs showed the influence of Italian opera. Mrs. Townshend Stith, one of the first women to sign her music, published "Our Friendship" (1830), a quasi-operatic song with an elaborately ornamented *bel canto* melody (see Example 7-2).

Inspired by the example of several Englishwomen whose songs first circulated in the 1830s, a few American women allowed their names to be used, protected by the canopy of music for the home. Parlor songs by women were published in *Godey's Ladies' Book* and other women's journals. At first their songs were unaccompanied or were harmonized by men, since women were almost always self-taught in composition, and harmony was considered a "scientific" skill they were incapable of learning.

By mid-century, a few composers emerged who were both more skillful and more professional than earlier composers of sentimental songs. Jane Sloman, born in England in 1824 to parents in the theatre, first became

EXAMPLE 7-2.    Mrs. Townshend Stith, "Our Friendship." Excerpt from *American Women Composers, before 1870,* copyright © 1983 by Judith Tick, is reprinted by permission of UMI Research Press, Ann Arbor, MI, p. [97].

known as a solo pianist at the age of seventeen. Yet she felt compelled to embrace Victorian standards of ladylike behavior when she modestly informed her audiences that only after the most strenuous urging by others did she consent to appear in public. Sloman's song "The Maiden's Farewell" (1842) has a highly ornamented, chromatic melody for its sentimental subject, a young woman's conflicts upon marrying and leaving her mother. Yet the words also express the close bond between mother and daughter typical of the Victorian era.

Susan Parkhurst (1836–1918), a member of the next generation, had an active career in the 1860s. Widowed in 1864, she supported herself and her daughter by performing and composing. Her works, published under the name Mrs. E. A. Parkhurst, include variation sets for piano—among them "Yankee Doodle," "Blue Bells of Scotland," and her own "Sweet Evalina"—and "Funeral March to the Memory of Abraham Lincoln." In addition to piano music, Parkhurst wrote gospel hymns, parlor songs, and topical songs on abolitionist, patriotic, and temperance themes, among them "I'll Marry No Man If He Drinks."

Faustina Hasse Hodges (1822–95) came from a more elitist tradition. She was the daughter of Edward Hodges, an organist and church composer who came to America from England in 1838. She also worked as a church organist, in addition to teaching organ, piano, and voice at Troy (N.Y.) Seminary. Her works include keyboard music and sacred and secular songs. Like other composers of her day, Hodges wrote many of her song texts herself. Two of her most successful songs were "Dreams" and "The Rose Bush," both with sentimental texts. Tick explains that "fading roses and fading dreams were typical conceits of parlor culture in the 1850s" and calls Hodges "a gifted musical genre painter."[20]

Marion Dix Sullivan (fl. 1840–50) was the first American woman to write what today would be called a hit song, her ballad "The Blue Juniata" (1844). Often reprinted, the song was mentioned by Mark Twain in his *Autobiography* and inspired variation sets by at least two composers. In addition to individual songs, Sullivan published two collections, *Bible Songs* (1856) and *Juniata Ballads* (1870), the latter a book of fifty simple, unaccompanied school songs.

Augusta Browne (1821–82) was both the most professional and the most prolific of the mid-century composers: her compositions number around 200. She supported herself by performing on organ and piano and by her own writings, both musical and literary. Her articles on music appeared frequently in popular periodicals of the day; later she also championed equal rights for women. Having married late and been widowed soon after, Browne was acutely aware of the hardships women faced when trying to make a living. She was a skillful composer, writing most of her music between 1840 and 1855. One of her best-known works, "The War-Like Dead in Mexico," was published in 1848 and dedicated to Henry Clay. It is atypical in its masculine subject and its dramatic martial rhythms.

The songs of Carrie Jacobs-Bond (1861–1946), the most successful song composer of the late nineteenth and early twentieth centuries, blend two traditions, the parlor song and the art song.[21] Carrie Jacobs was born in Janesville, Wisconsin. A precociously talented child, at four she played by ear, at nine she learned Liszt's Second Hungarian Rhapsody by ear, and at fourteen she decided to become a serious student after hearing Rivé-King play the same rhapsody. Because of family setbacks, musical training for Jacobs was restricted to lessons on the piano. In addition, her childhood was clouded by poor health, and illness dogged her throughout her life. Her twenties were marred by a failed marriage and financial struggles to support herself and her son. Her second marriage, which was happy, was troubled by economic disaster in the Panic of 1893 and ended with her husband's premature death.

Torn between expectations of a traditional woman's role and her musical ambitions, Jacobs-Bond decided in 1893 to bring some money into the household through her music. She arranged with a Chicago publisher to issue two of her songs, launching her career as a composer. Most of her 200 works are songs she published herself, painting the decorative title pages and promoting them by her own performances. "A Perfect Day" (1910), her biggest hit, sold eight million copies and five million records and appeared in sixty editions. Jacobs-Bond said that her aim was to write "the simple songs for the people rather than intricate and curious pieces which only the critics extol for their eccentricities." Although originally intended for the recital stage, her music became part of the popular culture.

Mary Turner Salter (1856–1938) began as a concert and oratorio singer, but after marriage she retired from performance and became a successful writer of parlor songs. Her most famous was the sentimental "The Cry of Rachel," a favorite encore of the contralto Ernestine Schumann-Heink, who measured the song's success by the number of listeners it moved to tears.

Although women were widely accepted as composers for the parlor, the composition of art music was a skill considered appropriate only for men. Women, critic George Upton wrote in 1880, should be content to function as men's Muses or inspirations. Furthermore, a prevailing theory, social Darwinism, placed women lower on the evolutionary scale than men, incapable of creating high art because they lacked intellectual ability. Hence there was serious doubt that women could create art music of real value under even the most favorable conditions. Yet support from the women's movement and the long, slow rise of women as composers in the nineteenth century prepared the way for the emergence of women as creators of art music, especially Clara Kathleen Rogers (1844–1931), Helen Hopekirk (1856–1945), Margaret Ruthven Lang (1867–1971), and Amy M. (Mrs. H. H. A.) Beach (1867–1944).

These four women were accepted members of Boston's Second New England School of composition, led by two composer-teachers, John Knowles Paine (1839–1906) of Harvard and George Whitefield Chadwick (1854–1931) of the New England Conservatory of Music. All four women lived in Boston, where support came from the dozens of extraordinary Boston women active as abolitionists, suffragists, social activists, educators, poets, writers, painters, physicians, lawyers, and architects. Further, Boston's intellectual and social elite was proud of its own composers, whether male or female, and regularly turned out to hear their music. Additional support came from the publisher Arthur P. Schmidt, who issued many of their works soon after they were composed.[22] Most important, ensembles such as the Boston Symphony Orchestra, the Handel and Haydn Society, and the Kneisel String Quartet performed their works, often more than once.

Rogers was the first of the four to have her music published and performed. Born Clara Kathleen Barnett, she was the youngest child of England's leading opera composer, John Barnett. At the age of twelve she was admitted to the Leipzig Conservatory as a student because of her musical gifts as a singer and pianist. She was also gifted in composition— during her student years she wrote a string quartet—but was refused entry into the composition class because she was female. Because of her example, however, the conservatory later established a composition class for women.

Clara Kathleen Rogers. Billy Rose Theatre Collection. Reproduced by permission of the New York Public Library, Astor, Lenox and Tilden Foundations.

After graduating with honors at the age of sixteen and faced with a choice between singing and playing the piano, Clara Barnett chose opera, as many multitalented women before and after her have done. At once highly competitive and demanding, opera nevertheless was a preferred field for women. First and foremost—and unlike instrumental performance—opera *required* the participation of women. As members of opera companies, women were part of a community of artists and had a certain continuity of work. Those who made it to the apex as prima donnas collected higher fees than any other performing musicians.

Rogers spent ten years as a prima donna in Italy, singing under the name of Clara Doria, chaperoned the entire time by her mother. Then she returned to England, sang in concert and oratorio, and finally toured the United States with the Parepa-Rosa Opera Company. She married Henry Munroe Rogers, a lawyer from Boston, and settled there, where she sang, taught, and finally had time to compose songs and an occasional instrumental work. Most of her compositions were published by Schmidt, beginning in 1883.

Her music shows a substantial lyric gift. Indeed, Rogers described the process of composition as "a supreme delight—amounting at times almost to intoxication." Yet she believed that with training in composition she would have tackled the larger forms as well:

> As I look back, I cannot help deploring that when I was a student in Germany there were no facilities accorded to women for learning orchestration, or in fact, for obtaining any guidance whatever in original composition. Had I obtained early in life a good technique in writing for instruments I really think I might have accomplished something worth while in orchestral composition.[23]

Example 7-3 contains an excerpt from her setting of one of Shakespeare's lyrics.

Helen Hopekirk wrote songs, piano solos, chamber music, and music for piano and orchestra. She was first a successful concert pianist, having toured England, continental Europe, and the United States for a number of years, playing solo recitals and appearing with leading orchestras. Like Rogers, Hopekirk had studied in Leipzig, making her debut there in 1878. More and more drawn to composition, Hopekirk twice interrupted her performing career to study and compose. With her husband, who was also her concert manager, she settled in Boston in 1897, where she lived for the rest of her life, teaching piano, playing, and composing. Her interest in folk songs from her native land led to her collection *Seventy Scottish Songs* (1905), for which she made the arrangements for voice and piano. That

EXAMPLE 7-3.    Clara Kathleen Rogers, "She Never Told Her Love" (Boston: Arthur P. Schmidt, 1882).

Helen Hopekirk. © C. H. Hall. Reproduced from Constance Huntington and Helen Ingersoll Tetlow, eds., *Helen Hopekirk 1856–1945* (Cambridge: privately printed, 1954).

interest also was reflected in her original compositions, many of which, like the song in Example 7-4, have a distinct Scottish folk influence.

In 1893, the Boston Symphony Orchestra gave the first performance of Margaret Ruthven Lang's *Dramatic Overture,* Op. 10—the first time a major American orchestra played a work by a woman. This was the first of seven orchestral works by Lang—now lost—that were performed in the 1890s by the Boston Symphony and other orchestras. Lang, like Rogers, was the daughter of musicians. Her mother was known as an "exquisite singer," and her father, Benjamin Johnson Lang, was a leading musician in Boston—teacher, frequent soloist on piano and organ, organist with the Handel and Haydn Society and the Boston Symphony Orchestra, and conductor of choruses and instrumental ensembles. B. J. Lang was also his daughter's teacher, and later he sent her to Munich to study violin and composition. On her return she continued composition studies with Chad-

EXAMPLE 7-4.    Helen Hopekirk, "The Bandriudh" (Song of Spring), from *Five Songs* (New York: G. Schirmer, 1903).

wick and Paine. Her father was also her mentor, and she regularly sought his approval of her works before she submitted them to Schmidt for publication. Her father also presented many of her works at his own concerts. But Lang had other sources of support—from leading singers and conductors and from music and women's clubs. Her song "Ojalà" was performed on a program of representative American works in Paris during the Exposition of 1889. Although Lang stopped composing many years before her death at age 104, singers and choral groups continued to perform her music, often giving entire programs of her works.

Margaret Ruthven Lang. Billy Rose
Theatre Collection. Reproduced by per-
mission of the New York Public Library,
Astor, Lenox and Tilden Foundations.

Like others of the Boston School, Lang's primary influence was German. On the other hand, her most famous song, "An Irish Love Song," Op.
22 (1895), is one among a number of her works written in a folk idiom. It
also exemplifies the widespread interest in folk song among contemporary
American composers of art music. Finally, some of her late works show
French influence, especially *Wind,* a beautiful and atmospheric double
chorus for women's voices.

Amy Marcy Beach (née Cheney, 1867–1944), an outstanding composer of the period, was born the same year as Lang. She came to Boston
from Henniker, New Hampshire, as a child. The Marcy side of the family
was quite musical, and her mother, Clara Imogene (Marcy) Cheney, had
performed as a singer and pianist before her marriage. Thus she was well
qualified to recognize her infant daughter's remarkable talent: "Her gift for
composition showed itself in babyhood—before two years of age she would,

EXAMPLE 7-5.      Margaret Ruthven Lang, *Wind,* Op. 53 (Boston: A. P. Schmidt, 1913).

when being rocked in my arms, improvise a perfectly correct alto to any soprano air I might sing."[24]

At four the child played by ear any music she had heard and also composed her first pieces for the piano—in her head and away from the instrument. Two years later she began piano lessons with her mother; she then studied successively with two German-trained pianists, the second a student of Franz Liszt. At sixteen she made an eagerly awaited debut with a Boston orchestra. At least fifteen local critics covered the concert, and all agreed that she was an outstanding talent with technical ability to match. For the next two years she played regularly in Boston and environs, and was as regularly admired by the critics. By the time she made her debut with the Boston Symphony Orchestra in 1885, the critics were calling her a master musician.

Her training in composition had not been totally neglected. In 1882 Amy Cheney studied harmony and counterpoint with an outstanding Boston teacher. After her debut, she sought advice about a composition teacher from the conductor of the Boston Symphony, Wilhelm Gericke, who recommended that she teach herself. Such a suggestion may have been influenced by public perceptions that men wrote out of their intellects, women out of their feelings, and that therefore women would not respond to training.

Amy Marcy Cheney Beach. Elizabeth Porter Gould Collection, Division of Rare Books and Manuscripts, Boston Public Library. Used by permission.

Following that advice, Amy Cheney taught herself, and very well indeed, by studying the scores of the masters. Throughout her youth she had continued to improvise and compose, and two of her songs were published under her birth name: "The Rainy Day" (Oliver Ditson, 1883) and "With Violets," her Op. 1, No. 1 (1885), the first piece of hers issued by Arthur P. Schmidt.

The year 1885 marked the beginning of her long association with Schmidt, her exclusive publisher for twenty-nine years. This year also saw her marriage at eighteen to Dr. Henry Harris Aubrey Beach, who was then forty-three and clearly delighted to have as his wife such a promising creative talent. They agreed that she would concentrate on composition and limit her performing to an occasional recital, the proceeds of which would go to charity. This arrangement was in some ways ideal for a composer. During the next twenty-five years, Beach turned out dozens of art songs, among them "Elle et moi," Op. 21, No. 3 (1893; see HAMW, pp. 161–65). Piano figurations depict the fluttering of the butterfly's wings, which are imitated as well in florid passages for the voice. Beach also wrote piano, chamber, and choral works, and several major compositions for orchestra, including Mass in Eb major, Op. 5 (1890); Symphony in E minor ("Gaelic"), Op. 32 (1897); and Piano Concerto, Op. 45 (1900).

The "Gaelic" Symphony (first movement in HAMW, pp. 166–203) was an important landmark in music, for it was the first symphony by an American woman to be performed anywhere. Indeed, during Beach's lifetime it had many performances by over a dozen orchestras in the United States and Europe. It was also important because it was the first symphony by an American composer to quote folk songs as themes. This work and many others that followed placed Beach within the nationalist movement in music (ca. 1893–1950), which was characterized by the use of folk and traditional music of the many native and immigrant groups in the United States.[25]

Following the deaths of her husband in 1910 and her mother in 1911, Beach again became active as a pianist while continuing to compose. Major works from the latter half of her life, composed in Beach's chromatic, post-Romantic style, include Theme and Variations for flute and strings, Op. 80 (1920); String Quartet in One Movement, Op. 89 (MS, 1929); a large number of choral works for the Protestant service, among them *Canticle of the Sun*, Op. 123 (1928) for chorus and orchestra; and many songs, including the superb "Rendezvous," Op. 120 (1928), with violin obbligato (Example 7-6).

Beach's numerous piano works include two written during her first residency at the MacDowell Colony (1921), "The Hermit Thrush at Eve" and "The Hermit Thrush at Morn," Op. 92, Nos. 1 and 2 (1922), based on bird calls Beach heard and notated at the Colony (see HAMW, pp. 204–10). Like folk songs, bird calls offered composers a fresh vocabulary that con-

EXAMPLE 7-6.     Mrs. H. H. A. Beach, "Rendezvous," Op. 120, for voice, violin, and piano (Boston: Oliver Ditson, 1928).

tributed to the changes in compositional style that took place in the twentieth century.

During her lifetime Beach's works had wide currency: in addition to the popularity of her symphony, her songs were sung by leading opera stars, her chamber music was featured by many ensembles, and her choral music occupied an important place in church repertoires. Despite her many successes, much contemporary critical commentary dwelt on the fact that Beach was a woman, hence her works could not be compared to those of mainstream male composers. At the same time, her colleagues in the New England School believed that she was the most gifted composer of the group. Her compositions crowned a century of progress by American women in music. Beach became a heroine to American women and her example a beacon to light the way for the coming generation of female composers.

## NOTES

1. Information in this section was generously provided by Susan L. Porter from *Musical Theatre in Post-Revolutionary America* (Washington, D.C.: Smithsonian Institution Press, forthcoming).

2. Information on composers is summarized from Judith Tick, *American Women Composers before 1870* (Ann Arbor: UMI Research Press, 1983), pp. 58–59, and from Porter.

3. Information on opera troupes is summarized from Katherine Preston, "Travelling Opera Troupes in the United States, 1825–1860," Ph.D. diss., City University of New York, 1989.

4. Information about Clara Kellogg is from her autobiography, *Memoirs of an American Prima Donna* (New York and London: G. P. Putnam, 1913; reprinted 1938).

5. Ibid., p. 30.

6. Tick, p. 30.

7. Information about Julia Crane and the Crane Normal Institute comes from the Archives of the Crane School of Music, SUNY-Potsdam.

8. Amy Fay, *Music Study in Germany,* edited by Mrs. Fay Pierce (New York: Macmillan, 1880; reprints 1965, and New York: Da Capo, 1979).

9. Mabel Wheeler Daniels, *An American Girl in Munich (Impressions of a Music Student)* (Boston: Little Brown & Co., 1905), quoted in Carol Neuls-Bates, ed., *Women in Music* (New York: Harper and Row, 1982), pp. 219–22.

10. Eva Munson Smith, ed., *Women in Sacred Song. A Library of Hymns, Religious Poems and Sacred Music by Women* (Boston: D. Lothrop, 1885). The collection also includes temperance and suffrage songs.

11. *History of the Handel and Haydn Society*, vol. 1, edited by Charles C. Perkins (1883; reprint New York: Da Capo Press, 1977), pp. 50–51.

12. *The New Grove Dictionary of American Music,* s.v. "[Fisk] Jubilee Singers," by Geneva H. Southall.

13. See Marta Milinowski, *Teresa Carreño: By the Grace of God* (New Haven: Yale University Press, 1940).

14. Information on Julie Rivé-King is from M. Leslie Petteys, "Julie Rivé-King, American Pianist," D.M.A. thesis, University of Missouri–Kansas City, 1987.

15. Harold Schonberg, *The Great Pianists* (New York: Simon and Schuster, 1963), p. 249; quoted in Petteys, pp. vii–viii.

16. Information from Diana Ruth Hallman, "The Pianist Fannie Bloomfield Zeisler in American Music and Society," M.M. thesis, University of Maryland, 1983.

17. See Susan Kagan, "Camilla Urso: A Nineteenth-Century Violinist's View," *Signs* 2/3 (Spring 1977):727–34.

18. Information from Karen A. Shaffer and Neva Garner Greenwood, *Maud Powell, Pioneer American Violinist* (Arlington, VA: The Maud Powell Foundation, 1988; distributed by Iowa State University Press).

19. Henry Roth, "Women and the Fiddle," *The Strad* 83 (March 1973):557.

20. Tick, p. 171.

21. Information on Jacobs-Bond comes from Phyllis Ruth Bruce, "From Rags to Roses: The Life and Works of Carrie Jacobs-Bond, an American Composer," M.M. thesis, Wesleyan University, 1980.

22. On Schmidt's support of women composers, see Adrienne Fried Block, "Arthur P. Schmidt, Music Publisher and Champion of American Women Composers," in *The Musical Woman: An International Perspective,* vol. 2, edited by J. L. Zaimont et al. (Westport, CT: Greenwood Press, 1987).

23. Clara Kathleen Rogers, *The Story of Two Lives: Home, Friends and Travel* (Norwood, MA: Plimpton Press, 1932), p. 81.

24. Copy of letter from Clara Cheney to "Cousin Anna," dated April 27, 1898, from 28 Commonwealth Avenue, Boston, in Box 4, F. 25, Beach Collection, University of New Hampshire at Durham.

25. On the relation of this work to the nationalist movement in the United States, see Adrienne Fried Block, "Dvořák, Beach, and American Music," in *A Celebration of American Music: Words and Music in Honor of H. Wiley Hitchcock,* edited by Richard Crawford, R. Allen Lott, and Carol J. Oja (Ann Arbor: University of Michigan Press, 1990).

## SUGGESTIONS FOR FURTHER READING

Block, Adrienne Fried. "Why Amy Beach Succeeded as a Composer: The Early Years." *Current Musicology* 36 (1983):41–59.
Handy, D. Antoinette. *Black Women in American Bands and Orchestras.* Metuchen, NJ: Scarecrow Press, 1981.
Kagan, Susan. "Camilla Urso: A Nineteenth-Century Violinist's View." *Signs: Journal of Women in Culture and Society* 2/3 (Spring 1977):726–34.
Loesser, Arthur. *Men, Women, and Pianos: A Social History.* New York: Simon and Schuster, 1954.
Morath, Max. "May Aufderheide and the Ragtime Women." In *Ragtime: Its History, Composers, and Music,* edited by John Edward Hasse. New York: G. Schirmer, 1985.
Tawa, Nicholas E. *Sweet Songs for Gentle Americans: The Parlor Song in America, 1790–1860.* Bowling Green, OH: Bowling Green University Popular Press, 1980.

# Modern
## Music around
## the World

# VIII.
# Contemporary
# British Composers

## Catherine Roma

During the early years of the twentieth century, an unusual number of British women composers were born. The first decade alone saw the births of Priaulx Rainier, Elizabeth Poston, Grace Williams, Elisabeth Lutyens, Elizabeth Maconchy, Imogen Holst, and Phyllis Tate. Most of these composers attended the Royal College of Music (RCM) in the twenties, and many were students of Ralph Vaughan Williams or Gustav Holst. They reacted to and were affected by the English Musical Renaissance and were considered more open than many in their generation to musical currents from the Continent. All struggled with their careers, not only because they were forward-looking composers but also because they were women. None felt they had experienced discrimination at the RCM. However, once out in the professional world, many felt the need to band together and to organize performances where their works could be heard. Anne Macnaghten, in collaboration with conductor Iris Lemare and composer Elisabeth Lutyens, established the still-functioning Macnaghten-Lemare series as a platform for performances of modern British music. Distinguished soloists were approached for help; voices were solicited for a chorus; and Lemare conducted a chamber orchestra made up of amateurs and students.[1] By the 1960s, when a favorable musical climate in London and the momentum of their past efforts and successes came together, these women had become well known. In fact, the Society of Women Musicians, an organization founded in 1911 to deal with the problems of invisibility among women composers and performers, disbanded in the early 1970s, believing it had met its objectives.

Thea Musgrave (b. 1928) stands alone in the next generation of composers. Not until the 1960s and early 1970s, when London had emerged as one of the international centers of new music, did the RCM and the Royal Academy of Music (RAM) see another generation quite like the one at the beginning of the century. Women composers, including Nicola LeFanu, Erika Fox, Judith Bingham, Judith Weir, and Diana Burrell, have benefited from the ground-breaking work of their predecessors. Yet Nicola LeFanu, the daughter of Elizabeth Maconchy, strongly believes that the 1980s have seen a rapid decline in opportunities for women in music because of the growing conservative political climate.[2] As a result a new organization, Women in Music, was formed in 1987 to address many of the problems created by that decline.

## THE FIRST GENERATION

### *Elisabeth Lutyens*

Elisabeth Lutyens (1906–83) was born in London, the fourth of five children of the distinguished architect Edwin Lutyens and Lady Emily Lytton. Though they were not a musical family, they did not actively disapprove of her interest in music. Lutyens studied both piano and violin, practiced many hours a day, and began to compose in secret. Strongly impressed by "the exciting flavor of new music from France—Debussy and Ravel—that was beginning to filter through the fog of English programmes,"[3] she persuaded her parents to let her go to Paris to study at the École Normale. She then entered London's Royal College of Music and was assigned to Harold Darke—though she might have been placed with Ralph Vaughan Williams or John Ireland, composers whom, in retrospect, she relegated to "the cowpat school of composition."[4] Darke's encouragement was central to the eventual development of her own highly individual compositional style.

In the 1930s, Lutyens had two experiences that influenced her greatly: she was introduced to Purcell's contrapuntal string fantasias, which she said led her to discover serial composition; and she heard a performance of Webern's "Das Augenlicht," which she found unforgettable. Lutyens turned permanently to serial technique with her Concerto for Nine Instruments (1940). Her new musical language developed naturally out of the rigor of her compositional attitudes, and her fascination with mathematical relationships placed her outside Britain's musical mainstream. Life for Lutyens was extremely difficult during and after World War II. In 1933 she had married Ian Glennie, with whom she had three children, but she later left him for Edward Clark, a well-known champion of contemporary music.

Though Clark played many roles in her life, he did not provide financial support. At first Lutyens made a meager living copying music, but writing music for documentary films eventually became a major source of her income, and she produced over one hundred such scores.

*O Saisons, O Châteaux!* (1946), for soprano, mandolin, guitar, harp, solo violin, and strings, presages Lutyens's mature style. Setting a poem from Rimbaud's *Les Illuminations,* Lutyens creates an extraordinary atmosphere, expressed directly in beautiful, highly articulate melodic writing. Another side of Lutyens can be seen in her Stevie Smith songs of 1948; light and humorous, these cabaret songs capture the essence of Smith's poetry. At forty-seven, Lutyens solidified elements in her compositional style and emerged a mature composer. Marks of her style include the use of palindromic structures and a progressive paring down of materials and gestures. Her harmonic language becomes consistent and her musical structures more tightly organized. Despite her rigorous approach to composition, she has an instinct for keeping the music varied. Her vocal music is most impressive—both solo and choral works are characterized by a wide-ranging choice of texts and a sensitive musical reaction to the words themselves.

*Motet (Excerpta Tractati-Logico-Philosophici),* Op. 27 (1953), is one of Lutyens's most remarkable compositions. For her text Lutyens selected a series of statements from Ludwig Wittgenstein's *Logisch-philosophische Abhandlung* (1912), a tract that poses the questions: How is language possible? How can a person, by uttering a sequence of words, say something? And how can another person understand? The formal, abstract nature of the text frees Lutyens from any necessity to interpret the words. Hence her motet is not a setting of words so much as a realization of Wittgenstein's philosophical ideas through her technique of musical composition. Though the motet uses twelve-tone aggregates, combinations, and serial techniques, it is not dodecaphonic in the strict sense of the word. This taut, complex, lyrical work, full of choice and craft, is not without the performance difficulties typical of all Lutyens's works.

Two important works from the 1960s are *And Suddenly It's Evening* (1966) and *Essence of Our Happinesses* (1968). In the 1970s, after focusing on dramatic and vocal works, Lutyens wrote a series of instrumental pieces entitled *Plenum (Plenum I:* piano; *Plenum II:* solo oboe and thirteen instrumentalists; *Plenum III:* string quartet; and *Plenum IV:* organ). In them Lutyens increased the flexibility of her notation and continued to reduce musical events. She always had a loyal following, and during the last decade of her life her closest friends were avant-garde musicians younger than she. These were the people who appreciated her music, her uncompromising spirit, her fearlessness, and her commitment to new music.

## Elizabeth Maconchy

Elizabeth Maconchy was born in 1907 in Broxbourne, Hertford, north of London. Although both her parents were Irish, the family lived in Buckinghamshire for several years before moving to Dublin after World War I. When her father died, the family returned to England. In the same year, at the age of sixteen, Maconchy was accepted into the Royal College of Music, where she studied composition with Charles Wood and Ralph Vaughan Williams. She worked with the latter for many years and acknowledges the central influence on her music of both Vaughan Williams and the Hungarian composer Béla Bartók.

During her six years at the RCM, Maconchy won the Blumenthal and Sullivan scholarships. In 1929, on being awarded the Octavia Traveling Scholarship, she visited Vienna and Paris and then spent two months in Prague studying with Karel Jirák. Her music aroused much interest, and she returned in 1930 when her piano concerto was premiered by the Prague

Elizabeth Maconchy. Photo by Suzie Maeder. Used by permission.

Philharmonic. Maconchy later traveled to Prague (1935), Cracow, and Warsaw (1939) for performances of her works by the International Society for Contemporary Music (ISCM). Her first major performance in London came in 1930, when Sir Henry Wood conducted her suite, *The Land,* at the Prom Concerts. Yet despite favorable press notices and recognition from people in important places, her early career did not flourish as one might have expected. Maconchy remained a private person, with a strong, quiet nature; and her hard-fought struggle with tuberculosis restricted her activities. However, in her solitude she was able to develop her own way of thinking, and she never stopped composing. She focused on chamber music, concentrating specifically on the string quartets that form the core of her output.

Between 1933 and 1984 Elizabeth Maconchy wrote thirteen string quartets, becoming the modern English composer most closely associated with this medium. Like the quartets of Bartók, Maconchy's reveal highly contrapuntal textures, short chromatic motives, and canonic procedures. However, her compositions are not derived from folk music, as are those of Bartók, Vaughan Williams, and Janáček—composers with whom she is constantly compared. For Maconchy, the string quartet is the perfect vehicle for dramatic expression, as if four characters were engaged in statement and comment: "The clash of their ideas and the way in which they react upon each other."[5] Her early quartets, those most often compared to Bartók's, follow a Classic multimovement format, but the later ones tend to be more compact, often in one continuous movement, with very economical use of material.

In the mid-1950s, after having experienced what she called a creative block, Maconchy began to write operas, and she produced three one-act works in a ten-year period (1957–67). She also wrote several pieces for children's voices: operas, extravaganzas, *scenas,* and musical theatre works. Her interest and enthusiasm for setting text also led to a rich outpouring of choral music and music for solo voice and instrumental ensemble, including *Ariadne* (1970), for soprano and orchestra, and *The Leaden Echo and the Golden Echo* (1978), for mixed chorus, alto flute, viola, and harp. Her integrity as a composer comes from knowing current trends, supporting other musicians, participating in contemporary music organizations, and quietly writing because she has to. Maconchy has achieved a balance of craft and control with insight.

## Grace Williams

In the history of music in Wales, Grace Williams (1906–77) occupies a position of first importance, and her reputation is undisputed. She came from a musical family and fondly remembered the days when she played violin in a family trio. After studying music at the University of Cardiff, she went on to the Royal College of Music, as did her friend Elizabeth Maconchy; there she studied composition with Ralph Vaughan Williams. Upon completion of her degree, she traveled to Vienna to study with Egon Wellesz. Back in London, Williams taught at the Camden School for Girls and composed music. She remained in London a total of twenty years (1926–46) before returning to Wales, where she spent the rest of her life. Highly self-critical, she later purged many of her earliest highly experimental pieces: her journal of May 10, 1951 reads, "DAY OF DESTRUCTION. Examined all my music manuscripts and destroyed nearly all which I considered not worth performing." Yet this early period also saw the creation of two of her most frequently performed works, *Fantasia on Welsh Nursery Tunes* (1941) and *Sea Sketches* (1947), a suite of five pieces inspired by the coastline near her home. *Fantasia,* which quotes eight traditional melodies, immediately became popular and was soon recorded. The work did much to make Grace Williams known, and for this it occupies an important position in her output.

The years between 1955 and 1961 were richly creative and productive. *Penillion* (1955), a suite for orchestra, is closely related to an indigenous, improvisational form of singing in Wales known as *cerdd dant;* it retains the recurring form ABAB, the narrative style, and the rhythmic and melodic characteristics of the traditional *penillion.* In the last ten years of her creative life, most of Williams's compositions involved voice in some way. At the age of sixty Williams wrote an opera, *The Parlour* (1966), adapting her own libretto from Guy de Maupassant's short story "En famille." In *Missa Cambrensis* (1971) she incorporates nonliturgical material into the Latin rite. The sound of bells and the interval of the tritone color the score, and the work as a whole shows the influence of Benjamin Britten's *War Requiem.* The Marian hymn *Ave Maris Stella* (Hail star of the sea, 1973), for unaccompanied mixed chorus, is perhaps her most impressive work. The first three words of the hymn form a refrain that opens every stanza; and the plastic rhythms reflect the ebb and flow of the sea, as do the undulating melodic lines and the skillful changes in vocal color. Williams was a communicator whose command of orchestral writing and skilled handling of voices make her contribution to Welsh music inestimable.

## Priaulx Rainier

Priaulx Rainier (1903–86), born in South Africa, was largely a self-taught composer. Her musical language combined twentieth-century forms with the sounds she heard on the borders of Natal and Zululand during her childhood. In 1920 Rainier was awarded a Cape University Overseas Scholarship to study violin at the Royal Academy of Music. After graduation she remained in London, where she taught and performed. While recovering from a serious car accident, she composed her first work, a duo for piano and violin, which was performed at Wigmore Hall in 1936. This successful premiere was followed by "Three Greek Epigrams" for soprano and piano (1937) and a string quartet (1939). Trademarks of Rainier's early style are apparent here: a wide variety of textural contrasts and ostinato-like rhythmic structures reminiscent of African music and dance.

In the autumn of 1937, Rainier studied for several months with Nadia Boulanger; these were her only formal composition lessons. Though composing did not come easily to Rainier, she found her own way and was able to forge a refined, disciplined, meticulously crafted, highly personal idiom. By the mid-1940s she had become a professor of composition at the RAM.

In 1953 Peter Pears commissioned the first of two works from Priaulx Rainier: *Cycle for Declamation*, for unaccompanied tenor voice, on fragments from John Donne's *Devotions*. Pears's second commission produced *Bee Oracles* (1970), Rainier's largest chamber work. This accessible and attractive piece, written for voice, flute, oboe, violin, cello, and harpsichord, is frequently performed; its text, by Edith Sitwell, draws on Indian philosophical thought. Rainier's only choral work is a powerful and prophetic Requiem (1955) for unaccompanied chorus and tenor solo. The text, by David Gascoyne, is a warning for prospective victims, a requiem for the ideals and hopes of the world. Rainier's choral writing is homophonic and stark in its rhythmic strength. The incantatory tenor solo acts at times as an integral part of the chorus, while at other times it provides a connection between choral sections and dramatic recitative.

The Requiem was the culmination of Rainier's early work; a change can be detected in her style during the early 1960s, when her compositions became more abstract, compressed, and chromatic, with frequent use of semitones and minor ninths. A strong rhythmic energy, employed with great sophistication, still pervades her works. Rainier's mature style can be heard in *Pastoral Triptych* (1960), for solo oboe, and *Quanta* (1962), for oboe and string trio. The title of *Quanta*, the first of her BBC commissions, refers to the quantum theory of energy existing in space, independent of matter. Though Priaulx Rainier's output is not large, it is meticulously crafted, and her music is complex, with highly charged dissonances and fragmented rhythms.

## THE MIDDLE GENERATION

### *Thea Musgrave*

Thea Musgrave was born in Barnton, Midlothian, near Edinburgh, Scotland, on May 27, 1928. Though music was an essential part of her childhood, not until she had begun a premedical course at Edinburgh University did she choose to make it her life's work. A postgraduate scholarship enabled her to work with Nadia Boulanger, from whom she learned the fundamental principles of discipline and economy and "the importance of every bar."[6] In 1952, Musgrave received the coveted Lili Boulanger Memorial Prize in composition, the first Scottish composer to be so honored. The next year she fulfilled her first commission—from the Scottish Festival at Braemar—with *A Suite o'Bairnsangs* for voice and piano. Her first major success came with *Cantata for a Summer's Day* (1954), a work commissioned by BBC Scotland and scored for chamber ensemble, narrator, and small chorus. Thereafter, Musgrave's works show a gradual movement toward serial technique. Her first fully serial piece is a setting for high voice and piano of "A Song of Christmas," a declamatory *scena* written in 1958.

The period 1961–65 marks a break in her development. Without commission or prospect of performance, Musgrave embarked on her first full-length opera, *The Decision,* and worked on it for two years, to the virtual exclusion of everything else. Its successful world premiere in 1967 at Sadler's Wells in London led Musgrave in a new direction as a composer. She became preoccupied with an instrumental style she describes as dramatic-abstract: dramatic in the sense that certain instruments take on the character of *dramatis personae;* abstract because there is no program. In several of the twenty-seven instrumental compositions written between 1964 and 1972, soloists are required to stand and move around the stage, engaging in musical dialogue or confrontation with other performers. While all the parts are fully notated, they need not be exactly coordinated with other parts or with the conductor; such a technique is described as asynchronous music. The first of Musgrave's dramatic-abstract works is the Chamber Concerto No. 2 (1966). The piece, in homage to Charles Ives, uses the character of Rollo, represented by the viola, who disrupts the general calm of the piece with phrases from popular melodies.[7] The concerto, in one uninterrupted movement divided into six short sections, is written for five players performing on a total of nine instruments.

A natural outgrowth of Musgrave's interest in the dramatic aspects of instrumental music was her return, in 1973, to operatic composition. In *The*

*Voice of Ariadne,* a three-act chamber opera, the asynchronous techniques of the concerti are carried over into the vocal ensembles. During the late 1970s Musgrave wrote two operas, *Mary Queen of Scots* (1977), one of her most significant works to date, and *A Christmas Carol* (1979), her most frequently performed work. The musical idiom of *Mary* is accessible and often tonal. The orchestral textures are always inventive, and the chorus is used very resourcefully, on and off stage. The title character's soliloquy (see HAMW, pp. 367–74) provides powerful insight into her strength and determination. A drama of conflict and confrontation, *Mary* highlights Musgrave's keen sense of dramatic timing and her rich theatrical imagination. Musgrave's opera *Harriet the Woman Called Moses* (1985) is based on the life of Harriet Tubman, whose exploits as a conductor on the Underground Railroad made her a major heroine in American history. Musgrave uses authentic folk songs and spirituals as she tells of Harriet's escape from slavery and of the many people who helped her. The work opens and closes with a thundering chorus built around two chords that carry the "freedom" Leitmotiv of the opera, and the chorus is almost always on stage to observe, comment on, or participate in the action.

In addition to her accomplishments as a composer, Musgrave has become a welcomed lecturer and a respected conductor of her own works. She was the third woman to conduct the Philadelphia Orchestra since its inception in 1900 and the first to conduct one of her own compositions, the Concerto for Orchestra, with the Philadelphia. She has directed the New York City Opera, the Los Angeles Chamber Orchestra, the San Diego and San Francisco Symphony orchestras, the St. Paul Chamber Orchestra, the BBC Symphony Orchestra, and London's Royal Philharmonic Orchestra. Musgrave is fortunate to have had almost all her works performed soon after they were written. She recognizes what a valuable lesson this is for any composer, for only then can she gain confidence and begin to explore new and individual paths.

## THE NEW GENERATION

### Nicola LeFanu

Nicola LeFanu, the daughter of Elizabeth Maconchy, was born in Essex in 1947. She remembers that her mother would play the piano every evening and compose music; thus, "It never entered my head that to be a woman composer was unnatural."[8] LeFanu studied composition with Egon Wellesz at St. Hillary's College, Oxford, from which she graduated in 1968 with a Bachelor of Arts honors degree in music. Her other teachers include Goffredo Petrassi, Peter Maxwell Davies, and Earl Kim.

The music of Nicola LeFanu covers a broad range of genres. She has written for orchestra, for chamber ensemble with and without voice, for solo voice, for chorus, and for solo voice accompanied by one instrument. Many people think of her as a composer of vocal music since her works for solo voice are popular with singers, over half of her works include voice, and she has always demonstrated a keen interest in theatre and poetry. In 1989 she was working on a children's opera, to be followed by a full-length opera.

*The Same Day Dawns* (1974), one of LeFanu's most performed works, is scored for soprano and five players, and uses texts drawn from Tamil, Chinese, and Japanese poems. The work is a cycle of very short, atmospheric songs that reflect the mood and color of the words with a conciseness reminiscent of oriental art. Though only eleven pieces are written, the set in fact includes fifteen, since four of the first five are repeated in reverse order toward the end of the cycle. *The Old Woman of Beare* (1981), a dramatic monologue for soprano and thirteen instruments based on a medieval Irish poem, was written to celebrate the fiftieth anniversary of the Macnaghten Concerts (formerly the Macnaghten-Lemare Concerts). The score alternates between highly dramatic, narrative lines and sung lines requiring a wide range and an agile singing voice. Shifting colors in the instruments support the texture and timbre of the old woman's story as it is presented in song.

LeFanu leads an extremely busy musical life, juggling marriage, two children, a university teaching job, and her own career as a composer. An activist serving and supporting contemporary music, she believes that opportunities for women composers in Britain have declined and that having women as role models is very important.

## *Judith Weir*

Born in Cambridge in 1954, Judith Weir grew up believing that music was something spontaneous and homemade. Her family, originally from Scotland, were enthusiastic amateurs and often played Scottish folk music. Weir began composition lessons while still in high school, and her experience as an oboist in the National Youth Orchestra influenced and inspired her. Before going to Kings College, Cambridge, in 1973, she spent six months at the Massachusetts Institute of Technology, where she sat in on computer music classes with Barry Vercoe. She also benefited from study with Gunther Schuller at Tanglewood.

The catalogue of publicly performed works by Judith Weir begins in

1972, though she has already withdrawn pieces she feels are not up to standard. Until her extremely successful opera, *A Night at the Chinese Opera*, most of her compositions were for small forces, and almost half of them used voice. From the start of her career Weir has preferred to fashion her music for specific performers (often her friends), for she feels that this is a natural, organic way of working and thinking. Constant sources of inspiration include the music of Stravinsky and the ever-surprising elements in the music of Haydn. Restrictions and parameters inspire her and set her going, as in "King Harald's Saga" (1979) for soprano Jane Manning. This unaccompanied, ten-minute *scena* is a colorful description of the Norwegian king's unsuccessful invasion of Britain in 1066. Weir captures the essences of eight colorful characters, all depicted by the soprano, through economy, clarity of text setting, and a keen sense of the sung word.

Judith Weir catapulted to international prominence with *A Night at the Chinese Opera* (1986–87), which was commissioned by the BBC for Kent Opera. Already intrigued by the Chinese music-dramas of the thirteenth century, she constructed her own libretto and created a three-act opera for eleven singers and modest orchestra. The outer acts are fully scored, staged, and sung, while Act II is a fast-moving, musically stylized reconstruction of the Chinese music-drama. The plot traces the adventures of a young canal builder in Kubla Khan's China who sees his career mirrored in the play. The opera moves at a very rapid pace, for Weir has cut her text to a minimum. The orchestral forces in the central act are greatly reduced and the sound is starkly oriental, while the orchestral writing in the outer acts is vivid and striking. Weir makes use of minimalist techniques, and her thematic economy and precision illuminate the situation on stage.

Weir believes that the labels "minimalist" and "eclectic" certainly capture some aspects of her work, although she believes the former is a loaded word these days. She does not rule out any musical device and sees each piece as a fresh beginning. Her work is a diary of what happens to her, and "should I meet people I want to work with, I will. I don't like to get too scheduled up too long in advance, because you change."[9]

### NOTES

1. Ernest Chapman, "The Macnaghten Concerts," *Composer* (Spring 1976): 13–18.

2. Nicola LeFanu, "Master Musician: An Impregnable Taboo?" *Contact* 31 (Autumn 1987):4–8.

3. Elisabeth Lutyens, *A Goldfish Bowl* (London: Cassell and Co., Ltd., 1972), p. 9.

4. Elisabeth Lutyens, unpublished article, July 2, 1971.
5. Elizabeth Maconchy, "A Composer Speaks," *Composer* 42 (Winter 1971–72):28. All thirteen quartets have been recorded by Unicorn Kanchana, under the supervision of the composer.
6. Donald L. Hixon, *Thea Musgrave—A Bio-Bibliography* (Westport, CT: Greenwood Press, 1984), p. 3.
7. Musgrave notes in the score: "Rollo was an imaginary character invented by Ives and represented the Victorian Conservative; 'one of those white-livered weaklings,' unable to stand any dissonance."
8. Nicola LeFanu, interview with Catherine Roma, London, England, February 27, 1989.
9. Judith Weir, interview with Catherine Roma, London, March 8, 1989.

### SUGGESTIONS FOR FURTHER READING

Baxter, Timothy. "Priaulx Rainier: A Study of Her Musical Style." *Composer* 60 (1977):19–26.
———. "Priaulx Rainier." *Composer* 76–77 (Summer–Winter 1982):21–29.
Boyd, Malcolm. *Grace Williams*. N.p.: University of Wales Press, 1980.
Bradshaw, Susan. "The Music of Elisabeth Lutyens." *Musical Times* 112 (1971):563–66.
———. "Thea Musgrave." *Musical Times* 104 (1963):866–68.
Carner, Mosco. "Phyllis Tate." *Musical Times* 105 (1964):20–21.
Dreyer, Martin. "Judith Weir, Composer: A Talent to Amuse." *Musical Times* 122 (1981):593–96.
East, Leslie. "The Problem of Communication—Two Solutions: Thea Musgrave and Gordon Crosse." In *British Music Now,* edited by L. Foreman. London: P. Elek, 1975. Pp. 19–31.
Kay, Norman. "Phyllis Tate." *Musical Times* 116 (1975):429–30.
Macnaghten, Anne. "Elizabeth Maconchy." *Musical Times* 96 (1955):298–302.
Opie, June. *Priaulx Rainier: A Pictorial Biography*. Penzance: Alison Hodge, 1988.
Pendle, Karin. "Thea Musgrave: The Singer and the Song." *Journal of the National Association of Teachers of Singing* 43/2 (November–December 1986):5–8, 13.
Roma, Catherine. "The Choral Music of Twentieth-Century Composers Elisabeth Lutyens, Elizabeth Maconchy, and Thea Musgrave." D.M.A. thesis, University of Cincinnati, 1989. Westport, CT: Greenwood Press, forthcoming.
Routh, Francis. *Contemporary British Music*. London: Macdonald & Co., 1972.
Saxon, Robert. "Elisabeth Lutyens at 75." *Musical Times* 122 (1981):368–69.

# IX.
# Composers of Modern Europe, Australia, and New Zealand

*Robert Zierolf*

Compared with Great Britain and the United States, continental Europe in the twentieth century has in many ways been slower to include women in music. Relatively fewer women hold posts in symphony orchestras, and many otherwise reputable music schools in Germany and Italy enroll no women composition students. Sociopolitical reasons for this situation include wars, which occupied the time and attention of leaders inside and outside of government—time and attention that without war might have led to more humanistic endeavors; the musical traditions and accumulated symphonic and operatic mainstream repertoires of Germany and Italy, repertoires and networks built almost exclusively by men as composers and music directors; and the public prominence of so many men and so few women in the other arts. The United States and Great Britain were different in important ways—the United States because it suffered no armed conflict on its own soil and had no long-standing musical traditions or repertoires; Great Britain because, before the twentieth century, its musical tradition was meager compared with those of Germany, Italy, or France and because the head of state in England had often been a woman.

One must also consider the effects of war, politics, and other social issues on the production of European artists, male and female. Some composers choose, as much as is feasible, isolation from society; others choose immersion in social issues as an avenue to creativity. For many in the twentieth century it has been impossible to ignore the conditions of life that intrude upon the solitude necessary for musical composition. Armed conflict, air raids, forced marches, ideological clashes, incarceration, martial law, repressive bureaucracies, censorship, and economic chaos and deprivation have been all too frequent in European society (both Eastern and Western, but especially the former) in the twentieth century. As we approach the end of the millennium, a more humanistic life seems possible even in the most troubled areas. But the damage done to, and interruption of, careers is irreparable.

A solution for some was to emigrate, temporarily or permanently, to the United States. Nadia Boulanger and Germaine Tailleferre spent some of the World War II years in America; both returned to France to resume their careers. Before her journey, Boulanger had donated her conducting and performing talents to the French Relief Fund. Betsy Jolas, a teen-ager at the beginning of the war, completed high school and undergraduate degrees in the United States before returning to France for further study at the Paris Conservatoire. People in the United States were beneficiaries of these temporary relocations in that these musicians' talents could be observed at close range. Close personal and artistic associations were formed, associations that would otherwise have been unlikely. These three Frenchwomen are examples of those who chose to leave strife for saner, safer situations, however temporary. Others chose to stay through the tough times, either because they lacked the money or the connections necessary for emigration, or because loyalty and duty made leaving their countries an insurmountable moral issue.

Whatever the reasons, Grazyna Bacewicz chose to stay in Poland during the war despite dangers and hardships endemic to her native country. It was not that she lacked contacts elsewhere, having just returned from Paris as the war broke out. (It was just as well; Paris would soon become relatively inhospitable, else Boulanger, Jolas, and Tailleferre would not have left.) Bacewicz's performing and composing were curtailed during the war, and her creative efforts were less extensive than would have been the case if the war had not intervened.

So why stay? Personal, individual considerations are always to the point and relevant here. But in general, Eastern and Central Europeans are more likely than Western Europeans to remain in their homelands in stressful times. It may be geography, history, language, or something less tangible, but whatever the reason their allegiance remains more definitive than pragmatic.

Until recently, political and personal restrictions on the people of Europe have been considerably more severe in the East than in the West; attempts to attenuate artistic expression have been likewise more repressive in the Eastern bloc. Nevertheless, few composers have chosen to leave. Some have been able to maintain dual residences or at least places to hang their hats in both East and West (Marta Ptaszynska, for example), so for them the repressive atmosphere is ameliorated somewhat by relative freedom in the United States. Even those for whom communism is the preferred ideology found a tremendous difference when emerging from behind the Iron Curtain; communism in Italy, for example, is quite different from that which formerly dominated Poland. Social and political issues are not simply stratified; they are multidimensional in general and with specific references to creativity and artistic expression.

Finally, feminism is an additional ingredient in all social and political situations, East and West. Women's roles, in general, and as composers, in particular, are not defined by politics alone, but also by cultural history and attitudes and myriad other factors. In Poland, for example, artificial barriers (meaning those based on gender) for women seem to have all but disappeared, while in much of continental Europe they frequently remain formidable, if muted. This too is changing, not rapidly enough, but changing nonetheless. It is clear that as more of women's music is being (re)discovered (for instance, Bacewicz's late works or Gubaidulina's strikingly original compositions), some will enter the repertoire on purely musical merits. The pedantic, mannerist pieces will find their rightful place in oblivion; the worthwhile will enrich the repertoire in proportion to their worth.

## FRANCE

Women in French arts have been associated with courts and elite society in ways different from their other European counterparts. Though few were actually titular heads of government, their influence on and participation in cultural affairs has been exemplary. Elisabeth-Claude Jacquet de la Guerre was favored by Louis XIV, as is evident by the privileges she enjoyed and the music she composed during his reign. From the Enlightenment through Chopin's days in Paris, salons headed by wealthy, socially prominent women played a leading role in musical activity.[1] Many of these learned women were themselves performers and composers, although few were recognized for their musicianship outside their intimate circles, and fewer still had their music published.

### Nadia Boulanger

Though she began her career as a composer, in the mid-1920s Nadia Boulanger (1887–1979) decided to turn from composition to teaching, and the world is doubtless the better for this decision. An accomplished conductor[2] and organist, she became famous for uncompromising standards and the ability to nurture creativity in composers as stylistically diverse as Elliott Carter, Aaron Copland, Thea Musgrave, and Philip Glass. Her command of traditional subjects—harmony, counterpoint, form—was never the impediment to learning and teaching modern music that plagued so many of her colleagues at the Paris Conservatoire and elsewhere. Her suspicion of atonal music—"There are dangers in atonal music. There is nothing to surprise one"[3]—did not extend to all. She claimed that "Stravinsky's use of twelve-tone elements in the *Canticum Sacrum* is not an experiment. It is an accomplishment."[4] Her humanistic attitude toward life and art, combined with enormous talent, directly inspired hundreds of students and thousands more through her legacy. Her composition classes often included extraordinary numbers of women, although it is curious that none became as well known as her most successful male students. Boulanger's eyes and ears for talent were acute, and her ability to encourage compositional ability in her women students was one of the most valuable, if most overlooked, attributes of her long service to the arts. For this as well as for many other reasons, one cannot overestimate Nadia Boulanger's contribution to twentieth-century music.

Given the long history of distinguished musicians in her family, Boulanger's musical talent might be seen as a birthright. Most of this lineage was Parisian, going as far back as her grandparents Frédéric and Marie-Julie Hallinger, both prize-winners during their student days at the Conservatoire. Her father, Henri-Alexandre-Ernest Boulanger, also attended the Conservatoire, where his winning of the Grand Prix de Rome supported his travels to Rome and Florence. After his return to Paris, Boulanger composed operas while teaching at the Conservatoire. There he met the talented eighteen-year-old Russian singer Raissa Mychetskaya, whom he married when he was sixty-two; Nadia was born ten years later.

A fluent talent and a penchant for work were evident early: by the age of sixteen Nadia had won every prize available at the Conservatoire. Composition came easily; two years after her first composition, *La Lettre de mort* (1906), she won second place in the Prix de Rome competition with *Sirène*. Composition study with Gabriel Fauré, Louis Vierne, Charles Marie Widor, and others was combined with organ lessons. She excelled in the latter as well as in classroom subjects, and she succeeded the brilliant Fauré as organist at the Madeleine Church after his death in 1924. By this time Boulanger had decided to forego composition. Despite some success and some prominent performances, she believed: "If there is anything of which I am very sure, it is that my music is useless."[5] Whether this would have been true is impossible to ascertain; but what is sure is that Boulanger would have needed one masterpiece after another even to approach the brilliant career she enjoyed as a pedagogue.

In the early 1920s Boulanger not only began a career as an organist but also began her long tenure at the American School at Fontainebleau and, often concurrently, professorships at the Paris Conservatoire and the École Normale. Indefatigable, she combined performance, touring, and writing criticism with teaching. From 1921, her first year at Fontainebleau, she attracted an international class; but it was the talented young Americans who made her reputation so quickly. George Antheil, Aaron Copland, Roy Harris, Walter Piston, and Virgil Thomson studied with her in the 1920s and, along with Walter Damrosch, brought their enthusiasm for her musicianship back to the United States.

By the late 1930s Boulanger was conducting major orchestras in important performances. In 1937 she conducted the Royal Philharmonic in London; in 1939 the Boston Symphony, the New York Philharmonic, and the Philadelphia Orchestra. She was probably the first woman to conduct these distinguished ensembles, but she seems not to have paid much attention to that fact but instead made music with her usual magnificent ease. Like many others, Boulanger spent some of the war years in the United States, conducting, performing, and teaching at Juilliard and other prestigious institutions. Her associations were with the best of the times: Walter Damrosch, Leopold Stokowski, Serge Koussevitzky, Darius Milhaud (then at Mills College), and Igor Stravinsky most of all. Her reputation with Americans had been made in Paris in the 1920s; it was solidified and extended in the United States in the 1930s and 1940s.

Perhaps because she was not a composer in her later years, or perhaps because she was not flamboyant or eccentric, Boulanger was more highly regarded by composers outside of France than by those in her native country. Rosters of students show far fewer French than other nationalities, a curious fact given the nationalistic enrollment policies of the Paris Conservatoire. It can be fairly said that the American School at Fontainebleau was where she ruled; in Paris she was overshadowed first by Fauré and Ravel, then by Olivier Messiaen and Pierre Boulez. It probably did not help that Boulanger promoted American music, especially that composed by former students, but it seems also that many were jealous of her reputation and talents. In addition, her skepticism of dodecaphonic technique was at odds with the postwar fervor for Schoenberg and Webern as promoted by Boulez and René Leibowitz; twelve-tone technique had a brief but potent hold on young French composers. Boulanger was exegetical in her thinking about all music, believing that thorough study was the only way to proper criticism. In the end, she was no different with regard to serialism.

Whatever the demands of her profession, Boulanger frequently made time for worthy social causes. With her sister, Lili, she worked for government and private supporters during World War I; while in Paris during World War II she performed and conducted benefit concerts for the French Relief Fund. She was active in the French League of Women's Rights and gave benefit performances for this and similar organizations. Her favorite cause was her sister's music, the preservation and dissemination of which was one of her favorite activities. From the early 1950s until her death in 1979, Boulanger devoted herself primarily to teaching at Fontainebleau and at the Paris Conservatoire. She accepted an amazing diversity of talent and held seminars in major music centers throughout Europe. She was honored and decorated in public and private by the leading musicians of the 1970s, and her reputation as the greatest composition teacher of the twentieth century—perhaps of any century—is unassailable.

## *Germaine Tailleferre*

Germaine Tailleferre (1892–1983) was the only woman in Les Six[6] and one of its most conservative members. The individuals in this famous group actually had little in common aesthetically; their work covered the gamut from Poulenc's pop-influenced style to Milhaud's exoticism to Tailleferre's classicistic conservatism. Over her father's objections but encouraged by her mother, Tailleferre entered the Paris Conservatoire in 1904 and remained there until 1915, winning several prizes for her prowess in harmony, solfege, counterpoint, and accompanying. After meeting Satie, she came into contact with the other young composers under his influence—George Auric and Darius Milhaud, with whom she studied briefly—and eventually with the others who constituted the group first labeled "Les Nouveaux Jeunes" by Satie and eventually "Les Six" by the critic Henri Collet, who was attempting to establish a corollary to the Russian Five. Never as unified musically as the Five, Les Six sought instead a new mode of expression in opposition to Wagnerian Romanticism, which was detested by most French musicians, and also in reaction to the Impressionism of Debussy. Satie was not someone to be emulated aesthetically as much as philosophically; his purposeful iconoclasm had much general but little direct influence on the music of Les Six. As a group they produced an album of individual piano pieces and one collaborative score (without Durey), the incidental music for Jean Cocteau's *Les Mariés de la Tour Eiffel*. For personal, musical, and sociological reasons the group ceased to exist after a couple of years, although several maintained contact and supported one another's efforts even as each composer took a separate musical direction.

Tailleferre's compositions attracted several important performers in Paris in the 1920s and 30s. Alfred Cortot played her piano music, including the Concertino in D, at concerts in London. Ravel was influential as Tailleferre's orchestration teacher and for his clarity of form and precise use of musical materials. Tailleferre's *Sicilienne* for piano (1928) is a neoclassical piece stylistically similar to Ravel's *Tombeau de Couperin*. Her Violin Sonata (1921, published in 1923; see HAMW, pp. 262–67 for the first movement), Ballade for piano and orchestra (1926), String Quartet (1918) and other chamber music, *Six French Chansons* and other songs, film scores, and music for the stage, including operas and ballets, were performed with some frequency.

Extended tertian sonorities, with mild excursions into polytonality, were often attractive to Tailleferre, but she experimented only briefly with progressive techniques such as serialism. Her craft is evident throughout her works, and their natural musicianship and evidence of solid, traditional training at the Conservatoire became her hallmarks. Musicality and individualism are less evident than are the secure control of form and articulation of events. Music by Tailleferre sounds mild by comparison with that of her contemporaries, and she preferred neoclassicism to the more radical experiments of her day. Self-deprecating and uninterested in the avant-garde after the demise of Les Six, she remained the French classicist even in her later years.

Except for the war years, when she resided in the United States, Tailleferre lived in France, finding employment as an accompanist, teaching privately, and, from 1970 to 1972, at the Schola Cantorum. She composed a large number of pieces, the most noteworthy being the short *Pastorale* for flute and piano and the Concertino for harp (ca. 1926, published in 1928). She died on November 7, 1983, the last of Les Six to be laid to rest.

## Claude Arrieu

Claude Arrieu (given name, Louise Marie Simon; b. 1903) is one of the most prolific French composers of the twentieth century. Her more than 200 compositions include both sacred and secular music and range from solo pieces, chamber music, vocal music, and instrumental works to opera and incidental music. Arrieu composes in classical forms—sonata, concerto, suite, symphony—as well as in programmatic and modern idioms. In general, her style is best described as personal neoclassicism. She learned much from the French neoclassic tradition prevalent during her formative years, but her music is not so much reminiscent of Ravel or Poulenc as it is a corollary to their styles.

Along with most other well-known composers of her generation, Arrieu studied at the Paris Conservatoire. Even as a student she won several important prizes in composition; eventually she was named to the prestigious Legion of Honor. In 1946 she began a long relationship with French radio and television studios, and she was one of the first composers to work with Pierre Schaeffer at Radiodiffusion français. Schaeffer is usually credited with inventing *musique concrète,* an early phase of electronic music in which acoustic sounds are manipulated electronically. Arrieu quickly lost interest in this experimental music, composing but one piece, *Fantastique lyrique* for *ondes Martenot* (1959), as her contribution to the electronic genre. Nevertheless, the studio experience was ultimately valuable as an apprenticeship for composing media scores. At least thirty film scores and more than forty radio scores attest to Arrieu's interest in and facility with the media. The most widely recognized is the score for the radio drama *Frédéric Général,* which won the Italia Prize in 1949, the year of its composition. Her many commissions, most notably the one from the French government for the opera *Les deux rendezvous* (1947), suggest a high degree of respect for Arrieu as a composer.

## Betsy Jolas

Betsy Jolas (b. 1926) has combined composition with simultaneous careers as conductor, editor, and writer. She is an excellent example of the French-American connection in twentieth-century music, but in ways different from those of Nadia Boulanger and Germaine Tailleferre. Born in France to American parents, Jolas moved to New York City with her family at the outbreak of World War II. She completed high school and college in the United States, earning a Bachelor of Arts from Bennington College before returning to France in 1948. She attended the Paris Conservatoire and studied composition with Milhaud and Messiaen, subsequently becoming the latter's assistant. She has since resided in France, and the titles of her pieces indicate her French leanings. Currently on the faculty at Fontainebleau, she is greatly admired for her teaching and musicianship. The prizes she has received for conducting and composing have been rewarding, and her multidimensional career has brought much acclaim, although less than had she concentrated on only one activity. Jolas writes for traditional as well as somewhat unusual ensembles, an example of the latter being *Quatuor II* (1964) for singer and string trio. Her eclectic techniques of composition range from Renaissance-style polyphony to atonality and aleatory music.

France is exceptionally rich with practicing women composers.[7] Many are also performers, conductors, critics, and teachers, reflecting the broad training emphasized at the Conservatoire. Their work runs the gamut from traditional music to the avant-garde, from Anne Marie Mimet's saxophone pieces (French composers have produced more repertoire for this instrument than have composers of any other nationality) to the *ondes Martenot* compositions of Yvonne Loriod and the early electronic works by Mariana Scriabin (daughter of the Russian composer Alexander Scriabin).

## Germany

Lists and other sources of information on twentieth-century German women composers indicate that they are less well represented both quantitatively and qualitatively than those of many other Western nations. None has achieved the status of a Lili Boulanger, a Thea Musgrave, a Marta Ptaszynska, or a Joan Tower. It is difficult to ascertain the reason for this unhappy situation, one that is clearly at odds with the relative success of some nineteenth-century German women as well as with the long and distinguished musical tradition Germany has enjoyed since the Middle Ages.

Although one may argue the point, it seems that sexist prejudice in the performing and other arts is still more pervasive in Germany than in similarly developed countries, and in any case more prevalent than it ought to be. For example, a tremendous row ensued when the late Herbert von Karajan, music director of the Berlin Philharmonic, chose a woman clarinetist for the orchestra. Although she was clearly the best player to audition, her gender was unacceptable to many members of the orchestra. (In general, European orchestras hire fewer women than do American orchestras.) Karajan threatened to cancel concerts and lucrative recording sessions until the woman was hired, but she did not take the job after all.

Hitler's agenda and its inhuman ramifications presented almost no opportunities for women in the arts. First of all, progressive new music was banned during his rule, and few earlier twentieth-century women had become successful anyway. After World War II Darmstadt, the most important center for progressive music and musical experimentation in Germany, was run and populated predominantly by men, with little attempt to include women composers and theorists in the resurrection of modern music. Even today, the students enrolled in composition programs in German music schools are overwhelmingly male.

As is almost always the case, a few women have managed to invade the compositional arena, often through their own performance skills or private settings. Born in Austria, Grete von Zieritz (b. 1899) studied piano and composition in Graz before honing those skills in Berlin. After winning the Mendelssohn Prize in 1928, von Zieritz toured as a pianist and taught at music schools in Germany and Austria. Approximately half of her large output is vocal—choral or solo; the other half is orchestral or chamber music. Her *Japanische Lieder* are particularly interesting, colorful songs; other songs are based on Dutch, German, Portuguese, or Spanish texts. In 1958 von Zieritz was awarded a government prize for composition, the first woman of her country ever recognized for this sort of creativity.

Ilse Fromm-Michaels (1888–1986) was a virtuoso pianist with a passion for Mozart, as is evident by the more than twenty cadenzas she composed for Mozart's concertos. Much less prolific than von Zieritz, Fromm-Michaels composed a modest amount of music and taught piano at the Musikhochschule in her native Hamburg. Ruth Zechlin (b. 1926) is also a keyboardist and conductor; her compositions have won the Goethe Prize, the Hanns Eisler Prize, and the German Democratic Republic Arts Prize. Zechlin has taught piano and composition in Berlin and Leipzig. Philippina Schick (1893–1970) composed several songs, sonatas, and other pieces in traditional forms. She taught music theory and English at the University of Munich and wrote books on harmony and counterpoint. As founder of the German and Austrian women composers' alliance (GEDOK), Schick provided impetus for women's music in countries that all but ignored and discouraged compositional efforts by women.

More recently, German composers and performers have banded together in an attempt to promote women's music on an international level. In 1978 the Internationalen Arbeitskreis Frau und Musik was founded by composers Barbara Heller and Siegrid Ernst and church musician and conductor Elke Mascha Blankenburg. Frau und Musik, which draws its membership from many European countries, has since sponsored international festivals for the performance of women's music of past and present generations. It has also backed the publication of helpful guides to women's music, prepared under the direction of Antje Olivier and Karin Weingartz-Perschel.[8] In 1981 Frau und Musik began an international women's music archive in Düsseldorf for scores and recordings. Cofounders Heller (b. 1936) and Ernst (b. 1929) exemplify their generation's energetic advocacy of new music. Ernst, whose output concentrates on instrumental music, studied with Stockhausen and Ligeti in Darmstadt and currently teaches at the Bremen Conservatory, where she has founded a Studio for New Music. Heller, also a pianist, is well known as a performer of music by women and as the organizer of the first large-scale women's music festival in Germany (1980, Bonn and Cologne). Of the younger generation, Rumanian-born Adriana Hölszky (b. 1953) has become one of the most performed German woman composers and has received recognition throughout Europe. Her output is particularly strong in chamber music for instrumental ensemble and for solo voice with one or more instruments.

## POLAND

For centuries beset by war, civil strife, and borders changed forcibly by powerful external forces, Poland remains a country with a vibrant artistic presence in the international community. Polish music has often been the leading edge of progressive trends, and even in the repressive political climate and economic deprivation of the past few decades, Poles remain a people with a great love of music. Advanced electronic music facilities are available, and composers' organizations support their members as best they can. Today, opportunities for women in Poland are better than for their counterparts in many Western European countries. Their music is heard frequently at the Warsaw Autumn Festivals and in other venues. Styles and compositional procedures range from neoclassic to avant-garde, but on the whole they are more progressive than reactionary.

This relatively happy situation was not always the case. Wanda Landowska (1879–1959) left Warsaw in the early 1920s for Western Europe and the United States, where she lived for the remainder of her life. She was the most highly acclaimed harpsichordist of her generation, with recordings of much of Bach's keyboard music to her credit. Prominent composers, including Poulenc, composed especially for her, and she was in constant demand as a performer and lecturer. However, her compositions remain largely in obscurity. Her Serenade for Strings and Bourrées d'Auvergne are particularly worthy of rediscovery.

### Grazyna Bacewicz

Grazyna Bacewicz (1909–69) was for a time better known as a violinist than as a composer, and she performed regularly into the 1950s. Her musical training (she also studied philosophy very seriously) always included equal parts of composition and performance. Even after her undergraduate years in Warsaw, Bacewicz continued both disciplines at a very high level, studying composition with Boulanger and violin with Carl Flesch, a famous pedagogue and author of method books on violin playing. From the early 1940s through the mid-1950s, Bacewicz performed solos with major orchestras and was a frequent judge of major violin competitions, including the Wieniawski International in Poland. She served for two years as concertmaster of the Polish Radio Orchestra. Also an accomplished pianist, she played the premieres of several of her compositions, including the Second Sonata.

It was probably her ability as a violinist that led Bacewicz to compose so much for strings. Seven string quartets, two piano quintets, and five violin sonatas constitute the bulk of her chamber music; four symphonies, several concertos, other orchestral music, and choral pieces with orchestral accompaniment are the heart of her large works. *Music for Strings, Trumpets, and Percussion* (1958) is one of several prize-winning compositions and is one of her most frequently heard works in Europe.

Clearly delineated structures are a prominent feature of all of Bacewicz's scores, regardless of style or medium. Her music through the early 1950s is tonal to varying degrees and in many ways has been considered to be her strongest music. Her experiments with atonality and other modern idioms have met with less critical success. But a reappraisal of these notions is definitely in order. The quartal harmony in the last movement, Toccata, of her Sonata II for piano (1953; see HAMW, pp. 300–18) sounds confident in context, if a bit derivative of Bartók and Hindemith. The opening of the third movement of her String Quartet No. 7 exhibits quartal harmony less pervasively, and the first movement contains some dodecaphonic sections in a larger tonal setting. This quartet and other late works are more difficult to perform and comprehend than her earlier, neoclassical compositions. But normal growth, unfettered by external, nonmusical influences, was not Bacewicz's lot. This unusual dichotomy of style and abrupt changes coming late in her creative life may be explained by the social and political difficulties that Bacewicz, along with most other Europeans, encountered during World War II, obstacles that continued in Eastern and Central Europe long after the war.

Bacewicz returned to Warsaw from Paris at the outbreak of World War II. She and her family left the city immediately, taking refuge in rural areas and smaller cities. Although her music making did not stop completely, survival amid the horrors of war interrupted her creative efforts to an appreciable extent. Returning to Warsaw after the war, she found the city in rubble and artistic organizations in disarray. It was soon obvious that rebuilding would be supervised by Soviet bureaucrats and the military, and that the arts would come under close supervision. This was to be true of all Soviet bloc countries, and it is the reason that composers such as Bartók and Ligeti left Central Europe for the relative freedom of Western Europe and the United States. Composers of music considered by authorities as too "modern" (read dissonant, atonal, discontinuous) were labeled "formalist" and were often harshly censured. Much progressive new music was banned from public performance, as it had been by Hitler during the war, and what little was heard in private settings lacked either adequate performance or, worse, a context for critical evaluation. Polish musicians banded together to promote composition and dissemination of new ideas, and these led eventually to magnificent festivals such as the Warsaw Autumn. But the youthful energy of an international Darmstadt, for example, was not available to Poles.

Bacewicz composed prolifically, but it is a mistake to label her progressive music reactionary when in fact she came late to others' new musical styles and absorbed whatever she found valuable after it was considered passé by those who had no such disadvantage. In other words, it is quite likely that Bacewicz would have contemplated atonality and some other, newer idioms much sooner had she been able to avoid the suffocating political situation. Serious analytical study and repeated quality performances will show that Bacewicz was in fact progressive in an intuitive, contemplative sense. Bacewicz's later music is vigorous, well crafted, and confident, and it deserves study by specialists. It might very well supplant or add to her better-known earlier pieces and bring her more to the forefront of mid-century composition.

## Marta Ptaszynska

Marta Ptaszynska (b. 1943) is one of three living Poles, the others being Witold Lutoslawski and Krzystof Penderecki, whose music is regularly performed and studied throughout the world. Ptaszynska is a multitalented woman. An accomplished percussionist, she often plays her own or others' percussion pieces. Although she specializes in contemporary techniques, she has been a regular member of the Warsaw Philharmonic percussion section.

After study at the Warsaw Conservatory and in Poznan, Ptaszynska studied with Nadia Boulanger in Paris and with Donald Erb at the Cleveland Institute of Music, where she also earned an Artist Diploma in percussion. Her skill as a performer led to many compositions being written especially for her. She appears frequently as a featured artist, and is repre-

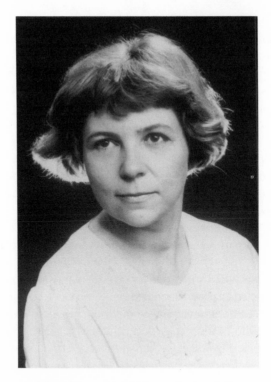

Marta Ptaszynska. Photo courtesy of the composer.

sented as a composer at international concerts and festivals, including the World Music Days of the International Society for Contemporary Music, the Aspen Music Festival, and, of course, the Warsaw Autumn. Since the early 1970s Ptaszynska has lived both in Poland and abroad, with a current residence in Pennsylvania. Often sought as a composer-in-residence, she has spent all or substantial parts of years on the faculties of Bennington College, the Berkeley and Santa Barbara campuses of the University of California, and Indiana University. Guest lectures at many other American and European universities and conservatories, combined with professional engagements, have brought her solidly into the musical mainstream.

The list of Ptaszynska's published works is impressive for the number and breadth of genres, but even more impressive is the list of solo and chamber performers and large ensembles that regularly program her pieces. (The Cleveland Orchestra and the Cincinnati Symphony Orchestra are exemplary of the latter category.) Among her more popular works are Concerto for Marimba (1985), Concerto for Percussion and Orchestra

(1974), and *Moon Flowers* for cello and piano (1986), dedicated to the Challenger astronauts who perished in the explosion. Her opera *Oscar of Alva* (1972), originally written for television, can also be performed live and was featured at the 1989 Salzburg Festival. Many of her chamber works include percussion. The large number of pieces for children are especially welcome at a time when little worthwhile contemporary music is being written for young people.

Style is a predominant feature of her music, regardless of medium. Not that Ptaszynska has only one style—in fact, her music exhibits a multiplicity of styles when viewed as a whole—but that her music is always engaging, provocative, and genuinely personal. Sonic ramifications are always a surface element to be considered consciously. At various times she has embraced such diversities as light projections to accompany music, oriental art and Zen philosophy, and painting techniques (as well as actual paintings) by a wide variety of contemporary artists. She eschews modernity for its own sake, preferring to follow her instincts. For the initiate, there is no mistaking her music for anyone else's, and no semblance of an attempt to take measure of even the best of her contemporaries' work. She explains:

> The most outstanding and best works of present-day music aren't and weren't in their time necessarily "supermodern"; on the contrary, they have often been written in a technique which we would call outright traditional. What, however, makes them stand out from among hundreds of other compositions are their lasting aesthetic values which won't allow them to be wiped off from the memory of the following generations quite regardless of their musical language. In any case the language of music of present-day composers will be no longer modern in a few hundred years from now, and only lasting and indisputable aesthetic values of their music will decide whether they will be performed, just so as e.g. the Viennese classics are performed today.[9]

Ptaszynska's music will doubtless be performed for many years to come.

Women composers in Poland now have the same opportunities for success as men do, and their music is heard frequently in excellent settings by competent performers. Ptaszynska is the foremost but by no means the only representative Polish woman. Bernadetta Matuszcak (b. 1937) studied with Nadia Boulanger and has won several important prizes. She frequently includes a reciting voice in a variety of media, and her mostly vocal music includes settings of texts by a broad array of writers, including Gogol, Rilke, Shakespeare, Tagore, and ancient anonymous authors. In contast, Krystyna Moszumanska-Nazar (b. 1924) writes mostly instrumental music. She teaches at the State College of Music in Cracow. It would seem that as the hope for a better life for all Poles becomes a reality, women are poised to lead the necessary teaching, performing, and composition activities. Even if negative political and social circumstances should prevail, the musical endeavors of Polish women have already created a legacy for all who follow to emulate.

## Soviet and Eastern European Composers

Composers in the Soviet Union have experiences vastly different from those of their Western counterparts. From the revolutions in the first decades of the twentieth century, through the Stalin era, World War II, and the Cold War, tribulations unimaginable to most Westerners have placed before them burdens as well as unique opportunities. For many years, what was published and performed was controlled by the Soviet Composers Union, with style and taste often arbitrated by lesser talents, even nonmusicians. Information on new music and composers, especially those censored as "formalist" for their progressive or avant-garde works, was next to impossible for outsiders to obtain. Much modern music, including everything by Bartók, Hindemith, and the Second Viennese School, was banned during the 1930s and 40s. The first serial piece by a Soviet composer was Andrei Volkonsky's *Musica stricta* (1956); composers were strongly urged to compose music for the "people" under the guidelines of socialist realism. Under Gorbachev, exchange of information, composers, and performers has for the first time allowed an international view of music from a group of countries, both ethnic Russian and other, with long, colorful musical heritages. Women composers are few but are increasing in number.

One Soviet woman, Sofia Gubaidulina (b. 1931), stands as the leader, at least with respect to the international scene, and her music is remarkable for its stunning originality. The progress of her style extends from early tonal pieces (most Soviet composers and their immediate predecessors wrote in a tonal style as students, before moving on to more progressive idioms, as can be seen by the first symphonies by Prokofiev, Shostakovich, and Stravinsky) to atonality (serial and free) to electronic music to eclecticism. A strong spiritual element is evident in Gubaidulina's music whatever its style or idiom. Gubaidulina achieves a powerful effect through the utterances of humans manifest in the cries, screams, whispers, and other nonmusical inclusions in her sonic palette. Pieces receiving important performances and praise include *Quattro* for brass ensemble; *Perception* for string sextet and male and female singers; a violin concerto, *Offertorium; De Profundis,* a performance-art piece for solo accordion; and two string quartets. The Kronos and Muir quartets play her music, and the Boston Symphony has recorded *Offertorium.* Surely *glasnost* and Western curiosity about Soviet music and life will provide significant opportunities for Gubaidulina's music to be heard by a large audience. Some other music by Soviet women is worth noting: a clarinet sonata by Elena Firsova and songs by Lesia Dychko, Margarita Ivanova Kuss, and Gaziza Zhulanova.

A scarcity of scores, recordings, and live performances has also inhibited our ability to describe and evaluate women's musical activities in Eastern Europe. Recordings suggest that Romania's Violeta Dinescu (b. 1953) can be counted as a major young talent. Born in Bucharest, she began winning composition prizes while still a student at the conservatory there. Though she has written a great deal of chamber music, her output also features music in many other genres, including opera and ballet. Her airy textures and her feeling for subtle shifts of instrumental color are distinctive features of her style. The fact that she has lived in Germany since 1983 undoubtedly has contributed to her ability to make herself and her music known.

Numerous other Eastern European women boast repertoire lists that invite further attention now that many of their homelands are opening their doors to the West: Hungary's Erzsébet Szönyi (b. 1924), for instance, and Czech composers Elena Petrova (b. 1929) and Ivana Ludová (b. 1941). Among the older generation, Yugoslavia's Ivana Lang-Beck (1912–83) and Bulgaria's Jivka Klinkova (b. 1924) will still be new voices to Western ears.

## AUSTRALIA AND NEW ZEALAND

Australia is a fascinating country in many ways: geographically closer to Asia than to Europe, yet largely British in manners and culture; home to one of the most interesting indigenous populations anywhere, but one only recently acknowledged and accommodated in all its richness; location of great modern cities, yet possessing some of the most desolate, unpopulated, vast expanses of open land on this planet.

Australia's art world is similarly dichotomous. Development of conditions conducive to concert life did not take place in Australia until the latter half of the nineteenth century. (In this, Australia and the United States are somewhat comparable.) European music, primarily English, was programed sporadically, and schools of music patterned after British models opened in the few major cities. In the 1890s, two songs for women's chorus by a Miss Woolley from Sydney were published (by Novello) and performed; and about the same time Mona McBurney's *The Dalmatians* was heard, the first opera by a woman to be performed in Australia. In the second half of the twentieth century a semblance of what might be called

Australian music has developed, with several composers enjoying national and international reputations. However, much instructional material in music is still very British, and many composers, even the younger ones, still travel to London for advanced musical studies.

One of Australia's most eminent composers, Peggy Glanville-Hicks (1912–90) exemplifies these eclecticisms. She traveled widely and lived in Europe and the United States. Studies with Vaughan Williams at the Royal College of Music in London, with Egon Wellesz in Vienna, and with Nadia Boulanger in Paris provided a broad background for her fertile musical imagination. Eastern Mediterranean culture was a further, if less noticeable, influence. The widely discussed opera *The Transposed Heads* (1953) is indicative of Glanville-Hicks's unique style, and a large number of other pieces in a variety of genres have established her international stature. More than any other composer, Glanville-Hicks epitomizes the unique culture and world vision that is Australia.

Despite a very different sort of musicality and life style, Margaret Sutherland (1897–1984) shares with Glanville-Hicks some elements in education. After attending the Albert Street Consortium in Melbourne, Sutherland won scholarships to study with Sir Arnold Bax in London. After a brief period in Vienna, she returned to Melbourne determined to enhance dramatically the quality of Australian concert music and to build the facilities and administrative apparatus necessary for performance at an international level. She succeeded, as is evident by the well-appointed arts complex on the banks of the Yarra River. The Spoleto Festival is but one of many major international arts attractions to make use of this facility. In addition, Sutherland maintained an active teaching schedule and a career as a chamber music pianist. In recognition for her eminence in Melbourne's cultural life, she was awarded an honorary doctorate from the University of Melbourne in 1969.

Sutherland's best music is post-tonal, with synthetic scales, polytonality, and quartal harmony employed in a personal, engaging style. Sophisticated imitative counterpoint occurs in her two string quartets; the second, entitled *Discussion* (1954), is interesting for its modern techniques in an accessible language.

Dulcie Holland and Miriam Hyde attended Australian music schools, then studied further at the Royal College of Music in London. Holland studied composition with John Ireland, Hyde with Gordon Jacob. Both women had some success in England. Holland won several prestigious prizes, including the Cobbett Prize for Chamber Music; Hyde performed the solo role in her piano concertos with the BBC and London Philharmonic orchestras. Miriam Eagles, a pianist and composer who also studied in

London; Mirrie Solomon Hill, composer of songs and piano music and teacher of theory and piano at the New South Wales Conservatorium; Esther Rofe, composer of the operetta *Magarzea;* and Helen Gifford also contributed much to the repertoire of music by Australian women.

Most composers traveled to London for advanced study, then returned to Australia. Jennifer Fowler (b. 1939) is one of the few who has made London her permanent residence. After completing preliminary studies at the University of West Australia, in 1968 Fowler won a grant from the Dutch government to study electronic music at the University of Utrecht. Since 1969 she has lived in London, composing in avant-garde idioms, including aleatory and nontraditional sounds. Her best-known work is *Ravelation* (1971, revised 1980), a string quartet. She often leaves performance details to the performers, and her penchant for indeterminacy is evident in *Ring Out the Changes* for strings and bells (1978), and in *Voices of Shades* (1977).

Like Jennifer Fowler, Alison Bauld has also settled in London. Her ballad opera, *Nell,* for which she wrote both the text and the music, was performed at the 1988 London International Opera Festival. Born in Sydney in 1944, Bauld received training in acting and music, and for a time she made her living as a professional actress. In 1969 she came to England to study composition, first with Elisabeth Lutyens, then with Hans Keller; and she received her doctorate from York University. Since then she has been particularly active working with dance companies, including the Laban Centre for Dance at the University of London. Commissions have come to her from various sources, including the BBC, which underwrote her radio opera *Once upon a Time,* also to her own text. The majority of Bauld's works involve voice and drama in some way. *Banquo's Buried* (1982), for example, is a ten-minute monologue for mezzo-soprano based on the words of Shakespeare's Lady Macbeth. Rhythmically complex, it involves sung declamation and both rhythmicized and free speech over an evocative piano accompaniment. British soprano Jane Manning, whose promotion of the music of living composers is well known, has premiered several of Bauld's works, including "Dear Emily," "Mad Moll," and "One Pearl" (all 1973), and "I Loved Miss Watson" (1977).

Gillian Whitehead (b. 1941) was born in New Zealand to musical parents, and studied music in Auckland and Wellington. She moved to Australia and then to London for graduate study (no graduate programs in music composition are available in New Zealand) with Peter Maxwell Davies. Her many grants and commissions have come from foundations in New Zealand, England, and Australia. She held a series of fellowships and temporary appointments in England and Australia before taking a permanent position at the New South Wales Conservatorium in Sydney in 1982.

Whitehead has absorbed influences from the Maori people (who are indigenous to New Zealand) and from many twentieth-century composers from Debussy to Webern. This prolific composer is a gifted listener, and thus she exhibits a plethora of styles resulting from diverse experiences. But the most remarkable element of Whitehead's music is her strength in many different genres. From the operas *Tristan and Iseult* (1975) and *The King of the Other Country* (1984) to solo and chamber pieces to orchestral music, Whitehead infuses a rare individuality into each work. Acclaim has come from respected critics on three continents, and it seems certain that Whitehead's place as one of Australia's most brilliant composers is assured.

## NOTES

1. E.g., Countess d'Agoult was responsible for bringing together the most adventuresome and famous people in the arts, notably, Chopin, Delacroix, George Sand, and Pauline Viardot.

2. When Stravinsky was unable to conduct the premiere of the Dumbarton Oaks Concerto because of illness, Boulanger was his personally chosen replacement.

3. Donald Campbell, *The Master Teacher* (Washington, D.C.: The Pastoral Press, 1984), p. 80.

4. Ibid.

5. Ibid., p. 31.

6. Other members of Les Six were George Auric, Louis Durey, Arthur Honegger, Darius Milhaud, and Francis Poulenc.

7. See Aaron I. Cohen, *International Encyclopedia of Women Composers,* 2d ed. (New York and London: Books and Music, 1987), p. 554, for an extensive list of French women composers of the twentieth century.

8. See Antje Olivier and Karin Weingartz, eds., *Frauen als Komponistinnen,* 2d, expanded ed. (Düsseldorf: Internationaler Arbeitskreis Frau und Musik, 1987); and Antje Olivier and Karin Weingartz-Perschel, *Komponistinnen von A–Z* (Düsseldorf: Tokkata Verlag, 1988).

9. Marta Ptaszynska, "Autumn Reflections," translated by Anna Staniewska, Warsaw Autumn Festival program booklet, 1987.

## SUGGESTIONS FOR FURTHER READING

Antheil, George. "Peggy Glanville-Hicks." *Bulletin of the American Composers Alliance* 4/1 (1954):2–9.

Best, Michael. *Australian Composers and Their Music.* Adelaide: Elder Music Library Series, 1961.

Callaway, Frank, and Tunley, David, eds. *Australian Composers in the Twentieth Century*. Melbourne: Oxford University Press, n.d.

Cortot, Alfred. "Les Six et le piano." *La Musique française de piano*, 3me série. Paris: Presses Universitaires de France, 1948.

Hayes, Deborah. *Peggy Glanville-Hicks, a Bio-Bibliography*. Westport, CT: Greenwood Press, 1990.

Kendall, Alan. *The Tender Tyrant: Nadia Boulanger*. London: Macdonald and Jane's, 1976.

Kratsewsa, Iwanka. "Betsy Jolas." *Schweizerische Musikzeitung* 114 (1974):342–49.

*Lili and Nadia Boulanger*. Special issue of *La Revue musicale* 353–54 (1982).

Mandel, William. *Soviet Women*. Garden City: Anchor Books, 1975.

McCredie, Andrew D. *Catalogue of 46 Australian Composers*. Canberra: Australian Government Printing Office, 1969.

Mitgang, Laura. "Germaine Tailleferre: Before, During, and After *Les Six*." In *The Musical Woman*, vol. 2, edited by J. L. Zaimont, C. Overhauser, and J. Gottlieb. New York: Greenwood Press, 1987.

Monsaingeon, Bruno. *Mademoiselle: Conversations with Nadia Boulanger*. Translated by Robyn Marsack. Manchester: Carcanet Press, 1985.

Orchard, W. Arondal. *Music in Australia*. Melbourne: Georgian House, 1952.

Rosen, Judith. *Grazyna Bacewicz, Her Life and Works*. Los Angeles: Friends of Polish Music, University of Southern California School of Music, 1984.

Rosenstiel, Léonie. *Nadia Boulanger*. New York: Norton, 1982.

Stevens, Elizabeth Mruk. "The Influence of Nadia Boulanger on Composition in the United States." D.M.A. thesis, Boston University, 1975.

Thomas, Adrian. *Grazyna Bacewicz: Chamber and Orchestral Music*. Los Angeles: Friends of Polish Music, University of Southern California School of Music, 1985.

Trickey, Samuel Miller. "Les Six." Ph.D. diss., North Texas State University, 1955.

# Modern Music in the Americas

# X.
# North America since 1920

*J. Michele Edwards*
*with contributions by Leslie Lassetter*

## AMERICAN VOICES

Ratification of the Nineteenth Amendment to the United States Constitution, on August 20, 1920 marked the culmination of decades of work by women activists. However, with the right to vote secured, the intensity of collective activity among American women diminished. According to historian Sara M. Evans, "The twenties formed an era when changes long under way emerged into an urban mass culture emphasizing pleasure, consumption, sexuality, and individualism."[1] These traits were present in the popular music, e.g., jazz and the Charleston, which emerged from black culture and spread into the dominant white culture. Perhaps even the plurality of styles within American music was an outgrowth of a social context focused on individuality and the diversity within American life. Consider, for example, the various piano styles represented among the following performers and composers: Lovie Austin's accompaniments for blues singers, Lil Hardin Armstrong's performances and recordings with many leading jazz artists, *From the New Hampshire Woods* by Marion Bauer, and the piano preludes of Ruth Crawford Seeger.

### Marion Bauer and Mary Howe

The musical language of Marion Bauer (1897–1955) and Mary Howe (1882–1964) remained strongly rooted in the Western European harmonic tradition. Rather than follow the Second New England School, which favored abstract instrumental forms, Bauer and Howe are descendants of Edward MacDowell's emphasis on coloristic harmony, programmatic titles, and narrative through-composed forms. Both women traveled in Europe during the early twentieth century, and Bauer was probably the first American composer to study with Nadia Boulanger. In exchange for harmony lessons in 1906, Bauer provided English lessons to both Nadia and Lili Boulanger as well as to the daughter of Raoul Pugno, Bauer's violin teacher.

Bauer's *From the New Hampshire Woods* is firmly grounded in periodic rhythm, tertian harmony, and an integrated melodic-harmonic unit, yet it is colored with tints of Impressionism. Written just over two decades later, *Turbulence* for piano (1942) moves further away from functional tonality with more complex harmonies. Rhythmic energy, more than harmonic seduction, propels this work. Howe's orchestral tone poem *Spring Pastoral* (1937) was originally a setting of a poem by Elinor Wylie for women's chorus. In the orchestral version, lush string writing supports the soloistic treatment of french horn and woodwinds. Both Howe and Bauer composed character pieces for piano as well as orchestral tone poems, e.g., Howe's *Dirge* (1931), *Sand* (1932), *Stars* (1937), and *Potomac* (1940); Bauer's *Sun Splendor* (1929; orchestrated 1944). Leopold Stokowski led a performance of *Sun Splendor* by the New York Philharmonic in 1947; it was the only work by a woman the orchestra had performed for a quarter of a century.

Both Howe and Bauer produced many of their compositions at the MacDowell Colony in Peterborough, New Hampshire. Howe spent summers there almost every year from 1927 onward. Bauer, who first visited in 1917, expressed her gratitude to Mrs. Edward MacDowell for founding "a haven where many other composers, writers, and painters have shared with me the extraordinary opportunity and privilege of doing creative work in peaceful, stimulating and beautiful surroundings."[2] For Howe, Bauer, and many others, the MacDowell Colony was a very stimulating "room of one's own"—a necessary component for creative activity by women, according to Virginia Woolf.

Howe and Bauer also made substantial contributions to American musical life beyond composition. Howe, one of the founders of the Association of American Women Composers, was active in many artistic and philanthropic organizations. Bauer, a champion of American music, was the only woman among the founders of the League of Composers. She was editor of the *Musical Leader,* author of many articles and several books, and a professor at New York University for twenty-five years.

## Undine Smith Moore

In a self-conscious effort to find an American voice and to establish artistic independence from the Central European tradition, some composers in the 1920s and beyond cultivated musical nationalism, incorporating elements from vernacular or ethnic music. Undine Smith Moore (1904–89) drew conspicuously on her African-American heritage in many of her compositions. Asked what made her music uniquely black, she responded:

> Musically, its rhythms; its choice of scale structures; its use of call and response; its general use of contrapuntal devices . . . ; the choice of timbres; melody as influenced by rhythms, timbres, scalar structure. When the harmony is non-tertian, it is apt to use the 4ths and 5ths so often sung by black people in the churches of my youth; the deliberate use of striking climax with almost unrestrained fullness.
> Philosophically . . . I have often been concerned with aspiration, the emotional intensity associated with the life of black people . . . [and] the capacity and desire for *abundant, full* expression as one might anticipate or expect from an oppressed people determined to survive.[3]

Moore, whose favorite medium is *a cappella* choir, is best known for choral compositions and spiritual arrangements. One of her most frequently

Undine Smith Moore teaching during a summer festival, "The Black Man in American Music," at Virginia State University, ca. 1972. Photo courtesy of Mary Easter.

performed spirituals, "Daniel, Daniel Servant of the Lord" (1952), is more a theme and variations than an arrangement. "Mother to Son" (1955), which sets a Langston Hughes poem for alto solo and mixed chorus, is one of Moore's own favorites and an example of her providing "music of good quality, interesting and fresh"[4] for performers in amateur, church, and school ensembles. "Lord, We Give Thanks to Thee" (1971), written for the hundredth anniversary of the Fisk Jubilee Singers, employs African-American melody and rhythm and builds to intense climaxes. *Scenes from the Life of a Martyr (to the Memory of Martin Luther King, Jr.)* (1982), an oratorio for narrator, chorus, and orchestra, was nominated for a Pulitzer Prize in 1982; Moore calls this her most significant work.

While not all of Moore's vocal music is overtly rooted in black styles, some of her instrumental works are. "Love Let the Wind Cry . . . How I Adore Thee" sets a poem by Sappho in Western European art-song tradition, celebrating love between women in a dramatic and affirming voice. *Afro-American Suite* (1969), for flute, cello, and piano, presents spirituals and includes syncopation typical of black musical traditions. Moore's harmonic practice is generally rooted in tonal language, sometimes freely treated or extended through modal references. However, the first and third movements of *Three Pieces for Flute (or Clarinet) and Piano* (1958) explore twelve-tone writing.

Moore, a graduate of Fisk University, continued her musical studies at the Juilliard, Eastman, and Manhattan schools and at Columbia University. She contributed to the education of many musicians during her forty-five years at Virginia State College (1927–72); among her students were such notables as jazz pianist Billy Taylor and opera singer Camilla Williams. Moore's commitment to education was deep; even after her retirement, she continued lecturing, giving workshops, and teaching as a visiting professor at various colleges. Moore was also cofounder and then codirector (1969–72) of Virginia State's Black Music Center, which was established to spread information about and cultivate appreciation for black music of all types.

## Depicting the American Scene

Works by white composers also included the experiences and music of black Americans. Mary Howe's *Chain Gang Song* (1925), for chorus and orchestra (originally piano), was her first major composition to be performed publicly. It incorporates three tunes sung by a crew of black prisoners in the mountains of western North Carolina. In her autobiography, *Jottings,* Howe describes the experience that prompted this composition:

[I was] rounding a bend on horseback . . . and coming on a gang of twenty or so black convicts in striped clothes. . . . iron ball and chain on many feet, and they sang while they drilled the hole for the dynamite charge. One man held and aimed the iron drill, and two more slugged at it with heavy shoulder weight iron hammers, rhythmically, so the three could know inevitably when the hammer blows would fall.[5]

White composers from other regions of the United States also participated in the American music movement through conscious inclusion of American themes and musical materials. Two Texans, Julia Smith (b. 1911) and Radie Britain (b. 1903), incorporated musical idioms typical of the rural West and Southwest—hoedowns, songs of the rodeo and range, Spanish-American elements, and desert themes. Smith's *American Dance Suite* (1936), an orchestral work, is based on four folk tunes and was later arranged for two pianos. *Cynthia Parker* (1939), an opera based on the fascinating and tragic story of a young white girl lovingly raised by Comanches and forcibly "repatriated" by whites, quotes Native American melodies. The descriptive titles of Britain's works bring to life her native Texas, e.g., *Ontonagon Sketches* (1939), *Red Clay* (1946), and *Cactus Rhapsody* (1953). Spanish-American rhythms are prominent in *Rhumbando* (1975) for wind ensemble.

Mary Carr Moore (1873–1957), active as an organizer of several societies to promote American music, employed materials from the Northwest and California, areas in which she spent most of her adult life. Two of her operas, *Narcissa* (1909–11) and *The Flaming Arrow* (1919–20), make extensive use of American themes and Native American materials. Moore and her mother, who prepared these librettos, worked hard to understand Native Americans—their music, their culture, and the shameful ways in which European Americans had treated them. *Narcissa,* based on the 1847 massacre of missionaries Marcus and Narcissa Whitman in the Pacific Northwest, is original in presenting the drama through a woman's eyes. Both dramatically and musically, Narcissa's character is the most fully and deeply drawn within the opera. In Moore's opera *David Rizzio* (1927–28), another strong woman is the focus: Mary, Queen of Scots.

# AMERICAN EXPERIMENTAL MUSIC

## Ruth Crawford Seeger

Ruth Crawford Seeger (1901–53) took a different yet thoroughly American path: she separated her compositional activity from her work

Ruth Crawford Seeger sings folk songs with children at a cooperative nursery school in Silver Spring, MD, ca. 1941–42. Photo courtesy of Michael Seeger and the Estate of Ruth Crawford Seeger.

with folk materials. During the late 1920s and early 30s Crawford was one of the most innovative ultramodern American composers (along with Henry Cowell, Edgard Varèse, and Carl Ruggles). Then, from the mid-1930s she concentrated on folk music. She worked with Alan and John Lomax, transcribing American folk songs found at the Library of Congress (*Our Singing Country*, 1941); created piano arrangements and accompaniments for folk songs (*Folk Song U.S.A.*, 1947, with the Lomaxes and Charles Seeger); compiled and edited materials for children (*American Folk Songs for Children*, 1948 and 1950, and *American Folk Songs for Christmas*, 1953); and consulted on folk music in the United States and the Dominican Republic. In one composition Crawford did utilize folk melodies: *Rissolty, Rossolty* (1941) was written for a radio series on folk music and was her only concert piece composed during the 1940s. Two of Crawford's children, Michael and Peggy, became professional folk singers.[6]

Crawford's eight years of study in Chicago offered many opportunities for an emerging composer: participation in the new music circle that gathered at Madame Herz's salons, acquaintanceship with Carl Sandburg, and, perhaps of greatest impact, her professional relationship with Henry Cowell. Cowell published several of Crawford's works in his influential series, *New Music*. He is also credited with arranging her move to New York in 1929 and her year of study with Charles Seeger, whom she later married.

Crawford's compositions from the 1920s show influences from Scriabin's music, which she had studied with Djane Lavoie-Herz, her piano teacher and a Scriabin disciple. In nine preludes for piano written between 1924 and 1928 (see HAMW, pp. 271–75 for Prelude No. 2), Crawford's use of melodic cells, dissonance, and irregular phrasing forecast her later stylistic directions. *Suite for Five Wind Instruments and Piano* (1927, revised 1929), an intense and dramatic work, is rhapsodic—presenting divergent musical ideas and a wide emotional spectrum. Crawford's demanding piano writing suggests her technical skill as a pianist and demonstrates her understanding of the piano's expressive capabilities.

From 1930 Crawford's compositions realized in sound the ideas and theories that Charles Seeger articulated primarily with words. He called for a procedure that would reverse or negate tonal organization to allow greater importance for nonpitch parameters. Crawford first cultivated this approach, called dissonant counterpoint, in four *Diaphonic Suites* for one and two instruments and *Piano Study in Mixed Accents,* all composed in 1930. Employing Seeger's principles, Crawford created independent musical lines, described by Seeger as "'sounding apart' rather than 'sounding together'— diaphony rather than symphony."[7] Her innovative structures employed an economy of melodic material to create organic wholes; elevated the importance of rhythm, dynamics, accent, and timbre; and enacted a role reversal between consonance and dissonance. In parameters other than pitch, Crawford and Seeger defined dissonance (or "dissonating") as the avoidance of patterns established through repetition and predictability.

Crawford used a serial rotation with a ten-note set in the fourth movement of String Quartet (1931; see HAMW, pp. 285–90 for the third and fourth movements), coupled with a layered pattern of long-range dynamics and a palindrome structure. Dynamics are also the primary organizing element in the third movement, which Crawford described as a "heterophony of dynamics."[8] The String Quartet, which she considered her most representative work, was composed during the productive year she spent in Europe on a Guggenheim Fellowship, the first ever awarded to a woman.

*Three Songs* (1930–32), for contralto, oboe, piano, and percussion (see HAMW, pp. 276–84 for "Rat Riddles"), is one of Crawford's most innovative works and employs experimental techniques that only decades later became widely used. In addition to continued use of dissonant counterpoint and palindromic structures that govern rhythm and dynamics, Crawford's compositional techniques include vocal performance in "somewhat (though not too much) of the 'sprechstimme' mode of execution"[9] for the declamatory vocal line; tone clusters in the piano part; and optional instrumental ostinati spatially separated from the primary performers. The level of independence among the four *concertanti* performers is remarkable, yet Crawford created an expressive musical whole consistent with the Carl Sandburg poems she set.

## Vivian Fine

Vivian Fine (b. 1913) continued in the experimental vein of her first theory teacher, Ruth Crawford. Fine studied with Crawford for four years, beginning at age twelve, and began composing at thirteen. *Four Pieces for Two Flutes* (1930) and *Four Songs* for voice and string quartet (1933) show an affinity with compositions by Crawford. In each of these early works Fine skillfully employs dissonant counterpoint. The third song, "She Weeps over Rahoon," involves carefully planned serialized pitch sets that are not related to twelve-tone technique. According to Steven Gilbert, this song "shows a remarkable degree of pitch and timbral control—this in addition to its being a very moving piece of music."[10]

Fine, an accomplished concert pianist, received a scholarship to study piano at Chicago Musical College with Djane Lavoie-Herz, one of Crawford's teachers, when she was only five years old. In 1931 she moved to New York to begin her career. In addition to premiering much new music, she earned her living as a dance accompanist. Her experience and success in this area led to collaborations with many leading modern dancer-choreographers: Doris Humphrey, Charles Weidman, Hanya Holm, and Martha Graham. Between 1937 and 1944, when Fine was most actively composing for dance, her writing moderated to display a more diatonic style, as in *The Race of Life* (1937), a humorous and popular ballet score, and *Concertante* for piano and orchestra (1944). Subsequent scores returned to atonality but with less sharp dissonance. In the fourth movement of a 1960 ballet score, *Alcestis* (see HAMW, pp. 347–54), a prominent melodic motive rises in a succession of perfect fourths. Here intervallic consistency and a rhythmic motive (a fanfare-like triplet) replace the hierarchical structure of tonality in providing unity to the composition. *After the Tradition* (1988), commissioned and premiered by the Bay Area Women's Philharmonic in celebration of Fine's seventy-fifth birthday, honors her Jewish origins, although the composer calls this a nonreligious work. The first movement is a Kaddish in memory of cellist George Finkel; the second movement takes its title ("My heart's in the East and I at the end of the

West") from Yehuda Ha-Levi, a twelfth-century Spanish poet; and the final movement exhibits much vitality.

Several of Fine's compositions highlight feminist issues, e.g., *Meeting for Equal Rights 1866* (1976) and the chamber opera *The Women in the Garden* (1978). *Meeting,* for chorus, soloists, narrator, and orchestra, sets excerpts from nineteenth-century debates on women's suffrage. Although the work is highly complex (it requires three conductors), it still received favorable audience response. One reviewer described it as

> a stirring and timely piece devoted to the unhappily still struggling cause of Equal Rights. Taking a feminist viewpoint that is full of righteous rage— which is understandable—and compassion—which is more important— *Meeting for Equal Rights 1866* . . . augments and dramatizes the conflicts and hopes of countless generations.[11]

*The Women in the Garden* brings together on stage Emily Dickinson, Isadora Duncan, Gertrude Stein, and Virginia Woolf, quoting from their writings and interacting to create an evocative drama.

## SERIAL MUSIC

Many American men composers who reached prominence before World War II produced at least some serial compositions during the postwar years (e.g., Roger Sessions, Arthur Berger, and Aaron Copland) and many men composers of the mid-1950s and 60s established their reputations using serial procedures (e.g., Milton Babbitt, Charles Wuorinen). In composer Jacob Druckman's assessment, "not being a serialist on the East Coast of the United States in the sixties was like not being a Catholic in Rome in the thirteenth century. It was the respectable thing to do, at least once."[12]

### Louise Talma

Louise Talma (b. 1906) was among the composers who shifted to the path of twelve-tone writing. Talma, whose early compositions are neoclassical and tonal, first adopted twelve-tone serialism in *Six Etudes* (1953–54). In a general way, she perhaps took her cue from Igor Stravinsky's gradual incorporation of twelve-tone procedures after the death of Arnold Schoenberg (1874–1951). As a long-time student of Nadia Boulanger and as the first American to teach at Boulanger's Fountainebleau School in France,

Talma was strongly influenced by Stravinsky's music. Like Stravinsky's twelve-tone works, Talma's music retains tonal qualities, and serialism is absorbed as an additional unifying factor. Further, Talma indicates she was influenced by Irving Fine's String Quartet, composed in 1952, the same year that Stravinsky made his first move toward serialism in *Cantata*.

Talma's treatment of pitch material is not limited to strict twelve-tone ordering procedures. Talma often creates focus through emphasis on subsets, intersecting rows, and combinatoriality. She has utilized this process in various mediums: the choral work *La Corona* (1955; see HAMW, pp. 321–32); *The Alcestiad* (1955–58), an opera in collaboration with Thornton Wilder; and *Textures* (1977) for piano. In an analysis of *The Tolling Bell* (1969) Elaine Barkin concludes that:

> Although the work may indeed be "freely serial" [Talma's description], it is not casual, not "indeterminate"; very carefully determined junctures are articulated, critical constraints have been imposed upon all dimensions of the work at "initiating moments" and "points of arrival," the text-music associations are quite clear—neither overstated nor concealed.[13]

The text of *Have You Heard? Do You Know?* (1974–80), like the libretto for *The Alcestiad,* offers ample opportunity to critique gender stereotypes and to raise larger feminist issues. During its seven scenes, we meet Della and Fred (a white, middle-class, suburban couple) and their neighbor Mildred. Analogous musical treatment for Fred's concern about the ups and downs of the stock market and Della's over similarly moving hemlines gives parity to traditional male and female experiences. Their desire for a "quiet place" is also handled nonhierarchically with closely related music. However, the work as a whole reinforces gender stereotypes, seems uncritical of the emptiness of their conversations, and glorifies the desire for material things. Stylistically *Have You Heard?* accompanied by a mixed chamber ensemble, returns to neoclassicism with melodic recurrence, tonal referents, and ostinatos reminiscent of Stravinsky.

## Joan Tower

Before 1974, the music of Joan Tower (b. 1938) employed various serial procedures. *Prelude for Five Players* (1970) opens with twelve pitch classes, subsequently handled as an unordered aggregate. According to Tower, *Prelude* "is divided into six sections which are differentiated by changes in tempo, texture, register and dynamics which, for the most part, are associated with various hierarchizations of the 12-tone set structure."[14] During the early 1970s Tower gradually moved away from serial procedures: *Hexachords* (1972) is based on a six-tone unordered chromatic series, and *Breakfast Rhythms I* and *II* (1974–75) completes the shift. Many of the works that follow are more lyrical, often inspired by images: *Amazon* (1976), prompted by the almost constant flow and motion of the Brazilian river; *Wings* (1981), drawing on the flight patterns of a large bird; and *Noon Dance* (1982), which explores the parallels between dancing and the "choreography" of playing chamber music. After focusing on sonority during the 1970s, Tower gave more attention to rhythmic aspects in the 80s. For example, *Petroushkates* (1980) not only quotes Stravinsky's ballet but paraphrases the very fabric of his score, much in the manner of a sixteenth-century parody Mass.

Tower has worked primarily in chamber music, both as a pianist and a composer. Most of her compositions are for a medium she knows intimately as pianist of the Da Capo Chamber Players, which she founded in 1970. In 1981 the American Composers Orchestra commissioned *Sequoia* and presented its premiere under Dennis Russell Davies. It was subsequently performed by the San Francisco Symphony under Davies, by Zubin Mehta conducting the New York Philharmonic, and by Leonard Slatkin leading several major orchestras. During 1985–86 Tower was composer-in-residence with the St. Louis Symphony, and in 1986 Elektra/Nonesuch issued a recording of *Sequoia* with the St. Louis Symphony under Slatkin's direction.[15] Tower's increased visibility since 1981 demonstrates the career importance of writing symphonic works that receive performances by major orchestras led by established conductors. Since the success of *Sequoia*, her first orchestral composition, Tower has written several other works for orchestra, including *Music for Cello and Orchestra* (1984) and concertos for piano (*Homage to Beethoven*, 1985) and flute (1989). Tower won the 1990 Grawemeyer Award, a $150,000 prize for a large orchestral work, for *Silver Ladders* (1985).

## Barbara Kolb

Barbara Kolb's (b. 1939) handling of serial techniques in *Appello* (1976) for piano shows how a personal style can emerge from this compositional procedure. Each of the four movements of *Appello* is based on a series from Book 1a of Pierre Boulez's *Structures* (1952), and the third movement "involves a strict time-point organization for control of the rhythmic acceleration that progresses throughout the movement."[16] *Appello*, however, stands in sharp contrast to Boulez's *Structures*. Kolb's work is a rich, often dense, expressive work in comparison to the sparse pointillism of *Structures*. Kolb integrates serialism into a larger stylistic repertoire that combines performer freedom (dynamics, pedaling, and indeterminate clusters) with composer control. As in many of Kolb's compositions, texture and timbre remain extremely important expressive means. Her choice of title, which means "call" in Italian, and the poetic references at the beginning of each movement suggest a focus on expressive import, while Boulez's title and subdivisions are pointedly abstract. According to Kolb, each movement is a different call—one that is "reaching and enticing, rather than insistent or demanding."[17]

# SOUND-MASS

During the first several decades of the twentieth century the domination of music by functional tonality was challenged in a number of ways. Initially these procedures preserved pitch as the foreground compositional element, but gradually compositions refocused attention on other parameters. Sound-mass minimizes the importance of individual pitches in preference for texture, timbre, and dynamics as primary shapers of gesture and impact. As part of the exploration and expansion of sonic materials, sound-mass obscures the boundary between sound and noise. Emerging from tone clusters in the piano works of American experimentalists in the early twentieth century, sound-mass moved into orchestral composition most noticeably by the late 1950s and 60s. Many works that involve sound-mass also include other aspects of sonic exploration, e.g., extensive use of muted brass or strings, flutter tonguing, wide vibrato, extreme ranges (especially highs), and glissandos (a form of microtonal writing). Early choral explorations of sound-mass occur in *Sound Patterns* (1961) by Pauline Oliveros and *From Dreams of Brass* (1963–64) by the Canadian Norma Beecroft (b. 1934). Beecroft blurs individual pitches in favor of a collective timbre through the use of vocal and instrumental clusters, choral speech, narrator, and a wash of sounds from an electronic tape. Both Barbara Kolb and Nancy Van de Vate have written compositions that rely heavily on sound-mass; however, their compositions also include an array of sources melded into personal stylistic syntheses.

## Barbara Kolb

Continuing the American experimental tradition, Kolb centers her compositional activity on unconventional ensembles as much as on unorthodox styles. Although she has written one piano solo (*Appello,* see above) and occasionally for full orchestra, most of her compositions are for nontraditional chamber ensembles, some with voice. She has also created a series of works combining prerecorded (nonelectronic) sounds with various instruments, e.g., *Spring River Flowers Moon Night* (1974–75), for two live pianists and a tape that involves an unusual group—mandolin, guitar, chimes, vibraphone, marimba, and percussion; and *Looking for Claudio* (1975), with guitar and tape of mandolin, six guitars, vibraphone, chimes, and three human voices. Stylistically, both her stimuli and her creations are diverse. *Three Place Settings* (1972) offers unusual wit and humor in a three-movement work for violin, clarinet, string bass, percussion, and narrator; *Trobar Clus, to Lukas* (1970) borrows a repeating structure from the eleventh or twelfth century; *Solitaire* (1971) uses quotations from Chopin; *Homage to Keith Jarrett and Gary Burton* (1976) draws on jazz and improvisation; *Cantico* (1982) is a tape collage for a film about St. Francis of Assisi; and *Millefoglie* (1984–85) combines computer-generated tape with chamber orchestra.

In *Crosswinds* for wind ensemble (1968) Kolb makes extensive use of sound-mass as it explores the metaphorically loaded title. The work unfolds after the opening segment presents the principal gestures of the whole. Relatively stable blocks of sound (later with more flutter and motion) alternate with soloistic lines suggesting chamber music. The use of mutes creates greater unity between brass and woodwind timbres, contributing to the indistinct quality of the sound-mass and highlighting timbre and density as the primary compositional elements. The release after the first major climax exposes a single alto saxophone, reminiscent of the opening bassoon solo in Stravinsky's *The Rite of Spring*. Here again Kolb writes for an ensemble outside the musical establishment.

## Nancy Van de Vate

Nancy Van de Vate (b. 1930), whose catalogue is large and varied, has pursued an active career as composer, educator, and promoter of contemporary music. In the mid-1950s she redirected her plans as a professional pianist when she moved to Oxford, Mississippi, with her husband and infant child. She felt performance opportunities were limited there and that she could not commit to the necessary daily routine of practice. "I changed to composition, then became so totally engrossed in it that I never again wished to direct the major part of my time and energy to any other aspect of music."[18] Van de Vate taught piano privately and then at several colleges and universities throughout the southern United States and in Hawaii, and has expressed a desire to communicate with a broad public. After leading the Southeastern Composers League for a decade, she founded the League of Women Composers in 1975 (renamed the International League of Women Composers in 1979) and served as its chair for seven years. She moved to Indonesia in 1982, where she developed enthusiasm for gamelan music. She now lives in Vienna, Austria.

*Journeys* (1981–84) and *Chernobyl* (1987) are among Van de Vate's works for orchestra that utilize sound-mass. Like Kolb, Van de Vate integrates many different techniques and styles. In addition to massive textures, *Journeys* combines minimalist aspects, melodic focus of soloist lines, extended string sonorities, an enlarged percussion battery (especially mallet instruments), and development of motivic material (C, B, C, Db). According to Van de Vate, *Chernobyl* was written "to express universal feelings about the event [an explosion at the Soviet nuclear power plant at Chernobyl] and its meanings for all peoples. . . . [It] is not intended to tell a story, but rather to evoke images and feelings."[19] The first half of the composition layers coloristic, dense, static clusters, while the second half is more diatonic and conventional in the treatment of harmony, rhythm, and melody. A descending minor second, which Van de Vate calls a "weeping motif," is prominent during the second section. It evokes the closing of the Revolution Scene in Modest Mussorgsky's *Boris Godunov,* where a similar string figure of repeated pairs frames the short conclusion by the Simpleton. In a prophetic lament, the Simpleton, alone on stage, warns of the impending disaster of war for the Russians. The affinity between these musical gestures is strengthened through the similarity of timbre, rhythm, pace, and range along with contextual links: the setting in Russia and the potential devastation.

Two trios by Van de Vate offer considerable contrast with the orchestral works just discussed: *Music for Viola, Percussion and Piano* (1976) and Trio for bassoon, percussion, and piano (1980, revised 1982). Timbre remains an important compositional consideration—occasional clusters occur in the piano parts, the upper bassoon range is explored, and percussion batteries add coloristic elements. However, tuneful melodies and periodic metrical organization also play important roles, and texture is not a primary component.

## SONIC EXPLORATION

The expansion of sonic resources during the twentieth century can be viewed as an intersection of events, including the enrichment of instrumental and vocal resources throughout the Western European tradition and the century's craving for newness. Further, independence of timbre as a primary compositional parameter emerges from what George Rochberg described as the shift from a temporal to a spatial concept of music, and it is closely tied to the move away from a melodic-harmonic treatment of pitch material.[20] Finally, the newness of sounds is part of music's expressive import through its confrontation of the sounds, and thus the ideology, of dominant culture.

Annea Lockwood (b. 1939) challenges the line between sound and noise in her compositions. A native of New Zealand, Lockwood came to the United States in 1973 after living in England for twelve years. Although she was trained in electronic music, directed the Hunter College Electronic Music Studio, and teaches electronic music composition at Vassar, Lockwood prefers to work with acoustic sounds. Around 1966 she moved away from instrumental music to create *Glass Concerts,* using industrial glass as the sound source:

> I began to feel that electronic timbres, that is, the classic studio timbres, were simplistic by comparison with acoustic timbres and spectra, and not satisfying, not intellectually stimulating, not interesting to work with. . . . I needed to refine my hearing and my audio sensitivity. . . . What fascinates me still about acoustic phenomena is the large area of unpredictability about them.[21]

Since then her compositions often include *musique concrète,* environmental sounds, theatrical elements, ritual, and improvisation. *Tiger Balm* (1970) effectively combines acoustic sounds of a cat purring, a heartbeat, gongs, jaw's harps, a tiger, a woman, and an airplane, using minimal manipulation. The sound installation *A Sound Map of the Hudson River* (1983) is part of an ongoing project called *River Archives,* to record all the rivers of the world. *A Sound Map* condenses a river journey, with each short segment focused on the sound of one geographic place.

The range of timbres on acoustic instruments has multiplied during the second half of the century, and the literature mentioned here gives only a hint of the scope and breadth of activity. Lucia Dlugoszewski (b. 1931), inventor of the timbre piano in 1951, has consistently worked with expanded acoustic sounds using conventional and invented instruments. She composed *Suchness Concert* (1958–60) and *Geography of Noon* (1964) for an ensemble of one hundred of her newly invented percussion instruments. *Space is a Diamond* (1970), for solo trumpet, virtually catalogues extended techniques for this instrument. A specialist in extended techniques and improvisation, harpist-composer Anne LeBaron (b. 1953) breaks stereotypes of harpists and harp music in her improvisation *Dog-Gone Cat Act* (recorded in 1981) for prepared harp.

Although some timbral exploration moves in the direction of noise and high intensity, other compositions highlight quiet, refined effects. *Translucent Unreality No. 1* (1978) by Darleen Cowles Mitchell (b. 1942), for prepared piano, flute, and wind chimes, unfolds slowly and calmly, like the ephemeral flowers mentioned in its epigraph. Relative, nonproportional rhythmic durations contribute to the mood of fluid impermanence. *From My Garden No. 2* (1983, revised 1988) by Ursula Mamlok (b. 1928), another delicate piece, is scored for oboe, french horn, and piano. The piano part includes pizzicato effects inside the instrument, and each performer also plays a crotale (a thick metal cymbal with definite pitch) by bowing as well as striking it.

At the beginning of the twentieth century both percussion and the allied parameter of rhythm were largely untapped resources in music of the Western European tradition. Percussion now enjoys prominence through its own ensembles as well as an expanded role in orchestras and chamber groups. Before composing *Amazonia Dreaming* (1988), for solo snare drum, Annea Lockwood thought of this medium as limited; however, she discovered it is capable of making "wonderful, animal-like sounds . . . as well as great beauty in its own natural resonances."[22]

In Julia Perry's *Homunculus C.F.* (1960; see HAMW, pp. 335–44), harp and celesta/piano join an ensemble of eight percussionists. According to Perry (1924–79), the title derives from the name of a character created by alchemy in Goethe's *Faust* and is the Latin word for "little man." Sections focus successively on rhythm (with nonpitched percussion), melody (essentially duets for harp and timpani or celesta), and harmony (vertical emphasis with increasing density), with the concluding segment recapitulating elements from the three earlier portions. Perry creates a precarious balance between pitch (melodic and harmonic) and rhythm. Although percussion is the principal timbre, the macrostructure is based on a single harmonic unit: a chord of the fifteenth (C.F.), rising from an E. And although pitched instruments offer melody and harmony, the instruments chosen (harp, timpani, vibraphone, and even celesta) do not produce sounds with particularly clear pitch focus.

In 1973 Perry suffered several strokes, which left her right side paralyzed. Although she learned to write with her left hand and continued to compose, she lived her last years in seclusion and did not publish further. Perry's extensive catalogue reveals her familiarity with two worlds: the neoclassicism of the white, European tradition and the religious music of her African-American heritage.

Performers as well as composers have been active participants in extending sonic resources, particularly in cases of close collaboration (e.g., Bethany Beardslee and Milton Babbitt; Jan DeGaetani and George Crumb; Cathy Berberian and Luciano Berio). Interestingly, the leading vocalists of contemporary music and especially music with extended techniques are almost exclusively women, including performance artists Laurie Anderson, Joan La Barbara, and Meredith Monk. Many of the compositions exploring vocal resources also call for virtuosic performance skills and a reevaluation of text and the human voice as components of musical expression.

Jan DeGaetani (1933–89), noted for both technical skill and artistic performances of contemporary music, surely influenced and shaped composition for voice. Jacob Druckman, Peter Maxwell Davies, György Ligeti, and Pierre Boulez composed works for her. The link between DeGaetani and composer George Crumb is particularly striking and covers more than two decades. She premiered and recorded most of his music for voice, including *Madrigals* (1965 and 1969) and *Ancient Voices of Children* (1970). As professor of voice at the Eastman School of Music and Artist-in-Residence at the Aspen Music Festival for many years, DeGaetani was influential on the next generation of performers.

Like DeGaetani, Cathy Berberian (1925 or 1928–83) was a virtuosic performer. She was born in the United States of Armenian parents. She developed strong theatrical abilities, and her dramatic presence remained powerful even when illness forced her to perform from a wheelchair. Her vocal skills influenced compositions not only by Luciano Berio, her husband from 1950 to 1966, but also by John Cage, Igor Stravinsky (the final version of *Elegy for JFK*), and numerous Europeans (Sylvano Bussotti, Henri Pousseur, Bruno Maderna, Hans Werner Henze). A large portion of Berio's output was written for Berberian: *Chamber Music* (1953), *Circles* (1960), *Sequenza III* (1965), and *Recital I (for Cathy)* (1972). Berberian's voice is also crucial in Berio's dramatic electronic work, *Thema (Omaggio a Joyce)* (1958), and to *Visage* (1961), which links violence and the erotic in disturbing ways. Even after their divorce Berberian and Berio continued to collaborate musically.

Berberian's own compositions—*Stripsody* (1966), *Awake and Read-Joyce* (1972), and *Anathema con VarieAzioni* (1972)—were also written with her own voice in mind. *Stripsody,* which deals with comic strips as cultural discourse, is a collage verbalizing onomatopoeic words from the comics. Inserted into this witty texture are very short scenes from comic strips (e.g., "Peanuts") or stereotypic movie scenes.

## PERFORMANCE ARTISTS*

Pushing the boundaries of performance and composition still further, performance art unites the roles of composer and performer and generally

*This section, through p. 236, was written by Leslie Lassetter.

incorporates a variety of media. Theatricality, vocal experimentation, multi-media events, Eastern philosophy, dance, and storytelling are among the elements included in the diverse styles and musical approaches. Performance art, along with minimalism and neotonality, is one of the new directions of the 1970s that seek to reengage the public. Women—including Pauline Oliveros, Laurie Anderson, Joan La Barbara, and Meredith Monk—are especially active leaders in this trend.

## Pauline Oliveros

Theatricality, humor, feminism, meditation, audience participation, and experiment are all important aspects of the music of Pauline Oliveros (b. 1932). Her family was musical: her mother and grandmother taught piano, and her grandfather collected instruments. After studying piano with her mother, Oliveros took up her brother's instrument, the accordion. Later she learned tuba and french horn, but her lifelong affinity with the accordion has remained central to her compositions and improvisations. Her studies at the University of Houston (1949–52) included accordion and composition. From Houston she transferred to San Francisco State College, to study composition with Robert Erickson, and received her B.A. there in 1957.

Oliveros's early works show a tendency toward experiment. Trio for Flute, Percussion, and String Bass (1963) has a Webern-like texture but uses nontraditional notation with and without indication of exact pitches. In contrast, Aeolian Partitions (1970) has approximately one page of notated music and several pages of instructions, including a list of the required performers and their props (a broom for the cellist, a newspaper and flashlight for the pianist, etc.) and a very detailed scenario. Aeolian Partitions also calls for telepathic improvisation.

> Each performer concentrates on another single performer. When he hears an interval or a chord mentally, he plays one of the pitches and assumes that he is sending the other pitch or pitches to the other performer by mental telepathy.[23]

Aeolian Partitions is one of many theatre pieces Oliveros has written. Her earliest work in this genre was Duo for Accordion and Bandoneon with Possible Mynah Bird Obbligato (1964). She added her pet mynah bird because it joined in during rehearsals; since the bird added a visual element, Oliveros asked Elizabeth Harris to design stage sets. Harris created a wooden seesaw with revolving chairs, which made reading a score impossible; so Oliveros replaced her original music with a set of simple instructions. The instructions for *Pieces of Eight* (1965) are more elaborate, calling for stage movement, costumes, cash register, skull and crossbones, and a bust of Beethoven with flashing red lights for eyes. Other theatre pieces include *George Washington Slept Here, Participle Dangling in Honor of Gertrude Stein, Double Basses at Twenty Paces,* and *Link* (renamed *Bonn Feier*).

Oliveros has also experimented with electronic music. In 1961, along with Morton Subotnick and Roman Sender, she founded the improvisation group Sonics, later renamed the San Francisco Tape Music Center. When the Center relocated to Mills College in 1966, Oliveros became director. Her commitment to electronically produced sound has influenced even her music for traditional performance forces. *Sound Patterns* (1961), which won a Gaudeamus prize, calls for an *a cappella* choir, yet it mimics tape devices such as white noise, filtering, ring modulation, and percussive envelope. *Bye Bye Butterfly* (1965) is an improvised piece realized by Oliveros with two oscillators, two live amplifiers, turntable, a recording of Puccini's *Madame Butterfly,* and two tape recorders in delay setup. In 1966 Oliveros experimented with compositions whose fundamental tones were outside the range of human hearing, so that the only musical sounds perceived were the overtones. This use of subaudio and supersonic oscillators to create music was so unprecedented, says Oliveros, that "I was accused of black art."[24] Her *I of IV* is based on the very nature of electricity.[25]

In the early 1970s Oliveros became involved with T'ai Chi, karate, dreams, mandalas, and Asian culture. Through a synthesis of her study of consciousness, martial arts, and feminist sociology she developed a theory of sonic awareness in which the goals of music are ritual, ceremony, healing, and humanism; beauty, rather than the goal, is the by-product. Using a parallel to Jung's viewfinder archetype based on sound—sound actively made, imagined, heard at present, or remembered—Oliveros created twenty-five *Sonic Meditations.* The three most suited to beginners appear in HAMW, pp. 364–66. The first, "Teach Yourself to Fly," is an exercise in tuned breathing; Meditation XIV, "Tumbling Song," calls for descending vocal glissandi beginning at any pitch. "Zina's Circle" (Meditation XV) is more complex and involves hand signals between the performers. All three of these *Sonic Meditations* call for the participants to stand or sit in circle formation; there is no separate audience.

Though Oliveros wrote her *Sonic Meditations* for participants only, she incorporated some of their elements into pieces intended for public performance. In the ceremonial mandala piece *MMM, a Lullaby for Daisy Pauline* (1980), for instance, she invited the audience to participate with humming sounds and audible breathing.[26] Still later works harken back to earlier composition techniques. At a 1985 performance of *Walking the Heart,* the hall illuminated only by candles, the whirling dancer, and the digital delay device recalled both the theatrical aspects and the electronically manipulated sounds of her early works. *The Roots of the Moment* employs not only an interactive electronic environment but also an accordion tuned to just intonation.

Oliveros has won a respectful following among composers as an experimenter and a forerunner in the now widely accepted field of electronic music. Through her many residencies at colleges and universities she has spread her ideas about a music based on listening to a younger generation of composers. Her concern with meditation and Eastern philosophies recalls the ideas of John Cage, though her music does not. Most poetically stated, Pauline Oliveros is, in her commitment to feminist principles and her exploration of a new language of sounds, a musical Gertrude Stein.[27]

## Laurie Anderson

Laurie Anderson (b. 1947), unlike the other musicians in this section, never had to give up a preconceived style of composition. As a young adult she was a student not of music but of art history and sculpture, though she studied violin throughout her youth. In reaction to her sculpture and performance art, with its great emphasis on music and sound, her teachers at Barnard College and Columbia University used to ask her if she was in the wrong department. One early sculpture looked like a mere table. With elbows resting on the table and hands cupped over the ears, however, the viewer could hear music. Anderson began making her own instruments in 1974.

Both sound and the art of the storyteller have always been an integral part of Anderson's work, and her music has very often served a story. Yet the visual element remains ever important. As is true of Meredith Monk's work, the art of Laurie Anderson can only be appreciated fully when one sees her perform. With the magical-elfin quality of the spectacle she creates, Anderson is truly an entertainer. In *O Superman,* a video, a light placed inside her mouth shows eerily through her closed lips and glows when she opens her mouth to sing. In live performance her charm, wit, inventiveness, and intellectual sarcasm—when at its best—captivate audiences. By means of slide projections, film, video, altered vocal sounds, and various self-invented instruments, Anderson's concerts take on the alternating qualities of comedy club, rock concert, and magic act. In the sophistication of her stories Anderson is like a trobairitz, and many of her tales are partly autobiographical.

In the mid- to late 1970s Anderson performed throughout the United States and Europe in art galleries and museums, including Berlin's Akademie der Kunst, settings where she could use intimate lighting effects. For example, she once projected a slide out of sight onto a ceiling. When she whisked her violin bow through the beam of light, for an instant the image came into view. She also created haunting music using a violin equipped with a tape-recorder head. Music sounded when her bow, strung not with horsehair but with prerecorded magnetic tape, touched the head. The song "Juanita" uses such a violin. Still another self-invented instrument, a white electric violin, sounded like thunder when played with a neon bow.

Anderson's magnum opus, the four-part, two-evening *United States I–IV*, was given its premiere in 1983 at the Brooklyn Academy of Music. This set of "visual songs" took several years to create: "My main intention is to make a portrait of a country. At first I thought it was just the United States, but it's not turning out to be that way. It's a portrait of any highly technological society."[28] The work was inspired by the many questions people asked Anderson about her country while she was on tour in Europe. It is documented both on record and in book form.[29]

Anderson has also written music for choreographers, such as *Long Time No See*, which was made into the dance *Set and Reset* (1983) by Trisha Brown. Anderson's work often has a very feminine, even feminist, undercurrent. The lyric from *Example #22*, sung in a pathetically painful tone of voice, provides one instance.

> The sun is shining slowly,
> The birds are flying so low.
> Honey you're my one and only,
> So pay me what you owe me.[30]

In her 1989 *Empty Spaces* concert at the Brooklyn Academy of Music, Anderson sang *Beautiful Red Dress*, in which the lyrics symbolized menstruation. To support the verbal imagery (red wine, red dress, etc.), the white tile walls became redder and redder as the song progressed.[31]

Despite the multifaceted aspects of Anderson's work—the humor, the homemade violins, the songs, the monologues, the toy saxophone, and the video, film, and light-shows—the central point of it all is the text. As she says: "I've never been a filmmaker or musician in the classic sense. . . . I use film and music . . . to be a subtext for the stories. The real subject, the real work, is the spoken words. I feel that's what I'm best at."[32]

## *Joan La Barbara*

Joan La Barbara (b. 1947), a noted interpreter of new music and champion of avant-garde vocal technique, has premiered the works of John Cage, Charles Dodge, Philip Glass, Steve Reich, Alvin Lucier, David Behrman, Roger Reynolds, Morton Feldman, and her husband, Morton Subotnick, among others. Her own music exploits the virtuosity she has developed in her vocal practice. One of her most celebrated pieces, *Circular Song* (1975), demonstrates a vocal technique inspired by (though not technically identical to) the circular breathing used by wind players. Following a graphic score (Example 10-1), La Barbara vocalizes on both the exhalation and the inhalation of breath. The effect is a series of siren-like glissandi on different vowels and vocal timbres, i.e., the production of more than one pitch simultaneously. *Voice Piece: One-Note Internal Resonance Investigation* (1974) takes its substance from the various ways in which La Barbara creates multiphonics from a single pitch. The composer calls such early works tightly controlled studies on specific ideas.

Aurally more intriguing in its greater musical variety is *Vocal Extensions,* written in 1974. La Barbara calls this work a

EXAMPLE 10-1.    Joan La Barbara, *Circular Song* © 1975 (Wizard Records, RVX 2266). Used by permission of the composer.

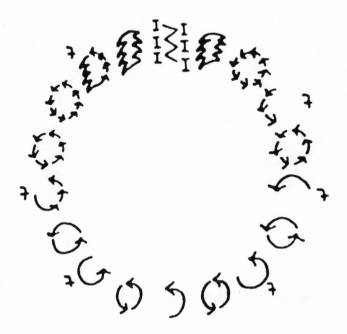

stretching [of] the voice, using sounds I've discovered in earlier experiments and expanding these possibilities by feeding the voice signal through a phase shifter, pitch modulator, and echo unit to shape a sound fabric based on the natural rhythmic flow of thought.[33]

*Cathing* (1977), which begins with a scathing interview of another singer (Cathy Berberian) who does not use some of the new, extended, twentieth-century vocal techniques, has similar electronic techniques and multitrack sound. In places La Barbara's vocal effects have the sound of various jungle animals responding to the droning, mantra-like chords of an oriental priesthood. One can also hear the influence of different cultures—Hebrew cantillation, American Indian wailing, and Japanese Kabuki speech.

La Barbara's more recent works tend toward larger performance forces than the earlier accompanied and *a cappella* solos and taped pieces. *Vlissingen Harbor* (1982), for amplified voice and seven instruments, was premiered in Los Angeles, as was *The Solar Wind,* for amplified voice and ten instruments, which was sponsored by the National Endowment for the Arts. One critic calls this piece a one-movement concerto for voice and orchestra in a minimal style. In *Chandra* (1983), La Barbara expands her tonal palette further to include solo voice, chamber orchestra, and male chorus.

## Meredith Monk

Meredith Monk (b. 1942)[34] is an artist in the broadest sense of the word. Her work breaks the dividing lines of dancer-choreographer, singer-composer, actress-stage director, and filmmaker-storyteller. Some of her titles have an anthropological ring: *Dolmen Music* (1981), *Recent Ruins* (1976), *Quarry* (1976), *The Plateau Series* (1978), for example. Others sound like medieval history: *Our Lady of Late* (1973), *Book of Days* (1989); or modern whimsical fantasy: *Needle-Brain Lloyd and the Systems Kid: A Live Movie* (1970) and *Candy Bullets and Moon* (1967). In the tradition of other contemporary New York artists,[35] she has named the company that performs her theatre pieces The House. The program for "Tour 8: Castle" in 1971 describes Monk's company as follows:

"The House is a group of artists, actors, dancers and a scientist who are committed to performance as a means of expression and as a means of personal and hopefully social evolution. We seek to unite our life and our work without losing our . . . individuality. Our work is full of remembered things and dreamed things and felt things that aren't seen and things that are seen outside and things that are only seen inside. . . ." That description of The House still holds . . . and The House, itself, is still standing. . . . Meredith is the director, the hub.[36]

As a child Monk studied piano, and at boarding school she sang in the chorus. Her career as a dancer and choreographer began after an intensely creative training period at Sarah Lawrence College. There she studied dance (with Bessie Schoenberg, Judith Dunn, and Beverly Schmidt), music, acting, writing, and literature. Speaking of her college days, Monk says:

> I was encouraged to work with a feeling, an idea . . . and let the medium and the form find itself. It seemed that finally I was able to combine movement with music and words all coming from a single source . . . a total experience.[37]

If Wagner approached the *Gesamtkunstwerk,* or total artwork, from the vantage point of a composer, Monk created what she has called composite theatre from the vantage point of a dancer steeped in all the creative arts. In her work, "the total art experience becomes more important than the significance of a singular message."[38]

In the sixties, critics labeled Monk's work *Blackboard* (1965) anti-dance and *16 MM Earrings* (1966) mixed-media. Like Oliveros, Monk experimented with music beyond the range of human hearing. Part of the score for *Duet with Cat's Scream and Locomotive* (1965) included sound

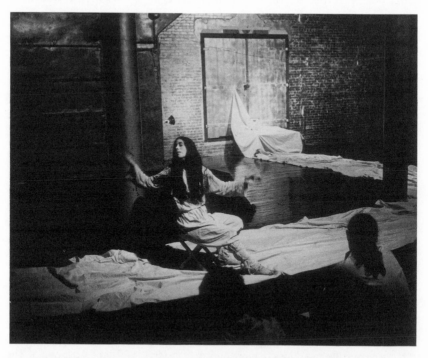

Meredith Monk in *Education of the Girlchild*. Photograph © 1973 by Peter Moore.

waves perceived by the brain but inaudible to the human ear. In her theatre pieces *Juice* (1969) and *Vessel* (1971), Monk experimented with moving the audience to different geographic locations in lieu of changing the sets on stage.

*Education of the Girlchild* (1973) is among Monk's most celebrated theatre pieces. Nancy Goldner, writing for the *Christian Science Monitor*, calls *Girlchild* a theatre piece about movement and stillness. A video of the work reveals just how still and motionless much of *Girlchild* is. The beginning of Part I is like an extended exercise in staring, and there are no words or dialogue to break the stillness. Goldner interprets a synopsis as follows: In Part I, a girl is born; she is educated by her female companions. By eating at table with them, she becomes socialized. Next she studies bricks and learns about the world. Finally, she experiences initiation into the cult of the ancestress. Part II is a long vocal solo in which Monk evolves from old age into youth. Her solo's "running vocal commentary of strange animalistic sounds" is a type of "sound-singing [that] draws one back to a pre-linguistic state."[39] Goldner's synopsis is referred to here as an interpretation because *Girlchild* has few words: Monk and her mostly female cast do not create, in Part I, a simple pantomime that makes the story line self-evident. In this sense there could exist as many synopses for Part I as there are viewers. In contrast, Part II, the seminal portion of *Girlchild*, first performed in 1972, is universally recognized as a backward movement through time beginning from the protagonist's old age. Monk performed *Girlchild* several times in New York and then in Paris; she revived it in 1979 and again in the 1991–92 season. A few years after *Girlchild* she created *Quarry* (1975–76), which received an Obie Award; this time she added film as one more element in her theatrical palette.

In her vocal music Monk is interested in exploring the voice like an instrument, allowing it the same flexibility as a dancer's spine. Asserting that music is a universal means of communication, she hints at the reason most of her music is without words: "People can respond directly, without having to go through language. I'm trying to approach a vocal music that's both primordial and futuristic. Maybe there won't be language differentiation in the future."[40] In addition to her concert career, she has made several recordings, among them *Our Lady of Late* (1974); *Dolmen Music* (1981, recipient of a German Critics Award for Best Record); and *Turtle Dreams* (1983).

Monk has not confined her collaborations to the world of modern dance (including various projects with Ping Chong since 1972), concertizing, and avant-garde theatre. In 1987 she and popular singer Bobby McFerrin sang a concert together at the Next Wave Festival at Brooklyn Academy of Music. Monk's most recent works include the film score *Fayum Music* (1988) for voice, hammer dulcimer, and double ocarina; the music theatre piece *The Ringing Place* (1987), first presented at the Brooklyn Academy of Music; and her feature-length film *Book of Days* (1989), which played at the New York Film Festival and in a shorter version on the PBS series "Alive from Off Center." Monk presented a short, live version of *Book of Days* at the Minnesota Opera in May 1988, and Houston Grand Opera premiered her theatre piece *Atlas* in February 1991.

John Rockwell has called Meredith Monk "the archetypical multimedia artist, having managed to work—one art at a time or in combination—in dance, theatre, film, and video"[41]—not to mention composing for her own vocal ensemble and maintaining her solo concert and recording career. Indeed, Monk stands apart and shoulders above many other personalities in the performing arts by the very breadth of her creative activity.

## ELECTRONIC AND COMPUTER MUSIC

The gender stereotype that suggests that women avoid technology and machines is quickly dispelled by the number of women actively involved in electronic music. Historically, Bebe Barron (b. 1928) and her husband, Louis (b. 1923), established one of the earliest classical electronic music studios in 1951, the same year that the studio at Westdeutscher Rundfunk in Cologne opened. They had experimented with the manipulation of taped sounds since 1948, simultaneously with and independent of Pierre Schaeffer, who is usually named as the innovator of *musique concrète*. *Heavenly Menagerie* (1951), the Barrons' first composition using the electronic oscillators they built, employed collage techniques like those later used by John Cage. The Barrons are better known for their electronic film scores, e.g., *Bells of Atlantis* (1953) and *Forbidden Planet* (1956), an MGM science fiction movie that helped establish the early association of electronic music with science fiction and outer space. The Barrons also prepared approximately 600 recorded sounds used by John Cage in *Williams Mix* (1951), which involved extensive tape splicing.

Currently, women are involved in virtually every aspect of electronic music. In the early 1980s Beverly Grigsby, herself a composer of electronic music, identified forty women in the United States composing with "electronically generated, processed, or manipulated music (using both analog and digital computers),"[42] and the list continues to grow. About half of these composers teach electronic music at colleges and universities; some are directors or founders of studios, e.g., Ruth Anderson (b. 1928) at Hunter College and Jean Eichelberger Ivey (b. 1923) at Peabody. Women have designed equipment (Daria Semegen), developed computer hardware or software (Laurie Spiegel, Suzanne Ciani), and created electronic instruments (Laurie Anderson).

Stylistically, women's works cover a wide range, from the extended neoclassicism of Trio for flute, oboe, harpsichord, and electronic tape (1973) by Emma Lou Diemer (b. 1927) to the experimental collages *DUMP* and *SUM (State of the Union Message)* (1973) by Ruth Anderson; and from the integration of nature sounds in *Beneath the Horizon* (1977–78) by Priscilla McLean (b. 1942), for processed whale sounds and tuba quartet, to computer voice synthesis in *Voices* by Tracy Peterson. Most composers have combined electronic music with live performance, either with acoustic sounds or with other media, such as film (Pril Smiley) or dance (Laurie Spiegel, Diane Thome). Aesthetic approaches vary radically: from Ivey, who moved to electronic music because she considered the unpredictability of live performance a drawback, to Spiegel, who claims that machines are nonsexist and therefore politically liberating; and from Diemer, who wished to incorporate conventional melodic and rhythmic patterns into electronic music as well as to revitalize her acoustic style, to Pauline Oliveros, who saw live electronics as a way to get "noise" into her works.

The emergence of electronic music at mid-century may be viewed as the convergence of interests in composer control (as seen in serialism), virtuosity, and timbre used for its expressive potential. However, it has also provided opportunities for composers who wish to explore chance or improvisational elements. Still other compositions reveal concern for communication, whether through meditation (Laurie Spiegel's *The Expanding Universe*, 1975) or through dramatic presentation of text (Joyce Mekeel's tape score for Gertrude Stein's *Yes Is For A Very Young Man*, 1965).

Ivey, who wants the immediacy of visual stimuli, often combines live and electronic media in dramatic ways. She has sometimes chosen texts with prominent roles for women. In *Testament of Eve* (1974), for mezzo-soprano, orchestra, and tape, Ivey reinterprets the biblical temptation story: in Ivey's text, Eve's actions are a conscious choice for knowledge and growth. In the program notes for the premiere, Ivey points out the bias of traditional interpretations: "[Eve] is very like Prometheus; and yet while Prometheus is usually seen as heroic, Eve in a patriarchal culture was often dismissed as silly, sensual, bad."[43] A year earlier, in *Hera, Hung from the Sky* (1973), Ivey completed another composition dealing with a woman's quest for equality with a male deity.

## AMERICAN SYMPHONIST: ELLEN TAAFFE ZWILICH

In the midst of much experimentation and a proliferation of styles in the late twentieth century, the music of Ellen Taaffe Zwilich (b. 1939) continues the American symphonic tradition with ties to neoclassicism and the "Great American Symphonists" of the 1930s and 40s. Zwilich updates this tradition, yet she retains a primary focus on pitch, relies on recurring and predictable patterns, and employs developmental forms. Discussions of her music frequently mention both her craft and the music's appeal to concert audiences and musicians.

After completing a master's degree in composition at Florida State University, Zwilich moved to New York and worked as a free-lance violinist. A year later, in 1965, she began a seven-year tenure with the American Symphony Orchestra, gaining important experience for her compositional activity. In 1975 she became the first woman awarded a D.M.A. in composition from Juilliard, where she studied with Roger Sessions and Elliott Carter, the most important influences on her music.

In 1983, Zwilich won the Pulitzer Prize for Symphony No. 1 (1982), becoming the first woman to receive this important recognition. The first movement of Symphony No. 1 (see HAMW, pp. 377–401), an organic elaboration of the initial fifteen measures, establishes tonal stability through motivic reiteration, decorated tertian harmony, and pedal points. The intervallic persistence of thirds (especially minor thirds) also contributes to its coherence. String Trio (1981), written just a year earlier, is noticeably more angular, abstract, dissonant, and virtuosic. A similar contrast between a large-scale public work and a more intimate composition is also apparent from the recording of *Symbolon* (1988), for full orchestra. This work unfolds in broad, simple gestures, in contrast to the more intense *Double Quartet* (1984), for string ensemble. By January 1990, *Symbolon,* which had been commissioned by the New York Philharmonic and was premiered by that orchestra in the Soviet Union, had been performed twenty-three times. Although handled conventionally, Zwilich's orchestration is often vivid (*Celebration,* 1984) and her string writing virtuosic (*Prologue and Variations* for string orchestra, 1983).

## MUSIC OF RELIGION AND RITUALS

The diversity of religious practice and belief in the United States provides a rich musical resource. African-Americans have consistently drawn on the music of their church roots—spirituals and gospel music—and contributed to the repertoires of church and school choirs as well as vocal soloists. Florence B. Price (1888–1953), Margaret Bonds (1913–72), Julia Perry, Undine Smith Moore, Evelyn Pittman (b. 1910), Betty Jackson King (b. 1928), and Lena McLin (b. 1929) acknowledged their religious-musical heritages in choral/vocal settings. Price, the first black woman to gain recognition as a major composer and whose Symphony in E minor (1931–32) was among the earliest by an African-American to be performed by major orchestras, did not quote preexisting tunes but employed melodic elements and rhythms characteristic of the black idiom.

Music for worship, once the province of professionals and the arena for stylistic innovation, is often performed now by amateur choirs, thus necessitating conservative melodic-harmonic writing. For example, the choral writing and arrangements of Gena Branscombe (1881–1977) and Alice Parker (b. 1925) rely on triads and tuneful melodies. In addition to writing literature appropriate for Protestant services, both have also composed much secular choral music. Branscombe, a native of Canada, came to the United States to study as a teen-ager and became a citizen in 1910. A proponent of American music and women composers, she often focused activities around amateur music making, e.g., her women's chorus (1933–54, called the Branscombe Choral) and women's music clubs. Her last composition was a commission for a special service at Riverside Church, New York: *Introit, Prayer Response, and Amen* (1973). Parker set approximately 400 hymns, carols, and folk songs (from various ethnic and racial traditions) for the Robert Shaw Chorale between 1949 and 1968, and many have received widespread performance. Parker's first opera, *The Martyrs' Mirror* (1971), recounts the lives of four Swiss Anabaptists executed for their religious beliefs. It was written for church performance and is partially based on Mennonite hymn tunes.

Louise Talma, born a Protestant, was an atheist when she began her studies with Nadia Boulanger. After hearing Boulanger identify "priest" as the top profession, Talma read extensively about religion, and at the age of twenty-eight she converted to Catholicism. This remains a foundation for her life. Although Talma has not composed much liturgical music (*Mass in English*, 1984), her convictions are revealed by her choice of texts from the Bible and poems that address religious issues, e.g., *The Divine Flame* (1948), *La Corona* (1955; see HAMW, pp. 321–32), *The Tolling Bell* (1969), and *Voices of Peace* (1973).

Miriam Gideon (b. 1906) holds a special place in Jewish music. She has been on the faculty at Jewish Theological Seminary since 1955 and was the first woman to receive a commission for a complete synagogue service,

*Sacred Service (for Sabbath Morning)* (1970). Although she does not want to be limited by labels such as "Jewish" or "woman" composer, Gideon acknowledges that some of her most interesting commissions have come from synagogues and temples. She has been consistently active in Jewish musical life as well as in a broad range of compositional spheres throughout her long and busy career. Gideon spent her teen years with an uncle, Henry Gideon, music director at the largest Reform temple in Boston, and learned much about that tradition playing organ at Temple Israel. Twenty years after completing undergraduate school, Gideon received her master's degree in 1946; and she was awarded a doctorate in composition from Jewish Theological Seminary in 1970. She has successfully combined teaching in several academic institutions with her work as a composer.

Gideon is not a "Jewish music literalist," but in *Sacred Service* she infused her personal, atonal style with "shofar calls, pentatonicism, asymmetrical rhythms, melodicles and chantlike effects, all reminiscent of numerous aspects and essences of genuine Jewish musical materials from a variety of traditions."[44] Among other works with specific Jewish links are *How Goodly Are Thy Tents* (1947), a setting of Psalm 84 for women's voices; *Adon Olam* (1954), which uses the accentuation of the Hebrew text; *Three Masques* (1958), using cantillation motives; *Shirat Miriam L'Shabbat* (1974) for Sabbath evening, which shifts away from dissonance through quartal harmony and freely uses cantillation, prayer modes, and Palestinian shepherd songs; *The Resounding Lyre* (1979), which includes one of Gideon's husband's poems; and *Woman of Valor* (1982), which uses Hebrew texts from Psalms and Proverbs. Even in *The Hound of Heaven* (1945; see HAMW, pp. 293–97), which sets a poem about conversion to Catholicism, Gideon selected verses with particular relevance and timeliness for Jewish people. In Gideon's opinion the lines she set tell how "we must suffer or be charred, as the poem says, in order to live deeply."[45]

In keeping with a general tendency in the twentieth century, some composers and their work are outside religious institutions yet still connected with spiritual issues and values. Especially for women, this is not surprising, since institutional religion has often been hostile to their active participation. Vivian Fine describes her *Missa Brevis* (1972) as a personal religious statement:

> Preserving a traditional sense of ritual, it uses both Latin and Hebrew texts. The voice sections—a collage of four separate tracks previously recorded by Jan DeGaetani—are a counterpoise to the parts played by the four cellists.[46]

Women's spirituality, concerned in part with holistic healing, meditation, and environmental issues, has stimulated production of music specifically for the recording medium, e.g., Kay Gardner's *A Rainbow Path* (1984) and *Garden of Ecstasy* (1990). On the other hand, Annea Lockwood's verbal-visual score for *Singing the Moon* (1981) is strictly a participatory sonic meditation.[47] Heidi Von Gunden's *Whistle Music: A Sonic Exorcism* (1980) infers performers and audience in more traditional terms, yet the "performance" involves meditative focusing of attention on the removal of evil spirits from the people present and the performance space.[48]

## POST–AVANT-GARDE SYNTHESIS

Increasingly in the twentieth century, plurality has been expanding not only through successive and concurrent styles, but through the coexistence of diverse styles within the output of a single composer and even within a single composition. While this repertoire does not focus on the most radical idioms, it also does not reject traditional materials. This fusion focuses on expression—often dramatic in nature—and has been especially hospitable to compositions on social themes or consciously feminist works.

. . . *to piety more prone* . . . (1983, revised 1985), by Elaine Barkin (b. 1932), is a powerful "assemblage" for four live speakers plus taped voices and musicians, including blues singers Bessie Smith, Ida Cox, Ma Rainey, and Ethel Waters. In addressing American society's response to violence committed by women, this hybrid work discloses gender stereotypes. *Susanna Does the Elders* (1987), by Susan McClary, reworks Alessandro Stradella's seventeenth-century oratorio *La Susanna*, whose central scene is itself an erotic revision of the apocryphal story of Susanna. In Stradella's oratorio, listeners may well imagine a striptease as they hear the seductive singing used to justify the attempted rape. McClary's music-theatre piece offers a feminist critique by placing seventeenth-century music—it is all Stradella's—within a new theatrical context. McClary asks:

> What do you do with music of theatrical power but which is antifeminist? . . . I want the dilemma to be thrown out to the audience. I'm opposed to censorship, but how do we deal with intolerance, of this or any sort, in "great art"?[49]

*Frankenstein, the Modern Prometheus* (1990), a multimedia opera by Libby Larsen (b. 1950), revitalizes this traditional genre with extensive and essential video as well as audio technology. The video presents multiple visual and emotional viewpoints, including the monster's perspective and intense closeups. Larsen's compelling drama, based on Mary Shelley's novel, probes dilemmas of technology. It is concerned, according to Larsen,

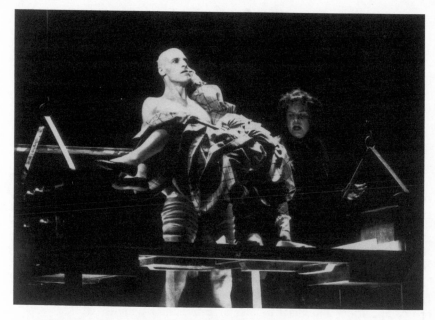

A silent monster is only one of the innovations in Libby Larsen's high-tech musical drama, *Frankenstein, the Modern Prometheus*. Photo by Susan Nelson. Reproduced by permission of the Minnesota Opera Company.

with human beings "who, by succumbing to intellectual egotism and ambition, become aliens in the society they wish to enrich."[50]

In the late 1970s, Beth Anderson* (b. 1950) experienced an abrupt about-face, and her music took on a more-traditional sound. *The Praying Mantis and the Bluebird* (1979–80) shows this shift toward neoromanticism. Contemplative in character, it is a simple, lyric piece for keyboard or harp (the praying mantis) and treble instrument (the bluebird). In her chamber and orchestral works of the 1980s, Anderson tends to quote from earlier music (hymns, opera, etc.) and to create melodies reminiscent of folk music. *Pennyroyal Swale* for string quartet (1985) opens with a fragment of a fiddle tune, then continues in a folklike style as indicated by "country fiddle" in the score. *Revelation* (1981), similar in its folk character, exudes a gypsy spirit.

The composer explains and defends this major shift in her music in an article entitled "Beauty Is Revolution":

> The idea that beauty is revolutionary is a revelation to me. I once believed that the concept of the music was more important than its sound. . . . it is a very liberating feeling to come back to my childhood definition of music, i.e.,

*Information on Beth Anderson has been provided by Leslie Lassetter.

writing down my inspiration. I've rediscovered the part of my brain that can't decode anything, that can't add, that can't work from a verbalized concept, that doesn't care about stylish notations, but that does make melodies that have pitch and rhythm. . . . Beauty is enough. . . . Beauty means perfect to me, but it also has an additional meaning having to do with being pleasurable rather than painful.[51]

What Beth Anderson has so aptly described is not only her personal manifesto but also the spirit that many of today's composers have chosen to follow. "Difficult music," as Laurie Anderson calls it, is no longer in the vanguard.

The music of Joyce Mekeel (b. 1931) melds an array of resources and often emerges from a dramatic or linguistic catalyst. Several of her works include multilingual texts: *Corridors of Dreams* (1972), *Serena* (1975), and *Alarums and Excursions* (1978), which works with material in eight languages. In *Corridors*, mostly sung or spoken in German or English, the execution of the text is an integral part of the composition. The first words are spoken partially through the flute, linking the timbre with the *shakuhachi* and the following Japanese Noh-style recitation by mezzo-soprano. Later the conductor declaims a marching song in counterpoint with dense instrumental gestures and the singer's stage whisper. Reaching back to earlier musical and literary eras, Mekeel also incorporates simpler materials. *Alarums and Excursions,* which refers to an Elizabethan stage direction, includes a tonal, Elizabethan-like tune, interrupted by an insistent twentieth-century violin gesture and a Gregorian-style recitation tone in stacked perfect fourths. These coexist with gamelan-like sounds from prepared piano and dense microtonal string glissandi. *Planh* (1975), for solo violin, whose title refers to a lament from the troubadour/trobairitz lyric tradition, suggests improvisation through short-term melodic repetitions and the avoidance of regular phrasing. Among Mekeel's instrumental works, the sound of words remains a part of her timbral resources, as in *Rune* (1977), for flute and percussion, and in *An Insomnia of Owls* (1984, revised 1985), for woodwind quintet. Mekeel's stylistic synthesis is well matched by her reliance on media outside primary institutional music organizations (such as the orchestra), which are more amenable to innovation.

## ORCHESTRAL PERFORMERS

In the first half of the twentieth century, especially during the 1930s and early 1940s, women's orchestras in the United States offered skilled players and conductors experience and employment in the symphonic field.

Women created their own opportunities because they could not obtain positions in all-male ("standard") orchestras. The Woman's Symphony Orchestra of Chicago and the New York Women's Symphony Orchestra were the best known nationally. The first white women—often harpists—were admitted to professional American symphonies in the mid-1920s, and a handful were hired during the 1930s. Many major orchestras hired no full-time women players until quite recently: the Boston Symphony in 1945 and the New York Philharmonic in 1966. In 1964, when pianist Patricia Jennings joined the Pittsburgh Symphony, she became the first black woman under contract with a major orchestra in the United States. After more than two decades of free-lance work, timpanist Elayne Jones won a principal position with the San Francisco Symphony in 1972 and became the first black person to hold a first chair with a major American orchestra.

Because of labor shortages caused by World War II, the 1940s brought increased employment opportunities for women. Consistent with this national trend, major orchestras hired increased numbers of women beginning with the 1942–43 season. Although women were generally viewed as temporary replacements, after the war musicians, unlike women in many other professions, retained much of their gain. Because women found positions with mixed orchestras, many of the all-women symphonies disbanded during the war years. In 1947, eight percent of the players with major American orchestras were women. Since the 1940s women have made substantial progress in gaining access to professional symphony positions. In 1964–65, 18.3 percent of the players in the eighteen largest-budget orchestras were women. In 1974–75, nearly one-quarter (24.9 percent) of the performers in thirty-one major symphonies were women, and by 1983, the figure was 27.8 percent. Gains for women orchestral players in the late 1980s appear to have reached a plateau in terms of percentages: in 1986–87, women constituted 30.8 percent; in 1987–88, 30.1 percent; and in 1988–89, 30.8 percent.[52] The publication of vacancy notices, legislation against discrimination practices, and blind auditions behind a screen have contributed to the increased numbers of women hired.

Participation of women in orchestras is in inverse proportion to orchestra budgets: the bigger the budget, the fewer women are engaged. Among the "Big Five" orchestras (Boston, Chicago, Cleveland, New York, and Philadelphia), in 1972 only thirty-eight (7.2 percent) of the players were women; there were fifty-one (9.7 percent) women in 1977; and one hundred (19.4 percent) in 1988. On the other hand, the percentage of women in regional and metropolitan symphonies (with budgets in 1987–88 of $1 million–$3.6 million and $280,000–$1 million respectively) is larger, reaching 46.3 percent and 47.1 percent for the 1988–89 season.

In the 1970s and 80s women formed alternative musical organizations, such as the now-defunct New England Women's Symphony and the thriving Bay Area Women's Philharmonic, from a different motivation: to foster women conductors and to provide a forum for performance of compositions by women. The Bay Area Women's Philharmonic is working to change the orchestral repertoire through the recovery of music by women of the past, commissioning new works by women, and promoting performances of these repertoires.

## CONDUCTORS

During the 1920s and 1930s, increased conducting opportunities for women were linked with the peak in activity for all-women orchestras. Conductors such as Frédérique Petrides (1903–83) developed careers leading women's orchestras but were unable to establish themselves with all-male orchestras. Petrides founded the Orchestrette Classique (later called Orchestrette of New York, 1932–43), a women's orchestra, and later devoted herself to outdoor concerts, which attracted large audiences as well as critical and popular acclaim. In order to gain conducting opportunities, a significant number of women have founded ensembles, e.g., Antonia Brico, Eve Queler, Ethel Leginska, Sarah Caldwell, Margaret Hillis, and Gena Branscombe.

Although Margaret Hillis (b. 1921) has conducted the Elgin (Illinois) Symphony since 1971 as well as other orchestras, she is best known for her work as a choral conductor. During her undergraduate days at Indiana University, Hillis conducted her first choral performance. Because of her success, she was encouraged to pursue a conducting career—specifically one in choral music, which was deemed possible for a woman. Hillis recalled her composition teacher's assessment:

> "You are a conductor, but there is no place for a woman in orchestral conducting." . . . So [Bernard Heiden] advised me to go into choral conducting. [He said,] "There a woman is acceptable. Otherwise, you're going to go down the drain." I almost had a nervous breakdown, almost a complete functional breakdown. All of a sudden my world fell apart, this world I had lived in and had lived for.[53]

Hillis took his advice and began her studies of choral music at Juilliard with Robert Shaw and Julius Herford.

After attending a rehearsal of her American Concert Choir and Orchestra of New York in 1954, Fritz Reiner employed Hillis and her ensemble with the Chicago Symphony during the next three seasons. In 1957 Hillis founded the Chicago Symphony Chorus at Reiner's request, and she continues to lead this ensemble. Through four decades Hillis has contributed extensively to the stature of choral music and to raising its performance standards through her leadership in the American Choral Foundation as well as her conducting.

Other women known for their work as choral conductors include Elaine Browne, Gena Branscombe, and Margaret Hawkins. In 1948 Browne founded Singing City Choir (Philadelphia), a multiracial/multicultural/multireligious ensemble dedicated to achieving peace and harmony among diverse people. She continued as its director until the summer of 1987 and has remained active as a guest conductor and workshop leader.

A typical path to the podium in opera is from rehearsal pianist to coach, then to chorus preparation and to conductor. Since rehearsal pianists in the United States are frequently women, we should expect to find more women than we do as opera conductors and music directors. Eve Queler (b. 1936) was hired as rehearsal accompanist and coach at New York City Opera in 1957, just six months after the birth of her first child. The time demands of these two areas of her life created conflicts, and her contract was not renewed for the following year. Queler returned to school to study conducting, then spent the next several years coaching and doing studio work. Her desire to conduct led her to found the New York Opera Workshop, later called the Opera Orchestra of New York, with which Queler has received international acclaim for her concert versions of rarely performed operas.

In the 1960s and 70s, Judith Somogi (1937–88) also moved through the ranks from rehearsal pianist and coach to become a conductor at New York City Opera. She was hired in 1966 and conducted her first production in 1974. After establishing her reputation with this company, Somogi conducted at the Pittsburgh Opera and served as principal conductor of the Frankfurt Opera from 1982 to 1988. She was a frequent guest conductor of major opera companies across the United States, including live telecasts with New York City Opera. After her orchestral debut with the Los Angeles Philharmonic in 1975, she appeared as guest conductor of various American orchestras and was musical director of the Utica (New York) Symphony during the 1980s.

Both Ethel Leginska (1886–1970) and Antonia Brico (1902–89) established prominent conducting careers during the 1920s and 30s. They appeared with major orchestras in the United States and Europe, as well as with various all-women symphonies. By the late 1930s, however, the novelty of women conductors had declined and most of their conducting opportunities disappeared. Leginska moved to Los Angeles and taught piano. Brico moved to Denver, where she taught and coached privately. She also conducted a semiprofessional orchestra, eventually named the Brico Symphony, for over thirty years. After the release of *Antonia: A Portrait of the Woman* (1974), a documentary film about her life, Brico received some renewed conducting opportunities with major orchestras.

In 1988 twenty-four women held conducting posts with professional orchestras that are members of the American Symphony Orchestra League; yet only two women have held even associate conductor positions with major symphonies in the United States and Canada. Catherine Comet, associate conductor of the Baltimore Symphony from 1984 to 1986, was the first. A year later, JoAnn Falletta became the second, when she was appointed associate conductor of the Milwaukee Symphony. Falletta resigned that post at the end of the 1988 summer season. Frenchwoman Comet, appointed music director of the Grand Rapids Symphony in 1986, was also the first woman music director of a fully professional orchestra.

In 1990 women still held few conducting positions with the ninety-nine United States and Canadian orchestras whose annual budgets are in excess of one million dollars. Only four women were principal conductors: Iona Brown, leading the Los Angeles Chamber Orchestra from the principal violin seat; Catherine Comet; Catherine Coriet, Music Director, American Symphony Orchestra; and JoAnn Falletta, Conductor, Long Beach Symphony Orchestra. Five more women held positions in the second rank: Marin Alsop (associate conductor, Richmond Symphony); Dianne Pope (Music Advisor, Des Moines Symphony Orchestra); and Tania Leon (conductor of community concerts, Brooklyn Philharmonic). Alsop, who was already conductor of Concordia, a New York chamber orchestra that she founded, has gained considerable responsibility with two more recent appointments: music director designate, Long Island Philharmonic, and music director and conductor, Eugene (Oregon) Symphony.

By 1990 several women held assistant conductor positions with major orchestras (Dallas, Houston, and Calgary), and others were music directors with smaller-budget professional orchestras: Victoria Bond (Roanoke Symphony) and Rachael Worby (Wheeling Symphony). During the late 1980s, women in the early stages of their conducting careers became more visible. Women constitute a growing percentage in conducting workshops sponsored by the American Symphony Orchestra League, in the summer program at Tanglewood, and in important events such as the Stokowski Conducting Competition.

At age seven JoAnn Falletta (b. 1954) began her musical training with guitar lessons because her family's apartment did not have enough room for a piano. When she was about twelve, her immigrant parents began taking JoAnn and her sister to concerts. From this time forward she knew she wanted to be a conductor, although as a teen-ager she was told this was impossible because no woman had previously worked as a conductor. In spite of this misrepresentation, Falletta continued to pursue her career plans. Falletta's comments in interviews reveal her awareness of gender in relationship to conducting. On the subtlety of gender issues, she claims, "The more I got into conducting, the more I had to come to terms with how I was raised as a young Catholic girl. We were taught to be supportive, nurturing, gentle, kind."[54] Falletta discovered that traditional socialization led women to apologize for making demands, and that this was a problem for a conductor. During her doctoral study with Jorge Mester at Juilliard she learned to avoid phrases and a tone of voice that could sabotage her on the podium. Falletta, who married in 1986, acknowledges the tension between career and family. Although many men have had both with the help of a support system from their wives, only a few woman conductors, e.g., Comet, have been able to sustain both an active career and motherhood.

Falletta has received considerable acknowledgment of her skill on the

JoAnn Falletta is part of a new generation of orchestra conductors. Photo by Niel Erickson. Reproduced by permission of JoAnn Falletta.

podium. In 1985, she won first prize in the Leopold Stokowski Conducting Competition and also received the Toscanini Conductors Award. In addition to her former position with the Milwaukee Symphony, she is currently conductor or music director of the Long Beach Symphony, the Bay Area Women's Philharmonic, the Denver Chamber Orchestra, and the Queens (N.Y.) Philharmonic. Since she joined the Bay Area Women's Philharmonic, whose repertoire is about eighty percent by women composers, Falletta has learned much music by women and has programed some of it with other orchestras she conducts.

## Neighbors to the South: Mexico and Latin America

Even in the twentieth century, women's participation in concert music has emerged only gradually in Latin America. Speaking about Mexico, Esperanza Pulido claims that *malinchismo* (an inferiority complex) and *machismo* (an exaggeration of masculinity or male pride) have hampered women as performers and composers.[55] Self-taught composer Maria Grever (1894–1951), the first Mexican woman to achieve fame as a composer, became a United States citizen in 1916 and later composed for Hollywood films and Broadway shows. In 1952 only seven Mexican women were active in commercial music. By 1982, at least forty-seven women had contributed regularly in this area and played an important role in shaping musical style and topics covered, e.g., Emma Elena Valdelamer and Laura Goméz Llanos.

Mexico became home for European-born composers Emiliana de Zubeldia (b. 1898) and Maria Teresa Prieto (1895–1982), both from Spain, and a temporary haven for Ruth Schonthal (b. 1924), who studied there after fleeing the Nazis in 1941 and before moving to the United States in 1946. Zubeldia adopted the harmonic theories of Augusto Novaro and used his acoustical principles to tune the pianos for performances of her compositions, as in *Sonatine* for two pianos and *Eleven Tientos*. Using extended tonality and later twelve-tone technique, Prieto composed much symphonic music: *Sinfonía Asturiana*, *Sinfonía Breve*, and *Chichén-Izá*. Schonthal, who supported herself playing in nightclubs, composed some works with Hispanic titles during her years in Mexico: *Concerto romantico* for orchestra (1942) and *Capriccio español* for piano (1945).

In the classical field, Mexican women, like their counterparts in the United States, often combine composition with teaching and performing. Rosa Guraieb Kuri (b. 1931), who is involved in all three areas, composes for voice and chamber ensemble as well as for her own instrument, the piano. She began composing after study with Carlos Chavez. Her chamber music includes two string quartets (1978, 1982); *Canto a la paz* (1982) for oboe, bassoon, and piano; and *Reencuentros* (1985) for violin, cello, and piano. Alicia Urreta (1935–86) first developed a career as a concert pianist, then began composing in the mid-1960s. She wrote music for dance (*Cubos, Luiz megra, Tantra,* and *Mujer flor*), electronic works, and instrumental pieces (a piano concerto and *Rallenti,* for orchestra). Urreta organized annual festivals of contemporary Mexican and Spanish music in Mexico City and Madrid. Marta Garcia Renart (b. 1942) is an accomplished pianist, choral conductor, and composer. Her compositions include choral works and music for a children's play. Graciela Morales de Elias (b. 1944) and Graciela Agudelo Murguia (b. 1945) compose primarily for chamber ensemble and reveal an interest in more experimental paths. Lilia Vázquez (b. 1955), a bassoonist and pianist, is a promising younger composer, if one can judge by the reception of her orchestral work, *Donde habita el Olvido* (1984).

Women born in Central America or in the Caribbean include Roció Sanz, born in Costa Rica but pursuing her career in Mexico; and Ninón de Brouwer Lapeiretta (b. 1907) and Margarita Luna de Espaillat (b. 1921) from the Dominican Republic. Lapeiretta has become known at home and abroad for her ballet score, *La reina del Caribe;* works for piano; two capriccios for wind ensemble; and *Absominación de la espera* for soprano and orchestra. A professor of music history and theory, Espaillat has created chamber music; piano pieces; an oratorio called *Vigilia eterna;* and *Elegie* for choir, narrator, and orchestra.

Three musicians born in Cuba must also be mentioned. As a pianist, Cecilia Arizti (1856–1930) concentrated her compositions around her instrument. Olga De Blanck (b. 1916) published several musical comedies between 1942 and 1944: *Vivimos hoy, Hotel Tropical, Rendez-vous de tres,* and *Cuento de Navidad.* Tania Leon (b. 1944), of African descent (her grandmother was a slave in Cuba), was trained in Cuba as a musician and an accountant. Later she studied in the United States, where she settled and has been associated with the Dance Theatre of Harlem since 1968. Leon, who was music director for television in Havana (1965–66) and conductor and musical director for the Broadway musical *The Wiz* (1977), frequently appears as guest conductor in the United States and Europe. In 1986 she joined the faculty at Brooklyn College Conservatory. *Tones* (1970) received its first New York performance in 1974 by the Symphony of the New World with Leon as piano soloist. Her other orchestral compositions include *Latin Lights* (1979), *Pet's Suite* (1980), and *Batá* (1985).

## NEIGHBOR TO THE NORTH: CANADA

In the early part of the twentieth century, Canadians retained their heavy reliance on study and compositional styles in England and France. During the second and third decades, Canadian composers generally followed one of two traditions: French as exemplified by Claude Champagne, or English as exemplified by Healey Willan. Since the late 1940s, most Canadians have studied composition in the United States or in Europe and have participated more in the so-called international styles of music.

Although Violet Archer (b. 1913) began composition study with Champagne, her early works are linked with the English late-Romantic tradition. After studying with Béla Bartók in New York in 1942, her compositions, which she called "a neo-classic, perhaps neo-baroque style,"[56] became more dissonant. They work within a new tonal language, juxtaposing and combining various modes but avoiding functional tonality. Following coursework with Paul Hindemith at Yale in 1947–49, her works became more austere but still retained their clarity and reserve. Archer identifies her Sonata for French Horn and Piano (1965) as a turning point toward greater abstraction and economy of materials. By the 1960s her compositions were heightened dramatically through the inclusion of expressionism, and some works from the 1970s incorporate electronic elements.

Archer has been a prolific composer, writing for many different media and for performers ranging from young amateurs to highly skilled professionals. Her interest in *Gebrauchsmusik* and her desire to contribute to the literature for various solo instruments and piano are among the many influences stemming from her association with Hindemith. Sonata for Alto Saxophone and Piano (see HAMW, pp. 357–63), which Archer identifies as a work that pleases her very much, is one of her most popular instrumental pieces.

Jean Coulthard (b. 1909) first studied piano with her mother, a professional musician, and later absorbed the English tradition from Ralph Vaughan Williams in London. Her music focuses on lyrical melody with an extended tonal vocabulary. Among her major works for piano are Sonata for Piano (1947), *B-A-C-H Variations* (1951), *Aegean Sketches* (1961), *Requiem Piece* (1968), *Sketches for the Western Woods* (1970), and *Ecology Suite* (1974). Many of her works draw on Canadian poetry or find their inspiration in the Canadian countryside: *The Pines of Emily Carr* (1969) for soprano, narrator, string quartet, timpani, and piano, for example, refers to the landscapes of the famed Canadian painter.

Barbara Pentland (b. 1912) became a composer despite the objections of her parents and problems with a serious heart ailment. In addition to work with Aaron Copland, three years at Juilliard, and an important summer in Darmstadt, Pentland studied with several women musicians: Cécile Gauthiez (in Paris, 1929–30), Eva Clare (in Winnipeg, 1930s), and Dika Newlin (at the MacDowell Colony, 1947 and 1948). Pentland's style has evolved significantly during her long career. Her early compositions, from the late 1930s, were in a neoclassical style. *Octet for Winds* (1948) was her first work to utilize aspects of twelve-tone technique. *Symphony for Ten Parts* (1957), a concise and transparent work, reveals the influence of Anton Webern's music from her study at Darmstadt in 1955. By the late 1960s Pentland employed aleatory elements and microtones. Although she became interested in unusual timbral combinations through her study of Webern, sonority became the organizing element in her music by the late 1970s. Dramatic works, especially on topics of social concern, also emerged during the 70s. *News* (1970), for voice and orchestra, is a deeply felt response to the casual reporting and audience acceptance of the violence during the Vietnam war. In *Disasters of the Sun* (1976), for mezzo-soprano, chamber ensemble, and tape, Pentland sets a text by Dorothy Livesay that critiques male domination. In its scenario, the Sun (man) is defeated by the Moon (woman), and Pentland's treatment of woman's victory is calm and understated as if inevitable.

Each of these women has played an important role in Canadian musical life and through her teaching has had a strong influence on younger musicians. Archer chaired the music theory and composition area at the University of Alberta from 1961 to 1978; Coulthard taught composition and theory at the University of British Columbia from 1947 to 1973; and Pentland was a university professor there from 1939 to 1963. In addition to their compositional work for advanced players, both Archer and Pentland have written teaching pieces for piano.

Electronic music appears to be an important medium for many women composers in Canada. Norma Beecroft (b. 1934), a flutist, has written extensively for electronic tape, especially in combination with live performers. During the 1970s Ginette Bellavance (b. 1946) composed a large number of electronic works for film and theatre. She was also involved in music as perception and with a pop-music research group, Yul. Micheline Coulombe Saint-Marcoux (1938–85) studied electronic music with the Groupe de Recherches Musicales de l'O.R.T.F. in Paris and has composed for electronic tape alone and with live performers. Her work for acoustic instruments is atonal and employs sound-mass, e.g., *Heteromorphie* (1970). Timbral exploration has led her to use the *ondes Martenot* in *Modulaire*

(1967) for orchestra and in *Séquences* (1968) for two *ondes Martenot* and percussion. Ann Southam (b. 1937) frequently combines live and electronic music in lyrical scores for dance. Diana McIntosh and Alexina Louie (b. 1949) are among the numerous younger Canadian composers. Louie, named Composer of the Year in 1986 by the Canada Music Council, wrote *The Ringing Earth* for the opening of Expo in Vancouver in 1986.

## FOR FUTURE CONSIDERATION

This chapter focuses primarily on women composers and performers; however, women have been active during the twentieth century in virtually every avenue of music. They work within traditional institutions as well as create their own organizations and venues. They are teachers, music therapists, philanthropists, arts administrators, publishers, and members of the recording industry. For a comprehensive understanding of the scope and breadth of women's contributions and influence in music, additional research in these and other areas is needed. As we grasp more fully the activities of women, we will gain a deeper understanding of the shape of North American music history.

### NOTES

1. Sara M. Evans, *Born for Liberty: A History of Women in America* (New York: The Free Press, 1989), p. 176.
2. Madeleine Goss, *Modern Music-Makers: Contemporary American Composers* (New York: E. P. Dutton & Co., 1952), p. 125.
3. As quoted by Herman Hudson with David N. Baker and Lida M. Belt, "The Black Composer Speaks. An Interview with Undine Smith Moore," *Helicon Nine* 14–15 (1986):175.
4. Ibid., p. 184.
5. Mary Howe, *Jottings* (Washington, D.C., privately published, 1959), p. 89, as quoted in Christine Ammer, *Unsung: A History of Women in American Music* (Westport, CT: Greenwood Press, 1980), p. 119.
6. Michael and Peggy Seeger are joined by their sister Penny and four of Crawford's grandchildren in a recording of fifty-three songs from Crawford's *American Folk Songs for Christmas,* Rounder CD 0268/0269 (Cambridge, MA: Rounder Records Corp., 1989).
7. Charles Louis Seeger, "On Dissonant Counterpoint," *Modern Music* 7 (June–July 1930):28.
8. Ruth Crawford to Edgard Varèse (letter and analysis), January 8, 1948, Ruth Crawford Seeger Collection, Library of Congress, Item 8m.
9. Crawford, "Notes" to "Rat Riddles" in *Three Songs,* New Music Orchestra Series, no. 5 (San Francisco: New Music Edition, 1933).

10. Steven E. Gilbert, " 'The Ultra-Modern Idiom': A Survey of *New Music*," *Perspectives of New Music* 12/1–2 (Fall/Winter 1973–Spring/Summer 1974):310.

11. Byron Belt, *Long Island Press,* May 21, 1976, as quoted by Jane Weiner LePage, *Women Composers, Conductors, and Musicians of the Twentieth Century,* vol. 2 (Metuchen, NJ: Scarecrow Press, 1983), p. 86.

12. Jacob Druckman, interview, *Soundpieces: Interviews with American Composers,* edited by Cole Gagne and Tracy Caras (Metuchen, NJ: Scarecrow Press, 1982), p. 156.

13. Elaine Barkin, "Louise Talma: 'The Tolling Bell,' " *Perspectives of New Music* 10/2 (Spring/Summer 1972):151.

14. Joan Tower, liner notes for *Prelude for Five Players,* CRI SD 302 (New York: Composers Recordings, 1972).

15. Elektra/Nonesuch 79118-1 (LP) or 79118-4 (cassette).

16. Barbara Kolb, Program Notes to *Appello* ([New York]: Boosey & Hawkes, [1978]). Further, Boulez had borrowed his series from an unordered pitch set in Olivier Messiaen's pioneering work, *Mode de valeurs et d'intensité* (1949). The pitch-class set used is: E♭, D, A, A♭, G, F♯, E, C♯, C, B♭, F, B.

17. Kolb, Program Notes to *Appello.*

18. Nancy Van de Vate, as quoted in an interview by Jane Weiner Lepage, *Women Composers, Conductors, and Musicians of the Twentieth Century,* [vol. 1] (Metuchen, NJ: Scarecrow Press, 1980), p. 257.

19. Nancy Van de Vate, liner notes for *Chernobyl,* Conifer Records CDCF 168 (CD) (London, 1988), pp. 3–4.

20. George Rochberg, "The New Image of Music," *Perspectives of New Music* 2/1 (Fall/Winter, 1963):1–10.

21. Tony Coulter, "[Interview with] Annea Lockwood," *Ear Magazine* 13/4 (June 1988): no pagination.

22. Ibid.

23. Pauline Oliveros, *Aeolian Partitions* (Bowdoin: Bowdoin College Music Press, 1970), p. 5.

24. Pauline Oliveros, "Some Sound Observations," *Source,* January 1968, p. 79; quoted in Heidi Von Gunden, *The Music of Pauline Oliveros* (Metuchen, NJ: Scarecrow Press, 1983), p. 59.

25. For a thorough discussion of this work, see Von Gunden, pp. 59–63.

26. For a description of how moving this lullaby can be, see Tom Johnson, "Two Transcendental Experiences," *Village Voice,* June 23, 1980, pp. 66, 68.

27. For a stream-of-consciousness comparison of Oliveros, Gertrude Stein, and Sappho, see Jill Johnston, "Dance Journal: The Wedding," *Village Voice,* January 14, 1971, pp. 33–34.

28. David Sterritt, "Laurie Anderson Multimedia Blitz," *Christian Science Monitor,* January 31, 1983, p. 17.

29. Laurie Anderson, *United States Live* (Warner Bros., WB 25 192-1, 1985); and *United States* (Harper and Row, 1984).

30. Laurie Anderson, *Big Science* (Warner Bros., WB 3674-2, 1982).

31. Laurie Anderson, *Strange Angels* (Warner Bros., WB 4-25900, 1989).

32. David Sterritt, "Laurie Anderson Considers the Heart of Her 'Performance Art' to Be Storytelling," *Christian Science Monitor,* October 24, 1983, p. 26.

33. Joan La Barbara, *Voice Is the Original Instrument* (Wizard Records, RVW 2266, 1975).

34. Monk was born in 1942 in New York, not in 1943 in Peru while her mother was on a performance tour, as cited in *The New Grove Dictionary of American Music,* s. v. "Meredith Monk."

35. The Kitchen, formerly located on Broome Street in New York, is a gallery

and performance space where Robert Ashley, Laurie Anderson, and others performed early in their careers. The Living Room is the recording studio partially owned by Philip Glass.

36. Lanny Harrison, p. 1 of a two-page typescript, written September 19, 1975. New York Public Library, Lincoln Center, clipping file.

37. L. K. Telbert, "Meredith Monk: Renaissance Woman," *Music Journal*, September–October 1979, p. 9.

38. Sue Snodgrass, "Meredith Monk: Solo Performance," *New Art Examiner*, March 1985, p. 59.

39. Nancy Goldner, "Stillness Becomes Movement in Monk's 'Education of the Girlchild,'" *Christian Science Monitor*, November 14, 1973, p. 18.

40. David Sterritt, "When Meredith Monk Sings, the Whole World Understands," *Christian Science Monitor*, January 18, 1982, p. 14.

41. John Rockwell, quoted in *Current Biography Yearbook*, 1985 edition, s.v. "Monk, Meredith."

42. Beverly Grigsby, "Women Composers of Electronic Music in the United States," in *The Musical Woman*, [vol. I] (Westport, CT: Greenwood Press, 1984), p. 151; see also complete article, pp. 151–96.

43. As quoted by Jane Weiner LePage, *Women Composers, Conductors, and Musicians of the Twentieth Century*, [vol. I], p. 96.

44. Albert Weisser, "Miriam Gideon's New Service," *American Jewish Congress Bi-Weekly* (New York), June 30, 1972, p. 23.

45. Albert Weisser, "An Interview with Miriam Gideon," *Dimensions in American Judaism* 4 (1970):40.

46. Vivian Fine, liner notes for *Missa Brevis*, CRI SD 434 (New York: Composers Recordings, 1982).

47. Annea Lockwood, *Singing the Moon* (score), *Ear Magazine East* 6/3 (April–May 1981):20.

48. Heidi Von Gunden, *Whistle Music: A Sonic Exorcism* [verbal instructions], *Heresies* 3/2 (No. 10, 1980):45.

49. Susan McClary, as quoted by Carla Waldemar, "Looking at Women and Great Art. Oh, Susanna," *Twin Cities Reader*, July 8, 1987, p. 17.

50. Libby Larsen, notes for the premiere program, Minnesota Opera, May 25 to June 3, 1990, p. 11.

51. Beth Anderson, *Ear Magazine* 6/3 (April 1981), New York Edition, quoted in press release of February 22, 1981, American Music Center, clipping file.

52. Statistics from the American Symphony Orchestra League.

53. Interview with Hillis, February 23, 1982, as quoted by Kay Donahue Larson, "Women Orchestral Conductors: Factors Affecting Career Development," M. M. thesis, Michigan State University, 1983, p. 59.

54. Ibid.

55. Esperanza Pulido, "Mexican Women in Music," *Latin American Music Review* 4/1 (Spring–Summer 1983):120.

56. Interview by Harvey Don Huiner, quoted in "The Choral Music of Violet Archer," Ph.D. diss., University of Iowa, 1980, p. 217.

Special thanks are due to those who provided research assistance for this chapter: Jane Lohr (University of Iowa graduate student), Melissa Hanson (Macalester College, class of 1990), Jill Edwards (Macalester College, class of 1991), Lia Gima (Macalester College, class of 1990), and Victoria O'Reilly (American Symphony Orchestra League); and to Sonya Sezun

(Macalester College, class of 1990) for translations from Spanish. I am also grateful to colleague and friend Dorothy Williams for her suggestions and support.

## SUGGESTIONS FOR FURTHER READING

Bailey, Walter B., and Bailey, Nancy Gisbrecht. *Radie Britain: A Biobibliography.* Westport, CT: Greenwood Press, 1990.

Brown, Cynthia Clark. "Emma Lou Diemer: Composer, Performer, Educator, Church Musician." Diss., Southern Baptist Theological Seminary (Louisville), 1985.

Eastman, Sheila, and McGee, Timothy J. *Barbara Pentland.* Toronto: University of Toronto Press, 1983.

Edwards, J. Michele. "All-Women's Music Communities: Fostering Leadership and Creativity." In *Bridges of Power: Women's Multicultural Alliances,* edited by Lisa Albrecht and Rose M. Brewer. Philadelphia: New Society Publishers, 1990. Pp. 95–107.

Fertig, Judith Pinnolis. "An Analysis of Selected Works of the American Composer Miriam Gideon (1906–  ) in Light of Contemporary Jewish Musical Trends." M.M. thesis, University of Cincinnati, 1978.

Gaume, Matilda. "Ruth Crawford: A Promising Young Composer in New York, 1920–30." *American Music* 5 (1987):74–84.

––––––. *Ruth Crawford Seeger: Memoirs, Memories, Music.* Metuchen, NJ: Scarecrow Press, 1986.

Harris, Carl, Jr. "Conversations with Undine Smith Moore, Composer and Master Teacher." *Black Perspective in Music* 13 (1985):79–90.

Jackson, Barbara Garvey. "Florence Price, Composer." *Black Perspective in Music* 5 (Spring 1977):30–43.

Koplewitz, Laura. "Joan Tower: Building Bridges for New Music." *Symphony Magazine* 34/3 (June/July 1983):36–40.

Long, Janice. "Alice Parker: Analytical Notes on the Cantatas." DMA thesis, University of Cincinnati, 1979.

McClary, Susan. *Feminine Endings: Music, Gender, and Sexuality.* Minneapolis: University of Minnesota Press, 1991.

MacMillan, Keith, and Beckwith, John. *Contemporary Canadian Composers.* Toronto: Oxford University Press, 1975.

Moore, James, Jr. "The Choral Music of Undine Smith Moore." DMA thesis, University of Cincinnati, 1979.

Muennich, Rose Marie. "The Vocal Works of Jean Eichelberger Ivey." Ph.D. diss., Michigan State University, 1983.

Nelson, Mark D. "In Pursuit of Charles Seeger's Heterophonic Ideal: Three Palindromic Works by Ruth Crawford." *Musical Quarterly* 72 (1986):458–74

Nicholls, David. *American Experimental Music.* Cambridge: Cambridge University Press, 1990.

Perle, George. "The Music of Miriam Gideon." *Bulletin of the American Composers Alliance* 7/4 (1958):2–9.

Proctor, George. *Canadian Music of the Twentieth Century.* Toronto: University of Toronto Press, 1980.

Riegger, Wallingford. "The Music of Vivian Fine." *Bulletin of the American Composers Alliance* 8/1 (1958):2–6.

Roth, Moira. *The Amazing Decade: Women and Performance Art in America, 1970–80.* Los Angeles: Astro Artz, 1983.

Smith, Catherine Parsons, and Richardson, Cynthia. *Mary Carr Moore, American Composer.* Ann Arbor: University of Michigan Press, 1986.

Sordo Sodi, Carmen. "Composito ras Mexicanas de Musica Comercial." *Heterofinia* 15 (1982):16–20.

Teicher, Susan. "The Solo Piano Works of Louise Talma." DMA thesis, Peabody Conservatory, 1982.

Tischler, Alice. *Fifteen Black American Composers: A Bibliography of Their Works.* Detroit: Information Coordinators, 1981.

Wilding-White, Ray. "Remembering Ruth Crawford Seeger: An Interview with Charles and Peggy Seeger." *American Music* 6 (1988):442–54.

Zaimont, Judith Lang, and Famera, Karen. *Contemporary Concert Music by Women.* Westport, CT: Greenwood Press, 1981.

# XI.
# American Popular Music

*S. Kay Hoke*

Since the early twentieth century the history of popular music in America has been one of interplay between musical styles and technological advances in sound reproduction. Of the many influences affecting the popular music scene, two are especially noteworthy: the introduction of microphones and amplifiers, allowing performers to project their sound without mastering the same techniques used by performers of art music; and the movement of mainstream popular music from a European-inspired written tradition to a vernacular style derived from oral tradition.

Until the 1920s the primary consumers of popular music were the literate middle and working classes, who had both the ability to read music and the means to buy a piano on which to reproduce it at home. The emergence of affordable electronic sound reproduction made popular music accessible to a broader audience unconstrained by the necessity for musical training. By 1925, control of the popular music industry had begun to shift from publishing houses to radio stations, record companies, and manufacturers of sound-reproduction equipment. Popular music in the United States has always been dominated by the so-called mainstream audience: urban middle-class whites. In the first half of the century their music was the product of Tin Pan Alley; in the second half it has been rock. But styles particular to other groups in the population have attracted broad-based audiences as well—for example, the music of rural whites, first known as hillbilly and later as country, and the music of black Americans, which includes blues, jazz, and gospel.

The study of popular music provides much information about women. They have excelled mainly as virtuoso singers but have also made significant contributions as instrumentalists and composers. Unlike art music, which is known primarily through its composers, popular music is known primarily through its performers; therefore the number of preeminent women in the field has been exceptionally large.

## TIN PAN ALLEY

What music historian Charles Hamm identifies as the "golden years of Tin Pan Alley" are those bounded by the United States's participation in the two world wars. The songs of Tin Pan Alley, written primarily by Jewish Americans living in New York City and grounded in the European classical tradition, maintain important links with European art music. Some of the men who composed these songs—Irving Berlin, Jerome Kern, George Gershwin, Harold Arlen—continue to be revered. Throughout the Big Band Era, many bands featured female singers, who performed the best of this repertoire. One classic type, referred to as a "canary," was a consummate stylist, cultivating a distinctive stage persona. Beautifully coifed and made up, costumed in an elegant gown, she performed in clubs, lounges, and, at the peak of her career, concert halls. The heyday of the canary was ca. 1940–55; among the many songbirds achieving commercial and artistic success were Jo Stafford (b. 1920), Patti Page (b. 1922), Dinah Shore (b. 1917), Kay Starr (b. 1922), Rosemary Clooney (b. 1928), Margaret Whiting (b. 1924), and Peggy Lee (b. 1920).

### Peggy Lee

Dubbed America's "premiere *chanteuse*" by Peter Reilly and "the Queen" by Duke Ellington, Peggy Lee is unarguably the most successful popular singer of her generation. Born Norma Dolores Engstrom on May 26, 1920, in Jamestown, North Dakota, she was encouraged by church choir directors and high school teachers to pursue a career in music. When she began to work as a radio singer, the station manager of WDAY in Fargo gave her the stage name Peggy Lee. Lee went on to perform in Minneapolis, St. Louis, Palm Springs, and Chicago, where Benny Goodman offered her a job as vocalist with his band. In 1942, still with Goodman's band, she recorded "Why Don't You Do Right?" a song that sold over one million copies. "Why Don't You Do Right?" "Fever," "Baubles, Bangles, and Beads," and "I'm a Woman" are considered her standbys, songs associated with her for over thirty years.

Despite a lack of formal musical training, Lee has either written or collaborated on hundreds of songs. Some of the best known are "It's a Good Day," "I Don't Know Enough about You," and "Mañana," a song with a

Peggy Lee. The Frank Driggs Collection.
Used by permission.

distinctive Latin beat. Although she has received many accolades throughout her career, true recognition as a serious artist came only in 1962, when
she was invited to appear in Philharmonic Hall at Lincoln Center. For this
concert she wrote a program entitled "The Jazz Tree," tracing the development of jazz as an American art form.

The professionalism and perfectionism of Lee are well known. She
prepares for each performance meticulously, recording every aspect of
the event in a large black notebook. For a major performance she culls approximately thirty songs from a list of over one hundred by her favorite
writers. Lyrics, arrangements, notes on instrumentation, observations
about the songs, and the gestures she will use to convey their meaning
are carefully entered, along with directions for lighting, her entrances and
exits, and her wardrobe and hairstyle. Nothing is left to chance; improvisation, musical or otherwise, is not her style. The result is a refined performance by a woman of queenly bearing. Because her voice is small and its
range is limited to about an octave and a half, Lee has perfected the sub-

tler aspects of her art. One might call her a scupltor of song, a musical artist who works delicately with color, inflection, emotion, and clarity of enunciation.

## Country Music

Country music is a commercial arm of folk music of the rural South that was originally handed down through oral tradition in the nineteenth and early twentieth centuries. Although its origins are in the folk music of British settlers, the evolution of country music has been shaped through contact with African-American and various types of ethnic and urban commercial music. The roots of country music as an industry reach back to the 1920s, when barn dance programs began to be broadcast on radio. The most important of these shows, originating in Nashville, Tennessee, was "Grand Ole Opry." Recordings date from 1927, when the Carter Family and a former railroad worker from Mississippi, Jimmy Rodgers, made their first discs for Victor.

### The Carter Family

A country music trio composed of Alvin Pleasant Carter (1891–1960), his wife, Sara Carter (1898–1979), and their sister-in-law, "Mother" Maybelle Carter (1909–78), the Carter Family became one of the most influential and popular country music groups in America. Their repertoire of Anglo-American folk songs, country ballads, religious songs, and sentimental parlor songs was very large. Their musical style—three-part harmony sung to simple chordal accompaniments of Maybelle's guitar and Sara's autoharp—was known and respectfully imitated by other groups. Maybelle, with her distinctive technique of playing the melody on low strings and strumming chords on upper strings, helped to popularize the guitar as a country music instrument. Although the trio did not perform together after 1943, its influence continued into the 1960s, when such singers as Joan Baez learned and performed the group's songs. Mother Maybelle continued to perform with her three daughters, Helen, June, and Anita, on "Grand Ole Opry" and with singer Johnny Cash, June's husband, on television and in road shows.

Because population shifts in the 1940s necessitated by the war effort brought people from the rural South and West together with people from the urban North and Midwest, traditional rural styles fused with urban popular styles. By 1950 Nashville was established as the commercial center

The Carter Family. The Frank Driggs Collection. Used by permission.

of the now-national entertainment of country music. In the 1970s and 1980s country music mirrored the growing homogeneity of American life and represented the way changes take place within the framework of a strong tradition. The lyrics of the songs remain traditional: familial love and traditional values, disappointed love, hard work, hard times, the man who leaves his woman, and old-time religion; the change is reflected in the mixture of country with popular and rock styles and the attraction of an international audience. Originally the instrumental ensemble comprised a fiddle, a five-string banjo, and a guitar; a mandolin, a string bass, and a steel guitar were added later. In the 1930s drum and piano were incorporated, and, over time, electric instruments appeared. By the 1970s, electric instruments had largely replaced acoustic ones.

## Kitty Wells

For most of its history country music has been men's music performed by men. Traditionally, women singers sang the sad songs, and few women emerged as top performers until Kitty Wells (b. 1919) made a decisive statement with "It Wasn't God Who Made Honky-Tonk Angels," a pointed reply to Hank Thompson's "Wild Side of Life." Though Thompson's song held women responsible for the fall of man, Wells countered by blaming men for their own downfall and for dragging women down with them. Her song, which made a new statement in country music, marked the turning point in her career and made her the first "Queen of Country Music." With a career spanning some three decades, Kitty Wells served as an inspiration to later stars. She fashioned the singing style that most women country singers have adopted—twangy and nasal, but clear and subtly ornamented. Her later hits, "Release Me" and "I Can't Stop Loving You," were made famous for the mainstream audience by rhythm-and-blues singer Ray Charles.

## Patsy Cline

The other country queen of the 1950s, Patsy Cline (1932–63), reached her audience in part through the new medium of television. Her singing style, influenced by contemporary popular music, helped her gain a crossover audience. She is best remembered for her song "I Fall to Pieces." Cline, whose life ended tragically in a plane crash in 1963, provided the model for women who wanted solo careers apart from male partners or family groups.

The 1960s and 70s ushered in new trends for women performers. Many of them broke with their male partners and became stars with independent identities. They began to sing about subjects formerly taboo to them: divorce, female adultery, contraception, the experience of sex, and womanly independence. The singing itself was sometimes strongly influenced by mainstream popular styles. Some women began wearing clothes that in earlier times would have caused a scandal. What is true for the best-known stars, however, is not the norm. Most country women still sing about the long-suffering woman who tolerates the weaknesses of her man and whose place is still at hearth and home, caring for the children—the public and lyrical myth of domesticity.

## Loretta Lynn

Loretta Lynn has lived the life of the women depicted in many country music songs. Born one of twelve children to a coal-mining family in Butcher Hollow, Kentucky, some time in the mid-1930s (she will not reveal the exact date), Loretta Webb married Oliver Vanetta "Mooney" Lynn, a veteran and former coal miner, at the age of fourteen and was the mother of four by the age of eighteen. Like most mothers, Lynn sang lullabies she remembered from her own childhood. Mooney Lynn was so impressed with his wife's singing ability that he bought Loretta an inexpensive guitar, possibly the most prudent investment he ever made. Loretta taught herself to play basic chords and began making up simple songs of her own. These early attempts at songwriting convinced Mooney all the more of her exceptional talent. His boasting that Loretta was a better singer than any country queen except Kitty Wells led to her first opportunity to perform professionally, an invitation in 1960 to sing with a country band on a local radio show in Bellingham, Washington. She was an immediate success.

Lynn taught herself to "compose" in the age-old manner of learning others' songs and respectfully imitating their styles. Over time she developed a style of her own and recorded a demonstration disc of a song she wrote, "I'm a Honky Tonk Girl." In order to promote the song, she and her family drove over 75,000 miles from radio station to radio station, persuading disc jockeys to play it. Their unorthodox scheme worked. The Lynn family was able to move to Nashville, and Loretta was engaged to appear on "Grand Ole Opry." She also performed on the Wilburn Brothers' syndicated television show and was paired with Conway Twitty as one of country music's most popular duos. No female country singer before her had been able to gain such national recognition.

A key element of Lynn's tremendous success was her talent for writing honest, direct lyrics about the realities of women who, like herself, married young, became mothers sooner and oftener than they had intended, and knew daily life in all its tedium and drudgery. Hers are earthy songs emanating from the heart but revealing in their plain language and often outspoken and courageous manner a kind of homespun philosophy. Among Lynn's best-known songs are "Don't Come Home A-Drinkin' with Lovin' on Your Mind," "One's on the Way," "You Ain't Woman Enough to Take My Man," "The Pill" (banned from many radio stations because of its stand favoring birth control), "Bargain Basement Dress," "I'm Gonna Make Like a Snake," and "Your Squaw Is on the Warpath" (Lynn is part Cherokee). Because she cannot read music, Lynn sings her songs into a tape recorder and writes the lyrics on whatever paper is available. Her melodies are shaped to fit the mood of the lyrics.

Though Lynn modeled her early vocal sound on that of Kitty Wells, she has since developed her own style, making her strong but touching voice slide like a steel guitar. As she has become one of country music's most prominent crossover artists, her voice has lost some of the twangy harshness that was part of its early charm. Today one might better describe it as warm and vibrant. After winning top honors in three categories at the Country

Music Association Awards in 1972, she appeared on the cover of *Newsweek*. Country music had finally been absorbed into mainstream popular culture in America.

## Dolly Parton

Like Loretta Lynn, Dolly Parton (b. 1946) was one of twelve children whose family lived in a two-room wooden shack. Her childhood in Locust Ridge, Tennessee, centered around singing and the church where her grandfather was a preacher. At the age of eight she was given a guitar on which she learned to accompany herself when she sang alone in church and with her uncles on the "Farm and Home" television show in Knoxville. Determined to become a country music star, Dolly boarded the bus for Nashville the day after her high school graduation.

Although she was able to find singing jobs immediately, Parton was not allowed to sing "hard" lyrics because of her high, childlike voice; she therefore began recording a country-rock blend known as rockabilly. Her career began to flourish when she joined Porter Wagoner's band and became his protégée. Her seven years on his television show (1967–74) and concert appearances with his band gained her national exposure. Even after Parton left the band for a successful solo career, Wagoner continued to produce and arrange for her.

In 1977 Parton began a conscious attempt to appeal to a wider audience. She traded a back-up band consisting entirely of relatives for one composed of eight professional Nashville musicians experienced in pop, rock, and country, and she replaced her Nashville manager with a Hollywood firm. By the time she and the new band, Gypsy Fever, opened at the Bottom Line in Greenwich Village, they were playing to enthusiastic houses with such prominent stars as Mick Jagger and Bruce Springsteen in attendance. In a review for the *New York Post* (May 14, 1977) Carl Arrington referred to the show as "the hottest ticket in New York" and observed that media people had been "gobbling up seats." A successful crossover album released the same year, *New Harvest, First Gathering,* reached the top of the country chart and near the top of the popular chart. Parton has also had success as an actress and as host of television variety shows.

A gifted songwriter, Parton often draws on her Tennessee heritage for inspiration. Among her autobiographical songs, "Coat of Many Colors" stands out as a particularly poignant memory of her impoverished childhood. The song, filled with biblical imagery, tells of a coat her mother pieced together for her from scraps of fabric. Other widely known songs with references to her childhood are "In the Good Old Days (When Times

Were Bad)," "Daddy Was an Old Time Preacher Man," and "My Tennessee Mountain Home." John Rockwell accurately noted that Parton's music is often shaded by the modalities and rhythmic idiosyncracies of English folk song, a link to the music she learned as a child. Like Loretta Lynn, Parton cannot read music, and her method for writing songs is to sing the tunes and lyrics into a tape recorder. She describes her compositional process as "trancelike" and feels that she is spiritually inspired.

A soft Appalachian twang is distinct in Dolly Parton's pure, accurate soprano voice. The voice itself is childlike, shivering with a rapid, controlled vibrato, but it can also be made to sound sheer, delicate, sweet, tender, or passionate. Parton displays a wide range of emotions in her songs, from the haunting "Falling Out of Love with Me" to the raucous, knee-slapping "Muleskinner Blues." The surprising flexibility of her voice has allowed her to perform many types of music, from mountain ballads to religious songs to rock-influenced popular tunes, and to elicit deep emotional responses from her audiences.

# GOSPEL

Although gospel music originated in both black and white fundamentalist churches of the rural South, the more compelling musical style has been that of black congregations. Like ragtime, blues, and jazz, black gospel emerged at the end of the nineteenth century, transforming staid Protestant hymns through the rhythmic techniques of syncopation and reaccentuation, the melodic techniques of note-bending and blue notes, the harmonic techniques of quartal and quintal chords, and performance techniques that called on performers to "sing" with their entire bodies. Modern gospel style, which dates from the 1920s, continues an older tradition of singing, shouting, and preaching. There are two discrete practices: quartet, dominated by male performers and characterized by singing in precise harmonies, often *a cappella*, by voices ranging from deep, resonant bass to falsetto; and gospel, dominated by female performers and making use of soloists, groups, and choirs. Gospel is sung with full voice and can sound strained, rasping, or guttural. The performers seek emotional power by singing at the extremes of their ranges, though performers in the 1970s and 80s began to use the middle range more extensively. Long melismas by the soloist alternate in antiphonal fashion with brief, staccato exclamations by the background group. In one special technique, originated by Mahalia Jackson and called the vamp, the soloist improvises while the accompanist and the background group repeat a chord progression and phrase respectively in ostinato fashion. The piano, the main accompanying instrument from the 1920s, was replaced by the electric organ in the 1950s. Accompanists, who are viewed as virtuosos in their own right and often have long-standing relationships with particular singers, play in a style that combines syncopations derived from ragtime with the left-hand octaves of stride technique and hymnlike chords in the right hand.

With few exceptions, the greatest individual artists have been women. Outstanding among them are Willie Mae Ford Smith (b. 1906), Sallie Martin (1896–1988), Roberta Martin (1907–69), Clara Ward (1924–73), Marion Williams (b. 1927), and the undisputed queen, Mahalia Jackson (1911–72). Women also attained eminence in gospel recording. Gospel recordings date from the mid-1920s and the initial hit from 1938. "Rock Me," a blues-inflected version of an earlier song, "Hide Me in Thy Bosom" by Thomas A. Dorsey, was performed by Sister Rosetta Tharpe (1915–73), the first gospel performer to achieve a national reputation. Nine years after Tharpe had demonstrated the commercial potential of gospel, Mahalia Jackson's "Move On Up a Little Higher" (1947) became the first such recording to sell a million copies. Jackson's deep, rich voice conveyed the music's message in a way that spoke meaningfully to both black and white audiences. Throughout her enormously successful career, Jackson remained essentially a church singer, but she freely acknowleged a stylistic debt to the "Empress of the Blues," Bessie Smith, whom she called her favorite.

# THE 1950s: ROCK'N'ROLL

American popular music changed markedly when two musical styles, one black and one white, came together. Black rhythm and blues had in common with white country music strong, insistent instrumental backgrounds that urged listeners to dance; the prominent use of the guitar— acoustic, electric, or steel; and a down-home vocal style proud of its rough edges. This new music, which we now know as rock, was known in its early history as rock'n'roll and was the first American music to cut across cultural and racial lines. The name "rock'n'roll" was a black euphemism for sexual intercourse; the connotative meaning was lost on neither the white male performers who dominated the early history of the style nor their youthful audiences.

Most of the well-known performers who shaped early rock'n'roll were male: Bill Haley, Elvis Presley, Jerry Lee Lewis, Buddy Holly, Chuck Berry, and Little Richard. There was, however, one woman, a black rhythm-and-blues singer named Big Mama Thornton, who deserves special mention as a powerful influence on rock'n'roll's most successful star, Elvis Presley. The daughter of a Montgomery, Alabama, preacher, Willie Mae Thornton (1926–84) was weaned on gospel before moving on to blues. Throughout the 1940s she sang in clubs and theatres in the South. By the early 1950s she was touring the entire United States. In 1952 she recorded the song "Hound Dog," which so appealed to black audiences that it became No. 1 on the rhythm and blues chart in 1955. With the emergence of rock'n'roll in the same year, Thornton's career went into a brief decline, while Elvis Presley's "Hound Dog," recorded in 1956 and clearly modeled on Big Mama's earlier version, became No. 1 on the popular, rhythm and blues, and country charts. Of the two recorded versions, Presley's pales in comparison to Big Mama's.

Thornton revitalized her career during the blues revival of the 1960s. Again she served as a model for a young white singer, this time rock star Janis Joplin, whose version of Big Mama's "Ball and Chain" helped propel her to stardom. Thornton herself achieved national recognition, appearing at the Monterey and Newport jazz festivals and at other jazz, blues, and folk festivals throughout the country. Her singing style comes out of the tradition of Ma Rainey and Bessie Smith—an earthy, somewhat coarse sound, which could be wrenchingly expressive.

The music industry resisted promoting early rock'n'roll for several reasons. The music was linked with societal problems ranging from juvenile delinquency and sexual promiscuity to racial unrest. It emerged at the same time as serious consideration of the issue of desegregation in American society and attracted racially mixed audiences. More important, however, it brought on a power struggle between music publishers and recording companies, which the recording companies ultimately won. American popular song had always belonged to a written tradition, whereas rock'n'roll sprang from two oral music traditions and was dependent on technological advances that made the shift in power irrevocable.

Rock'n'roll became an umbrella term for numerous styles in the late 1950s, including popular ballads, love songs, dance music, jazz, gospel, and even California surfing music. Much of the music was performed by squeaky-clean whites, women and men, who became teen idols. Most of these "idols" were boys intended to appeal to adolescent girls, but the two most important female performers of the late 1950s and early 60s, Connie Francis (b. 1938) and Brenda Lee (b. 1944), were women whose appeal was primarily musical. Francis's strong contralto voice was ideal for romantic ballads, such as "Who's Sorry Now?" and "My Happiness," but it was also effective in the novelties "Stupid Cupid" and "Lipstick on Your Collar." Though Brenda Lee's roots were in country music, her repertoire ranged from rock to ballads to country. Among her best-known songs are "Dynamite," "Rockin' around the Christmas Tree," "I'm Sorry," and "The Cowgirl and the Dandy." Her powerful voice and diminutive size earned Lee the moniker "Little Miss Dynamite."

By the late 1950s, the Brill Building in the center of New York's music district housed a group of songwriters attempting to bridge the gap between the coarse music of rock'n'roll and the sophisticated songs of Tin Pan Alley. This successful attempt, which came to be identified as the "Brill Building sound," began as the brainchild of Al Nevins and Don Kirshner, the founders of Aldon Music. Some of their writing teams were already well established, but others were young unknowns, among them Cynthia Weil and Carole King. The Brill Building writers were talented professionals who believed a good song could carry the singer; their songs set a new qualitative standard in rock'n'roll.

## Carole King

It seems as if Carole King (b. 1942) has had two separate and successful careers in popular music. In the 1960s she wrote teen-idol music, rhythm and blues, soul, and rock; during the 1970s she helped develop, write, and perform a style called "soft rock," which emphasized the lyrics rather than the beat. Her first career began when she dropped out of college to marry Gerry Goffin, who was also interested in popular music and wrote lyrics for fun. They began almost immediately to turn out hits, especially ballads sung by black vocal groups and marketed for urban teen audiences. "Will You Love Me Tomorrow?" (recorded by the Shirelles in 1960) and the sophisticated "Up on the Roof" (recorded by the Drifters in 1962) exemplify their best and most famous early songs. In the mid-1960s they wrote a soul tune entitled "Natural Woman," which became one of Aretha Franklin's biggest hits. By the time King and Goffin dissolved their writing partnership and their marriage in 1968, they were probably the most popular and prolific of all the Brill Building teams.

King began a second career on the West Coast, where she moved with her two daughters. She began performing with a rock group called the City, which she formed in Los Angeles in 1968. The group was not successful, but other sides of her career flourished. King began to work with lyricist Toni Stern, who wrote biting, realistic, and not particularly optimistic texts. This change in the sort of text King set to music proved beneficial to her writing. Another boon to her career was an invitation to tour with James Taylor, who encouraged her as both performer and writer and added some of her songs to his repertoire. She recorded two solo albums in rapid succession.

The second, *Tapestry* (1971), which was still on the charts in 1977 and eventually sold some fourteen million copies, was one of the greatest success stories in the history of recorded music. In it the new Carole King revealed herself as a gentle balladeer, singing about home, lost youth, friendship, painful separations, and the pleasures of physical love. In the same year, she and Taylor made a tour of the United States that ended at Carnegie Hall. Writers began referring to King as the "queen of rock" and successor to Janis Joplin. The albums that followed could never measure up to the success of *Tapestry*, although several—*Music, Fantasy, Diamond Girl,* and *Simple Things*—were gold albums, and *Carole King Thoroughbred* received a Grammy. Her career then went into a decline, but King attempted a comeback with a new album, *City Streets* (1989), her first in nearly a decade.

King's songs are characterized by a dominating bass line, simple harmonic progressions with gospel inflections, and shapely melodies with their roots in Tin Pan Alley. As a performer, King is an effective interpreter of her own material. Her plain, rather small voice is deceptively strong but lacks the energy and edge provided by the young black singers who made her earlier songs hits. She compensates somewhat for these deficiencies with good technique.

# The 1960s: Urban Folk Revival

By the beginning of the 1960s early rock'n'roll had vanished, and new trends—among them folk-derived music—recalled musical and social elements of the American past. Bob Dylan (b. 1941) was one of the first prominent figures in the urban folk revival to compose most of his own material. Among those who followed Dylan's new direction were three women—Judy Collins, Joan Baez, and Joni Mitchell—whose careers began in the coffeehouses and nightclubs that were urban sanctuaries for folk singers. Collins (b. 1939) composed some of her own music, but she also sang songs by Dylan and the Canadians Joni Mitchell and Leonard Cohen. She also expanded her repertoire to theatre songs, popularizing Stephen Sondheim's "Send in the Clowns" from *A Little Night Music.* Baez and Mitchell represent the beginning and the end of the urban folk style. Baez, the first woman folk singer to become a star, began her career in the late 1950s and always remained true to folk music; Mitchell, who composes most of her own material, is a product of the late 60s and has been able to adapt creatively to changing times.

## Joan Baez

The original folk madonna, Joan Baez has always viewed her musical career and her political life as one. In 1967, when the Daughters of the American Revolution would not allow her to perform in Constitution Hall because they viewed her protest of the Vietnam conflict as unpatriotic, she gave a free concert at the Washington Monument, which drew ten times as many people. Baez has been allied with civil rights, antiwar, and antinuclear movements, and much of the income from her concerts has gone to these causes.

Baez began to sing in coffeehouses in the Boston area after dropping out of Boston University. In 1959 she was invited to appear at the Newport Folk Festival, where she met and befriended the black folk singer Odetta (b. 1931), who also became one of the prominent figures in American folk music. Although Baez's name did not even appear on the festival program, her performance made a tremendous impact. In 1960 Baez returned to Newport as a star. Her first album, *Joan Baez,* the most popular folk album ever recorded by a female singer, also dates from 1960. On November 23, 1962 she was *Time* magazine's cover story. Audiences were attracted to her supple soprano voice, described as pure, vibrant, and haunting. Its range of about three octaves allowed her to perform some songs, notably Spanish ones, in an alto range. Baez has had no formal training in voice and taught herself to play guitar. Her approach to performance has always been spare and informal. Assured and self-contained, she wears comfortable clothing, little or no makeup, and a simple hairstyle. Unlike most stars, Baez places limits on her career, refusing to record more than one album a year. Anglo-American folk songs comprised her early repertoire; soon she added protest songs. One of the first established folk singers to promote Bob Dylan's songs, Baez felt his music spoke to her social consciousness, clarifying for her what political action to take.

Baez has written some songs but does not consider composition a particular strength. Ironically, as her popularity faded in the 1970s, she composed some quite effective songs, four of which appear on her last important album, *Diamonds and Rust* (1975). Although she continues to perform, Baez now devotes herself mainly to political activism. In 1979 she established a pacifist group, Humanitas International, an organization committed to peace and world unity.

## Joni Mitchell

Arguably the most innovative woman songwriter to emerge in the late 1960s, Joni Mitchell, with her penchant for minor-mode melodies and texts with multilayered images, grew stylistically over two decades from folk to rock to jazz to jazz fusion. Now a mature artist, she can shift easily among these styles. Born Roberta Joan Anderson (1943) in Fort MacLeod, Alberta, Mitchell first performed in Toronto, then Detroit. After the breakup of her marriage to Chuck Mitchell, also a folk performer, she moved to New York, determined to make her way. Here she met David Crosby (of Crosby, Stills, and Nash fame), who was impressed by her artistry and taught her the method of guitar tuning that makes her folk accompaniments unique. In 1968 the album *Joni Mitchell* (later renamed *Song to a Seagull*) was released; it was a critical but not a commercial success. *Clouds,* released the following year, included "Both Sides Now" (an alternative name for "Clouds"), which in a version by Judy Collins sold over one million copies; the album with Mitchell's interpretation of the song won the Grammy in 1970 for Best Folk Performance.

By the early 1970s Mitchell was beginning to earn a reputation as a songwriter of uncommon ability. Her songs were critically acclaimed for their beautiful melodies and transparent imagery. Some of her more complex, introspective works have been compared favorably to art songs. Examples of her striking originality as a composer and lyricist appear on the album *Blue* (1971). In "Little Green" Mitchell uses "green" to symbolize the child who has been born too soon to parents who are themselves still children, and to imply that the child named "Green" will be perpetually youthful. In 1978 she began a collaboration with jazz bassist and composer Charles Mingus in which Mitchell was to write lyrics to his jazz tunes. The project as envisioned was never completed because of Mingus's untimely death, but Mitchell's next album, *Mingus,* was in a jazz style and dedicated to him. Her work in the 1980s, marked by its social consciousness, takes a pessimistic look at American politics and addresses the problems of aging.

# Rock

From the outset, the new popular music called rock represented a cluster of styles connected by a common ideology, audience, and milieu. Rock belongs to the American political and social upheavals of the 1960s, when individuals and groups organized into movements to overcome political, social, cultural, racial, and sexual repression. Rituals, among them rock concerts and festivals of various types, arose to replace those deemed outdated and no longer viable, and the music itself became an instrument for change.

There are three striking ironies concerning the rise of rock. The first is that a music attached to emancipation movements and liberal ideology should attract a predominantly white middle-class audience and become mainstream music. The second is that the music industry did not cry out in moral outrage, as it had during the emergence of rock'n'roll, against music that celebrated anti-establishment values, but rather capitalized on its vast commercial potential. The third is that the reinvigoration of American popular music came from an unexpected source: the invasion of British groups such as the Beatles and the Rolling Stones, both of which paid homage to the roots of early rock'n'roll and gave a needed infusion of raucousness and rhythmic drive to the genre.

In the early 1960s bands emerged by the hundreds from San Francisco's then-obscure Haight-Ashbury district. Their music, while rooted in the past, was electric and used distorted, heavily amplified instrumental sounds, distinguishing it from rock'n'roll. As the music grew more sophisticated, it began to assimilate elements of Eastern music, especially Indian ragas. The song lyrics, the technique of sound distortion, and the light-shows at dance-concerts were intended to recreate the psychedelic experience, and audiences were intensely involved with the music. The year 1967 was the heyday for San Francisco rock, and by 1971 the local scene had all but disintegrated; but the musical style that arose there became a national phenomenon and provided the foundation for rock in the 1970s and 80s.

Electronic tone generation and amplification are the hallmarks of rock. The core instruments are electric guitars, supplemented by electronic keyboards (piano, organ, synthesizers), bass and drums, and lead singer with back-up group. Each performer has a separate microphone and amplifier, and the sound is normally fed into a central mixing board and out through powerful loudspeakers, electronically filtered and distorted through feedback. In recording studios it is possible to manipulate the music still further through splicing, overdubbing, and multitrack taping.

Rock was at first the strict province of males: exclusive, fraternal, misogynistic. The Grateful Dead, a group with a large following even today, represents the quintessential San Francisco rock band of the mid-1960s: all male, psychedelic (under the patronage of Owsley Stanley, an LSD chemist), with a full sound dominated by Jerry Garcia's guitar runs and some twenty-three tons of sound equipment. Women who entered the rock fraternity had to be tough "bad girls" who could compete equally with the boys. Only two women emerged from the San Francisco rock scene as superstars, Janis Joplin and Grace Slick (b. 1939). Lead singer and guitarist of Jefferson Airplane, Slick was responsible for the group's rise to national prominence with her song "White Rabbit," a drug-influenced variation on the theme of

*Alice in Wonderland.* She wrote songs uniquely suited to her penetrating voice—bitterly contemptuous songs that made her seem to be both man- and woman-hater.

## Janis Joplin

Janis Joplin (1943–70), whose celebrity no other female rock star approached, projected a vulnerability beneath a veneer of toughness. An alienated teen-ager who preferred reading, painting, and listening to the recordings of Bessie Smith, Odetta, and Leadbelly to typical teen-age activities, she joined the band Big Brother and the Holding Company in San Francisco in 1966. Universally acclaimed as the only white crossover artist to perform the blues convincingly, Joplin turned millions of white middle-class rock fans into blues enthusiasts. It was in fact her show-stopping rendition of Big Mama Thornton's "Ball and Chain" at the Monterey International Pop Festival in 1967 that made Joplin a national star.

Joplin created an onstage image to please herself. Her eccentric costumes were of feathers, fur, sequins, odd hats, and an equally odd array of jewelry. The counterculture image extended to her stage deportment. Janis swaggered onto the stage drinking Southern Comfort, her language peppered with profanity, as she talked to her audiences about war and peace, love and brotherhood. When she sang, she was totally unrestrained, gripping. Her powerful, anguished voice, welling up out of deep personal pain, worked in extremes—from whispers and moans to howls, groans, and shrieks—in a single song. Her renditions of the blues have a frenetic, driven quality. Joplin was at the peak of her brief career when she died of a drug overdose in 1970. The album she was in the process of recording, *Pearl,* contains her final best-selling song, "Me and Bobby McGee," written by Kris Kristofferson, and two of her own songs, "Mercedes Benz" and "Move Over." It is, however, the last song on the album, "Get It While You Can," that serves as a timely epitaph for Janis Joplin and the counterculture she represented.

## SOUL

The rise of the musical style known as soul, often described as rhythm and blues with gospel fervor, or secular gospel, coincided with the civil rights activism and the awakening of black pride in the early 1960s. The musicians who performed it succeeded in breaking down the barriers between white and black, making this black vernacular style a dominant force in popular music. Soul was about sincere feelings, compellingly expressed in music; it carried a message of promise, of expectations. It was music for dancing. Most of the singers had Southern roots and had once sung in black churches. Thus many of the musical characteristics and vocal techniques of soul are rooted in gospel but applied in a highly stylized manner to secular lyrics. A solid rhythm section provides an anchor for the often fluid vocal lines.

There were two prominent styles. The first, referred to as Southern, "raw," or Red Clay soul, was harsh, aggressive, visceral music with heavy blues inflections, a pulsing rhythm, and a sense of spontaneity. The studio musicians, working without written arrangements, took a sketch of a song from a writer or producer and shaped it with their own ideas as the rehearsal progressed. When they began to "feel" the music, the recording commenced. Because the music was recorded in Southern studios, the house bands were racially mixed and composed of authentic blues and country musicians.

Northern, also called "soft" or "sequin" soul, was the disciplined, polished style usually associated with Motown Records in Detroit. Rhythm was the driving force of this formulaic music. The meter was invariably 4/4 with emphasis on the percussion section. The baritone saxophone figured prominently in arrangements. A slightly later manifestation, called the soul ballad, was a romantic love song, elaborately arranged and indebted to Tin Pan Alley. Motown had a resident composing team—Brian Holland, Lamont Dozier, and Eddie Holland—who came to define Motown's style and produced twenty-eight top-twenty hits between 1963 and 1966. Although men produced the records and must be credited with developing both soul styles, women were the most important and successful artists. Many began their careers as gospel singers, thus standing in a line extending from Sister Rosetta Tharpe, Bessie Smith, and Ella Fitzgerald, through Dinah Washington, to Aretha Franklin.

## Aretha Franklin

The prima donna of Red Clay soul, Aretha Franklin (b. 1942) belongs to a female vocal tradition that mingles the sanctified with the worldly. Child of a Baptist minister and gospel singer, she grew up surrounded by musicians who came to stay at her family's home in Detroit when visiting or performing in her father's church. James Cleveland taught her gospel piano techniques; Mahalia Jackson, Clara Ward, Marion Williams, Dinah Washington, Lou Rawls, and Sam Cooke taught her about singing; and Dinah Washington, Sam Cooke, and Ray Charles served as crossover models for her career.

John Hammond, who had recruited Bessie Smith and Billie Holiday for Columbia Records, signed eighteen-year-old Aretha to a contract. Columbia wanted to mold her into a singer of torch songs and popular standards, but the plan failed miserably. After Jerry Wexler persuaded her to record for Atlantic, Aretha began to find her niche. She was allowed to choose her own material, which ranged from songs by Sam Cooke and Otis Redding to Carole King's "Natural Woman." Wexler took her to record in Muscle Shoals, Alabama, where she worked out arrangements with studio musicians who, like her, had grown up in gospel music. The result was electrifying. Five of her recordings were No. 1 hits, and her forceful version of Otis Redding's "Respect" won a Grammy in 1967. She had become one of the most successful singers in America and a powerful symbol to black audiences, who referred to the summer of 1967 as the time of "Retha, Rap, and Revolt." The following summer, Franklin's soul interpretation of the national anthem opened the tempestuous Democratic National Convention in Chicago.

Soul, like the blues of an earlier era, went out of fashion in the 1970s, but Franklin reached beyond its limits with her introspective album *Young, Gifted, and Black* (1972). Her powerful mezzo-soprano voice, with its range of about two and a half octaves, is vibrant, natural, and expressive. She exhibits great flexibility in register shifts and can change color and intensity as the lyrics demand. Her eloquence is best revealed when she is singing gospel. The 1980s witnessed a new blossoming of her career. In addition to attaining commercial and critical successes with new recordings, she starred in a television special for Showtime and was the subject of a PBS broadcast in the American Masters series (1989). Franklin has also released two gospel albums, *Amazing Grace* (1972) and *One Lord, One Faith, One Baptism* (1987), and has completed several tours.

## Diana Ross and the Supremes

The pinnacle of Motown success, the epitome of "sequin" soul, and the most famous of the many female singing groups of the 1960s, the Supremes had record sales of over twelve million—second only to those of the Beatles—and were the only group to have six consecutive gold records in a single year (1964). The Supremes were a true American success story—three friends growing up in the Detroit housing projects who were recruited by Berry Gordy and fashioned into a sophisticated, professional group. They were a perfectly polished act from their appearances, choreography, and stylized hand gestures to their onstage conversation. Mary Wilson (b. 1943), Florence Ballard (1943–76, replaced by Cindy Birdsong [b. 1939] in

1968), and Diana Ross (b. 1944) made up the famous group. The Supremes began to generate interest when they were paired with the writing team of Holland-Dozier-Holland, who tailored music to their voices. Their first hit, "Where Did Our Love Go?" provided the model for subsequent songs— simple structures in 4/4 meter with steady rhythm, accents on all four beats, and a soft, velvet vocal sound scored in close harmony with Ross's plaintive, little-girl voice singing vapid lyrics about teenage love. Among their most prominent successes were "Baby Love," "Stop in the Name of Love," and "Come See about Me." The Supremes sang their last song as a group, "Someday We'll Be Together," at a farewell performance in 1970, for Diana Ross had decided to begin a solo career. After her departure the group achieved only moderate success and finally disbanded in 1979.

Diana Ross soon sought to change both her feline image and her singing style. With gowns designed by Bob Mackie, she transformed herself into a glamorous vision. Her voice became more refined and the songs she recorded, while verging on the sentimental, were no longer about teen-age love, but rather about women whose independence had been obtained at a heavy cost. A number of these songs were commercial successes: "Reach Out and Touch (Somebody's Hand)," "Ain't No Mountain High Enough," "Remember Me," and "Do You Know Where You're Going To?" As a nightclub performer Ross has a wonderful stage presence, and she has been able to command top fees as an entertainer. She received critical acclaim for her portrayal of Billie Holiday in *Lady Sings the Blues* (1972). More recently she has worked closely with her former protégé, Michael Jackson, who has produced several of her albums and with whom she often performs.

## ROCK SINCE THE 1960s

During the 1970s and 80s rock styles have mushroomed to include folk rock, blues rock, hard rock, soft rock, southern rock, soul, jazz rock, art rock, punk rock, funk, disco, and New Wave. While the basic language of rock has undergone little alteration, it has taken on a new rhythmic vitality from influences without and within. Hispanic immigrants, especially those from the Caribbean basin, have brought a music with exciting rhythms. A second enlivening source has been a style of improvised rhymes with rhythmic accompaniment called rap, developed by street-wise black youths in New York City. Both influences represent the continuing movement away from melody and toward rhythm that began in early rock'n'roll. Rapid technological progress has been responsible for the most significant modifications in the production and transmission of rock: groups have added sophisticated electronic equipment, particularly synthesizers and digital sequencers.

Despite the shifting fashions in rock, there has always been a desire for songs that speak to the human condition with the human voice as messenger. Clear evidence of this need exists in two musical trends that thrive outside mainstream rock. One is the persistence of Tin Pan Alley styles—updated arrangements of older songs or new compositions based on models from the past. Among those who have fashioned successful careers in this style are Barbra Streisand (b. 1942) and Linda Ronstadt (b. 1946), who began her career in rock. Streisand, known for her emotionally exaggerated singing style, is an outstanding interpreter of popular standards. Ronstadt is a consummate stylist who has performed popular standards, operetta, opera, and songs by Philip Glass. Her three 1980s recordings of Tin Pan Alley songs were critical and commercial successes, as was her album of *rancheras*, songs sung to mariachi music, made as a tribute to her father.

A second type of music somewhat outside the rock mainstream, called women-identified music, arose out of the Women's Movement. A number of women musicians began to respond in creative ways to the misogyny expressed in rock lyrics and to the near-total control of the popular music industry by men. Strengthened by the Women's Movement, they began writing "women-identified music" or "women's music" in the 1960s as a conscious expression of the singular experience of a musician as a woman. That it is feminist music implies a political end—the redefinition of the status of women in popular culture and in the mass media.

The audience for this music consists of people who believe in a strong female ideal and in more expansive roles for women in society, and who support women's issues and humanist causes. The performers reach their audiences through recordings, concerts, and women's music festivals. The more traditional ways of communicating with an audience—recordings and concerts—have taken on nontraditional aspects. At concerts, for example, child care and signing for the deaf may be provided, and concert sites are made accessible to the disabled. Women's music festivals, which have proliferated since the first one in 1974 at the University of Illinois, are sometimes entirely closed to men.

The male-dominated music industry has resisted change on the question of equal rights for women. Women learned, as blacks had learned in the early 1960s, that the best way to transmit new or different musical ideas was to take control of both artistic and business ends of the industry. Since the early 1970s, women-identified music has grown from several grass-roots organizations to sophisticated enterprises totally controlled by women.

Blossom Dearie and Betty Carter had formed their own labels in an earlier era, but their motives were entirely artistic. More recently, women have formed companies for ideological reasons. Of these, which have names such as Ova, Urana, and Sweet Alliance, the most important is Olivia Records. Founded in 1973 as a women's collective, Olivia controls the process from writing the music to its production and engineering. Olivia's first entirely women-produced album was Meg Christian's *I Know You Know*. In 1978, Women's Independent Label Distributors (WILD) formed as a collective to promote national record distribution and concert tours of the recording artists. Today there are a number of promotion companies, among them Women on Wheels and Once in a Blue Moon.

Although the message is often radical, the style of women-identified music is mainly that of the mainstream idiom inspired by Tin Pan Alley. Performers' distinctive musical sounds derive more often from the way instrumental texture, vocal quality, and particular techniques are blended than from innovations of form. Lyrics, then, assume maximum importance; some are directed to a lesbian audience.

A pioneer musician who recorded on her own Cassandra label, Malvina Reynolds began writing songs in the 1940s that spoke to humanistic causes and were consciously political. Reynolds encouraged the use of her songs as advocacy pieces and allowed them to be performed without payment of royalties. The messages of some of the songs are evident from their titles: "Rosie Jane (Pregnant Again)" and "We Don't Need Men." The song for which she is best remembered, however, is "Little Boxes"; it describes the poorly constructed housing developments of the post-1945 era, for which she coined the term "ticky tacky."

Performers of women-identified music who emerged in the late 1960s and early 70s include the New Harmony Sisterhood, the New Miss Alice Stone Ladies' Society Orchestra, Deadly Nightshade, the New Haven Women's Liberation Band, Meg Christian, Holly Near, and Margie Adams. Meg Christian and Cris Williamson both record for Olivia; Holly Near records on her own Redwood label.

# ROCK AT THE END OF THE CENTURY

From the vantage point of the 1990s, one can look back over some thirty-five years in which rock has dominated popular music in the United States. Rock stars lead lives of great affluence and astonishing celebrity and have become role models for the young. The culture is saturated with rock music. Expensively produced videos serve as audio-visual equivalents of the

45 rpm records that represented the most current technological advance in the early days of rock'n'roll. MTV, cable television's most successful rock video channel, has been on the air since 1982. Madonna, arguably the most successful rock star of the 1980s, owes her meteoric rise in popularity in large part to a skillful use of the new technology.

## Madonna

A combination of brains, hard work, ambition, talent, and timing have made Madonna Louise Veronica Ciccone (b. 1959) the epitome of the late twentieth-century success story. A shrewd linking of the new—slickly produced music videos—and the old—an album of dance singles—helped bring about her leap to stardom in the early 1980s. Music video was the perfect vehicle for Madonna, who considers videos little movies in which she stars. Knowing that she must create an arresting image that will film well, she uses as her models glamorous female stars of an earlier era: Judy Holliday, Carole Lombard, Marlene Dietrich, and Marilyn Monroe. The result is an image that is both brazenly sexy and delicately feminine, with the veneer of a Catholic "bad girl" who wears the symbols of her church—rosaries and crucifixes—to adorn her revealing costumes.

The success of her debut album, *Madonna* (1983), was largely due to an aggressive promotional campaign using music videos. Madonna's second album, *Like a Virgin* (1984), contained three songs that became best-selling singles, including "Material Girl," the lyrics of which disdain romantic love in favor of "cold, hard cash." By 1985 the album had sold over six million copies, earning Madonna some cold, hard cash of her own. The music on her first two albums and on *True Blue* (1986) is light, girlish, fresh, and hip. Madonna's thin, breathy, slightly nasal, and nervously energetic voice drives the music forward and is ideally suited to the dance tunes of these early albums. *Like a Prayer* (1989), her most serious album to date, reveals a more sophisticated approach. Her voice is lower, darker, fuller, and truer to pitch. The songs, while retaining much of the tunefulness of her earlier work, are serious and self-revelatory. "Till Death Do Us Part" speaks to the painful and very public breakup of her marriage to movie idol Sean Penn. In "Promise to Try" Madonna attempts to deal with poignant memories of the mother who died while the singer was still a child. The music in some of the songs is referential; "Cherish," a song about lasting love, bows to the Association's song of the same name. Throughout the album Madonna draws effectively on her Catholic background. In the title song she skillfully alternates music of prayerful petition with a more typically Madonnaesque refrain of hard-driving dance music. She rounds out the album with "Act of

Contrition," a compelling song that begins with her quiet recitation of the rosary. It remains to be seen whether Madonna will come to occupy a place in popular music comparable to that of the female singers she most admires: Ella Fitzgerald, Joni Mitchell, and Patsy Cline. Still, she has clearly earned a niche in history as "Rock Queen of the 1980s."

## CONCLUSION

The popular music tradition embodies a multiplicity of styles, and though styles may change over time, nothing from the past ever goes away entirely. Today the most creative musicians often speak to contemporary concerns while enlivening their music by reinterpreting or evoking the best ideas from the past. One of the elements that has greatly contributed to enlivening popular music in the twentieth century is the talent of women musicians, vocalists, instrumentalists, and composers. Though the idea persists that women are incapable of making significant contributions except as singers or pianists, the historical facts document quite dramatically that women instrumentalists and composers were neither welcomed nor encouraged by the men inside the tradition or by society. Even singers, who were always considered more acceptable, were stereotyped as canaries, bad girls, folk madonnas, and the like. The handful of women who overcame such arbitrary obstacles must be perceived as grand exceptions to the rule. Nevertheless, since the so-called liberation movements of the recent past, much progress has been made in discrediting long-held sexual stereotypes in American society. Although today's world of jazz and popular music is far from providing equal opportunity to musicians of both sexes, women's chances for success are much greater than ever before.

SUGGESTIONS FOR FURTHER READING

Hamm, Charles. *Yesterdays: Popular Song in America.* New York: W. W. Norton, 1979.

Heilbut, Anthony. *The Gospel Sound: Good News and Bad Times.* New York: Limelight Editions, 1985.

Hirshey, Gerri. *Nowhere to Run: The Story of Soul Music.* New York: Times Books, 1984.

Malone, Bill C. *Country Music, U. S. A.* Rev. ed. Austin: University of Texas Press, 1985.

Miller, Jim, ed. *The Rolling Stone Illustrated History of Rock and Roll.* Rev. ed. New York: Rolling Stone Press, 1980.

Pavletich, Aida. *Rock-A-Bye, Baby.* Garden City, NY: Doubleday, 1980.

Pleasants, Henry. *The Great American Popular Singers.* New York: Simon & Schuster, 1974.

# XII.
# African-American
# Women in Blues and Jazz

*Michael J. Budds*

## INTRODUCTION

Beginning in 1619, Africans were brought to the American colonies to endure the humiliation of slavery. In most instances slaves were stripped of all traces of their native cultures, indoctrinated in European ways, and expected to worship in the European manner. Yet these adverse circumstances produced one of the most powerful musical developments in history. From the time when African slaves began to render European hymns according to the music-making practices of their homelands, a dynamic tradition of African-American music has evolved. Because this music developed as an oral tradition, much of its history has been lost. Yet even if the music had been written down, European notation cannot communicate its essence.

Although much African-American music, especially jazz, is often described as the combination of a European "what" and an African "how," such an explanation oversimplifies the complex process of acculturation. Among the most distinctive features of making music in African-American culture are an emphasis on improvisation and the use of preexisting musical patterns as the basis for elaboration; acceptance of the performer as a creative partner with the composer; the presence of "hot" rhythm and the cultivation of swing; acceptance of a heterogeneous sound ideal permitting a great variety of colors; and a range of emotional expression that dismisses mainstream society's notions of decorum and propriety. Texts in vocal music often mirror the lives of black Americans quite realistically.

The participation of women in the African-American music tradition has always been of vital importance. As wives, mothers, and caretakers of the family souls, African-American women found many opportunities to sing. Secular music, such as lullabies and play songs, and sacred pieces, such as spirituals, were passed from one generation to another, as was the distinctive style of performance. For worship services, talented women developed keyboard skills. Indeed, as a haven for honest expression and as the focus of community life, the Church must be recognized as the primary institution responsible for nurturing and preserving the black tradition in music. In addition, women assumed leading roles in religious practices in which African spirit beliefs and customs survived. "While men served 'aboveground' as preachers in the Afro-American churches, women held sway as 'underground' priestesses."[1] In the rites of Vodun, commonly known as voodoo, for example, the central figures were the so-called voodoo queens, and many songs celebrate the dynamic personalities and powers of these women. Such portrayals recur during the 1920s in the theatrical posing of blueswomen.

Yet the opportunities for women to pursue careers as musicians and entertainers were exceedingly few. Participation in the minstrel tradition after the Civil War affected only a small number of performers. During the twentieth century, however, as various streams of black music occupied a prominent place in the world of commercialized entertainment, black women became supremely successful as singers and rather well accepted as pianists, both functions enjoying the sanctions of tradition.

## THE BLUES

The blues, the primary stream of black folk music, arose in rural areas during the eighteenth and nineteenth centuries, its antecedents both secular (work songs and field hollers) and sacred (spirituals and singing sermons). Its practice was probably codified near the end of the nineteenth century, although regional and local dialects have been cultivated throughout its recorded history. In the twentieth century, a process of urbanization has taken the blues into the realm of popular music as well. The modern history of the blues is a distinctive one, but its influence on other strains of African-American music, such as jazz and gospel, has been fundamental. The blues has also influenced the white rural tradition (country) and, since the advent of rock'n'roll in the 1950s, the popular music of mainstream America.

Several features give the blues its special identity. The first relates to a state of mind. The term, which usually designates a highly personal condition of melancholy or depression, did not enter American usage until after the Civil War, and its application to music expressing the emotional state of American blacks may not have occurred until after 1900. The act of performing the blues is believed to be cathartic, an emotional release. Some also contend that, because of social conditions in the United States, only blacks can meaningfully perform the blues.

The blues is a form of improvised song. At the heart of the music is a flexible series of elemental chords, related to the harmony of hymns, popular songs, and the Amen cadence. A twelve-measure pattern has been widely adopted and has served as the basis for great elaboration; the distinctive melodic and harmonic language uses pitches outside the European tempered system. A characteristic aspect of performance is an antiphonal procedure from Africa known as call-and-response: the alternation of phrases or verses of text by the singer with purely instrumental fills. An extraordinarily compelling tradition has also arisen in the treatment of the improvised text in blues performances, and a vernacular language rich in imagery and double entendre has emerged. The blues deals with human existence at its most realistic; its point of view ranges from anguished to angered and from playful to defiant.

The blues tradition may be divided into two practices: rural and urban. Country (or rural) blues, the older form, is less regular because of the idiosyncracies of its self-taught, independent-thinking practitioners. The country blues typically takes the form of solo performance: a male vocalist singing to his own instrumental accompaniment. Whereas male performers have dominated this part of the tradition, women have been ever-present as the subjects of their songs. Remarkable among the few women who sang the country blues was "Memphis Minnie" McCoy (1896–1973), who also earned considerable respect for her forceful guitar playing.

When blacks migrated to cities in the early twentieth century, they took their music with them. In the process, the blues was transformed into a popular music and subjected to commercial influences. The so-called classic urban blues of the 1920s became a mainstay of black public entertainment. Charismatic women soloists who combined physical glamor, a bold social stance, and emotionally powerful singing, created a memorable repertoire that admitted a wide variety of instrumental accompaniments. Some of the most celebrated performances of the period featured Mamie Smith (1883–1946), Gertrude "Ma" Rainey (1886–1939), Bessie Smith (1894–1937), Clara Smith (1894–1935), Ida Cox (1896–1967), Beulah "Sippie" Wallace (1898–1986), Bertha "Chippie" Hill (1905–50), and Victoria Spivey (1906–76). These artists achieved celebrity status as captivating entertainers, both in personal appearances and on records. As they sang of lost love and broken dreams, of sexual politics and moments of glory, they were providing important models of independence for other black women.

Rhythm and blues, an umbrella term for a varied body of black popular music in the late 1940s, is thought to reflect the growing confidence among African-Americans following World War II. Although the melancholy of earlier blues was not dismissed, the rhythmic vitality, upbeat tempos, and emphasis on the good-time lyrics of rhythm and blues added new dimensions. The participation of women in rhythm and blues at this time may be symbolized by Willie Mae "Big Mama" Thornton (1926–84), whose career is described in the preceding chapter. Other significant women blues singers, such as Dinah Washington [Ruth Jones] (1924–63), Mabel Louise "Big Maybelle" Smith (1924–72), Etta James (b. 1938), and Cora "Koko" Taylor (b. 1938), have carried on this tradition. Whereas men dominated the rural blues and women reigned as the significant interpreters of the classic urban blues of the 1920s, both sexes have participated fully in the rhythm and blues tradition since the 1940s, although women have remained in the minority. The absence of women instrumentalists in the blues tradition is closely related to the social and professional prohibitions described below in the discussion of jazz.

## "Ma" Rainey

Mamie Smith may have been the first woman to record the blues, but it was Gertrude "Ma" Rainey who popularized the genre for mass audiences. She was Paramount Records' biggest-selling star of the 1920s, performing with some of the greatest instrumentalists of the era—Coleman Hawkins, Fletcher Henderson, Blind Blake, George Tom Dorsey, and Louis Armstrong. The woman now known as the "Queen of the Blues" was born Gertrude Pridgett in Columbus, Georgia, in 1886. Her parents were troupers in minstrel shows, and she followed in their footsteps from the age of fourteen. In 1904 she married Will "Pa" Rainey; they toured as the song-and-dance team of Ma and Pa Rainey, then as Rainey and Rainey, Assassinators of the Blues. Their repertoire consisted of minstrel and novelty songs, dancing, humor, and a little blues singing. For a while young Bessie Smith was a member of the ensemble and learned about blues from the Queen Mother herself. By 1917 "Ma," now billed as "Madame," had formed her own Georgia Jazz Band, and "Pa" was no longer her partner. From 1920 until 1935, when she retired from the stage, she performed chiefly in vaudeville, her repertoire including an ever-larger proportion of blues.

Rainey's recording career with Paramount began in 1923 and ended in

1928, when the company refused to renew her contract because her style of down-home singing and the blues had gone out of fashion. On her more than one hundred discs the accompaniments ranged from simple guitar and piano (in blues such as "Sweet Rough Man") to jazz ensembles of cornet, trombone, clarinet, bass saxophone, piano, and banjo (in "Chain Gang Blues"). Although recordings are an important legacy of Rainey's long career, her live performances are what moved her mainly poor, rural black audiences. These people understood they were hearing a woman who knew about their troubles firsthand. The usually frank lyrics dealt with loneliness, violence, men who do women wrong, prostitution, trouble with the law, drinking, and even sexual brutality. A stanza from Rainey's own "Bo-weavil Blues" illustrates the use of double meanings:

> I don't want no man to put no sugar in my tea.
> I don't want no man to put no sugar in my tea,
> Some of 'em is so evil, I'm 'fraid he might poisin [sic] me.

The earthy sound of Rainey's full-voiced contralto comes through even on the rather primitive recordings of the 1920s. Her voice could sound harsh, sometimes guttural, and it was often tinged with melancholy. The influence of rural African-American folk music is evident in her moaning style, which is sometimes echoed in the wailing instrumental accompaniments on her recordings. Rainey varied the melody and rhythm to suit her interpretive purposes and often held back a bit in the middle of a line or at the beginning of a repeated line for emphasis. Although she never learned to read music, "Ma" Rainey composed at least twenty-four of the songs she performed. One of her show-stoppers was "See See Rider," which, like "Bo-weavil Blues," exemplifies the classic AAB form of blues lyrics, where B serves as a kind of stinger or punch line. Among the other well-known songs she wrote are "Don't Fish in My Sea," "Weepin' Woman Blues," and "Moonshine Blues."

"Ma" Rainey was a total performer who wanted to please audiences with her appearance as well as with her music. With her smile shining with gold-capped teeth, she dressed flamboyantly in sequin and rhinestone gowns, often wore diamond jewelry, and carried an ostrich feather fan. One of her monikers, "The Golden Necklace of Blues," derived from her trademark necklace made of twenty-dollar gold pieces. A sound business-woman both on the road and, after her retirement, as the owner-manager of two theatres, she went home to Georgia in 1935, kept house for her brother, and joined the Friendship Baptist Church. It is no small irony that after such a long and successful career as a performer, her death certificate lists her occupation as "housekeeper." "Ma" Rainey died in December 1939 and was buried in the family plot in the town of her birth.

## Bessie Smith

The life of the woman known as the "Empress of the Blues" was itself a blues litany. The place of Bessie Smith's birth, Chattanooga, Tennessee, is not disputed, but dates differ. Most recent sources say 1894; 1895 is on her gravestone. An orphan by the age of eight, Bessie sang in the streets of Chattanooga for spare change before joining a minstrel troupe as a child performer. In 1912 she met and worked with "Ma" Rainey in Moses Stokes's Show. Her 1923 marriage to a Philadelphia policeman ended when he deserted her for another woman, although his leaving may have been caused in part by his wife's drinking problem. Her career reached its apex in the 1920s, when she performed for large audiences in both North and South, and frequently appeared at New York City's Apollo Theatre. Smith may have earned as much as $2,500 a week, making her one of the highest-paid black performers of the era. Yet she found herself earning half her usual salary following the stock market crash of 1929 and learned the

Bessie Smith. The Frank Driggs Collection.
Used by permission.

hard lesson of being out of fashion and without the resources to adapt to new trends. Bessie Smith's life ended in a car crash in Clarksville, Mississippi, in 1937. She was buried in an unmarked grave on the outskirts of Philadelphia.

Smith's recording career, like Rainey's, began in 1923. Although Smith recorded some 200 discs over the next decade, her prime recording years were 1923–28. Her first recording was a new version of "Down Hearted Blues," a song popularized by another famous blues singer, Alberta Hunter, and Lovie Austin, the equally famous female jazz pianist. Smith's rendition sold 780,000 copies in less than six months. Other recordings sold as many as ten million copies. Smith collaborated with various members of Fletcher Henderson's band, including Louis Armstrong, with whom she made a justly famous duet of W. C. Handy's "St. Louis Blues." Although she is best known for her slow blues, Smith also recorded Irving Berlin's "Alexander's Ragtime Band" and other up-tempo standards.

A blues singer who never betrayed her rural Southern roots, Bessie Smith preferred to play to live audiences, even in the North. Unfortunately, her refusal to "whiten" her act for urban middle-class audiences probably hastened her loss of popularity in the 1930s. Possessor of a warm, powerful, resonant voice, Smith could shout or moan, sound plaintive or languorous. Because she normally worked within an interval of a sixth, her range of an octave proved no limitation. She tended to concentrate on focal tones within the key, then embellish them with microtonal slides. The result is an expressive, personal shaping of the original tune. She further shaped songs by modifying the lyrics to enhance their meanings. Working contextually, she would eliminate words and interpolate "hmms" and "ahs," alter vowels, drop or add syllables, repeat or interject words. Her clear diction makes all this lyrical alteration extremely effective. In addition, Smith had a sure understanding of how and when to use rubato. She bent the rhythm by leaning into it and preferred to sing without a drummer so that she could control the rhythmic flow of a performance.

The liberties Smith took served the same expressive end. A recorded example illustrating her style is the popular song "Nobody Knows You When You're Down and Out." Cast in the typical Tin Pan Alley structure of verse and chorus, the song approximates the blues because of her particular interpretation. Her treatment of the verse is conversational, as if she is confessing her own sad story. At the beginning of the chorus Smith reshapes the well-known tune by sliding into, then stretching, its opening "nobody" and later by dropping syllables and phrases and inserting heartfelt "hmms" to enhance the absent lyrics. She also adds text, most noticeably at the end of the chorus, when she slides into "when you're down and out" as a tag line.

Smith had a regal presence on stage. She was good-looking, with a pleasant round face and dimples, and her shapely body swayed to the rhythm as she sang. "Empress" is a fitting title for her, as she dominated her own era. Among her most important legacies is the tremendous influence she had on contemporary and later generations of blues singers and jazz performers, such as Louis Armstrong, Billie Holiday, Mahalia Jackson, Willie Mae "Big Mama" Thornton, Dinah Washington, Odetta, and Janis Joplin. Her artistry survives through her recordings, which Columbia reissued in full in the early 1970s. For more than three decades after Smith's death, her grave at Mount Lawn Cemetery in Sharon, Pennsylvania, remained unmarked. When this became widely known, Janis Joplin and Juanita Green, a nurse who then headed the North Philadelphia chapter of the NAACP (and who had scrubbed Bessie Smith's floors as a child), bought a gravestone. The inscription reads: "The greatest blues singer in the world will never stop singing."

# JAZZ

Jazz is another significant stream of music created primarily by African-Americans since the early twentieth century. Although improvisation by individual performers is central to jazz, a variety of performance contexts have been embraced in a series of rapidly changing substyles. Throughout its history jazz musicians have drawn on the resources of folk music, popular music, and fine-art music and have, in turn, exerted an immeasurable influence on music outside the nebulous borders of jazz. Although black musicians must be identified as the major figures in the evolution of jazz, white musicians have worked successfully in this tradition almost from its beginning.

More than other musical traditions, jazz has been viewed by the musicians who produce it and by the society it serves as a male reserve. As late as 1973, an anonymous male pianist declared: "Jazz is a male language. It's a matter of speaking that language and women just can't do it."[2] More recently, in his discussion of "the gender problem" in jazz, the historian Neil Leonard observed: "Women function in secondary roles as pianists, singers, dancers, den mothers, homemakers, breadwinners, and sex objects, but seldom are first-line musicians."[3] The truth of these statements must be qualified, although women have been most successful and best accepted in the world of jazz as singers and pianists. Because jazz is primarily an instrumental music and because its history has been largely shaped by wind players, women have been at a considerable disadvantage. The direct precursors of jazz were the blues, ragtime,[4] and the marching band tradition, each of which is strongly associated with men and their fraternal pleasures. Although in mainstream society young women were encouraged to become proficient as singers and pianists, in part with the hope of making successful marriages, rarely were they encouraged to pursue careers. Playing wind instruments was not considered decorous, and the thought of women marching down the street as band members was inconceivable. Among the lower classes there were economic obstacles as well: instruments and lessons were luxuries, and money was rarely to be wasted on the education of girls.

In a sense, the very venues for jazz performance served as discriminatory social filters. Ragtime and early jazz found homes in the rough-and-tumble night spots of turn-of-the-century American cities, where a host of unsavory behaviors flourished by night. Because of its association with early jazz, Storyville, the pleasure district of New Orleans, has become legendary, but similar areas existed in other cities. If a woman, musician or not, valued her reputation, she would not be seen in such precincts. Indeed, the initial objections of the Establishment to ragtime and jazz were based on their African-American origins and their whorehouse associations.

In subsequent decades the factors that contributed to the jazz musician's precarious lifestyle continued to inhibit the participation of women. The scarcity of musical opportunities, the instability of employment, the resulting financial insecurity, the loose code of morality that flourished in night spots, and the temptations of liquor and drugs were obstacles confronting all jazz artists. For women, additional challenges related to sexist notions prevailed in society. Men typically refused to take women seriously as gifted musicians and did not welcome them as competitors for jobs. At the same time, almost no role models existed for women as jazz artists, and their families seldom supported their career aspirations. One final circumstance made the barriers to a career almost insurmountable: jazz is fundamentally an oral tradition, which the young typically learn by playing with established figures. Systematically excluded from entry-level opportunities and denied the essential period of apprenticeship, women players were rarely able to develop their talents to a professional level, let alone establish themselves as viable jazz artists.[5]

One response to this dilemma was the formation of ensembles made up exclusively of women. In general, such an artificial solution contributed as much to the double standard as it strengthened the rights of women performers. Two ensembles, however, made important strides in improving the position of women jazz musicians, although both were forced to make concessions to sexism. The Melodears, formed in 1934 and led by singer Ina Ray Hutton [Odessa Cowan] (1916–84), became one of the popular swing bands of the decade. Although Hutton was billed as "the blonde bomb-shell" and was obliged to parade around in extravagant costumes, the members of her ensemble were highly competent and played arrangements comparable to those of male bands. Perhaps the most highly respected all-women big band was the International Sweethearts of Rhythm, formed in 1939 in Piney Woods, Mississippi. From the time of its debut at the Howard Theatre in Washington, D.C., in 1940 until it was disbanded late in the decade, the International Sweethearts of Rhythm was accepted not only as the premier female band but also as a first-rate ensemble. Through tours in the United States and Europe, and through such recordings as "Don't Get It Twisted," this band reached a broad audience and enjoyed real success.

Yet today's jazz legacy would not be as substantial as it is without the enduring contributions of women singers and pianists. Many, indeed, stand as artists of the highest calibre. In addition to Billie Holiday, Ella Fitzgerald, and Mary Lou Williams, notable women jazz performers include the singers Ethel Waters (1896–1977), Mildred Bailey (1907–51), Helen Humes (1913–81), Anita O'Day (b. 1919), Carmen McRae (b. 1922), Sarah Vaughn (1924–90), Cleo Laine (b. 1927), Betty Carter (b. 1930), and Nancy Wilson (b. 1937); the pianists Lovie Austin (1887–1972), Sweet Emma Barrett (1897–1983), Lil Hardin Armstrong (1898–1971), Hazel Scott (1920–81), Marian McPartland (b. 1920), Toshiko Akiyoshi (b. 1929), Alice Coltrane (b. 1937), and Carla Bley (b. 1938); and organist Shirley Scott (b. 1934). Several of these women were also active as composers.

## Billie Holiday

Struggle and misery mark the lives of many artists. Few, however, contain the elements of tragedy and pathos to the same degree as the life of Billie Holiday, the woman considered by many to be the most important singer in the history of jazz on the basis of her originality, artistry, and influence. The poverty of her childhood in the slums of Baltimore, the institutionalized racism and sexism of her time, the unforgiving nature of the entertainment business all exacted a powerful toll on her outwardly tough but inwardly fragile sensibility. Highly temperamental in both personal and professional dealings, she suffered from what has been called "a staggering lack of self-esteem."[6] Her private search for the love she sang about so eloquently yielded failed relationships that left her victimized and exploited. She did not possess the personal resources to sustain her own existence and retreated into the private hell of alcohol abuse and drug addiction. Her autobiography, *Lady Sings the Blues* (1956), and the film biography of the same name (1972), though marred by inaccuracies and sensationalism, succeed in communicating the sordid details of her life.

Born in 1915 to a teen-aged unwed mother and soon abandoned by her father, Eleanora Fagan was given little education. Reportedly raped at the age of ten and arrested for prostitution after following her mother to Harlem, she embarked on a career as a singer in the 1930s. Her only musical education took the form of listening to recordings of Bessie Smith and Louis Armstrong loaned to her by a madam for whom, as a child, she worked as a messenger. In 1933 Holiday was discovered by producer John Hammond and, with his assistance, began recording and performing in prominent New York clubs. Her collaborations with pianist Teddy Wilson, Lester Young, and others brought her greater recognition, though her public appeal never equaled the respect accorded her by musicians and musical connoisseurs. In 1937 she toured with Count Basie's band, and in 1938 she became one of the first black female soloists to cross the racial barrier by performing publicly as a member of Artie Shaw's band. In spite of her success, both affiliations were sources of great personal humiliation: for appearances with Basie, Holiday was forced to darken her face with makeup; and traveling with the all-white Shaw band presented a regular series of confrontations in restaurants, hotels, and nightclubs.

One must assume that the plaintive, almost wounded quality so characteristic of Holiday's singing and so much a part of her attraction to listeners was a musical mirror of her own personal anguish. Her assumed name—a combination of the names of her movie idol Billie Dove and guitarist Clarence Holiday, the father who abandoned her—makes an apt symbol of her suffering. Her nickname, "Lady Day," coined by saxophonist Lester Young, paid tribute to her dignified bearing. Her trademarks were a white dress and a white gardenia, worn in her hair.

The last years of her life were tainted by arrests for narcotics possession, a public trial, a prison term, and revocation of the cabaret card that permitted her to work in New York City. Her recordings in the 1950s bear witness to the ravages of liquor, drugs, and a deteriorating personal life on her voice. She died alone in 1959, her fortune dissipated by her own mismanagement and the expenses of her addictions.

Holiday, a singer of uncommon expressive power, lacked a naturally beautiful voice. Yet she created a dynamic, individual world of expression. By exploring the continuum between heightened speech and singing, by recasting well-known tunes to reach their essential musical qualities, by applying the jazz instrumentalist's manner of phrasing to her singing, and by interpreting sad songs with disarming personal emotion, she almost single-handedly raised the singer's role in jazz to the level of creativity expected of instrumental soloists. At the same time her singing was colored by the tonal inflections, urgency, and realism associated with the blues. Her primary vehicle was the torch song, which she transformed into some of the most immediate jazz of her time. Among many memorable performances, Holiday's renditions of "Them There Eyes," "All of Me," "I Can't Get Started," and "Georgia on My Mind" demonstrate her talents magnificently.

## Ella Fitzgerald

Perhaps no one symbolizes the very concept of a jazz singer as much as Ella Fitzgerald. For more than fifty years she has reigned as a superlative interpreter of the American popular song and has participated in the jazz tradition as one of its most versatile artists. In so doing, she has commanded the highest respect of musicians and the adoration of an international public. Her knowledge of musical style and her awareness of her own capabilities have resulted in stunning musical creations. She has the uncanny capacity to transform the most conventional melody and the most banal lyrics into memorable music.

Born in Newport News, Virginia, in 1918, Fitzgerald was reared as an orphan in Yonkers, New York. Youthful aspirations to become a dancer enticed her to enter an amateur contest at Harlem's famous Apollo Theatre in 1934. Too stagestruck to dance, she won by singing. This surprising turn of events brought her to the attention of drummer Chick Webb, who engaged her to sing with his ensemble. After his death in 1939, Fitzgerald led the band until 1942. Early success as a big-band singer not only brought her national celebrity, but provided invaluable on-the-job training during her teen years, as she heard instrumentalists improvise and explore the rhythmic and melodic subtleties of jazz.

Her solo career, which dates from 1942, acquired an important dimension in 1946, when Fitzgerald became associated with the impresario Norman Granz and his Jazz at the Philharmonic tours. In 1955, on Granz's new record label Verve, Fitzgerald embarked on a milestone venture—a series of albums devoted to the great composers of American popular song. This twelve-year project yielded a treasury of performances of some of the finest works of Arlen, Berlin, Ellington, Gershwin, Kern, Mercer, Porter, and Rodgers. Fitzgerald's discography ranks among the most impressive in the history of jazz.

Fitzgerald's universal and long-standing success as a singer can be attributed to a number of factors: a genuine and endearing personality; an appealing voice with true intonation and an extraordinary range; an intuitive knowledge of her own considerable vocal technique that allows her to emphasize her strengths; an impeccable sense of rhythm and harmony; and a seemingly inexhaustible gift for melodic invention. Whether Fitzgerald is embellishing a classic love ballad like Gershwin's "I've Got a Crush on You" or "Someone to Watch over Me," or astonishing her listeners with her justly famous virtuoso scat improvisations, as on "How High the Moon," her performances present a quality of musical rightness and inevitability that defies explanation.

## Mary Lou Williams

Pianist, composer, and arranger Mary Lou Williams must be remembered as a true pioneer. For much of her career she was regarded as the only female instrumentalist to demonstrate the highest level of achievement in jazz circles. Her full measure of success was often explained with the dubious justification that she "played like a man." In fact, although Williams was fully aware of the playing styles of many male pianists, she

Mary Lou Williams. The Frank Driggs Collection. Used by permission.

modeled herself after pianist and composer Lovie Austin (1887–1972). Williams was also exceptional for her important contributions to jazz arranging and composition. By the end of her long and multifaceted career, she had revealed not only a remarkable talent, unending resourcefulness, and a high sense of purpose, but an equally rare ability to move on with the times without losing touch with the historical foundations of jazz, especially the blues.

Born in Atlanta, Georgia, on May 8, 1910, Mary Elfrieda Scruggs learned about spirituals and ragtime literally on her mother's knee; from the age of four, she astonished her family and her neighbors with her piano playing. Claiming never to have received a formal lesson, she taught herself by listening closely to other musicians, then working out at the keyboard what she had heard. By the age of ten she performed publicly in Pittsburgh, where she was reared, and sat in with visiting bands whenever possible. At the age of fifteen, Mary joined a band led by saxophonist John "Bearcat" Williams, whom she married in 1926. In 1929, with him, she began her professionally rewarding association with Andy Kirk and his Clouds of Joy, a Kansas City–based band that featured both "hot" and "sweet" music. Many attribute a substantial part of the high reputation of Kirk's band to Mary's arrangements, compositions, and solos, such as "Froggy Bottom" (1936) and "Mary's Idea" (1938). Benny Goodman, Jimmie Lunceford, Earl Hines, Bob Crosby, Louis Armstrong, Tommy Dorsey, Duke Ellington, and Dizzy Gillespie also performed her polished arrangements.

With the ascendancy of the bop style, in 1942 Williams formed a combo with trumpet player Shorty Baker, her second husband, and became prominent on the New York scene. In 1945 she led a short-lived all-women ensemble, which included the talented guitarist Mary Osborne (b. 1921). After a brief stint as the staff arranger for Duke Ellington, Williams established herself as a soloist and trio player and toured at home and abroad. Except for a three-year hiatus (1954–57), she worked constantly as a performer and composer and ultimately as a teacher, notably at Duke University, until her death on May 28, 1981. Toward the end of her life, critics, scholars, and jazz lovers recognized her stature as a musician and her authority as a participant in much of the history of jazz. In addition, Williams served as president of her own recording company and established and guided the Bel Canto Foundation, a charitable organization dedicated to helping needy musicians.

The piano style of Mary Lou Williams is marked by experimentation and eclecticism. She established herself as a swing-era pianist with elements of the stride style and boogie-woogie. Her transition to the bop idiom, with its irregular and sometimes relentless "noodling," was accomplished with such convincing ease that it seemed natural. By the 1960s, moreover, she had enriched her vocabulary with gestures of rhythmic and harmonic intricacy not unlike those found in the creations of many of the so-called radicals of the day. Nevertheless, she never turned her back on "the beat."

Just as in her playing, Mary Lou Williams exhibited an unusually broad scope as a jazz composer in more than 350 works. Firmly grounded in spirituals, ragtime, the blues, and the swing-era style, she nevertheless embraced new ideas. Her first extended work, *Zodiac Suite* (1945), in twelve movements, was premiered by her trio on her New York radio show; in 1946 a part of this work was performed by members of the New York Philharmonic and the composer at Carnegie Hall. She collaborated with Milton Orent in creating a fairy tale in the bop style, *In the Land of Oo Bla Dee*, recorded by Dizzy Gillespie's big band. After her conversion to Catholicism in the mid-1950s, Williams often used her gifts for composition as a form of religious expression. Her most celebrated work in this sphere is *Mary Lou's Mass* (1969) for jazz combo and solo vocalists, which was commissioned by the Vatican, written in Rome, and choreographed by Alvin Ailey. This score has been praised as an encyclopedia of black music and has received many performances in both liturgical and concert settings.

Mary Lou Williams was willing to embrace new developments and was able to explore new idioms without sacrificing tradition. Through the force of her musicianship and the strength of her character, she was able to weather the storms of an inhospitable system and to flourish admirably in spite of it. For these reasons, during the later years of her life, she was often justifiably acknowledged as the "First Lady of Jazz."

## NOTES

1. Linda Dahl, *Stormy Weather: The Music and Lives of a Century of Jazz-women* (New York: Pantheon Books, 1984), p. 6.

2. Ibid., p. 3.

3. Neil Leonard, *Jazz: Myth and Religion* (New York: Oxford University Press, 1978), p. 24. Note the author's use of the present tense.

4. In spite of its origins, ragtime was quickly embraced in the parlors of middle-class American homes, and among its most-devoted consumers and champions in the first decades of the twentieth century were white women pianists. A number of women, most notably May Aufderheide (1890–1972), were active as ragtime composers. See Max Morath, "May Aufderheide and the Ragtime Women," in *Ragtime: Its History, Composers, and Music*, edited by John E. Hasse (New York: Schirmer Books, 1985), pp. 154–65.

5. In her important study, *Stormy Weather*, Linda Dahl discusses a number of women pioneers—instrumentalists and singers—who struggled to achieve recogni-

tion as jazz musicians. She also includes profiles of ten women who were enjoying successful careers in jazz at the beginning of the 1980s as well as a selective discography (pp. 307–54) devoted to women jazz musicians as vocalists, instrumentalists, and composers.

6. James Lincoln Collier, *The Making of Jazz: A Comprehensive History* (Boston: Houghton Mifflin, 1978), p. 310.

## SUGGESTIONS FOR FURTHER READING

Harrison, Daphne Duval. *Black Pearls: Blues Queens of the 1920s.* New Brunswick: Rutgers University Press, 1988.

Placksin, Sally. *American Women in Jazz: 1900 to the Present.* New York: Wideview Books, 1982.

Unterbrink, Mary. *Jazz Women at the Piano.* Jefferson, NC: McFarland, 1983.

# The Special Roles of Women

# XIII.
# Women's Support and Encouragement of Music and Musicians

## Linda Whitesitt

## INTRODUCTION

"Culture, like automobiles, lighting fixtures, and bread, is produced by the integrated actions of people filling a variety of roles."[1] Far from the Romantic ideal of art as the product of individual and isolated genius, musical culture is the outcome of actors in socially defined roles playing parts in socially constructed institutions. It is the result of performers, listeners, teachers, instrument makers, publishers, critics, ticket purchasers, managers, helpmates, fundraisers, administrators, and volunteers interacting in private and public institutions—family, church, court, salon, concerts, symphony orchestras, festivals, and conservatories. By transcending the myth of the great artist and looking at systems rather than individuals as the architects of art, women become visible as starring actors in the institutional creation of musical culture.

Limited by familial and societal conventions from entering the public professions of composition and performance, women have turned to other ways of participating in musical culture. In the private sphere of home, court, and salon, they have encouraged the musical education of their children, engaged the services of composers and performers, and promoted the careers of virtuosi. In the public sphere of symphony orchestras, music festivals, community recital series, and educational institutions, women have founded performing ensembles, coordinated fund-raising efforts, managed appearances of touring artists in their communities, started music libraries, donated land for music parks, established instrument collections, and joined together to solicit financial backing for large musical institutions.

Although women have viewed their support of music from a variety of vantage points, most have sought the role of friend to music for the same reasons: a deep love of music, a belief in the value of musical experiences in the life of a community, and an appreciation of the rewards of musical training in the education of the young. Many have come to their commitment of nurturing the lives of musical individuals and institutions from musical backgrounds, and many see their work as an opportunity to give back to the community and to music the enrichment they experienced as music students. Discouraged from entering the labor market, educated, and displayed as status symbols for their husbands, wealthy women with leisure time looked to involvement in cultural activities to escape the isolation of the home. Only in the twentieth century, with the necessity of coordinated group support for ever-larger musical institutions, have women of lesser means pooled their resources to support musical organizations.

Although much of their work has been in the form of financial subsidy, women's support of musical activities calls for a broader definition of patronage, one that includes the encouragement of child by mother and husband by wife; the donation of hours, energy, and organizational skill; and the fashioning of nurturing environments for musical culture. In view of the sheer number of women who have been active supporters of music and the lack of scholarly attention to the area of patronage in general, the scarcity of primary sources, the dearth of reliable secondary studies, and the invisibility of women's activities in historical documents, this chapter is but a brief exploration of what has been an unknown terrain. What follows is only a beginning—a brief chronological sketch of women's part in helping to create musical culture.

## SUPPORT IN PRIVATE INSTITUTIONS OF MUSIC MAKING

Until the development of public institutions of music making in the late eighteenth century, music was cultivated in the private institutions of church and court by persons holding positions of power. On occasion and under certain circumstances, these might include women. During the Middle Ages the most significant was Eleanor of Aquitaine (1122–1204), who, along with her family and her descendants, influenced the course of medieval music.[2] By the thirteenth century, Europe's feudalism began to be replaced by a hegemony based on royal dynasties. Numerous noblewomen of Europe's castles and manors directed musical courts where composers and performers flourished: Mary of Burgundy (1457–82) retained the services of chanson composer Antoine Busnois as her *prêtre chaplain;* Margaret of Austria (1480–1530) reestablished the musical brilliance of the Burgundian court with her special protégé Pierre de la Rue; and Mary of Hungary (1505–58) succeeded Margaret as Regent of the Netherlands and followed her lead as patron by nurturing an active musical chapel in Brussels.

The power enjoyed by some women under the feudal and monarchical system of western Europe was far less common in the sovereign states in Renaissance Italy. Nevertheless, two women exerted an enormous influence on the course of native Italian music in the sixteenth century: Lucrezia Borgia (1480–1519) in Ferrara and Isabella d'Este (1474–1539) in Mantua. Both women paid exclusive attention to secular music for voice and strings, but Isabella focused her patronage on a single type of music, the frottola, while Lucrezia concentrated on music for banquets and dances for court celebrations. In addition, both women employed one of the greatest frottol-

Leonardo da Vinci, drawing of Isabella d'Este. Paris, the Louvre. Photo courtesy of Alinari/Art Resource.

ists of the period, the composer Bartolomeo Tromboncino, who served Isabella from 1489 to 1505, when he left for Lucrezia's court. Both Isabella and Lucrezia encouraged Tromboncino to create musical settings of the poems of Petrarch and his most talented successors, thus raising the literary standards of the frottola. Because of Isabella's greater commitment to quality poetry, "and because her determined patronage stretches over a longer period than Lucrezia's, it may be that Isabella is the more important patron. Nevertheless, both women contributed profoundly to the rise of native Italian music and to its development."[3]

Women of noble rank continued to hold sway over the course of musical styles and composers' careers through the nineteenth century. In England, Elizabeth I (1533–1603) encouraged the flowering of keyboard music during her reign not so much by direct patronage as by her example as an amateur singer, dancer, and virginalist. In Rome, Queen Christina of Sweden (1626–89) gathered around her an incredible entourage of poets, musicians, artists, and intellectuals; they became the nucleus of the Arcadia, one of the most famous academies in Rome. As her *maestro di cappella* Christina employed Alessandro Scarlatti, who remained in her retinue from ca. 1680 to 1684. Scarlatti probably also provided music for Christina's successor as patron of the arts in Rome, Maria Casimira of Poland (1641–1715), who in 1696 settled into voluntary exile in that city. Her fifteen years of distinguished and far-reaching patronage in Rome included support of Alessandro's son, Domenico Scarlatti. Today Scarlatti's renown as a composer of keyboard sonatas is due to the woman he served first as teacher then as music master, the woman who commissioned for her own use most of the composer's 550 harpsichord sonatas: Princess Maria Barbara of Bragança (1711–58).

The revolutions at the end of the eighteenth century shook the social foundation of music making, dependent as it was on the wealth of the aristocracy. Now the growth of independent concerts, opera, and musical societies caused the structure of musical life to develop different institutions and social organizations. By the middle of the nineteenth century, the growing economic power and stability of the middle class supported a public world of commercial concert establishments, and "by 1870 there was little in the new concert world which would seem anachronistic today."[4]

The nineteenth century also witnessed the emergence of two different musical worlds: high art, the music of the German classical school; and music that was more popular, opera and music of the virtuosi. Each had its own public, institutions, and activities. Benefit concerts and salons provided a setting for the dazzling displays of the virtuosi and offered musicians the opportunity to build followings for themselves. Orchestral and chamber music concerts furnished an arena for classical music. Until the middle of the nineteenth century, concerts of popular music overshadowed concerts of classical music in London, Paris, and Vienna. Not until the 1860s did "serious" music encompass both the virtuosic and the German schools.

Given the close link between the popular-music world and the world of the family (benefit concerts grew out of salons centered in the home), women played a critical role in its foundations: they took charge of their children's musical education, continued their own musical training, and directed the salons. In the public world of classical concerts, however, "Males imposed . . . a lofty intellectual definition through which—thanks to the traditional conception that men were more serious than women—they excluded the other sex from leadership, even though women attended classical-music concerts just as much as men."[5] Women would not be awarded formal public authority over such concerts until the twentieth century.

With the soaring popularity of the piano at the turn of the nineteenth century and its importance as a woman's instrument, many composers made their livings by teaching and composing for women as well as by performing in women's salons. Beethoven honored many women with dedications: Eleonore von Breuning, Christiane Lichnowsky (1765–1841), Anna Luise Barbara Keglevich, Antonie Brentano, and Dorothea Ertmann, among others. His participation in the musical gatherings of Nanette Streicher and her husband, Johann Andreas Streicher, led to a close "motherly" relationship with Frau Streicher, a type of nurturing association characteristic of many of Beethoven's alliances with other women. Other sponsors in the nineteenth century include Countess Maria Wilhelmine of Thun-Hoherstein (mother of Christiane Lichnowsky), who was a patron of Haydn, Beethoven, and Mozart; Countess Delphine Potocka (1807–77), the dedicatee of many of Chopin's works; and Pauline Viardot-Garcia (1821–1910), who helped foster the careers of Gounod and Saint-Saëns.

In addition to arranging salons, women of wealth continued their private subsidy of composers. For Grand Duchess Elena Pavlovna (1807–73), sister-in-law of the tsar, Anton Rubinstein served as accompanist to palace singers (he jestingly referred to his position as "Janitor of Music"), lived as a guest at the Kàmennoi-Òstrov Palace, wrote a series of short operas to illustrate the differing nationalities of Russia, accompanied his patron to Nice, and helped the duchess plan the establishment of the Russian Musical Society and the Russian Conservatory. Another Russian composer, Tchaikovsky, was awarded a number of commissions followed by an annual allowance for fourteen years by the wealthy widow Nadezhda von Meck (1831–94), who later employed Debussy as her pianist. She and

Tchaikovsky had a unique association in that they never met; both needed the illusion of close emotional support without the obstructions an actual meeting might incur.

Women have long served as sources of support for their partners, dedication generally inspired by deep commitment and admiration for the artistic ability of their lovers or husbands both during their lives and after their deaths. Clara Schumann (1819–96) gave sustained emotional, financial, and artistic sustenance to Robert at the same time as she managed their household, bore eight children, and pursued her own successful composing and performing career. Other helpmates in the nineteenth century include George Sand (1804–76), pseudonym of the writer Amantine Lucile Aurore Dudevant (Chopin), Countess Marie d'Agoult (1805–76) and Princess Carolyne Sayn-Wittgenstein (1819–87; Liszt), Cosima Wagner (1837–1930), Giuseppina Verdi (1815–97), and Alma Mahler (1879–1964). A woman's negation of self on behalf of her partner's art is epitomized in Alma Mahler's acquiescence to her husband's wish that she abandon her own composing career:

> I buried my dream and perhaps it was for the best. It has been my privilege to give my creative gifts another life in minds greater than my own. And yet the iron had entered my soul and the wound has never healed.[6]

> I lived his life. I had none of my own. He never noticed this surrender of my existence. He was so self-engrossed that any disturbance, however slight, was unendurable. Work, exaltation, self-denial and the never-ending quest were his whole life on and on and forever.[7]

With the consolidation of modern concert institutions in the second half of the nineteenth century, salons declined in importance. However, the practice of inviting musicians to perform for guests in one's home continues until this day. Composers and performers of the early twentieth century won unwavering support from the woman whose salon became the crossroads in new musical developments in Paris: Princesse Edmond de Polignac (1865–1943), who for more than half a century promoted the talents of young performers, commissioned new works, and ensured the performance of new music. The list of those she supported reads like a register of the primary actors on the musical/artistic scene from 1880 to 1940: Gabriel Fauré, Ernest Chausson, Vincent d'Indy, Emmanuel Chabrier, Maurice Ravel, Ethel Smyth, Claude Debussy, Manuel de Falla, Jean Cocteau, Serge Diaghilev, Darius Milhaud, Igor Stravinsky, Erik Satie, Germaine Tailleferre, Karol Szymanowski, Nadia Boulanger, Paul Hindemith, Francis Poulenc, Kurt Weill, and Jean Françaix.

## SUPPORT OF PUBLIC INSTITUTIONS

Although individual women have continued to support composers in the twentieth century, much of women's gift-giving to music has been directed toward public institutions in their communities: concert and opera series, symphony orchestras, educational institutions, music festivals, and the like. Combining their view of music as necessary for the cultural life of their communities with their commitment to social services for the masses and education for the young, women have joined together to provide rich musical environments. Nowhere has this support been so vital as in the United States.

The role of cultural supporter was first championed for American women by Fanny Raymond Ritter (1830–90) at the 1876 meeting of the Association for the Advancement of Women:

> Every American lady who possesses the indispensable kindness of heart, refinement, generosity and culture, as well as influence,—the wives of men of intellectual power, inherited wealth, or great commercial prominence, more especially—can accomplish a great deal in her own small circle. . . .
>
> With lady amateurs, then, will chiefly rest the happy task of preparing, by a beneficent use of such abilities as they may possess, the soil which must foster the young germs of future American art. . . .[8]

In the United States there was a common notion that men guarded the precincts of business and politics while women oversaw the domains of home and culture. Many women triumphed in the socially sanctioned separate sphere of musical patronage without questioning the construct of separate spheres itself, and they did it, as Ritter suggests, "in [their] own small circle."

Women began their group patronage of music in women's music clubs and music departments of women's clubs, part of a long line of nineteenth-century women's organizations that included charitable and missionary societies, moral reform and welfare groups, and women's study clubs. Organized initially to provide a forum for women trained as musicians but unable to practice music as a profession, women's music clubs soon turned to stimulating the musical culture of their communities by sponsoring concerts of touring artists. They were so successful that by 1927 it was reported that, outside of large cities, individual clubs handled three-fourths of the concert engagements in the United States, spending approximately one million dollars to engage concert artists.[9] Club efforts were a major force in the growth and education of concert audiences at the turn of the century, and they played a significant role in molding the musical values of their communities and shaping the nature of concert life in America.[10]

One outstanding music club leader was Ella May Smith (1860–1934), president of the Music Club of Columbus (Ohio). Coming to the presidency of her club in 1903 from a career as a piano teacher, vocal coach, instructor of music, lecturer on music history, music journalist, composer, and author, Smith increased the membership of the once-disbanded club to 850 by the end of her first year and 3,500 by the end of her fourth. During her thirteen years as president (1903–16), this talented leader established a yearly series of six artists' and six members' concerts, free public organ recitals, a choir, the Altruistic Department, an exchange program with other clubs, extension lectures and recitals, a student organization, community music schools in settlement houses, and a music library and a trust for its continuation at the Columbus Public Library. The club also donated an organ to the city. Many women, using the experience gained in directing club activities, entered the world of music management and became role models for a growing number of women professional managers in a variety of arts organizations.

Women have been indispensable in championing the symphony orchestras in their communities, shaping their development, organizing financial support, and developing educational programs. Women have also been influential in the founding of orchestras. In Cleveland, Adella Prentiss Hughes (1869–1950) enlisted the aid of wealthy businessmen to bring conductor Nikolai Sokoloff to that city in 1918. She persuaded them to pay his salary, thus founding the Cleveland Orchestra, which she managed for fifteen years. Hughes helped raise money for operating expenses; encouraged the securing of Cleveland's first adequate concert auditorium, Severance Hall; arranged tours for the orchestra; and developed a comprehensive educational program. Likewise, Ima Hogg (1882–1975) engineered the founding of the Houston Symphony in 1913, served twelve terms as president of its board of directors, initiated the Women's Committee, and directed fund-raising campaigns.

Women were essential in the establishment and growth of symphony orchestras in other cities as well. In Cincinnati in 1894, the Ladies' Musical Club led the way in founding and supervising the Cincinnati Symphony Orchestra. Prominent in these efforts were Helen H. Taft (1861–1943), first president of the Orchestra Association Board; Bettie Fleischmann Holmes, a later president; and Annie Sinton Taft, who with her husband, Charles Taft, provided major financial support for the orchestra. In Washington, D.C., the Friday Morning Music Club was one of the founding members and a major financial supporter of the National Symphony Orchestra. Composer

Mary Howe (1882–1964) was important in this early relationship, and later in the century Marjorie Merriweather Post (1887–1973) donated more than one million dollars to the orchestra. Women exerted tremendous influence on the course of the New York Philharmonic:

> To anyone who examines without prejudice the history of the Philharmonic it is a perpetual source of wonder that, ever since that fateful moment in 1909 when Mrs. George Sheldon helped to marshal the forces that reorganized the old Philharmonic, the Society has been blessed with an unfailing supply of rich, hard-working, intelligent, loyal, and public-spirited women who have been willing to give their time and money for the good of the city's musical life. Some of them may have had nobler motives than others, but whether they did what they did out of generosity, or vanity, or love of music, or just to keep busy, the results for the Philharmonic have been always salutary and sometimes salvatory.[11]

In Philadelphia the early work of informal committees of women and the efforts after 1904 of the formal Women's Committees were integral to the success of the Philadelphia Orchestra. Such achievement has been echoed in women's work in symphony auxiliaries and on symphony boards throughout the United States.

Women have also been active in founding educational institutions. One of the first was Clara Baur (d. 1912), who in 1867 founded and directed the Cincinnati Conservatory of Music. Twenty years later, Jeannette Thurber (1850–1946) organized the ill-fated National Conservatory of Music in 1885 and persuaded Antonín Dvořák to assume its directorship in 1892; he remained for three seasons. In 1894, May Garrettson Evans (1866–1947) founded the Peabody Graduates' Preparatory and High School of Music, which was incorporated into the Peabody Conservatory as the Preparatory Department two years later. Close by, pianist Harriet Gibbs Marshall (1869–1941) founded the Washington (D.C.) Conservatory of Music in 1903. As the first black pianist to graduate from Oberlin Conservatory, Marshall's goal was to provide black students with a rigorous musical education. In Philadelphia the Curtis Institute of Music was founded in 1924 by Mary Louise Curtis Bok (later Zimbalist; 1876–1970), who served as president until 1969.

Women have been fervent advocates of music festivals. The first woman in the United States to found a music festival was Maria Longworth Nichols Storer (1849–1932). In 1871 she established the Cincinnati May Festival and convinced Theodore Thomas to conduct it. After two years of diligent planning and fund raising, the first festival took place in May 1873. America's first summer music festival, the Norfolk Music Festival, located in the Litchfield Hills of northwestern Connecticut, was founded by Ellen

Battell Stoeckel (1851–1939) and her husband, Carl, in 1900; it was a direct outgrowth of the Litchfield County Choral Union, which they had begun in 1899. A significant part of this festival was the commissioning of new works by such composers as George Chadwick, Victor Herbert, Horatio Parker, Samuel Coleridge-Taylor, Percy Grainger, and Jean Sibelius. Although the festival ceased in 1922, Ellen Stoeckel continued her generous gifts to music and her community. She willed much of her property for the use of Yale University, a bequest that led to the establishment of the Yale Summer School of Music and Art.

The Berkshires of western Massachusetts are the scene of two of America's best-known summer music festivals—South Mountain and Tanglewood. The first grew out of the efforts of Elizabeth Sprague Coolidge (1864–1953), whom many view as the most important patron of music in the twentieth century. Coolidge began her career as "Lady Bountiful of Chamber Music" with the founding of the Berkshire Quartet in 1916. Two years later, she established the annual Berkshire Festival of Chamber Music at South Mountain, near Pittsfield. The Berkshire Quartet and the new Coolidge-supported Elshuco Trio presented newly commissioned works alongside classical repertoire. The success of these festivals led her to sponsor similar festivals in cities throughout Europe.

Composer-conductor Henry Hadley's idea for an orchestral music festival, the Berkshire Symphonic Festival, was carried forward by three women: Gertrude Robinson Smith (1881–1963), Mrs. Owen Johnson, and Mrs. William Fulton Barrett. It opened its doors in August 1934, and in 1936 the Boston Symphony Orchestra was engaged as its permanent orchestra. In the same year, Rosamund Dixey Brooks Hepburn (Mrs. Andrew H.; 1887–1948) and Mary Aspinwall Tappan (1851–1941) donated a permanent home for the festival, the Tanglewood estate, which has since served as the site of an annual international festival of music.

Wolf Trap, the only national park in the United States dedicated to the performing arts, is the result of the creative imagination and financial backing of Catherine Filene Shouse (b. 1896). Donor of the land and the funds for both the outdoor and the indoor theatres, Shouse is dedicated to the educational and performing opportunities offered at the park. Other communities across the country have been blessed with women who have given or raised the funds for new arts centers. In San Francisco, Louise M. Davies (b. 1900) has given $5 million toward the erection of the concert hall that bears her name and an additional $3 million to the orchestra's endowment fund. Los Angeles's Dorothy Buffum Chandler (b. 1901) almost single-handedly raised $18.5 million for the building of the Music Center, then organized a company to float $13.7 million in bonds to finish the work.

The love of music has also been behind the generous patronage of Alice Tully (b. 1902), from her support of major cultural institutions and the careers of promising singers to her contribution to the chamber music hall at Lincoln Center that bears her name. On the occasion of her eighty-fifth birthday, Will Crutchfield addressed the nature of a patron's involvement in the outcome of her patronage:

> Some people adhere to the view that patrons ought simply to write their checks and never dream of influencing ("interfering in") artistic results. Miss Tully, bestowing her philanthropies from a highly discriminating point of view, has represented the opposite tradition. I prefer it.[12]

Many women have given financial backing and energetic support to composers through stipends, commissions, and moral encouragement. Elizabeth Sprague Coolidge shaped the course of chamber music in the twentieth century, first by founding the Berkshire Chamber Music Festivals, then, in 1925, by establishing the Elizabeth Sprague Coolidge Foundation at the Library of Congress, along with the auditorium that bears her name. Other women who have supported the creative efforts of composers and performers include: Mary Louise Curtis Bok (George Antheil, Samuel Barber, Gian-Carlo Menotti), Isabella Stewart Gardner (1840–1924; Charles Martin Loeffler, Clayton Johns), Gertrude Vanderbilt Whitney (1875–1942; Edgard Varèse), Alma Morgenthau Wertheim (Aaron Copland, Roy Harris), and Blanche Walton (1871–1963; Henry Cowell).

This brief survey of women's patronage has merely begun to suggest the richness of women's contributions to musical culture. Each woman's gift to music making is a story in itself, and the areas not discussed call for additional volumes of study. Women have built and supported retreats and working communities for musicians and artists (Katrina Trask, 1853–1922, Yaddo; Marian MacDowell, 1857–1956, the MacDowell Colony); donated scholarships for young composers and performers (the National Federation of Music Clubs); established grants for music making and scholarship (Martha Baird Rockefeller, 1895–1971); contributed to music libraries (Lila Acheson Wallace, 1889–1984, the Juilliard School Library); offered commissions in memory of loved ones; donated instruments to performers and collections (Gertrude Whittall, 1867–1965, the Gertrude Whittall Foundation and Pavilion at the Library of Congress); furthered music making through writing and editorial efforts (Minna Lederman, b. 1898, the journal *Modern Music*); founded publishing firms (Alma Wertheim, d.

1953, Cos Cob Press; Sylvia Smith, b. 1948, Smith Publications and Sonic Art Editions); and worked to support new music (Betty Freeman, b. 1921, patron of composers John Cage, Steve Reich, Philip Glass, Daniel Lentz, Ingram Marshall, and Paul Dresher).

## CONCLUSION

Other aspects of women's support remain to be examined. How have women of other cultures and other colors worked to facilitate the making of music? What has been the relationship between giver and recipient and what have been the effects of the gifts on the artists and the art? How have women's efforts been viewed by other contributors to musical culture—press, critics, teachers? How has patronage changed the lives of the patrons? Why have women seemingly failed to support women composers and performers? Conversely, how have they fostered the activities of other women? Many questions remain to be answered before we can begin to understand how women's supportive efforts have altered the fabric of our musical culture. By changing our perspective of music culture from one focused on individuals of genius to one centered on institutions of creative interactions, we have at last begun to ask the right questions.

### NOTES

1. Gaye Tuchman, "Women and the Creation of Culture," *Sociological Inquiry* 45 (1975):192.

2. Rebecca A. Baltzer, "Music in the Life and Times of Eleanor of Aquitaine," in *Eleanor of Aquitaine: Patron and Politician,* edited by William W. Kibler (Austin: University of Texas Press, 1976), p. 61.

3. For a detailed study of the patronage of these two Renaissance noblewomen, see William F. Prizer, "Isabella d'Este and Lucrezia Borgia as Patrons of Music: The Frottola at Mantua and Ferrara," *Journal of the American Musicological Society* 38 (Spring 1985):1–33.

4. William Weber, *Music and the Middle Class: The Social Structure of Concert Life in London, Paris and Vienna* (New York: Holmes & Meier Publishers, Inc., 1975), p. 7.

5. Ibid., p. 126.

6. Alma Mahler, *Gustav Mahler: Memories and Letters,* translated by Basil Creighton (New York: The Viking Press, 1946), p. 21.

7. Ibid., p. 104.

8. Paper written by Fanny Raymond Ritter and read by Mrs. Churchill at the Centennial Congress in Philadelphia of the Association for the Advancement of Woman (1876) and published in *Woman's Journal.* It is quoted here as it was

published (with additions) as *Woman as a Musician: An Art-Historical Study* (New York: Edward Schuberth & Co., 1876), pp. 15–17.

9. *Past Presidents Assembly (A Fraternity of Presidents) of the National Federation of Music Clubs. Blue Book* (N.p.: National Federation of Music Clubs, 1927), p. 1.

10. For more detail concerning women's concert management efforts, see Linda Whitesitt, "The Role of Women Impresarios in American Concert Life, 1871–1933," *American Music* 7/2 (Summer 1989):159–80.

11. Howard Shanet, *Philharmonic: A History of New York's Orchestra* (Garden City, NY: Doubleday & Company, 1975), p. 294.

12. As quoted in Dorle J. Soria, "A Wonderful Woman," *Opera News* 52/14 (March 26, 1988):44.

## SUGGESTIONS FOR FURTHER READING

Barr, Cyrilla. "The Faerie Queene and the Archangel: The Correspondence of Elizabeth Sprague Coolidge and Carl Engel." *American Music,* in press.

———. "The Musicological Legacy of Elizabeth Sprague Coolidge." *Journal of Musicology,* in press.

———. Biography of Elizabeth Sprague Coolidge. Champaign: University of Illinois Press, forthcoming.

Bernhard, Virginia. *Ima Hogg: The Governor's Daughter.* Austin: Texas Monthly Press, 1984.

Blair, Karen. *The Clubwoman as Feminist: True Womanhood Redefined, 1868–1914.* New York: Holmes & Meier, 1980.

———. *The History of American Women's Voluntary Organizations, 1810–1960: A Guide to Sources.* Boston: G. K. Hall, 1988.

Cossart, Michael de. *The Food of Love: Princess Edmond de Polignac (1865–1943).* London: Hamish Hamilton, 1978.

Keefer, Lubov. *Music Angels: A Thousand Years of Patronage.* Baltimore: Sutherland Press, Inc., 1976.

Martin, Theodora Penny. *The Sound of Our Own Voices: Women's Study Clubs 1860–1910.* Boston: Beacon Press, 1987.

Perry, Pamela J. "The Role of Women as Patrons of Music in Connecticut during the Nineteenth and Twentieth Centuries." D.M.A. thesis, Hartt School of Music, University of Hartford, 1986.

Rosaldo, Michelle Zimbalist, and Lamphere, Louise, eds. *Woman, Culture, and Society.* Stanford: Stanford University Press, 1974.

Viles, Elza Ann. "Mary Louise Curtis Bok Zimbalist: Founder of the Curtis Institute of Music and Patron of American Arts." Ph.D. diss., Bryn Mawr College, 1983.

Whitesitt, Linda. " 'The Most Potent Force' in American Music: The Role of Women's Music Clubs in American Concert Life." In *The Musical Woman.* Vol. III: *An International Perspective,* edited by Judith Lang Zaimont. Westport, CT: Greenwood Press, 1991.

# XIV.
# Women in
# Non-Western Music

## L. JaFran Jones

## INTRODUCTION

The music dealt with in most of this book constitutes a magnificent repertoire, a monument to human intelligence and creativity by any standards. It is important to understand, however, that it is still only a small part—not necessarily the best part—of a global phenomenon: the music produced by people in all different regions of the world. This is a difficult concept to grasp, because most people who love the music of their own culture—as we do, under the umbrella of European tradition and its extensions in the new worlds—have too little experience with the music of other cultures. It is also difficult because no adequate terminology has been developed to discuss the phenomenon. Cultural bias can be diminished by consciously seeking out the musics of other peoples and endeavoring to appreciate them on their own terms. This is certainly a prime directive for anyone who wishes to become musically literate in today's world. The problem of clarifying terminology and concepts is more difficult. It depends ultimately on a joint effort of music scholars throughout the world. It demands mutual understanding, mutual tolerance, and mutual agreement among diverse people united by their love for music as a human, not merely a national, heritage. Music is only in part a universal language, as humans are only in part a single race. Both appear at first a universe of diversity. Moving beyond this depends to a large extent on the future. It is a future toward which students of "Western" music should seriously consider contributing.

"Music" is a term at once too broad and too narrow to serve us without reservation. On the one hand, it encompasses a range of phenomena that few other cultures would crowd together under a single rubric. The gamut extends from natural sounds to certain events of the mind that no ear can perceive, and it includes activities in specially reserved spheres, such as religion. On the other hand, it may exclude everything that goes against our particular prejudices. Nevertheless, it is a term we have not learned to do without. Nothing more adequate has gained currency.

Until we have refined our conceptual tools, we must continue to use "music" with multiple caveats and awkward qualifiers. Thus the reader is advised to examine the context every time this word occurs and attempt to redefine it accordingly. Frequently the *ad hoc* definition will be more closely linked to presuppositions of the person using the term than to the subject at hand. Some help comes from the rough-shod qualifiers "Western" and "non-Western." They allow at least an initial distinction between musics, yet they fail to shed the trappings of chauvinism. "Western" music receives the affirmative tag, as if taken as the norm. "Non-Western" tends to place all other musics on the negative side of the equation. This is something like discussing race in terms of "white" and "non-white."

It must suffice here to point out some pitfalls in conventional terminology and to put the reader on guard. This is not the place to attempt a remedy. Thus the very terms we have found wanting appear in the title of this chapter and will continue to be used hereafter. Our concern is "non-Western music." Far from being that which is left over after "Western music" has been accounted for, it encompasses most of the music made by people on Earth. The genres that have grown out of the European art-music tradition constitute just one variety of music making among many others. We must be prepared for the realization that "non-Western" music is a vast sea within which the lovely vessel of our own music floats.

Among the new disciplines to emerge in the twentieth century, one is devoted to exploring the global phenomenon of music without the burden of occidental prejudices. English-speaking scholars call it "ethnomusicology." Like musicology, it deals with the technical details of music, intervals, rhythms, and structures. But it must approach these matters from the broadest point of view, for the canons of Western music theory constitute only a special case in the way people organize sound. It also studies instruments and genres, attempting to understand them on their own terms, without establishing hierarchies across cultural boundaries. Thus, the West African *kora* receives the same serious attention as our harp, and the Indonesian *gamelan* has all the respect accorded to a symphony orchestra.

Like ethnology, ethnomusicology focuses its attention on the cultures within which music is produced. Music making is an extremely culture-sensitive activity. It is an error to abstract music from its context. This does not mean that we cannot approach the music of another culture without delving into mountains of ethnographic detail. There are certain universal qualities to music that have appeal across cultural boundaries, and music is an open door to cultures we may otherwise find difficult to appreciate. It does mean that a serious study of any music requires an equally serious study of its specific culture. Ethnomusicologists must usually approach their target music as outsiders, a difficult position. For this reason, they must understand the culture as thoroughly as the music and must endeavor to hear a music through the ears of the culture that fosters it. Music is made by people; it does not exist by itself.

In pursuing the music, it is only marginally fruitful to look for specific compositions or performances. Individual pieces and events seem less important than the continua of which they are part. One attends to repertoires and contexts in which music is made. Thus, if one collects a particular song at a specific wedding and "wedding songs" are a valid primary category, one might err by dealing with them on a more atomic level. The field researcher asks, "What types of events involve music making?" and "What repertoires are associated with them?" Musical material is analyzed in generic terms—interval structure, range, cadenza types—and coordinated with conventional components of their events.

Beyond cultural background, event type, and musical characteristics, social functions of a repertoire must be considered. Sometimes music has a serious duty to perform, which is not apparent in its immediate context: training youth, reinforcing culturally prescribed roles, passing information, facilitating social transactions, and avoiding confrontations. Here it is important to consider texts as well as music. In addition, the music of one group may be directed at or variously affect another. For example, the study of women's music cannot ignore courtship songs sung by men, or the prohibitions attached to men's repertoires or to men's instruments.

## WOMEN AND MUSIC

Our knowledge of world music remains severely limited by lack of data. Ethnomusicology is a young discipline, still seeking valid theories and methods. Yet its subject matter is as old and as vast as human life on Earth. Specific studies on women's music are few and scattered. Thus it is too early to answer most of the questions that might puzzle us. Nevertheless, a few tentative generalizations may be suggested. Women make music, and men make music. Both can sing and play instruments. There is no evidence that one sex possesses more musical ability than the other or gains more enjoyment from music. Nor is there evidence that one sex produces more music makers. We know of no instruments or musical systems that one of the sexes is inherently incapable of mastering. We are not dogged by the question debated in Western music—why are there so many men and so few women?

There are, indeed, differences virtually everywhere between men's music and women's music. There are repertoires, instruments, and musical contexts exclusive to one gender and forbidden to the other. There are other societies besides our own where more men than women are seen making music in public. Perhaps no cases have been studied in sufficient depth to account unequivocally for the differences, but the bulk of evidence from ethnomusicology points to culture as the source of gender distinctions in music. Each culture defines "men" and "women" and prescribes the behavior (including musical behavior) appropriate to each. These unwritten cultural codes typically take only incidental account of the concrete, physical differences between the sexes. Thus it is valid to deal separately with women's music, whereas dealing with women's musicality may be motivated by prejudiced presuppositions.

## SURVEY

This overview is not intended to be comprehensive, but suggestive. Likewise, categories are informal and may not be rigorously drawn. Any scheme for breaking down a cultural continuum is necessarily artificial and must admit rough edges as well as troublesome crossover items that refuse to be neatly pigeonholed. The survey framework demands that things be taken out of their rich cultural context, from which they are, in principle, inseparable. The reader must indulgently assume the ample background of detail that would be needed in order to present each item adequately. Consistent with the prime importance of firsthand experience, I draw generously on my own extensive fieldwork in Tunisia, North Africa, and Malta, with some supplementary references to other scholars' work.

The printed page is far removed from real-life music. Yet it is the medium we must use here. Only a few musical examples are provided to stimulate the reader's appreciation of sound in relationship to culture. Time and key signatures are added to help the reader: most of the examples are modal, and there is flexibility within measures.

## Making Music

Most music is made by people who are not musicians and whose attention is not focused on the music itself. It is not a matter of performing/ listening, but of making music in the course of life's activities. If asked, "What are you doing?" someone who happens to be singing, humming, or whistling will probably not mention the music, but something else: just thinking, waiting, washing clothes, celebrating a wedding, worshipping. The repertoires used may well have been composed by individuals, but they are usually perceived as part of the cultural heritage. At any rate, one does not normally think in terms of composers and poets when in the shower, around the campfire, at a celebration: one sings or plays what comes to mind, what one likes, what is appropriate for the occasion. In music making one focuses on the context, the event, the activity, the mood. The music "goes along."

Music making is a basic and satisfying human activity. Everyone can do it. People often make music just for the fun of it, because they feel good, to while away the time, to soothe a troubled mind. Although they may not be doing anything else, they do not concentrate on the music, as in practicing an instrument or in singing someone a song. They are living their lives, and music happens in the process. This may be the underlying perception behind our verb "play," as it applies to music. Other terms express the same thing more consciously. The Sicilian name for jaw's harp is *cacciapensiri*—care chaser (a typically "male" instrument, incidentally).

Women make music in this way at least as much as men do, although rarely outside the family. Many cultures have restrictions on what women may do in public, and such impromptu music making frequently falls under the ban. At home, however, women do more singing and instrument playing than one might expect, particularly in societies where women appear generally repressed. Unlike other music situations, there is no fixed repertoire for this usage. Thus, considerable crossover into men's music may occur. Women sing songs that are normally forbidden them and play instruments that would be inappropriate for them in more formal contexts.

Obviously this sort of music is especially difficult to study and record. It requires an intimacy with family life that most ethnomusicologists are unable to achieve. One normally finds out about it from informants or from published memoirs. It is equally obvious, however, that female scholars have a better chance of penetrating the inner sphere of music life than do their male colleagues. Within a society, this "incidental" music, heard from mothers and female relatives, forms part of everyone's childhood memories.

Its importance in transmitting musical traditions to both girls and boys will be stressed below.

"Whistle while you work" is proverbial in our culture. Music helps make work lighter, quicker, and more pleasant. Although it is generally uncommon for women to whistle, there are sizeable repertoires of work songs for both women and men in most societies we study. They provide the most concrete examples of how music may be tailored to suit its context. Our study of this music must perforce center on traditional work, where tasks for women and men are clearly divided by the rules of the culture, where the activities are most conducive to music, and for which long-standing repertoires exist. Music appears to have lost currency in the modern workplace, and traditional repertoires are in danger of being forgotten. No doubt it is the workers—everyone—who stand to lose the most.

In Tunisia, for example, women work mostly in the home or in the company of other women. Their jobs are heavy and demanding: preparing food, making and maintaining clothing, taking care of the home compound, and raising children. Rural women have such additional burdens as fetching water, collecting firewood, processing grain, and tending domestic animals. Except in wealthy families it is rare to find any woman or girl completely idle. When there seems to be nothing else to do, a woman will take up her spindle and make yarn. Except for formal celebrations or ceremonies, when women get together, they work. Men may be rigorously excluded from women's work sessions, under penalty.[1]

The music women make while working depends largely on what the task is. Pounding food in a mortar and grinding flour are heavy, rhythmic tasks. The songs have a strong beat, with short, simple, often repetitive texts. The grain staple *kuksī* is often prepared in groups. Movements are still rhythmic, but slower and gentler. This affords the accompanying songs more latitude for melodic and textual elaboration. Often material from religious, ceremonial, or popular repertoires enters in. This music is more social and enjoyable. Often one woman or girl will keep time with traditional drumming patterns on a *darbūka* (vase-shaped clay drum) or a handy household utensil. Songs for spinning have an element of incantation. With charming melodies, the texts address the wool, the yarn, and the spindle, and they express wishes about the clothes to be made and the good fortune of those who will wear them.

Malta offers an example of free-rhythm, improvised work songs. Women often work on the flat roofs of their houses, washing and hanging clothes, for example. Roof repair is also a traditional women's task. The women hold singing "conversations" with each other from roof to roof. They elaborate on a few traditional (modal) melodic patterns with consider-

Women in southern Tunisia spinning wool and singing. From André Louis, *Douiret: étrange cité berbère* (Tunis: Société Tunisienne de Diffusion, 1975), p. 73. Reproduced by permission.

able ornamental improvisation. The texts, in verse, are also partly improvised and depend on the subject of the day's conversation. The singing involves an element of contest, where women try to surpass each other with clever turns of melody and phrase. This music belongs to the genre *bormliza*[2] and corresponds in some respects to the popular male "joust" singing, *spirtu pront*. In Example 14-1, note the descending lines of *bormliza*. The range is usually between a seventh and a ninth. Extreme melisma in descending patterns is the most striking characteristic of the genre. Voices are tense and must produce a considerable volume of sound.

This calls to mind a variety of improvised conversational singing practiced by the youth of some Bedouin tribes in eastern Libya.[3] It may more accurately be called "social singing," although it occurs in the context of work, at wells. Young women come to fetch water, and young men bring their animals to drink. Although normal social interaction between young men and women is frowned on, they may have singing exchanges in this context. The words are improvised within a body of conventional rules.

EXAMPLE 14-1.    *Bormliza* (Malta).

They must correspond to accepted standards of poetry in a rivalry of taunting and teasing. It is very important to be good at this type of singing. In this semiritualized framework, young people are allowed to become acquainted, to measure each other's qualities and, no doubt, marriageability.

Lullabies constitute a special category of women's work songs. Because of their very specific purpose, they display striking resemblances across cultural boundaries. This has given rise to a plethora of gratuitous theories about cross-cultural influences on the one hand and the "true nature" of women's music on the other. Marius Schneider displayed more ambition in contending that the use of "ra-ra-ra" as opposed to "na-na-na" vocables corresponded to the anthropologists' distinction between brachycephalic (short- or broad-headed) and dolichocephalic (long-headed) peoples.[4]

Beyond their immediate function and their pleasing musical qualities, lullabies have important roles in the lives of mother and child. They allow the mother to express hopes and dispel fears, and they constitute the child's first musical experience. Their effect also reaches older children in the family. Lullaby words reinforce cultural values and prejudices. Although the melodies may remain essentially the same, there are often striking differences between the texts sung to boys and to girls. Tunisians traditionally congratulate a woman when she has a boy and console her if she has a girl. This valorization is reflected in the lullabies she will subsequently sing.

Play songs for girls share the musical characteristics typical of children's songs, which, like lullabies, appear to have less culture specificity. The games girls play and the words they sing, however, are significantly different from those of boys. They center on domestic concerns, marriage aspirations, and women's place in society. They may be seen as powerful media for training and acculturation, as some interesting examples collected in Tunisia demonstrate.[5]

Crucial events in individuals' lives are typically solemnized with ceremonies and celebrations. These may involve only the family or include the broader community and possibly the religious establishment. They provide occasions for considerable music making, with many events where women play a leading or exclusive role. Each society has its own set of ritual occasions, but universally prominent for virtually all peoples are birth, marriage, and death. Rich musical repertoires and elaborate customs exist for these crucial celebrations, the proper execution of which may affect the good fortune of the individuals feted or of the entire community. Cultural heritage is here most evident and music most prominent.

Birth celebrations in Tunisia are typically restricted to family and close friends and are not elaborate, although they may be more so in the case of a first child. The sexes are quite naturally segregated. Men wait outside for the women's signal and generally have little to do with the affair. As mentioned, the birth is celebrated more joyously if the child is male. The principal actors in the parturition (besides the mother) are the childbirth professionals, a *shaddāda* to hold the mother steady and a *qābla* (midwife) to receive the child. They are not outsiders but are experienced women from the community who contribute to the success of the event by their concern for the mother and by the particular importance of their persons. There should also be an *'ashshāqa*, whose role it is to chant or shout certain conventional formulae that invoke blessing, protection, and good fortune on mother and child. She is armed with an incensor and at specific points of juncture circles it above the mother three times and pronounces her *ta'shīqa* (Example 14-2; this is also used on other propitious occasions and to ward off evil). The *'ashshāqa*, who may earn a few much-needed coins for her service, is also a woman distinguished by experience, piety, or other powers.

As important to the event as any conventional singing are the attendant women's *zaghrīṭ* and *tarḥība*. *Zaghrīṭ*, usually described as ululation, is an exclusively female vocalization typical of Middle Eastern, African, and (to some extent) southern European women. It is produced with a high-pitched, loud voice, accompanied by rapid movement of the tongue and the uvula.

EXAMPLE 14-2.    *Ta'shīqa,* a melodic (modal) invocation of blessing and good fortune (Tunisia).

(The right hand is usually extended horizontally over the upper lip.) It may simply be an expression of joy, but it is also an act of power. It would be most unfortunate for any significant event to pass without *zaghrīṭ*. Clearly women's monopoly of this device enhances their status. Most regions have conventions specifying greater length, more iterations, or more volume for the *zaghrīṭ* of a male birth. The *tarḥība* (welcoming) is a rhythmic fanfare (Example 14-3) produced by one or more women on *bandīr* (round, snared frame-drum) or *darbūka*. It likewise has ritual value and may not be omitted on this and other important occasions. Men are certainly capable of producing the *tarḥība,* and I know of no prohibitions or penalties, but it counts, like the *zaghrīṭ,* as the exclusive province of women.

The women also sing. The specific repertoire for birth celebrations is quite small, but many songs of well-wishing, religious praise, and thanksgiving, also used at weddings and circumcisions, are appropriate here. Most important is the *ta‘līla* for the occasion. This is a traditional song, considered to be of old and venerable vintage, whose melody summons nostalgia and whose text may contain obsolete or even "forgotten" words. Every important ritual occasion has a *ta‘līla* or (in the case of weddings) several *t‘allal* that are to be sung at appropriate moments.

Weddings are genuine community events and involve much more than the joining of a couple. They are the most elaborate, prolonged, and expensive ritual celebrations in Tunisian society. A full-scale, traditional Tunisian wedding may last up to seven days, each packed with events that require special food, special acts, and special music. The sexes are segregated for many of these events. Women's activities generally center on the bride's house, men's on the groom's. Often there is a kind of neutral ground as well.

The musical repertoire for Tunisian weddings is vast, rivaled perhaps only by that of Sufi religious groups, which may also play a prominent role at weddings. Music is ubiquitous, but there is very little "performance." Music making is a communal undertaking, inseparable from the other acts of celebration. *Zaghrīṭ* and *tarḥība* are *de rigueur* at specified moments. The *‘ashshāqa* is there, as are other wedding professionals, who may sometimes have selections to sing or play on instruments while others listen; but the tone throughout is that of collective music making, certainly never the performer/listener "concert" setting that pervades much of Western music.

EXAMPLE 14-3.    *Tarḥība,* a welcoming drum fanfare (Tunisia).

Principal women-only events are *līt al-ḥannā* (night of henna, when an herbal dye is applied to the hands and feet of the bride and, optionally, of members of the wedding party) and *līt al-jilwa* (night of glory, when the bride is displayed in all her finery). Each event has a set of ritual acts to be performed in prescribed sequence and a set of *t'alil* to be sung at specified points of the celebration. Women usually sing together, but occasionally there is antiphony between groups, such as the bride's attendants and the wedding guests. *Darbūka* or *bandīr* drums are always on hand and usually get passed around in the course of the evening. Example 14-4 *(ta'līlat al-'arūsa)* is sung in the bride's house by the women of both families, just before the bride takes leave of her parents and is borne in solemn procession by the groom's family to the house of her future husband. This song is ostensibly in 6/8 rhythm, but it has measures of hemiola within the verses. The melodic range is narrow, and small motivic patterns repeat.

Besides the *t'ālil* there are many other wedding songs, and the praise repertoire of Sufi groups enjoys great favor. Well-liked folk songs and popular mass-media songs come up as well. The women may also dance, usually as a group, with rhythmic body movements, as in Sufi events. Occasionally individuals come forward impromptu and dance before the others to display their finery and skill. Without the restrictive presence of men, these dances can become very sexually explicit, but this is hardly the rule.

Sometimes all-women ensembles are hired for their (particularly rhythmic) skills, their instruments, and their intimate knowledge of the

EXAMPLE 14-4.    *Ta'līlat al-'arūsa,* a special wedding song (Tunisia).

wedding repertoire. They are paid (or at least fed) and may be genuine professionals, but it is difficult to consider them performers in the Western sense. Their role is rather to enhance the music making of the group and to reinforce the good feelings and propitious tone of the occasion, perhaps also to display the wealth of the family or to encourage the flow of small contributions from the guests.

Women also have a leading role at times of death, particularly as mourners. Mourners may be hired professionals, family members, or the entire community, but they are usually only women. Mourning, like religious ceremony, involves what Western observers would readily label "music," although the participants may fail to see what it has in common with music making at festive events and may be offended by the implied comparison.

Elizabeth Mathias describes wake ceremonies in rural Sardinia, where women sing extemporaneous dirges.[6] Men may not be present, nor are they allowed to show signs of mourning. The information that comes out at a wake is equally important to them, but they are allowed to learn of it only secondhand. Women from the family predominate, telling in their song of the deceased's life and virtues, but also expressing their own problems and complaints. Wakes are very long, and all the women in the community have an opportunity to be heard. The wake thus fills an important social function, and it is a major source of power for women, since they control the flow of information in the community. Men have no similar opportunity to vent their feelings and needs, and must depend on women for this.

Control of official religion is often in the hands of men, who allow women only a helpmate role. Men have codified into religion curious notions about women, associating them with sin and evil and labeling them as distractions from men's higher spiritual aspirations. Religion is a source of many prohibitions against women's musical activities. Sīdī 'Abd as-Salām, a venerable North African saint of the fifteenth century, called women's religious ceremony the "ceremony of the devil" and forbade them to touch the sacred drums of his brotherhood.[7] Muslim tradition anathematizes the female voice to the extent of commanding women to clap their hands when answering the door, so that a caller will not be troubled by hearing their voices.[8] Jewish groups are not far behind, some forbidding women to sing, even religious songs, in front of men.[9]

Nevertheless, religion is a major context for women's music making, even within systems where orthodoxy is severe. There are many examples of women providing spiritual exercise, including music, for other women, and not infrequently their influence extends to male devotees. Tunisia has female groups within the Tijānī Sufi order. They operate loosely under a male grand *shaykh* but are largely independent, in both the content and the conduct of their ceremonies. Each group is led by a *mqaddma,* who fills the function of *shaykh.* She is normally an older woman of piety and experience whom circumstances (such as widowhood) have rendered relatively independent of male control. She shares her home with a circle of devotees, usually needy women who live from the contributions she collects. They are her assistants in ceremony and constitute a vocal/instrumental ensemble for the music.

Typically there are weekly ceremonies (Thursday or Friday) at a *zāwīya* (shrine) and many additional appearances at weddings or in the homes of women who have special (spiritual or health) needs. Their standard instrument is a large bowl-shaped drum with single laced head (*ṭabla,* or *ṭablat sīdī ḥmād*). They may use other instruments as well. The repertoire consists chiefly of songs in praise of the Prophet or of Sīdī Aḥmad, the founder of the order. The women share some repertoire with male brotherhoods, but most of it is their own. Tijānīya songs are much appreciated by women and are sung with or without occasion. An important function of the female Tijānīya ceremony is therapeutic. Through the blessings *(baraka)* of Sīdī Aḥmad, the personal powers of the *mqaddma,* and the beneficent effect of music and motion, many women seek relief from their physical and emotional afflictions. There are secular spin-offs of the Tijānīya, called *ḥadhriya,* who work weddings and celebrations, providing similar music but with little claim to spiritual powers.

There are also women's religious ceremonies in Tunisia involving spirit possession and oracular demonstrations (such as glossolalia), but this sort of musical/spiritual activity has been studied more elsewhere. In Korea, a *kut* (shamanic ceremony) is frequently led by a woman who can take on hundreds of different spirits. It is possible, but rare, for men to have this role. The style of ceremony may vary with the occasion, but there is always music. The female shaman *(mansin)* is accompanied by two double-head laced drums *(chango)* and a double-reed aerophone *(piri).* A woman may become a shaman by inheritance or by divine inspiration.

In the rich cultural heritage of Bali, spirits enter virtually every aspect of life. They function through both men and women mediums *(sadeg)* in a variety of ceremonies involving music. Young girls may also enter trance and become *sanghyang* vehicles of the spirits' musical utterances. Though not exclusive to women, practices of possession with song and dance constitute a significant context for women to make music and to assert their importance in society. The ceremonies are necessary to the community and important in the official, sanctified realm of the temple.

## Performing Music

Performance is the realm of the star, the diva, the virtuoso, the rock group; also of the sequestered composer and of the silent, appreciative audience. It is the stratified structure for music making perhaps most familiar to people in the West; and it is threatening to become a norm for the rest of the world, with the irresistible thrust of mass media. Lofty though its spiritual summits may be, it breeds atrophy in the musical laity, who risk losing a cherished boon companion for the delights and pains of their lives. I find the transformation palpable in my Tunisian friends. People who brought out their pipes and drums for my evenings with them fifteen years ago now offer me a cushion in front of the television.

The story of professional women performers outside the West is an old and curious one, with many turns we may not expect from the standpoint of our occidental bias. Yet it is similar in many respects to stories we know very well: women struggling to achieve a balance between their private and public lives; attempting to maintain respectability in the face of their obvious deviation from expected female behavior; revered for their artistic prowess and reviled for their violation of cultural norms; envied and admired for their freedom and allure and decried for their refusal to be normal. It is a story of women's lives that bears telling and retelling with each set of individual details in order to achieve its full impact on our consciousness, and for which bland generalizations appear a violation, a betrayal.

Other societies than ours have had their Maria Callas, their Billie Holiday, their Edith Piaf, and their fortunate ones. There are tales of ecstasy and of tragedy. But the stories are often told in tones of masculine mentality, with male fantasies and judgments. Women need to get behind the myths and retell these stories in terms of real life. Two recent essays have undertaken this in a general way,[10] but more specific focus on individuals is needed.

## Transmitting Music

Paco de Lucía is one of today's leading flamenco guitarists. Lucía is his mother. There may be many reasons why he chose this stage name, but we might surmise that one of them is an acknowledgment of his musical debt to a woman. Music, as we have stressed, is a basic human activity that all people may enjoy. Nevertheless, it must be learned. No one is born with the songs and tunes of her or his culture. Our society provides music education in schools and conservatories. In the world at large, however, throughout human history, very few people have received formal music training; yet music belongs to everyone. Many who gain much from music and who are able to give much are unschooled, but they have learned well.

A great many vectors combine in transmitting musical traditions; no one of them is sufficient by itself. It is obvious, however, that women have an immense share in this process. One might, indeed, assert that women are the principal transmitters of music. It would be difficult to dispute this claim, yet it has an odd ring to our ears, for it is still not common among us to attribute such strong roles to the "weaker" sex. Women's music receives relatively less public exposure, certainly less attention, than men's, and the scarcity of women among music's leading figures is proverbial. Yet it is largely women who give us music—our first melodies and much that we acquire thereafter. This is tacitly confessed even in our word "music," for the Muses were females. The great Orpheus learned his art from these divine women, a pattern that has been repeated countless times since then.

If Orpheus owed his music to the Muses, and Paco to Lucía, the same is true of many other men who have become prominent in music and for whom music has become a prominent part of life. It is also true, of course, for many women. In reminiscences of the great Tunisian *mālūf* composer Aḥmad al-Wāfī, 'Uthmān al-Ka"āk mentions that al-Wāfī's mother and sisters were skilled in *mālūf*. The boy Aḥmad first learned from his mother the instruments and repertoire for which he was to become famous, a music that she and her daughters would never have been able to perform in public. Al-Ka"āk further notes that al-Wāfī's older sister knew and loved Ṭayyibīya Sufi music, a male repertoire. It was from her that al-Wāfī first acquired this music. The same woman was also al-Ka"āk's grandmother. It is thus not surprising to read that when al-Ka"āk participated in his first Ṭayyibīya session, he already knew the repertoire.[11] Several Maltese men have told me that they learned *spirtu pront* from their mothers. *Spirtu pront* is a difficult improvisational art, demanding both musical and poetic virtuosity. Women do not engage in it publicly, but they are capable of teaching it to their sons. Such examples could be multiplied. One might say that the voice that sings at the cradle sets the tone for the world's music.

It is not only as mothers that women enrich the musical heritage of their own and future generations. They also perform an important service in cross-cultural fertilization. In the Arab-Islamic civilization of the Middle Ages it was customary for wealthy men to purchase "singing slave girls" from foreign climes, not infrequently from Christian lands, east and west. (The practice continued until the end of the nineteenth century in Tunisia and may still persist in some places.) These women were consummate virtuosi in their own music and fetched a high-price. They often became the teachers of musicians in their involuntarily adopted country. We know few of their names, but their legacy is with us. Much of the musical wealth of the Arab world was brought and bequeathed by these anonymous women slaves.[12] Examples of this process may be drawn from other cultures as well, including our own.

## CONCLUSION

The time is not ripe for conclusions. Serious gender studies in music are just beginning to emerge. Many old prejudices about women and music have yet to be unmasked. Much of the world's music still remains beyond our ken. If concluding words are to be spoken, they must come from a future generation of ethnomusicologists.

### NOTES

1. William Marçais and Abderrahman Guiga, *Textes Arabes de Takrouna*, vol. 1 (Paris: Imprimerie National Ernst Leroux, 1925), pp. 330–32.

2. Marcia Herndon and Norma McLeod, "The Bormliza: Maltese Folk Song Style and Women," *Journal of American Folklore* 88 (1975):81–100.

3. 'Abd as-Salām Ibrāhīm Qādridūh, *Ughnīyāt min bilādī* (Beirut: Matba'a Samaya, 1974), pp. 81ff.

4. Marius Schneider, "A propósito del influjo de la música árabe. Ensayo de etnografía musical de la España medieval," *Annuario Musical* 1 (1946):31ff. (Barcelona, CSK Instituto Español de Musicología).

5. Aṣ-Ṣādiq ar-Rizqī, *Al-Aghānī at-Tūnisīya* (Tunis: ad-Dār at-Tūnisīya lin-Nashr, 1967), pp. 284–90.

6. Elizabeth Mathias, "Funeral Laments and Female Power in Sardinian Peasant Society," in *Contributions to Mediterranean Studies* (Malta: Malta University Press, 1977), pp. 153–64.

7. Muhammad 'Umar Salīm Makhlūf, *Mawāhib ar-rahīm fī manāqib mawlānā ash-shaykh Sīdī 'Abd as-Salām Ibn Salīm* (Beirut: al-Maktaba ath-Thaqāfīya, 1966), pp. 197–99.

8. Abdelwahab Bouhdiba, *La Sexualité en Islam* (Paris: Presses Universitaires de France, 1975), p. 53.

9. Ellen Koskoff, "The Sound of a Woman's Voice: Gender and Music in a New York Hasidic Community," in *Women and Music in Cross-Cultural Perspective,* edited by Koskoff (Westport, CT: Greenwood Press, 1987), pp. 213–23.

10. L. JaFran Jones, "A Sociohistorical Perspective on Tunisian Women as Professional Musicians" (pp. 69–83), and Jennifer Post, "Professional Women in Indian Music: The Death of the Courtesan Tradition" (pp. 97–109), ibid.

11. *at-Turāth al-Mūsīqī at-Tūnisī* (Tunis: al-Ma'had al-Watanī lil-Mūsīqā wa-r-Raqs, n.d.), vol. 5, pp. 5, 9, 18.

12. Ḥ. Ḥ. 'Abd al-Wahhāb, "Taqaddum al-mūsīqā fi-sh-sharq wa-l-andalus wa-tūnis," in *Waraqāt* (Tunis: Maktabat al-Manār, 1966), vol. 2, pp. 196–205. Al-Ka"āk (note 11) also alludes to this on pp. 5, 11–12.

## SUGGESTIONS FOR FURTHER READING

Belo, Jane. *Trance in Bali*. New York: Columbia University Press, 1960.

Bergman, Billy. *Goodtime Kings: Emerging African Pop*. New York: Quill (William Morrow and Co.), 1985.

Covell, Alan Carter. *Ecstasy: Shamanism in Korea*. Elizabeth, NJ: Hollym International Corp., 1983.

Henry, Edward. *Chant the Names of God*. San Diego: San Diego State University Press, 1988.

Huhm, Halla Pai. *Kut. Korean Shamanist Rituals*. Elizabeth, NJ: Hollym International Corp., 1980.

Jackson, Irene V., ed. *More than Drumming: Essays on African and Afro-Latin American Music and Musicians*. Westport, CT: Greenwood Press, 1985.

Keil, Charles. *Tiv Song*. Chicago: University of Chicago Press, 1979.

Kendall, Laurel. *Shamans, Housewives, and Other Restless Spirits: Women in Korean Ritual Life*. Honolulu: University of Hawaii Press, 1985.

Koskoff, Ellen. "When Women Play: Musical Instruments and Gender Style." In *Violet Archer Festschrift*, edited by Regula Qureshi and Christopher Lewis. Edmonton: University of Alberta Press, forthcoming.

Nettl, Bruno. *The Study of Ethnomusicology*. Urbana: University of Illinois Press, 1983.

Nketia, J. H. Kwabena. *The Music of Africa*. New York: W. W. Norton and Co., 1974.

# XV.
# Recovering *Jouissance:*
# An Introduction to Feminist
# Musical Aesthetics

*Renée Cox*

Wa-oh-oh-oh . . .

—THE RONETTES

Although feminist criticism in art and literature has been developing during the last quarter of the twentieth century, feminist scholarship in music is just beginning to get off the ground. One reason is that the work of female musicians has been less evident to us than that of female artists and writers. There are many possible explanations for what seems to be a relative dearth of female composers, among them the lack of opportunity in the past for musical education, the lack of resources and access to the means necessary to get works performed, and the public nature of the discipline in cultures that sought to confine women to the home. (Much more than "A Room of One's Own" is needed to be a successful composer.) Another reason for the absence of feminist criticism in music has been the strong resistance within the academic disciplines in music to cultural criticism in general. A conservative discipline, musicology was concerned for some time largely with the "factual, the documentary, the verifiable, the analyzable, the positivistic"; with paleography, transcription, repertoire studies, archival work, bibliography.[1] The approach to the music itself in musicology and music theory has tended to be formalistic, with a concentration on the relations of tones in the works themselves rather than on texts and programs, social and cultural contexts, and aesthetic concerns.

But this is beginning to change. Music scholars are becoming more concerned with criticism and with cultural and aesthetic issues, and are engaging in dialogues with other disciplines. Researchers in music have begun to get serious about identifying, editing, analyzing, and recording music by women throughout history, considering the social circumstances in which women in music were active, and assessing the status of women in the various music disciplines. What is still needed in this stage of music research is more attention to the relationships of personal, social, and cultural conditions of the composers to the nature and structure of the musical compositions themselves. Approaching a woman's music formalistically, without situating it within the cultural and psychological conditions in which it was created, can lead to unrealistic assessments of her work. What follows is not meant to be an exhaustive or definitive consideration of feminist aesthetics, but rather an enumeration of some ways in which we might begin to evaluate musical practices from a feminist perspective.

A few examples exist of musical analyses that try to define the expression of feminine or masculine traits within the canonical masterpieces. Some opera composers seem to associate the sexual or powerful woman with tonal instability, resolved only when the woman is killed or appropriated into the patriarchy. In Mozart's *Die Zauberflöte*, for instance, the music of the dark, powerful Queen of the Night is predominantly minor, chromatic, and dissonant, while that of the wise and noble Sarastro (and of Tamino and Pamina, after they are initiated into Sarastro's kingdom) is diatonic, relatively simple, and regular. Catherine Clément has pointed out that in Wagner's *Tristan und Isolde,* chromaticism is associated with a seductive, deadly female sexuality. This association is also exemplified in Wagner's *Tannhäuser,* where the music of Venus, goddess of sensual pleasure, is beautiful but unstable, chromatic, unresolving, while that of Tannhäuser, the Pilgrims, and the saintly Elisabeth is predominantly diatonic and straightforward. Susan McClary has shown that in Bizet's *Carmen* the music of the heroine is predominantly chromatic and rhythmically syncopated, while Don José and the pure, chaste Micaëla sing diatonically. Because we tend to want the music of these nontraditional women to achieve clarity and order, we may subconsciously want them to be defeated, to die. And it is precisely when the heroines in these operas are destroyed that all the musical tension associated with them is resolved. Music thus may reinforce stereotypes about women, promoting fear, hatred, and subordination.[2]

Dramatic music, song, and programmatic music are ripe for gender analysis of this kind. Discerning the masculine and feminine in "pure" instrumental music (as in abstract art) will be more difficult, yet it may lend itself well to gender analysis once trends in the texted and programmatic works are established. Eva Rieger characterizes masculine music of the nineteenth century by "large intervals, rising arpeggios, volume, sforzandos, octave runs, fugues, full orchestral scoring and the proliferation of winds and brass instruments," while feminine music is lyrical, legato, and muted and has delicate instrumentation, small intervals gently rising and falling, and regular rhythms. She points out that the "thrusting, active male principle" of the first theme of sonata form triumphs over the passive, feminine second theme.[3] All this helps to explain why the work of Beethoven seems to be more masculine that the music of, say, Chopin or Debussy. Beethoven is musically authoritative, definitive, conclusive; opposites are reconciled, and chaos is conquered by the light. Chopin's music seems feminine not only in its immediacy, lyricalness, gentility, and sensuousness, but in its questioning, searching, inconclusive, and disruptive qualities. Most contemporary music scholars have avoided using the terms "masculine" and "feminine" in their discussions of music or musical themes, but because some of the composers themselves seem to have been thinking in these terms, and because these associations may be reinforcing stereotypes, it seems desirable to make such associations as explicit as possible.

Feminist aestheticians in literature and art have also considered the possibility of developing a feminine mode of writing or a "feminine sensibility" in art. Could music also be expressive of women's experience, and, if so, what would such music be like? We cannot distinguish women's music from men's at the present time, perhaps because we are not familiar enough with women's experiences, have not explored them enough to enable us to discern when they are being expressed. And because qualities associated with the feminine have traditionally been considered inferior and used against women, women composers may have had to adopt a masculine mode of expression in order to be taken seriously as artists. Women who seek to develop a female aesthetic or a women's culture, in contrast, choose to advance qualities traditionally associated with women and to celebrate the expression of these qualities. This is not to suggest that women cannot reach the highest levels of the discipline as it is presently defined. Women's cultures are for those who feel that the present culture is not conducive to what they have to offer or express, and that an examination of female experiences may help them to develop different, more authentic voices.

Because both music and writing are process-oriented, an examination of the nature of *l'écriture féminine,* a style of female or feminine writing characteristic of certain French feminists, should be instructive for the development of a women's music. This feminine writing is well exemplified by the following description of female experience by Hélène Cixous:

Unleashed and raging, she belongs to the race of waves. She arises, she approaches, she lifts up, she reaches, covers over, washes ashore, flows embracing the cliff's least undulation, already she is another, arising again, throwing the fringed vastness of her body up high, follows herself, and covers over, uncovers, polishes, makes the stone body shine with the gentle undeserting ebbs, which return to the shoreless nonorigin, as if she recalled herself in order to come again as never before. . . . She has never "held still"; explosion, diffusion, effervescence, abundance, she takes pleasure in being boundless, outside self, outside same, far from a "center". . . .[4]

Cixous asserts that feminine writing is impossible to define, cannot be theorized, enclosed, or encoded. Words used to describe such writing are gestural, rhythmic, spasmodic, heterogeneous, process-oriented, immediate, fluid, and elastic. A principle of continuous growth, proliferation, and development replaces expression as product or object.

In what sense could such writing be considered feminine? Both Cixous and Julia Kristeva stress that the feminine here refers to a mode that disrupts and explodes conventional culture and meaning, and can be found in the writing of either sex. Yet is is most likely to occur in the writing of women and in the speech of women when men are not around. Kristeva believes that the source of such writing is the rhythmic, presymbolic play of mother-infant communication in the infant's preoedipal stage of fusion with the mother. When traces of this *jouissance*—the pleasure of the preoedipal stage—arise from the subconscious and are set against conventional modes of discourse, feminine writing is the result. In not having to develop a gender identity different from that of the mother, girls can maintain the *jouissance* of the connection with her longer. Luce Irigaray has suggested that the continuity and openness of feminine writing also reflects women's sexual experiences: while phallocentric culture is based on singularity, identity, and specificity, women's sexual experience is indefinite, cyclic, without set beginnings and endings. Cixous writes that a woman's "rising" is not erection but diffusion.[5]

The process, continuity, and immediacy of music—music of all kinds by both sexes—seems analogous to the feminine writing discussed above, which seems more lyrical, more musical than traditional prose. A music modeled on feminine writing would engage the listener in the musical moment rather than in the structure as a whole; would have a flexible, cyclical form; and would involve continuous repetition with variation, the cumulative growth of an idea. Such music would serve to deconstruct musical hierarchies and the dialectical juxtaposition and resolution of opposites, disrupt linearity, and avoid definitive closures. In sung music, vocalization would be relaxed and make use of nonverbal or presymbolic sounds.

To date, musicologists have not looked at art music by women in this light, but there has been some consideration of the possibility of the musical expression of women's experience in the folk music of feminists, in the music of popular culture, and in ethnomusicology. The Michigan Womyn's Music Festival in Walhalla is attended by thousands of women annually. Composer Kay Gardner, who regularly performs at this festival, claims women's music is expressive of the sexual experience of women in its tendency toward "circular" musical forms, with the climax in the middle rather than at the end.[6] That music could be expressive of female sexuality has also occurred to rock critic Maggie Haselswerdt:

> The beat of rock and roll may be the beat of sexual intercourse, but for the most part, it's intercourse from the male point of view. Though female sexuality is one of the stronger flavors in the brew when it comes to the blues, soul and dance music, rock's driving beat, piercing guitar lines, pounding keyboards and expansive, stage dominating gestures mark the territory as male. Female sexual response . . . is slow building rather than immediate, diffuse rather than focused, buzzing rather than pounding, melting rather than hardening, and cyclical rather than constant. . . . The song . . . "Be My Baby" . . . owes its uncanny power to the wholesale appropriation of female patterns of sexual response. Phil Spector and the Ronettes weave a gauzy curtain around the sexual impulse, diffusing and romanticizing it, blurring the focus with walls of vibrating sound, highlighting the drama of the encounter with a series of minute yet heartstopping pauses. "So c'mon and be ... be my little baby" leads to the almost unbearably intense moment when Ronnie's famous "Wa-oh-oh-oh" is punctured by a reprise of the devastating opening beat. That's as close to what I mean by melting as mere vinyl can come.[7]

Not all women would identify with the playful description of female sexual experience Haselswerdt (or Gardner) offers. Yet her sense that female sexuality is at issue in "Be My Baby" seems appropriate in light of the historical context of the song. "Be My Baby" was written by Ellie Greenwich, Jeff Barry, and producer Phil Spector for the Ronettes in the early 1960s. Although Spector is white, he was attracted to the expression of feeling and physicality in black music, and he was responsible for the "multilayered, multitextural wall of sound" in the black "girl groups" of the period. These groups were designed to appeal to girls and young women, and they usually posited a sweet and sensitive man as an object of desire. The female "voice" in these songs is not usually a passive one; the young woman urging the man to "be my baby," for example, is gently aggressive, somewhat maternal, more choosing than chosen. The physicality of "Be My Baby" is reinforced by the boom da boom BANG of the percussion, which is imitative of a heartbeat. The prolonged "oooh"s and "aaah"s of the chorus, along with the end of the song, where Ronnie replaces the text with long and highly embellished "ohhh"s, is suggestive of the preoedipal stage.

Offering "Be My Baby" as reflective of a female sexual response is problematic, however, in that what is heard is not the direct experience of sexually liberated women, but at least partly the conception of a young white male expressed through the voices of young women who were dominated both professionally and personally. Presentations of women's experience in the work of relatively autonomous female musicians should prove more authentic. Susan McClary considers the music of Laurie Anderson from a feminist perspective and shows how she serves, in both her texts and her music, to break down patriarchal dualities and to celebrate female or feminine pleasure. An example of a celebration of female *jouissance* can be found in Anderson's "Langue d'Amour (The Hothead)," which evokes the Genesis account of creation in its story of a man, a woman, and a "snake with legs" on an island. Charmed by the snake's stories, the woman falls in love with the snake and becomes bored with the man, who no matter what happens is as "happy as a clam." When at the man's bidding the man and woman leave the island, the woman misses the snake and is restless, a hothead. The conclusion of "Langue d'Amour" consists of a prolonged section in which the woman's *jouissance* is expressed more with vocal sounds than with words: "Oooo là là là là. Voici. Voilà. Oooo là là là là. . . ." In the piece's "chromatic inflections that escape diatonic control and in rhythmic pulsations that defy regular metric organization," McClary suggests, Anderson sacrifices narrative—in text as well as music—for the sake of sustained pleasure; "unitary identity is exchanged for blurred, diffused eroticism."[8]

The expression of women's experience in art music is most likely to appear in contexts in which women and women's concerns and expressions are valued or at least tolerated: times like the present and the ancient past. (Feminists have pointed out that eras of humanism and "enlightenment" are likely to oppress and silence women.) Among recent women composers, Pauline Oliveros is preoccupied with circles, cycles, and mandalas.[9] Both the cyclic principle and the tendency in women's writing toward "continuous growth, proliferation and development" are characteristic of the music of Ellen Taafe Zwilich. Zwilich describes her music as "organic," as concerned with "the elaboration of large-scale works from initial material," material that "contains the 'seeds' of the work to follow," which is subjected to "continuous variation."[10] This predilection for musical organicism, for continuous growth and development, can also be found in the music of men, of course, and it is not found in all music by women. But it is especially meaningful in the music of women, for it has been associated with the female or feminine since ancient times. The goddess principle involves the continuous cycle of birth, growth, death and rebirth, gestation and nurture, proliferation and development. Although these are natural processes that apply to and can be observed in all living forms, they are processes that women who give birth and nurture children can experience directly and attentively.

Why all this emphasis on the female body and sexuality? One answer is that male response to female sexuality is the principal reason women have been oppressed. This is a problem that needs to be addressed, one that will not go away if we avoid or ignore it. Yet some feminists have expressed concern that the emphasis on the body and sexuality in some feminist theory and criticism is dangerous in that it can validate the patriarchy's reduction of women to their bodies and thus serve to feminize the irrational. In response to these stereotypes, many feminists would prefer to focus not on women's bodies and emotions but on women's ability to reason. The importance of the work of these feminists cannot be overestimated. In functioning principally or exclusively in the intellectual mode, however, some women have begun to feel that their voices are partial or disembodied, that in denying their bodies and emotions they are limiting their expression and their insights. Because of the nature of their bodies and their experiences, what women (and African-Americans of both sexes[11]) may have to offer is the integration of body and psyche, an integration of the mental, emotional, and physical. Such an integration can give rise to authenticity and creativity, a special kind of creativity concerned not with the production of aesthetic objects but with living a life aesthetically, with the integration of art and life.[12] Because such a creativity would be disruptive to the objectifying and controlling nature of the patriarchal order, the patriarchy is likely to identify any tendency toward exploration of the body as shameful, any emphasis on emotional life as irrational. In exploring their bodies, cycles, natural rhythms, sexuality, and emotional life, however, women can examine the impact of these aspects on their reason, the relationships among them, and their thought. Instead of the cool, disembodied reason that Cartesian dualism has created, women's reason will be informed by their bodies and their passions.

Perhaps the most difficult problem with the idea of a women's music lies in determining how to distinguish the expression of women's experience from the expression of male constructions of the feminine. Even in music by feminist women, can we distinguish women's experience from patriarchal conceptions of the feminine that women have internalized? Do women have any authentically female experience unconditioned by patriarchal oppression and constraints? Do the female processes or qualities identified above arise out of the very social conditions that we are trying to change, such that celebration of these qualities would limit women's progress?

Our descriptions and expressions of the feminine and of women's experience are similar to constructions of femininity offered by the patriarchy, first because we cannot avoid the influence of these constructions, and second because these constructions are probably not wholly unrelated to the ways women think, feel, and behave. In their proclivities toward dominating women, however, men have cast the characteristics they considered feminine in a negative light and have used these perspectives to silence and oppress women. Rather than attempt to separate themselves completely from male concepts of the feminine, undoubtedly an impossible task, feminists could expose these concepts or images and reformulate them in a positive light. As beautiful and compelling as Wagner's musical conception of femininity or feminine sexuality may be, an examination of his music-dramas makes it clear that Wagner views feminine sexuality as attractive yet deadly, and that the ideal woman is pure and chaste, and sacrifices herself for her man. In the popular music examined above, in contrast, images of femininity and female sexuality that have been traditionally viewed negatively are reconstructed and celebrated. Anderson's "Langue d'Amour" takes a belief that has been most powerful in silencing women—the idea that woman was responsible for the Fall, and that this Fall had something to do with her sexuality—and turns it around, posits a female protagonist who combines thought, emotion, and desire and delights in them, refusing to accept shame or guilt. (Though "Langue d'Amour" ends with the woman's *jouissance,* the woman on the island is intellectual in her curiosity, her desire for knowledge.) So even if the presentations of female sexuality offered in *Tristan und Isolde,* "Langue d'Amour," and "Be My Baby" are similar in their emphases on nonlinearity or tonal instability, we could distinguish them by saying that Wagner's presentation of the feminine is misogynist, that of "Be My Baby" is nonjudgmental, and that of "Langue d'Amour" is feminist (in effect, whether or not in intent). Feminist musicians have also critiqued or parodied traditional notions of the feminine (as folk singer Phrank does in her ironic rendition of "I Enjoy Being a Girl" from the album of the same name) or sought to express pure form or the "purely human" (a perspective that could be viewed either positively or negatively, as a transcendence of gender categories or as an insensitivity to women's oppression). Whether or not the feminist critic finds generalizations about the feminine or women's experience productive or oppressive, a feminist approach to music could identify, explicate, and critique such perspectives.

Scholars who choose to write on women and music will meet with resistance, both outside the feminist movement and within it. Tolerance of difference, and the offering and finding of support for musical or theoretical expressions and ideas, will be essential for productive work in this area. It is through examining our experiences as women, developing authentic musical and critical voices, and listening to and supporting one another that a feminist musical aesthetic will develop.

## NOTES

1. Joseph Kerman, *Contemplating Music: Challenges to Musicology* (Cambridge: Harvard University Press, 1985), p. 12.

2. See Catherine Clément, *Opera, or the Undoing of Women*, translated by Betsy Wing, Foreword by Susan McClary (Minneapolis: University of Minnesota Press, 1988), pp. 56–58; Susan McClary, "Sexual Politics in Classical Music," in *Feminine Endings: Music, Gender, and Sexuality* (Minneapolis: University of Minnesota Press, 1991), pp. 53–79; and Renée Cox, "A History of Music," *The Journal of Aesthetics and Art Criticism* 48 (Fall 1990):395–409.

3. Eva Rieger, " 'Dolce Semplice'? On the Changing Role of Women in Music," in *Feminist Aesthetics*, edited by Gisella Ecker, translated by Harriet Anderson (Boston: Beacon Press, 1985), pp. 139–40.

4. Hélène Cixous and Catherine Clément, *The Newly Born Woman*, translated by Betsy Wing, Introduction by Sandra Gilbert (Boston: Beacon Press, 1985), pp. 90–91.

5. See *New French Feminisms*, edited and with introductions by Elaine Marks and Isabelle de Courtivron (New York: Schocken Books, 1981); Julia Stanley and Susan Wolfe (Robbins), "Towards a Feminist Aesthetic," *Chrysalis* 6 (1978):57–76; Julia Kristeva, *Desire in Language: A Semiotic Approach to Literature and Art*, edited by Leon S. Roudiez, translated by Thomas Gora, Alice Jardine, and Roudiez (New York: Columbia University Press, 1980), chap. 5; Luce Irigaray, "This Sex Which Is Not One," in *This Sex Which Is Not One*, translated by Catherine Porter (Ithaca: Cornell University Press, 1985), pp. 99–106; and Cixous and Clément, *The Newly Born Woman*, p. 88.

6. Ruth Scovill, "Women's Music," in *Women's Culture: The Women's Renaissance of the Seventies*, edited by Gayle Kimball (Metuchen, New Jersey: Scarecrow Press, 1981), p. 158.

7. Maggie Haselswerdt, "Let's Talk About Girls . . .," *Rock and Roll Confidential* 63 (December, 1988):1–2.

8. Susan McClary, "This is Not a Story My People Tell: Time and Space According to Laurie Anderson," presented at the conference on Time, Space, and Drama in Recent Music, SUNY Stonybrook, 1989; published in *Feminine Endings*, pp. 132–47. "Langue d'Amour" is from Anderson's album, *United States*.

9. See Pauline Oliveros, *Software for People: Collected Writings 1963–80* (Baltimore: Smith Publications, 1984).

10. Quoted in James R. Briscoe, ed., *Historical Anthology of Music by Women* (Bloomington: Indiana University Press, 1987), pp. 375–76.

11. See Michael Ventura, "Hear That Long Snake Moan," *Shadow Dancing in the U.S.A.* (Los Angeles: J. P. Tarcher, 1985), pp. 103–63.

12. See Renée Cox, "A Gynecentric Aesthetic," *Hypatia: The Journal of Feminist Philosophy* 5/2 (Summer 1990):43–62. In the aesthetic envisioned, music

and dance serve to integrate intellect, emotion, and body and to unite the individual with the community and with nature. There is an integration of music and dance, spirituality, healing, and the erotic; and the erotic is expressed as a vital, positive force. Process and continuous creation in aesthetic activity are preferred to objectification; there is a synthesis of the arts, with no divisions of high or low art; everyone in the community is included in aesthetic and other activities; and the structure or process of music reflects the egalitarianism of the community in its unity of equal voices.

I wish to thank Anne Mellor and my fellow participants in her NEH seminar on Romanticism and Gender in English Literature (UCLA, summer 1989) for their valuable assistance. I am indebted to Susan McClary for permitting me to read three of her forthcoming papers, and grateful to Marcia Citron, Susan Cook, and Jeffrey Kallberg for sending me examples of their work.

### SUGGESTIONS FOR FURTHER READING

Berkeley, Ellen P., and McQuaid, Matilda, eds. *Architecture: A Place for Women.* Washington, D.C.: Smithsonian Institution Press, 1989.

Dolan, Jill. *The Feminist Spectator as Critic.* Ann Arbor: UMI Research Press, 1988.

"Editorial: Is There a Feminist Music Theory?" *In Theory Only* 9 (1987):3–4.

Frueh, Joanna. "Towards a Feminist Theory of Art Criticism." In Arlene Raven, Cassandra Langer, and Joanna Frueh, *Feminist Art Criticism: An Anthology.* Ann Arbor: UMI Research Press, 1988.

Greene, Gayle, and Kahn, Coppelia, eds. *Making a Difference: Feminist Literary Criticism.* London and New York: Methuen, 1985.

Harris, Ann Sutherland, and Nochlin, Linda, eds. *Women Artists, 1550–1950.* New York: Random House, 1976.

Parker, Rozsica, and Pollock, Griselda, eds. *Framing Feminism: Women and the Women's Art Movement, 1970–85.* London: Pandora, 1987.

———. *Old Mistresses: Women, Art and Ideology.* New York: Pantheon, 1981.

Penly, Constance, ed. *Feminism and Film Theory.* New York: Routledge, 1988.

Said, Edward. "Music." *The Nation,* February 7, 1987, pp. 158–60.

Sandow, Gregory. "Roll Over Opera: Open Letter to Will Crutchfield." *Village Voice,* June 16, 1987, p. 78.

# General Bibliography

SUGGESTIONS FOR FURTHER READING

The following resources are more general than the items listed at the end of each chapter or cover more than one period, country, or topic:

The New Grove series of dictionaries include much information about women in all areas of music. Check for general articles on "Women in Music" as well as specific articles on particular women in The New Grove Dictionary of Music and Musicians, The New Grove Dictionary of American Music, The New Grove Dictionary of Jazz, and The New Grove Dictionary of Opera.

Die Musik in Geschichte und Gegenwart, including its two-volume supplement, contains many articles on women. Short but informative articles can also be found in Riemann's Musiklexikon, Baker's Biographical Dictionary, and the Thompson Encyclopedia. For information on women singers or singing actresses, try Enciclopedia dello spettacolo.

Da Capo Press has published much worthwhile music of women of the past in its Women Composer Series.

BOOKS AND ARTICLES

Ammer, Christine. Unsung: A History of Women in American Music. Westport, CT: Greenwood Press, 1980.

Anderson, Bonnie S., and Zinsser, Judith P. A History of Their Own. 2 vols. New York: Harper and Row, 1988.

Block, Adrienne Fried, and Neuls-Bates, Carol. Women in American Music, a Bibliography of Music and Literature. Westport, CT: Greenwood Press, 1979.

Bowers, Jane, and Tick, Judith. Women Making Music. Urbana: University of Illinois Press, 1986.

Bridenthal, Renate; Koonz, Claudia; and Stuard, Susan, eds. Becoming Visible: Women in European History. 2d ed. Boston: Houghton Mifflin, 1987.

Briscoe, James R., ed. Historical Anthology of Music by Women. Bloomington and Indianapolis: Indiana University Press, 1987.

Carroll, Berenice A., ed. Liberating Women's History. Urbana: University of Illinois Press, 1976.

Chiti, Patricia Adkins. Donne in musica. Rome: Bulzoni, 1982.

Cohen, Aaron. International Encyclopedia of Women Composers. 2d ed. New York and London: Books and Music, 1987.

Edwards, H. Sutherland. The Prima Donna. New York: Da Capo Press, 1978.

Goss, Madeleine. Modern Music Makers. Westport, CT: Greenwood Press, 1952.

Hipsher, Edward Ellsworth. American Opera and Its Composers. Philadelphia: Theodore Presser, 1934; reprint New York: Da Capo Press, 1978.

Hixon, Donald L., and Hennessee, Don. Women in Music: A Bio-Bibliography. Metuchen, NJ: Scarecrow Press, 1975.

James, E. T.; James, J. W.; and Boyer, P. S., eds. *Notable American Women*. 3 vols. Cambridge: Harvard University Press, 1980.

Jezic, Diane Peacock. *Women Composers: The Lost Tradition Found*. New York: Feminist Press, 1988.

Kutsch, K. J., and Riemens, Leo. *Grosses Sängerlexikon*. 2 vols. Bern and Stuttgart: Francke Verlag, 1987.

Le Page, Jane Weiner. *Women Composers, Conductors, and Musicians of the Twentieth Century*. 3 vols. Metuchen, NJ: Scarecrow Press, 1980–

Lerner, Gerda. "Placing Women in History: Definitions and Challenges." *Feminist Studies* 3/2 (Fall 1975):5–14.

Lyle, Wilson. *A Dictionary of Pianists*. New York: Schirmer, 1985.

Manning, Jane. *New Vocal Repertory*. Basingstoke: Macmillan, 1986.

Marcus, Adele. *Great Pianists Speak with Adele Marcus*. Neptune, NJ: Paganiniana, 1979.

Migel, Parmenia. *The Ballerinas, from the Court of Louis XIV to Pavlova*. New York: Da Capo Press, 1980.

Neuls-Bates, Carol. *The Status of Women in College Music: Preliminary Studies*. Binghamton, NY: College Music Society, 1976.

————, ed. *Women in Music: An Anthology of Source Readings from the Middle Ages to the Present*. New York: Harper and Row, 1982.

Olivier, Antje, and Weingartz, Karin, eds. *Frauen als Komponistinnen*. 2d, expanded ed. Düsseldorf: International Arbeitskreis Frau und Musik, 1987.

Olivier, Antje, and Weingartz-Perschel, Karin, eds. *Komponistinnen von A-Z*. Düsseldorf: Tokkata Verlag, 1988.

Rasponi, Lanfranco. *The Last Prima Donnas*. New York: Knopf, 1982.

Reich, Nancy, ed. *Women's Studies, Women's Status*. CMS Report No. 5. Boulder: College Music Society, 1988.

Rieger, Eva. *Frau und Musik*. Frankfurt: Fischer Taschenbücher, 1980.

Rosen, Judith, and Rubin-Rabson, Grace. "Why Haven't Women Become Great Composers?" *High Fidelity/Musical America* 23/2 (February 1973):46, 51–52; 47–50.

Schonberg, Harold. *The Great Pianists*. New York: Simon & Schuster, 1963.

Shepherd, John. "Music and Male Hegemony." In *Music and Society: The Politics of Composition, Performance and Reception*, edited by Richard Leppert and Susan McClary. Cambridge: Cambridge University Press, 1987.

Showalter, Elaine, ed. *The New Feminist Criticism: Essays on Women, Literature, and Theory*. New York: Pantheon, 1985.

Silverman, Kaja. *The Acoustic Mirror: The Female Voice in Psychoanalysis and Cinema*. Bloomington and Indianapolis: Indiana University Press, 1988.

Sonntag, Brünhilde, and Mathei, Renate, eds. *Annäherung an sieben Komponistinnen*. 4 vols. Kassel: Furore, 1986.

Weissweiller, Eva. *Komponistinnen aus 500 Jahren*. Frankfurt: Fischer, 1981.

# Recordings

A companion set of three audio cassettes contains most of the music given in score in *Historical Anthology of Music by Women*, edited by James R. Briscoe (Bloomington and Indianapolis: Indiana University Press, book 1987; companion cassettes 1991). It includes the following works:

Kassia: "The Fallen Woman." Jessica Suchy-Pilalis, soprano cantor
Hildegard von Bingen: "In Evangelium." Shannon Huneryager, soprano
————: "Kyrie." Indianapolis Children's Choir, Henry Leck, director
Anne Boleyn: "O Deathe, rock me asleepe." Laurel Goetzinger, soprano; Anna Briscoe, harpsichord
Maddalena Casulana: "Morte—Che vôi—Te chiamo" (Madrigal VI). Butler University Madrigal Singers, Michael Shasberger, director
Francesca Caccini: "Maria, dolce Maria." Laurel Goetzinger, soprano; Anna Briscoe, harpsichord; Andrew Ross, cello continuo
————: "Aria of the Shepherd," from *La Liberazione di Ruggiero*. Laurel Goetzinger, soprano; Butler University Collegium Musicum
Isabella Leonarda: Kyrie, from *Messa Prima*. Schola Cantorum of the University of Arkansas, Jack Groh, conductor
Elisabeth-Claude Jacquet de la Guerre: *Semelé*. Carol Plantamura, soprano; Robert Bloch, violin; Deirdre Cooper, cello; Susan Erickson, harpsichord
Maria Margherita Grimani: "Sinfonia," from *Pallade e Marte*. New England Women's Symphony, Jean Lamon, conductor
Anna Amalie: "Adagio," from Sonata in F. Loretta Contino, flute; Andrew Ross, cello; Anna Briscoe, harpsichord
Marianne von Martinez: "Allegro," from Sonata in A. Anna Briscoe, piano
Maria Theresia von Paradis: "Morgenlied eines armen Mannes." André Aerne, tenor; Anna Briscoe, piano
Maria Agata Szymanowska: "Nocturne." Anna Briscoe, piano
Josephine Lang: "Frühzeitiger Frühling." Laurel Goetzinger, soprano; Anna Briscoe, piano
Fanny Mendelssohn Hensel: "Schwanenlied." Laurel Goetzinger, soprano; Anna Briscoe, piano
Clara Schumann: "Liebst du um Schönheit." Laurel Goetzinger, soprano; Anna Briscoe, piano
————: "Allegro moderato," from Trio in g. Hélène Boschi, piano; Annie Jodry, violin; Etienne Péclard, cello
Louise Farrenc: "Allegro deciso," from Trio in e. Katherine Hoover, flute; Carter Brey, cello; Barbara Weintraub, piano
Pauline Viardot-Garcia: "Die Beschwörung." Laurel Goetzinger, soprano; Anna Briscoe, piano
Amy Marcy Beach: "Elle et moi." Laurel Goetzinger, soprano; Anna Briscoe, piano
————: "A Hermit Thrush at Morn." Virginia Eskin, piano
Dame Ethel Smyth: Scene from *The Wreckers*. Butler University Chorale, Michael Shasberger, director

Lili Boulanger: "Je garde une médaille d'elle," from *Clairières dans le ciel.* Laurel Goetzinger, soprano; Anna Briscoe, piano

Alma Mahler: "Der Erkennende." Laurel Goetzinger, soprano; Anna Briscoe, piano

Rebecca Clarke: "Allegro," from Piano Trio. Aeolian Trio of De Pauw University— Dan Rizner, violin; Eric Edberg, cello; Claude Cymerman, piano

Germaine Tailleferre: "Modéré sans lenteur," from Sonata in c♯. Arnold Steinhardt, violin; Virginia Eskin, piano

Ruth Crawford Seeger: Prelude no. 2. Rosemary Platt, piano

———: "Rat Riddles." Beverly Morgan, mezzo-soprano; Speculum Musicae, Paul Dunkel, conductor

Miriam Gideon: *The Hound of Heaven.* William Metcalf, baritone; Isidore Cohen, violin; Karen Phillips, viola; Fred Sherry, cello; Fritz Jahoda, conductor

Grazyna Bacewicz: Sonata No. 2. Anna Briscoe, piano

Louise Talma: "La Corona," from *Holy Sonnets.* Dorian Chorale, Harold Aks, conductor

Julia Perry: *Homunculus C. F.* Manhattan Percussion Ensemble, Paul Price, conductor

Vivian Fine: "The Triumph of Alcestis," from *Alcestis.* Imperial Philharmonic of Tokyo, William Strickland, conductor

Violet Archer: "Preamble," from Sonata. William Hochkeppel, alto saxophone; Anna Briscoe, piano

Thea Musgrave: "Monologue of Mary," from *Mary, Queen of Scots.* Ashley Putnam, soprano; Virginia State Opera Association, Peter Mark, conductor

Ellen Taaffe Zwilich: First Movement, from Symphony No. 1. Indianapolis Symphony Orchestra, John Nelson, conductor

# Index

# Contributors

ADRIENNE FRIED BLOCK, a noted authority on American music, is co-director of the Project for the Study of Women in Music at the Graduate School, City University of New York. She is preparing a biography of Amy Beach.

Musicologist MICHAEL J. BUDDS is on the music faculty of the University of Missouri-Columbia. An expanded edition of his book, *Jazz in the Sixties: The Expansion of Musical Resources and Techniques* (1978), was published in 1990.

MARCIA J. CITRON, Associate Professor of Musicology at Rice University, is the author of books and articles on several women composers, including Fanny Mendelssohn and Cécile Chaminade. She has also written a feminist exploration of gender and the musical canon.

RENÉE COX teaches at the University of Tennessee-Chattanooga. Her ideas on the aesthetics of music have been published in several leading journals.

J. MICHELE EDWARDS is Professor of Music and former Director of the Women's/Gender Studies Program at Macalester College in St. Paul, MN. She also conducts Harmonia Mundi, a chamber ensemble in the Twin Cities that regularly performs compositions by women.

A professed generalist, S. KAY HOKE joined the music faculty at Butler University in Indianapolis in 1978. She has added musical and women's studies dimensions to the general studies course and has chaired the Committee on the Status of Women for the College Music Society.

BARBARA GARVEY JACKSON is Professor of Music at the University of Arkansas and a professional violinist. She is also founder and publisher of Clar-Nan Editions, a firm that specializes in performing editions of music by women of the seventeenth and eighteenth centuries.

L. JAFRAN JONES teaches ethnomusicology and directs two Balinese gamelan ensembles at Bowling Green (Ohio) State University. She has conducted field research principally in northern Africa, Malta, and southern Europe, and she has traveled to China to study and write about the cultural and social dimensions of Chinese music.

LESLIE LASSETTER is finishing her doctoral dissertation and working on a book about Philip Glass. She has served as a Junior Research Fellow at the Institute for Studies in American Music at Brooklyn College.

ANN N. MICHELINI is Professor of Classics in the College of Arts and Sciences, University of Cincinnati.

KARIN PENDLE is on the musicology faculty of the College-Conservatory of Music, University of Cincinnati. Her published work includes many studies of eighteenth- and nineteenth-century opera.

NANCY B. REICH is the author of *Clara Schumann: The Artist and the Woman* (1985), which has also been published in a German translation. She continues to work on nineteenth-century studies.

CATHERINE ROMA is an active choral director and clinician in the Cincinnati area, where she founded the nationally known women's choir MUSE in 1984. She also founded and directed the Anna Crusis Women's Choir in Philadelphia. She teaches at Xavier University and Wilmington College (Ohio).

NANCY STEWART received her Ph.D. in musicology from the University of Cincinnati and teaches at St. Lawrence University in Canton, NY.

LINDA WHITESITT teaches at Queens College (Charlotte, NC) and is director of orchestras for the Charlotte-Mecklenburg Public Schools.

ROBERT ZIEROLF, a theorist and critic, is head of the Division of Composition, Theory, and Music History at the College-Conservatory of Music, University of Cincinnati.